Dear Student:

You have chosen to begin a career as a business professional by majoring in a business discipline. If your experience is anything like mine, you will not regret your choice. Working in business leads to fulfilling and enjoyable experiences and relationships with interesting, quality people. Working in a company you admire that sells products or services in which you believe will enable you to feel positive about yourself, your contributions, and your professional life.

Do you want to be more than just another department manager? Do you see yourself as a future business leader? If so, the MIS course is THE most important course in the business curriculum. Are you surprised to read that? If you view the MIS course as the "Excel class" or the "Access course," that opinion is preposterous. But, as you will learn in Chapter 1, learning software is not the major goal of this class. Instead, you will learn how businesses use information systems and technology to accomplish their goals, objectives, and competitive strategy.

Think about any modern organization. How does Amazon.com ship millions of items per second, 24/7, worldwide? How does YouTube store and deliver thousands of hours of video every day? How do Facebook and MySpace connect you to your friends? They use information systems! And, those organizations succeeded primarily because they found innovative ways to apply emerging information technology.

Maybe you're thinking, "Not me! I'll leave that stuff to someone else." Well, you might leave the *development* of information systems to someone else, but if you leave the thinking about innovative applications of information systems to someone else, you're in trouble. In the twenty-first century, every business professional must be able to envision ways to gain competitive advantage using information systems and know how to collaborate with professionals to develop and maintain those systems.

To help you gain this critical knowledge, we have included three unique features in this book. First, every chapter is organized around a set of questions. Use these questions to manage your study time. Read until you can answer the questions. Second, every part and every chapter begins with a real-life scenario of a business professional who needs knowledge of information systems. Use those scenarios to understand how you can apply the knowledge of information systems to gain a personal competitive advantage. Finally, read the two-page boxed inserts, called "Guides." If possible, discuss the questions in these guides with other students. Such discussions will give you a chance to practice your listening skills and to learn to assert your own opinions in an effective manner.

Like all worthwhile endeavors, this course is work. That's just the way it is. No one succeeds in business without sustained focus, attention, desire, motivation, and hard work. It won't always be easy, it won't always be fun. However, you will learn concepts, skills, and behaviors that are essential for success in business in the twenty-first century.

I wish you, as an emerging business professional, the very best success!

Sincerely,

David Kroenke

Whidbey Island, Washington

THE GUIDES

Each chapter includes two *unique* guides focused on the issues in information systems that are currently most relevant. In each chapter, one deals with ethics, and the other deals with an issue related in some other way to the chapter topic. In business, you'll deal with issues similar to those presented and discussed in the guides, and you may be asked to recommend solutions to these problems. Each guide includes questions intended to stimulate thought, discussion, and active participation to help you develop your problem-solving skills.

Ethical issues abound in business, and as recent news stories indicate, some businesspeople are better than others at sorting through ethical conflicts. The "Ethics Guides" stimulate debate on how ethics apply to information systems issues. These guides will help you respond to future ethical dilemmas authentically and in a way that is consistent with your own values.

The other guides tackle topics that will help improve the quality of your thinking, which will improve any information system that you use and your ability to use MIS in your career. Some present ideas from cognitive science and

apply them to MIS. Others introduce you to someone who disagrees with one of the main ideas or methods in the chapter. In almost any business situation, you will find people with opinions contrary to the generally accepted wisdom. Having some practice managing opposing opinions will help you respond to them effectively. Finally, other guides state some strong personal opinions of the author. In business, people will differ in their opinions and then "agree to disagree"—they will back off, reflect, and sometimes alter their viewpoints. These guides will help you practice your reflection skills as you evaluate and discuss others' opinions.

All of the guides in the book will bring into your study thoughts and issues that will deepen your experience of MIS, both in the classroom and in preparation for helping you become a better business professional.

A listing of the guides follows, along with a page reference for its location in the book. The *Ethics Guide* in each chapter is indicated. (Twenty additional guides are available for instructional use at *www.pearsonhighered.com/kroenke*.)

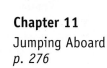

LEARNING AIDS FOR STUDENTS

We have structured this book so you can maximize the benefit from the time you spend reading it. As shown in the table below, each chapter includes a series of learning aids to help you succeed in this course.

RESOURCE	DESCRIPTION	BENEFIT	EXAMPLE
"This Could Happen to You" (located at the start of each part and each chapter)	Parts and chapters open with a running business scenario, the likes of which could entwine you in just a few years.	Sets up the chapter content and provides an obvious example of why the chapter is relevant to you.	Dee's blog at Emerson Pharmaceuticals, pp. 2 and 4; Majestic River Ventures, p. 158
Question-Driven Chapter Learning Objectives	These queries, and the subsequent chapter sections written around them, focus your attention and make your reading more efficient.	Identifies the main point of the section. When you can answer each question, you've learned the main point of the section.	pp. 43, 44, 45
Guides	Each chapter includes two guides that focus on current issues relating to information systems. One of the two deals with an ethical issue.	Stimulates thought and discussion. Helps develop your problem solving skills. Helps you learn to respond to ethical dilemmas in business.	pp. 106, 112
"MIS in Use" Cases	Each chapter includes an "MIS in Use" case that illustrates a situation that requires the topic of that chapter. Each leads to a Collaboration Exercise.	Provides you with an opportunity to apply the knowledge you have gained to a realistic situation.	pp. 126, 143
"How Does the Knowledge in This Help . . . You?" (near the end of each chapter)	This section revisits the opening scenario and discusses what the chapter taught you about it.	Summarizes the "takeaway" points from the chapter as they apply to the person in the story, and to you.	p. 58
Active Review	Each chapter concludes with a summary-and-review section, organized around the chapter's study questions.	Offers a review of important points in the chapter. If you can answer the questions posed, you will understand the material.	p. 59
Key Terms	Highlights the major terms and concepts with their appropriate page reference.	Provides a summary of key terms for review before exams.	p. 59
"Using Your Knowledge"	These exercises ask you to take your new knowledge to the next step by applying it to a practice problem.	Tests your critical thinking skills and keeps reminding you that you are learning material that applies to the real world.	pp. 59–60
Collaboration Exercise	A team exercise that applies the chapter's topic to the MIS in Use case for that chapter.	Use Google Docs & Spreadsheets, Microsoft Groove, Microsoft SharePoint, or some other tool to collaborate on collective answers.	pp. 60–61
Case Study	A case study closes each chapter. You will reflect on the use in real organizations of the technology or systems presented in the chapter and recommend solutions to business problems.	Requires you to apply newly acquired knowledge to real situations.	p. 61

RESOURCE	DESCRIPTION	BENEFIT	EXAMPLE
"International Dimension" (follows the final chapter in each part)	Each of the book's four parts closes with a module on the international aspects of the part topic.	Helps you understand international applications and issues relating to MIS.	pp. 146–147
"Consider Your Net Worth" (in the review section at the end of each part)	These exercises ask you to think about how you can use the text material in your career.	Helps you see ways that the knowledge from your study of the text can give you a competitive advantage in the marketplace.	p. 150
"Application Exercises" (in the review section at the end of each part)	These exercises ask you to solve business situations using spreadsheet (Excel) or database (Access) applications.	Helps develop your computer skills.	pp. 151–153
"Part Case" (at the end of each part)	A case study, similar to the case studies at the end of each chapter, demonstrates how real organizations use the technology or systems presented in the part.	Requires you to apply knowledge gained from several chapters to real business situations.	p. 154
Glossary (end of book)	A comprehensive list includes definitions of the key terms.	Provides one place for your quick review of terms and concepts.	p. 353
Video programs available	(1) All chapter opening scenarios are depicted in a series of short dramatizations that emphasize the importance of the chapter content. (2) Author David Kroenke gives tutorial discussions of key topics throughout the textbook.	(1) Bring to life the opening scenarios and put you right in the action. (2) Further discuss chapter material and help you develop better study skills.	These accompany each part opening and chapter opening. An icon in the margin of the book (e.g., see p. 5) indicates related video clips of the author.
MyMISLab	A student and instructor portal that contains an Online Microsoft Office 2007 tutorial, SharePoint collaboration tools and assignments, a class-testing program tied to AACSB standards, and classroom and tutorial videos.	Expands the classroom experience with valuable hands-on activities and tools.	**www.mymislab.com**
SharePoint Hosting	Pearson will host Microsoft SharePoint site collections for your university. Students need only a browser to participate.	Enables students to collaborate using the world's most popular collaboration software.	**www.pearsonhighered. com/kroenke**

MIS
ESSENTIALS

David M. Kroenke

Prentice Hall
Upper Saddle River, New Jersey 07458

Library of Congress Cataloging-in-Publication Data

Kroenke, David.
 MIS essentials/David M. Kroenke.—1st ed.
 p. cm.
 Includes bibliographical references and index.
 ISBN 978-0-13-607560-8 (pbk.: alk. paper)
1. Management information systems. 2. Business—Data processing. I. Title.
T58.6.K773 2009
658.4'038011—dc22

2008045329

Editor-in-Chief: Eric Svendsen
Executive Editor: Bob Horan
Director of Development: Stephen Deitmer
Product Development Manager: Ashley Santora
Editorial Project Manager: Kelly Loftus
Director of Marketing: Patrice Lumumba Jones
Marketing Manager: Anne Fahlgren
Permissions Project Manager: Charles Morris
Senior Managing Editor: Judy Leale
Production Project Manager: Ann Pulido
Senior Operations Specialist: Arnold Vila
Operations Specialist: Benjamin Smith
Design Director: Christy Mahon
Senior Art Director: Janet Slowik
Cover Design: Liz Harasymczuk Design
Cover Photos: Getty Images: Siri Stafford, Matthew Antrobus, Coco Marlet, and Thomas Barwick
Interior Design: Ilze Lemesis
Interior Illustrations: Amanda Duffy
Director, Image Resource Center: Melinda Patelli
Manager, Rights and Permissions: Zina Arabia
Manager, Visual Research: Beth Brenzel
Manager, Cover Visual Research & Permissions: Karen Sanatar
Composition: BookMasters, Inc.
Full-Service Project Management: Jen Welsch/BookMasters, Inc.
Printer/Binder: Courier/Kendallville
Printer/Cover: Lehigh-Phoenix Color/Hagerstown
Typeface: 10/13 Utopia

Credits and acknowledgments borrowed from other sources and reproduced, with permission, in this textbook appear on appropriate page within text.

Microsoft® and Windows® are registered trademarks of the Microsoft Corporation in the U.S.A. and other countries. Screen shots and icons reprinted with permission from the Microsoft Corporation. This book is not sponsored or endorsed by or affiliated with the Microsoft Corporation.

Pearson Education Ltd., London
Pearson Education Singapore, Pte. Ltd
Pearson Education, Canada, Inc.
Pearson Education–Japan
Pearson Education Australia PTY, Limited

Pearson Education North Asia, Ltd., Hong Kong
Pearson Educación de Mexico, S.A. de C.V.
Pearson Education Malaysia, Pte. Ltd
Pearson Education Upper Saddle River,
 New Jersey

Prentice Hall
is an imprint of

www.pearsonhighered.com

10 9 8 7 6 5 4 3 2 1
ISBN-13: 978-0-13-607560-8
ISBN-10: 0-13-607560-6

To C.J., Carter, and Charlotte

BRIEF CONTENTS

Chapter Extensions

CONTENTS

12 Information Security Management p. 286

▰▰▰ The International Dimension, Part 4

International IT Development and Management p. 312

TO THE STUDENT

*K*nowing the *Essentials of MIS* is important because no matter what you do in business, you will use information systems. And, if you are a business leader, you will need to be able to think innovatively about how to use MIS to advance your own and your organization's goals and objectives. Whether you work in accounting, marketing, finance, operations, management, human resources—whatever your business specialty—you need to know the essentials of MIS.

Because working with MIS is a given, the only important question is: How effective will you be? Will you be a helpless user, one who says, "I don't know anything about computers, and I don't want to?" Or will you be a manager who says, "I know there's a way to use information systems to improve the productivity of my employees?" Will you be someone who finds an innovative application of information technology to push your company ahead of the competition? Or, will you be the user who "just doesn't get it?"

Relating This Class to Your Business Career

Many students think this is "the computer class." It is not. MIS is not the same as computer literacy. Some students think the primary goal of this class is to teach you Excel or Access. Although you may learn about using those products in this class, you will do so on the way to learning something far more important: how to use computer-based systems to better accomplish business goals and objectives—your personal ones and those for the business in which you work.

Working with MIS is not something you will wait to do 20 years down the road when you are vice president of whatever. It starts your first day on the job. Imagine yourself that day, hired by the company you really want to work for. What happens that first day? Typically, your supervisor first gives you a desk and then assigns you a computer.

What are you going to do with that computer? Send emails to your parents? Surf the Web? IM your friends? Are you even allowed to use your work computer for personal email? (Maybe.) Can your employer read the email you send from work? (Yes, definitely.) *Will* your employer read the email you send from work? (Maybe.) But, more important, what are you going to DO with that computer to help your career? To help your department? To give your organization a competitive advantage?

Here's the good news: You don't have to wait until that first day to start. This book is designed to help you experience MIS right now—in school, where you can ask "silly" questions without ruining your business reputation. Use Google Docs & Spreadsheets, or Microsoft Groove, or Microsoft SharePoint, or some other software to facilitate your group and team assignments. Get involved with MIS now, where you can propose infeasible projects, and where you can develop ideas that are not just "out of the box," they're out of the universe. Do it now while you have the support of a department of knowledgeable professionals (your professors) who are there to provide you consulting, at no extra charge!

Using This Book

Every part and every chapter in this book start with a real-life business scenario of someone working with MIS. For example, you can read about Dee Clarke in Part 1 (page 2). Dee wanted to sponsor a blog to provide information to 450 very demanding salespeople. Her blog had to be private; she couldn't put it on some public space for competitors to look at. It also had to be very professional, and it needed the blessing of her internal computer department. How would you proceed if that idea occurred to you? How did Dee proceed? Each chapter will give you knowledge to apply to those scenarios.

The book consists of four parts and three chapters within each part. Every chapter starts with a list of questions. Read those questions. Read the text material. Apply the knowledge to the scenario. Do the activities in the "Active Review." You can stop reading when you know you can answer the list of questions.

Every chapter has two "Guides." These are two-page spreads that present some experience of MIS. One of the guides poses an ethical problem; the other one describes a scenario that will help you use MIS now, today, in the classroom. Your professor may use the guides for discussion in class, or may prefer that you read and think about them on your own. Whether you use them formally or informally in your course, talk about them with others. The experience of hearing others' ideas and sharing your own is good practice for almost any career you choose to pursue.

This book comes with two different video programs. One video series shows the people in the scenarios. You can see Dee in action. You can see why she's risen so far, so fast, and watch her maneuverings. In Chapters 7 through 12, you can meet the owner, employees, and clients of Majestic River Ventures, and learn, in part, how Majestic is attempting to use social networking to accomplish its competitive strategy.

The second series is a collection of videos of me explaining key concepts. The video icon Video in the margin of the book means there is a video available for that topic.

I hope you will get involved with MIS today, so that you are as ready as you can be to participate in the incredible opportunities coming your way. During your career, information systems will have a profound impact on business organizations. Business is a social activity. People "do business" with other people. In the coming years, computer networks and portable computing devices will radically change how people relate. Organizations will be virtual; people will work closely together, yet may never meet in person. Many jobs and tasks performed today will be eliminated, and jobs unforeseen today will become careers and professions. All this change will be animated by people using MIS.

So, start your experience. Turn to page 2 and read about Dee. Ask yourself what you would do if you were "in her shoes." And don't forget to have some fun—using MIS now!

David Kroenke
Whidbey Island, Washington

MIS
ESSENTIALS

MIS AND YOU

Knowledge of information systems will be critical to your success in business. If you major in accounting, marketing, management, or in another, less technical, major, you may not yet know how important such knowledge will be to you. The purpose of Part 1 of this textbook is to demonstrate why this subject is so important to every business professional today. We begin with a real-life case.

This could happen to you

Dee Clark is the Hospital Sales Marketing Director for the Academic and Hospital Division of Emerson Pharmaceuticals, a $4 billion pharmaceutical company.[1] Emerson employs a team of 450 salespeople to present its drugs and information about their effectiveness and use to doctors in many different settings. Dee's division focuses on doctors and pharmacists in medical schools and in hospitals. Emerson introduces dozens of new drugs each year. It is both difficult and very important for the salespeople to learn about the new products. To be effective, salespeople need to be able to discuss the characteristics, efficacy, dosage recommendations, and relevant research for each of these drugs.

The pharmaceutical industry is competitive. Many other companies compete for medical professionals' attention and business. The competitors, too, employ large professional sales forces. Dee's job is to ensure that all of her reps have the information they need to succeed in this very competitive environment. When one rep develops a technique that successfully presents a product, overcomes a doctor's or pharmacist's reluctance, or causes the professional to choose Emerson's drugs over those of the competition, Dee wants to disseminate that technique to as many other salespeople as possible.

Thus, a big part of Dee's job is to inform the salespeople about the drugs she markets and to make sure the salespeople have all the information they need to succeed. Dee sometimes invites doctors and other professionals to seminars

---

[1]The people and the events in this case are real. Everything related here actually happened. However, to protect the innocent, the guilty, and the publisher of this text, the name of the company and the company's industry have been changed. Dee does exist, and she does work with a 450-person sales force.

conducted by leading medical researchers, and sometimes she herself makes presentations to hospitals. She wants the sales force to know about these events and the sales that result from them.

In the fall of 2008, Dee was looking for better ways to connect with her salespeople. She was discussing this need with some of her friends, who suggested that she use a blog to disseminate the latest product news, current competitive threats and responses, recent successes, and other information. A **blog**, or **Weblog**, is an online journal. Blogs use information technology to publish information over the Internet. One of the first and most famous blogs is *www.drudgereport.com*. (If you are not familiar with blogs, visit that site now.)

Dee liked the idea of a blog, but time was pressing. Her friend suggested the blog in November 2008, and she needed the blog to be up and running by the company's national sales meeting in January 2009. As she pondered this idea, she asked herself questions like these:

- **Is this possible? Can I have it done on time?**

- **What will I need to learn? How hard will it be to post my thoughts, pictures, and other resources on the blog?**

- **How can I keep competitors from reading my blog?**

- **Will the salespeople use the blog? What can I do to make it easy for them to do so?**

- **What kind of computer do I need to support the blog?**

- **Where do I begin?**

Dee's situation illustrates why the knowledge in this class is vitally important to business professionals today. Dee is a *marketing manager*. In college, she majored in marketing. She is not an information systems professional, and she never thought she would need to know how to manage the construction of an information system. Yet that is exactly what her job now requires her to do.

Keep thinking about Dee as you read this text. This exact scenario could happen to you!

CHAPTER 1

IS in the Life of Business Professionals

Dee Clark does not know it, but she needs to build an information system (IS). As a marketing manager, she will not build the system herself. She will not buy the computer hardware and hook it up. She will not acquire or write any computer programs. She will, however, hire and manage the people who will do exactly that. As you will see, she will also be confronted along the way with the need for knowledge that she does not possess.

This could happen to you

Dee's lack of knowledge will cost her company, and it will impede her progress. Her ignorance about MIS (management information systems) will leave her at a disadvantage in conversations with technical people and make it difficult for her to do her job. Her uncertainty about what to do will delay the project and keep her from performing her other job tasks. Because of her lack of IS knowledge, she will work many extra hours and spend sleepless nights worrying about the success of her project. What's especially sad is that it didn't need to be this way. She just needed the knowledge that you are about to obtain.

For example, consider this question: What is an information system made of? When people say they want to build a new garage, you have some idea of what they're going to do. But when people say they're going to build a new information system, what are they going to build? We begin the book with that question.

I've got this great idea for a blog!

Study Questions

Q1 What is an information system?

Q2 What is MIS?

Q3 How does IS differ from IT?

Q4 How do successful business professionals use IS?

Q5 What new opportunities for IS are developing today?

Q6 What is your role in IS security?

Q7 What is this class about?

How does the knowledge in this chapter help Dee and you?

Q1 What Is an Information System?

A **system** is a group of components that interact to achieve some purpose. As you might guess, an **information system (IS)** is a group of components that interact to produce information. That sentence, although true, raises another question: What are these components that interact to produce information?

Figure 1-1 shows the **five-component framework** of **computer hardware, software,**[1] **data, procedures,** and **people**. These five components are present in every information system—from the most simple to the most complex. For example, when you use a computer to write a class report, you are using hardware (the computer, storage disk, keyboard, and monitor), software (Word, WordPerfect, or some other word-processing program), data (the words, sentences, and paragraphs in your report), procedures (the methods you use to start the program, enter your report, print it, and save and back up your file), and people (you).

Consider a more complex example, say, an airline reservation system. It, too, consists of these five components, even though each one is far more complicated. The hardware consists of dozens or more computers linked together by telecommunications hardware. Further, hundreds of different programs coordinate communications among the computers, and still other programs perform the reservations and related services. Additionally, the system must store millions upon millions of characters of data about flights, customers, reservations, and other facts. Hundreds of different procedures are followed by airline personnel, travel agents, and customers. Finally, the information system includes people, not only the users of the system, but also those who operate and service the computers, those who maintain the data, and those who support the networks of computers.

---

[1]In the past, the term *software* was used to refer to computer components that were not hardware (e.g., programs, procedures, user manuals, etc.). Today, the term *software* is used more specifically to refer only to programs, and that is how we use the term throughout this book.

FIGURE 1-1
Five Components of an
Information System

Hardware	Software	Data	Procedures	People

The five components in Figure 1-1 are common to all information systems. Dee will need these five components for the information system that will support her blog. Note especially the *people* and *procedures* components of her system. Dee and her product managers will contribute to the blog. They will need training and procedures to do so. The salespeople will need procedures for accessing the blog, and someone will need to support the hardware and software as well as administer the data contained in the blog.

Before we move forward, note that we have defined an information system to include a computer. Some people would say that such a system is a **computer-based information system**. They would note that there are information systems that do not include computers, such as a calendar hanging on the wall outside of a conference room that is used to schedule the room's use. Such systems have been used by businesses for centuries. Although this point is true, in this book we focus on *computer-based* information systems. To simplify and shorten the book, we will use the term *information system* as a synonym for *computer-based information system*.

Q2 What Is MIS?

Today, there are thousands, even millions, of information systems in the world. Not all relate to business. In this textbook, we are concerned with **MIS**, or **management information systems**. MIS is the development and use of information systems that help businesses achieve their goals and objectives. This definition has three key elements: *development and use, information systems*, and *business goals and objectives*. We just discussed *information systems*. Now consider *development and use* and *business goals and objectives*.

Development and Use of Information Systems

Information systems do not pop up like mushrooms after a hard rain; they must be constructed. You might be saying, "Wait a minute. I'm a finance (or accounting, or management) major, not an information systems major. I don't need to know how to build information systems."

If you are saying that, you are like a lamb headed for fleecing. Like Dee, throughout your career, in whatever field you choose, you will need new information systems. To have an information system that meets your needs, you need to take an *active role* in that system's development. Even if you are not a programmer or a database designer or some other IS professional, you must take an active role in specifying the system's requirements and in helping manage the development project. Without active involvement on your part, it will only be good luck that causes the new system to meet your needs.

To that end, throughout this text we will discuss your role in the development of information systems. In addition, we devote all of Chapter 10 to this important topic. As you read this text and think about information systems, you should ask yourself questions like, "How was that system constructed?" and "What roles did the users play during its development?" If you start asking yourself these questions now, you will be better prepared to answer them once you start a job, when financial, career, and other consequences will depend on your answers.

In addition to development tasks, you will also have important roles to play in the *use* of information systems. Of course, you will need to learn how to employ the system to accomplish your goals. But you will also have important ancillary functions as well. For example, when using an information system, you will have responsibilities for protecting the security of the system and its data. You may also have tasks for backing up data. When the system fails (most do, at some point), you will have tasks to perform while the system is down as well as tasks to accomplish to help recover the system correctly and quickly.

Finally, throughout your career you may from time to time be faced with ethical issues involving your use of information systems. To help you prepare for those challenges, in every chapter of this book we have included an *Ethics Guide*. These Guides will get you to start thinking about ethical dilemmas, which will help you clarify your values and make you ready to respond authentically to future ethical challenges.

The first *Ethics Guide*, on pages 8–9, considers what to do with information that comes your way but that was not intended for you.

Achieving Business Goals and Objectives

The last part of the definition of MIS is that information systems exist to help businesses achieve their *goals and objectives*. First, realize that this statement hides an important fact: Businesses themselves do not "do" anything. A business is not alive, and it cannot act. It is the people within a business who sell, buy, design, produce, finance, market, account, and manage. So information systems exist to help people who work in a business to achieve the goals and objectives of that business.

Information systems are not created for the sheer joy of exploring technology. They are not created so that the company can be "modern" or so that the company can claim to be a "new-economy company." They are not created because the IS department thinks it needs to be created or because the company is "falling behind the technology curve."

This point may seem so obvious that you wonder why we mention it. Every day, however, some business somewhere is developing an information system for the wrong reasons. Right now, somewhere in the world, a company is deciding to create a Web site for the sole reason that "every other business has one." This company is not asking questions like, "What is the purpose of the Web site?" or, "What is it going to do for us?" or, "Are the costs of the Web site sufficiently offset by the benefits?"—but it should be!

Even more serious, somewhere right now an IS manager has been convinced by some vendor's sales team or by an article in a business magazine that his or her company must upgrade to the latest, greatest high-tech gizmo. This IS manager is attempting to convince his or her manager that this expensive upgrade is a good idea. We hope that someone somewhere in the company is asking questions like, "What business goal or objective will be served by the investment in the gizmo?"

As a future business professional, you need to learn to look at information systems and technologies only through the lens of *business need*. Learn to ask, "All of this technology may be great, in and of itself, but what will it do for us? What will it do for our business and our particular goals?"

Again, MIS is the development and use of information systems that help businesses achieve their goals and objectives. Already, you should be realizing that there is much more to this class than buying a computer, writing a program, or working with a spreadsheet.

Q3 How Does IS Differ from IT?

Information technology and *information system* are two closely related terms, but they are different. **Information technology (IT)** refers to methods, inventions, standards, and products. As the term implies, it refers to raw technology, and it concerns only the hardware, software, and data components of an information system. In contrast, an information system is a system of hardware, software, data, procedures, and people that produce information.

IT, by itself, will not help an organization achieve its goals and objectives. It is only when IT is embedded into an IS—only when the technology within the hardware,

ETHICS GUIDE

Ethics of Misdirected Information Use

Consider the following situations:

Situation A: Suppose you are buying a condo and you know that at least one other party is bidding against you. While agonizing over your best strategy, you stop at a local Starbucks. As you sip your latte, you overhear a conversation at the table next to yours. Three people are talking so loudly that it is difficult to ignore them, and you soon realize that they are the real estate agent and the couple who is competing for the condo you want. They are preparing their offer. Should

you listen to their conversation? If you do, do you use the information you hear to your advantage?

Situation B: Consider the same situation from a different perspective—instead of overhearing the conversation, suppose you receive that same information in an email. Perhaps an administrative assistant at the agent's office confuses you and the other customer and mistakenly sends you the terms of the other party's offer. Do you read that email? If so, do you use the information that you read to your advantage?

Situation C: Suppose that you sell computer software. In the midst of a sensitive price negotiation, your customer accidentally sends you an internal email that contains the maximum amount that the customer can pay for your software. Do you read that email? Do you use that information to guide your negotiating strategy? What do you do if your customer discovers that the email may have reached you and asks, "Did you read my email?" How do you answer?

Situation D: Suppose a friend mistakenly sends you an email that contains sensitive personal medical data. Further, suppose you read the email before you know what you're reading and you're embarrassed to learn something very personal that truly is none of your business. Your friend asks you, "Did you read that email?" How do you respond?

Situation E: Finally, suppose that you work as a network administrator and your position allows you unrestricted access to the mailing lists for your company. Assume that you have the skill to insert your email address into any company mailing list without anyone knowing about it. You insert your address into several lists and, consequently, begin to receive confidential email that no one intended for you to see. One of those emails indicates that your best friend's department is about to be eliminated and all of its personnel fired. Do you forewarn your friend?

DISCUSSION QUESTIONS

1. Consider the questions in situations A and B. Do your answers differ? Does the medium by which the information is obtained make a difference? Is it easier to avoid reading an email than it is to avoid hearing a conversation? If so, does that difference matter?

2. Consider the questions in situations B and C. Do your answers differ? In situation B, the information is for your personal gain; in C, the information is for both your personal and your organization's gain. Does this difference matter? How do you respond when asked if you have read the email?

3. Consider the questions in situations C and D. Do your answers differ? Would you lie in one case and not in the other? Why or why not?

4. Consider the question in situation E. What is the essential difference between situations A through D and situation E? Suppose you had to justify your behavior in situation E. How would you argue? Do you believe your own argument?

5. In situations A through D, if you access the information you have done nothing illegal. You were the passive recipient. Even for item E, although you undoubtedly violated your company's employment policies, you most likely did not violate the law. So for this discussion, assume that all of these actions are legal.

    a. What is the difference between legal and ethical? Look up both words in a dictionary, and explain how they differ.

    b. Make the argument that business is competitive and that if something is legal, then it is acceptable to do it if it helps to further your goals.

    c. Make the argument that it is never appropriate to do something unethical.

6. Summarize your beliefs about proper conduct when you receive misdirected information.

software, and data is combined with the people and procedure components—that IT becomes useful.

Think about these statements from the standpoint of the information systems at your university. Do you care that the university network uses the latest, greatest technology to send messages across campus? Do you care that the university's Web site uses the latest, fastest hardware to show you available classes? Not really. It is only when the humans at the university (including you) use procedures to do something—to enroll in a class, for example—that the IT becomes useful to you.

Consider Dee and her blog. She will use IT, but that isn't her primary interest. Her goal is to combine the IT in hardware, software, and data with procedures to enable herself, Emerson's product managers, and her sales reps to accomplish their own goals and objectives.

Successful businesspeople understand this crucial difference between IT and IS, and they take advantage of it, as we show next.

Q4 How Do Successful Business Professionals Use IS?

Today, every business professional uses numerous information systems. Some people do little more than write email, access Web pages, and do instant messaging. Although the ability to use such basic information systems is essential, that level of knowledge and use does not give anyone a competitive advantage in the workplace.

To gain a competitive advantage, you need to do more. You need to learn to think about IT and IS when you consider the problems and opportunities that confront your department or organization. Dee Clark, the marketing manager at the start of this chapter, is an excellent example. She needs to rapidly and conveniently transmit the latest news, advice, and opportunities to the sales reps with whom she deals. She considered this need creatively and realized she could use a blog to disseminate that information. Doing so gave both her and her sales reps a competitive advantage.

Recent research supports this claim. The RAND Corporation (a famous technology institution that invented dozens of new technologies, including the design of the Internet) published a study on trends in the world workforce in the twenty-first century.[2] That study predicted strong demand for business professionals who have the ability to create innovative applications using emerging technology. Further, that demand will continue for the next 50 years.

To take advantage of this trend, you need not be a developer of technology. Rather, you need to think creatively about problems, challenges, and opportunities in your business and organization and be able to apply new technology to your business needs.

Amazon.com is a perfect example. Jeff Bezos, founder and CEO of Amazon.com, did not invent any technology. He was one of the first to see, however, that the emerging technology of the Internet, combined with existing database technology, enabled a new business model. He developed an organization that became one of the world's largest users of information systems. In fact, on December 14, 2005, the information systems at Amazon.com processed an average of 41 items per second for 24 hours. Truly, Amazon represents an innovative application of the technology that was emerging when Bezos founded the company.

Throughout this textbook, we will consider many different information system types and underlying technologies. We will show the benefits of those systems and technologies, and we will illustrate their successful implementations in *MIS in Use* cases, such as the one about YouTube in *MIS in Use 1*.

---

[2]Lynn A. Karoly and Constantijn W. A. Panis, *The 21st Century at Work* (Santa Monica, CA: RAND Corporation, 2004), xvii–xviii.

 **1 YouTube and You?**

You just read the sentence: "That study predicted strong demand for business professionals who have the ability to create innovative applications using emerging technology." Did you gloss over it? Was it just words?

In the spring of 2005, I taught an MBA-level database course structured on the premise that essentially free data communications and data storage would create new business opportunities. The students were assigned to groups and asked to develop the outline of a business plan for a company that would take advantage of one of those new opportunities. Alas, we did not develop any viable plan. The students graduated and went on with their lives.

Meanwhile, at the same time, another team *did* find a viable way to take advantage of near-free data communications and data storage. On February 15, 2005, Chad Hurley, Steve Chen, and Jawed Karim registered the domain "YouTube," and by April 23 had posted their first video. By November, YouTube had 200,000 registered users and was showing 2 million videos per day. In 9 months, YouTube had grown from nothing to 200,000 users.

By January 2006, YouTube was showing 25 million videos per day. By May 2006, YouTube was showing 43 percent of all videos viewed over the Internet. By July 2006, users were viewing 100 million videos and uploading 65,000 new videos per day. YouTube had a total of 30 employees.

Think about that: 30 employees were serving 100 million videos per day. That's 3.33 million videos *per employee*, all accomplished in just over 1 year.

That phenomenal success was capped by Google's $1.65 billion acquisition of YouTube in October 2006 (see Figure 1). In just 20 months, YouTube's founders had turned nothing but an idea into $1.65 billion. That's a rate of $2,750,000 of equity per day.

What's the point of this story? The opportunities were there in 2005, and they are still there today. Although it is unlikely that you, too, will have such success, think about it: How can you use free data communications and data storage in your business? Or, in a job interview, how might your prospective employer use such resources?

You and a team of your fellow students will have an opportunity to collaborate on this idea in the Collaboration Exercise at the end of this chapter (on page 20).

FIGURE 1
A Great IS Opportunity—
Google's Purchase of
YouTube for $1.62 Billion

Q5 What New Opportunities for IS Are Developing Today?

"That's fine," you might be saying. "That was then, and this is now. The Internet is old news. All the good opportunities are gone." If you think this way, you are wrong. In fact, there are great opportunities right now.

Two Opportunities, Right Now

Information technology has developed in such a way that, for all practical purposes, data storage and data communication are free. Of course, no business resource is free, but the costs of storage and data transmission are so low that, when compared to other business expenses, they are essentially zero.

Whenever an important business resource becomes free, new opportunities for using that resource abound. In the case of free data storage and free data transmission, consider Getty Images (*www.gettyimages.com*; see also *Part Case 1-1*, page 69). Getty Images sells pictures over the Internet. The pictures are electronic; they are made of binary digits (explained in Chapter 4). Because the cost of both data storage and data transmission is essentially zero, the variable cost of production of a new image to Getty is zero. (See the Getty image in Figure 1-2.)

Reflect on that statement: "The cost of production is zero." Any revenue that Getty makes on an image goes straight to the bottom line. Truly, this is a business that has found an innovative application of IT.

For another example, consider Media Partners *www.media-partners.com*, a partnership that produces video training and sells it to commercial organizations and the government. Recently, Media Partners has developed an online training program to teach the principles of customer service. In this program, the trainee takes a short exam, watches a video, and then takes another exam. Results of the tests are sent via email to the employee's supervisor.

This entire system is automated. Because the cost of data storage and data transmission is essentially zero, the variable cost of producing the program is essentially zero. All of the revenue from these programs goes straight to the bottom line. Media Partners harnessed IT to produce a veritable money machine.

FIGURE 1-2
Another IS Opportunity—Getty Images Supplies Photographic Images Electronically

Hans Bjurling/Getty Images – Johner Images Royalty Free

These opportunities are real, right now, but the best news is that there is no sign that technology development is slowing. New opportunities will continue to emerge, as predicted by Moore's Law.

Moore's Law

Gordon Moore is the cofounder of Intel Corporation, the world's leading manufacturer of computer chips and other computer-related components. In 1965, he said that because of technology improvements in electronic chip design and manufacturing, "The number of transistors per square inch on an integrated chip doubles every 18 months." This observation is known as **Moore's Law**. Moore's prediction has proved generally accurate in the more than 40 years since he made it.

The density of transistors on a computer chip relates to the speed of the chip, and so you will sometimes hear Moore's Law expressed as, "The speed of a computer chip doubles every 18 months." This is not exactly what Moore said, but it comes close to the essence of his idea.

Dramatic Reduction in Price/Performance Ratio

As a result of Moore's Law, the price/performance ratio of computers has fallen dramatically for years (see Figure 1-3). Computers have shrunk from multimillion-dollar, room-filling machines in 1968 to $300 small desktop devices in 2008. Along the way, the availability of increased computing power has enabled developments such as laser printers; graphical user interfaces, such as Windows; high-speed communications; cell phones; personal data assistants (PDAs); email; iPhones; and the Internet.

Moore's Law is the principal reason why data storage and data transmission are essentially free today. All indications are that the price/performance ratio of IT products will continue to fall. New opportunities for applying new technology will continue to emerge; you just need to learn to look for them!

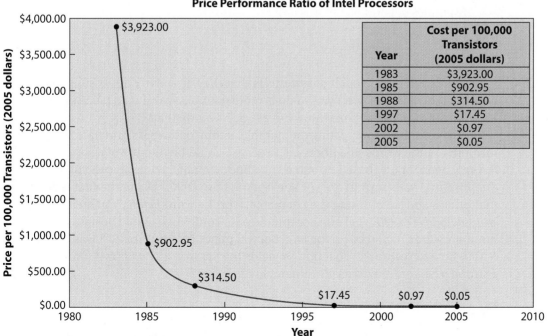

FIGURE 1-3
Computer Price/Performance Ratio Decreases

Q6 What Is Your Role in IS Security?

As you have learned, information systems create value. However, they also create risk. For example, Amazon.com maintains credit card data on millions of customers and has the responsibility to protect that data. If Amazon.com's security system were breached and that credit card data stolen, Amazon.com would incur serious losses—not only lost business, but also potentially staggering liability losses. Because of the importance of information security, we will consider it throughout this textbook. Additionally, Chapter 12 is devoted to security.

However, you have a role in security that is too important for us to wait until you read that chapter. Like all informations systems, security systems have the five components, including people. Thus, every security system ultimately depends on the behavior of its users. If the users do not take security seriously, if they do not follow security procedures, then the hardware, software, and data components of the security system are wasted expense. So, before we proceed further, we will address how you should create and use a strong password, which is an essential component of computer security.

Almost all security systems use user names and passwords. As a user of information systems in a business organization, you will be instructed to create a strong password and to protect it. *It is vitally important for you to do so.* (In fact, you should already be using such passwords at your university.)

Strong Passwords

So what is a strong password, and how do you create one? Microsoft, a company that has many reasons to promote effective security, defines a **strong password** as one with the following characteristics:

- Has seven or more characters
- Does not contain your user name, real name, or company name
- Does not contain a complete dictionary word in any language
- Is different from previous passwords you have used
- Contains both upper- and lowercase letters, numbers, and special characters (such as ~ ! @; # $ % ^ &; * ( ) _ +; − =; { } | [ ] \ : " ; ' <; >; ? , . /)

   Examples of good passwords are:

- Qw37^T1bb?at
- 3B47qq<3>5!7b

The problem with such passwords is that they are nearly impossible to remember. And the last thing you want to do is write your password on a piece of paper and keep it near the workstation where you use it. Never do that!

One technique for creating memorable, strong passwords is to base them on the first letter of the words in a phrase. The phrase could be the title of a song or the first line of a poem or one based on some fact about your life. For example, you might take the phrase, "I was born in Rome, New York, before 1990." Using the first letters from that phrase and substituting the character < for the word *before*, you create the password *IwbiR,NY<1990.* That's an acceptable password, but it would be better if all of the numbers were not placed on the end. So, you might try the phrase, "I was born at 3:00 A.M in Rome, New York." That phrase yields the password *Iwba3:00AMiR,NY,* which is a strong password that is easily remembered.

Password Etiquette

Once you have created a strong password, you need to protect it with proper behavior. Proper password etiquette is one of the marks of a business professional. Never write down your password, and do not share it with others. Never ask others for their passwords, and never give your password to someone else.

But what if you need someone else's password? Suppose, for example, you ask someone to help you with a problem on your computer. You sign on to an information system, and for some reason you need to enter that other person's password. In this case, say to the other person, "We need your password," and then get out of your chair, offer your keyboard to the other person, and look away while he or she enters the password. Among professionals working in organizations that take security seriously, this little "do-si-do" move—one person getting out of the way so that another person can enter a password—is common and accepted.

If someone asks for your password, do not give it out. Instead, get up, go over to that person's machine, and enter your password yourself. Stay present while your password is in use, and ensure that your account is logged out at the end of the activity. No one should mind or be offended in any way when you do this. It is the mark of a professional.

Q7 What Is This Class About?

Many students enter this class with an erroneous idea of what they will study. Often, students think of it as a computer class—or at least a class that has something to do with computers and business. Many students think this class is about learning how to use Excel or Access or Dreamweaver. Figure 1-4 lists a number of reasons that students have given me when explaining why they don't need to take this class. As you can see, opinions vary on what the class is about.

By now, you should have an idea that this class is much broader than just learning how to use Excel or Dreamweaver. You may, in fact, use those programs in this class, but the focus will not be on learning what keys to push to make the program work as you want. Instead, the focus will be on learning to use those tools *to accomplish a business purpose.*

The *Guide* on pages 16–17 shares my personal opinion about why these chapters—and this book—matter to you.

- "I already know how to use Excel and Word. I can build a Web site with FrontPage. OK, it's a simple Web site, but I can do it. And when I need to learn more, I can. So let me out of this class!"
- "We're going to learn how to work with information systems? That's like practicing the stomach flu. If and when the time comes, I'll know how to do it."
- "I'm terrified of computers. I'm a people-person, and I don't do well with engineering-like things. I've put this class off until the last quarter of my senior year. I hope it's not as bad as I fear; I just wish they didn't make me take it."
- "There's really no content in this class. I mean, I've been programming since high school, I can write in C++, though Python is my favorite language. I know computer technology. This class is just a bunch of management-babble mixed up with some computer terms. At least, it's an easy class though."
- "Well, I'm sure there is some merit to this class, but consider the opportunity cost. I really need to be taking more microeconomics and international business. The time that I spend on this class could be better spent on those subjects."
- "The only thing I need to know is how to surf the Web and how to use email. I know how to do those, so I just don't need this class."
- "What, you mean this class is not about learning Excel and FrontPage? That's what I thought we were going to learn. That's what I need to know. Why all this information systems stuff? How do I make a Web site? That's what I need to know."

FIGURE 1-4
Student Thoughts About Why "I Don't Need This Class"

Duller Than Dirt?

Yes, you read that title correctly: This subject can seem duller than dirt. Take the phrase, "development and use of IS in organizations." Read just that phrase, and you start to yawn, wondering, "How am I going to absorb hundreds of pages of this?"

Stop and think: Why are you reading this book? Right now in the Sea of Cortez, the water is clear and warm, and the swimming and diving are wonderful. You could be kayaking to Isla San Francisco this minute. Or, somewhere in the world people are skiing. Whether in Aspen, Colorado, or Portillo, Chile, people are blasting through the powder somewhere. You could be one of them, living in a small house with a group of friends, having good times at night. Whatever it is that you like to do, you could be doing it right now. So why are you here, where you are, reading this book? Why aren't you there?

Waking up should be one of your goals while in college. I mean waking up to your life. Ceasing to live according to someone else's plan and beginning to live your own plan. Doing that requires you to become conscious of the choices you make and the consequences they have.

Suppose you take an hour to read your assignment in this book tonight. For a typical person, that is 4,320 heartbeats (72 beats times 60 minutes) that you have used to read this book—heartbeats that you will never have again. Despite the evidence of your current budget, the critical resource for humans is not money but time. No matter what we do, we cannot get more of it. Was your reading today worth those 4,320 heartbeats?

For some reason, you chose to major in business. For some reason, you are taking this class, and, for some reason, you have been instructed to read this textbook. Now, given that you made a good decision to major in business (and not to kayak in Baja), and given that someone is requiring you to read this text, the question then becomes, "How can you maximize the return on the 4,320 heartbeats you are investing per hour?"

The secret is to personalize the material. At every page, learn to ask yourself, "How does this pertain to me?" and "How can I use this material to further my goals?" If you find some topic irrelevant, ask your professor or your classmates what they think. What's this topic for? Why are we reading this? What am I going to do with it later in my career? Why is this worth 1,000 (or whatever) heartbeats?

MIS is all-encompassing. To me, that's one of its beauties. Consider the components: hardware, software, data, procedures, and people. Do you want to be an engineer? Then work with the hardware component. Do you want to be a programmer? Write software. Do you want to be a practicing philosopher, an applied epistemologist? Learn data modeling. Do you like social systems and sociology? Learn how to design effective group and organizational procedures.

Do you like people? Become an IS trainer or a computer systems salesperson. Do you enjoy management? Learn how to bring all of those disparate elements together.

I've worked in this industry for almost 40 years. The breadth of MIS and the rapid change of technology have kept me fascinated for every one of those years. Further, the beauty of working with intellectual property is that it doesn't weigh very much—moving symbols around won't wear you out. And you do it indoors in a temperature-controlled office. They may even put your name on the door.

So wake up. Why are you reading this? How can you make it relevant? Jump onto Google, and search for "MIS careers" or use some other phrase from this chapter and see what you get. Challenge yourself to find something that is important to you personally in every chapter.

You just invested 780 heartbeats in reading this editorial. Was it worth it? Keep asking!

DISCUSSION QUESTIONS

1. Explain what it means to "wake up to your life."

2. Are you awake to your life? How do you know? What can you do once a week to ensure that you are awake to your life?

3. What are your professional goals? Are they yours, or are they someone else's? How do you know?

4. How does this class pertain to your professional goals?

5. How are you going to make the material in this class interesting?

Consider the definition of MIS again: the development and use of information systems that help organizations (and the people who work in them) accomplish their goals and objectives. Thus, to understand MIS, you need to understand both business and technology, and you need to be able to relate one to the other.

The table of contents of the chapters in this book will give you an idea of how we will proceed. In the next two chapters, we will discuss the relationship of business processes and information systems, and we will show how information systems can be used to gain competitive advantages. Then, in Chapters 4 through 6, you will learn about hardware, software, databases, and data communications technology. With that foundation, in Chapters 7 through 9 we will show how technology can be used in three different ways to gain a competitive advantage. Finally, you will learn about the management of systems development, IS resources, and security in Chapters 10 through 12.

How does the knowledge in this chapter help Dee and you?

This chapter should encourage Dee. She's on the right track: She's looking for innovative applications of emerging technology. She wants to use an information system (her blog) to find ways to give her sales force a competitive advantage.

Dee's work can be guided by the five components. She will need a computer with software and data to store and process her blog. She doesn't know yet how that will be done, but she knows that they need to exist. She also knows that someone will need to follow procedures to set up and administer her blog. She herself will need a computer with software to post entries to her blog, and she will need procedures (and training) for doing so. Finally, she knows that the salespeople will need procedures for accessing the blog and for sending her comments about various blog entries.

I've got this great idea for a blog!

Collaboration technology, as described in Chapter Extensions 1 and 2, may be of particular use to Dee and her salespeople.

She also knows that using the blog is not the end of the story. Technology will continue to develop and improve, and she'll need to think constantly about how she can use other technology in other systems to help her accomplish her goals and objectives.

Finally, Dee knows how to create a strong password. She will need one to control access to her blog—she certainly wouldn't want someone from the competition to post entries to her blog. But she also wants to block well-intentioned people from making unauthorized entries to the blog. She wants to control the timing, for example, of important news, and using security with a strong password will help her do that.

Active  Review

Use this Active Review to verify that you understand the material in the chapter. You can read the entire chapter and then perform the tasks in this review, or you can read the text material for just one question and perform the tasks in this review for that question before moving on to the next one.

Q1 **What is an information system?** List the components of an information system. Explain how knowledge of these components will guide Dee's work as she builds her information system.

Q2 **What is MIS?** List the three elements of MIS. Why does a nontechnical business professional need to understand all three? Why are information systems developed? Why is part of this definition misleading?

Q3 **How does IS differ from IT?** Define *IS*. Define *IT*. Does IT include IS, or does IS include IT?

Why does technology, by itself, not constitute an information system?

Q4 How do successful business professionals use IS? How will developing the blog help Dee? Explain the employment trend involving emerging technology. How does this trend pertain to Jeff Bezos, CEO of Amazon.com?

Q5 What new opportunities for IS are developing today? Explain what IT resources are essentially free today. Describe two opportunities for taking advantage of those free resources. Explain how the success of YouTube depends on these two resources.

Q6 What is your role in IS security? Summarize the importance of security to corporations like Amazon.com. Define *strong password*. Explain an

easy way to create and remember a strong password. Under what circumstances should you give someone else your password?

Q7 What is this class about? In your own words, tell what this class is about. Look at the table of contents of this book. What major themes does it address? How will those themes relate to you as a business professional? If you were (or are) employed and if you had to justify the expense of this class to your boss, how would you do it?

How does **the knowledge** in this chapter help **Dee and you?** How can Dee's plan for her blog be guided by the five components of information systems? Why does Dee need a strong password to control access to her blog?

Key Terms and Concepts

Blog (Weblog) 3
Computer hardware 5
Computer-based information
   system 6
Data 5
Five-component framework 5

Information system (IS) 5
Information technology 7
Management information
   systems (MIS) 6
Moore's Law 13
People 5

Procedures 5
Software 5
Strong password 14
System 5

Using Your Knowledge

1. Using your own knowledge and opinions as well as those listed in Figure 1-4 (page 15), describe three misconceptions of the purpose of this class. In your own words, describe what you think the purpose of this class is.

2. Describe three to five personal goals for this class. None of these goals should include anything about your GPA. Be as specific as possible, and make the goals personal to your major, interests, and career aspirations. Assume that you are going to evaluate yourself on these goals at the end of the quarter or semester. The more specific you make these goals, the easier it will be to perform the evaluation.

3. Consider costs of a system in light of the five components: costs to buy and maintain the hardware; costs to develop or acquire licenses to the software programs and costs to maintain them; costs to

design databases and fill them with data; costs of developing procedures and keeping them current; and finally, human costs both to develop and use the system.

   a. Over the lifetime of a system, many experts believe that the single most expensive component is people. Does this belief seem logical to you? Explain why you agree or disagree.

   b. Consider a poorly developed system that does not meet its defined requirements. The needs of the business do not go away, but they do not conform themselves to the characteristics of the poorly built system. Therefore, something must give. Which component picks up the slack when the hardware and software programs do not work correctly? What does this say about the cost of a poorly designed system? Consider both direct money costs as well as intangible personnel costs.

c. What implications do you, as a future business manager, recognize after answering parts a and b? What does this say about the need for your involvement in requirements and other aspects of systems development? Who eventually will pay the costs of a poorly developed system? Against which budget will those costs accrue?

Collaboration Exercise 1 ◎

Each chapter in this textbook concludes with a Collaboration Exercise like this one.

Before you start these exercises, you should read Chapter Extensions 1 and 2, which describe collaboration techniques and tools for managing collaboration tasks. In doing these exercises, consider using Google Docs & Spreadsheets, Google Groups, Microsoft Groove, Microsoft SharePoint, or some other collaboration tool.

To begin, reread *MIS in Use 1* on page 11. Then, collaborate with your team to answer the following questions.

1. How did the availability of near-free data communication and data storage facilitate YouTube's success? Would YouTube have been possible without them?

2. Even though the cost of data communication and data storage is very low, for the volume at which YouTube operates they are still substantial expenses. How did YouTube fund these expenses? (Search the Internet for "History of YouTube" to find information to answer this question.)

3. How does YouTube (now owned by Google) earn revenue?

Using the cases of YouTube, Getty Images, and Media Partners as a guide, answer the following questions:

4. Choose a large corporation located in the geographic vicinity of your college or university. In what ways is it already taking advantage of the low cost of data communication and data storage?

5. As a team, define *innovation*.

6. Using the corporation you identified in question 4 and your team's definition of innovation in question 5, identify three innovative ways that the corporation could take advantage of the low cost of data communication and storage.

7. Create an outline of the reasoning that you and your fellow team members could use in a job interview. Assume you wish to demonstrate a knowledge of the power of emerging technology as well as your capacity to think innovatively.

Case Study 1 V̇ideo

Requirements Creep at the IRS

The U.S. Internal Revenue Service (IRS) serves more people in the United States than any other public or private institution. Each year, it processes over 200 million tax returns from more than 180 million individuals and more than 45 million businesses. The IRS itself employs more than 100,000 people in over 1,000 different sites. In a typical year, it adapts to more than 200 tax law changes and services more than 23 million telephone calls.

Amazingly, the IRS accomplishes this work using information systems that were designed and developed in the 1960s. In fact, some of the computer programs that process tax returns were first written in 1962. In the mid-1990s, the IRS set out on a Business System Modernization (BSM) project that would replace this antiquated system with modern technology and capabilities. However, by 2003 it was clear that this project was a disaster. Billions of dollars had been spent on the project, and all major components of the new system were months or years behind schedule.

In 2003, newly appointed IRS commissioner Mark W. Everson called for an independent review of all BSM projects. Systems development experts from the Software Engineering Institute at Carnegie Mellon University and the Mitre Corporation, as well as managers from the IRS, examined the project and made a list of factors that contributed to the failure as well as recommendations for solutions. In their report, the first two causes of failure cited were:

- "There was inadequate business unit ownership and sponsorship of projects. This resulted in unrealistic business cases and continuous project scope 'creep' (gradual expansion of the original scope of the project)."

- "The much desired environment of trust, confidence, and teamwork between the IRS business units, the

BSM organization (the team of IRS employees established to manage the BSM project), the Information Technology Services (ITS, the internal IRS organization that operates and maintains the current information systems), and the Prime (the prime contractor, Computer Sciences Corporation) did not exist. In fact, the opposite was true, resulting in an inefficient working environment and, at times, finger pointing when problems arose."

By 2008, the public outcry against the waste of money had diminished, but the problem lingered. A few Internet services, such as modernized electronic filing, had been implemented, but the fundamental BSM project of automating the processing of any but the simplest returns had not been implemented. Because of budget reductions, the IRS decided to move most of the development from contractors to in-house IRS personnel. The Government Accounting Office (GAO) was not confident that this was a solution to the problem.

The BSM team developed the new system in a vacuum. Neither the existing IRS business units (the future users of the system) nor the existing ITS staff accepted, understood, or supported the new system that had been engineered by the BSM team. Consequently, the BSM team poorly understood the system needs, and that misunderstanding resulted in continual changes in project requirements, changes that occurred after systems components had been designed and developed. Such requirements creep is a sure sign of a mismanaged project and always results in schedule delays and wasted money. In this case, the delays were measured in years and the waste of billions of dollars. The bottom line: Users must be involved in both the *development* and *use* of information systems.

Questions

Back in 2004, in response to the problems that it identified, the IRS Oversight Board recommended the following two actions:[3]

- "The IRS business units must take direct leadership and ownership of the Modernization program and each of its projects. In particular, this must include defining the scope of each project, preparing realistic and attainable business cases, and controlling scope changes throughout each project's life cycle . . . "

[3]The report identified more than two problems and made more than two recommendations. See the "Independent Analysis of IRS Business Systems Modernization Special Report" at *www.irsoversightboard.treas.gov*.

- "Create an environment of trust, confidence, and teamwork between the business units, the BSM and ITS organizations, and the Prime . . . . "

1. Why did the Oversight Board place leadership and ownership of the modernization program on the business units? Why did it not place these responsibilities on the Information Technology Services (ITS) organization?

2. Why did the Oversight Board place the responsibility for controlling scope changes on the business units? Why was this responsibility not given to the BSM? To ITS? To Computer Sciences Corporation?

3. The second recommendation is a difficult assignment, especially considering the size of the IRS and the complexity of the project. How does one go about creating "an environment of trust, confidence, and teamwork"?

   To make this recommendation more comprehensible, translate it to your local university. Suppose, for example, that your College of Business embarked on a program to modernize its computing facilities, including computer labs, and the computer network facilities used for teaching, including Internet-based distance learning. Suppose that the Business School dean created a committee like the BSM that hired a vendor to create the new computing facilities for the college. Suppose further that the committee proceeded without any involvement of the faculty, staff, students, or the existing computer support department. Finally, suppose that the project was one year late, had spent $400,000, was not nearly finished—and that the vendor complained that the requirements kept changing.

   Now assume that you have been given the responsibility of creating "an environment of trust, confidence, and teamwork" among the faculty, staff, other users, the computer support department, and the vendor. How would you proceed?

4. The problem in question 3 involves, at most, a few hundred people and a few sites. The IRS problem involves 100,000 people and over 1,000 sites. How would you modify your answer to question 3 for a project as large as the IRS's?

5. If the existing system works (which apparently it does), why is the BSM needed? Why fix a system that works?

Business Processes, Information, and Information Systems

Before Dee could get very far with her project to create a blog for the sales force, she needed a budget. For that, she needed the approval of her boss. When Dee explained the idea to him, he was pleased that she was thinking innovatively, and he was positively inclined to support the project. However, he wanted more specifics and told her that before he would approve spending any money, he wanted answers to three questions:

- **"How will this blog impact the sales process?"**

- **"How will the salespeople use it?"**

- **"How will it help us gain sales?"**

Dee began her career as a salesperson, and she is intimately acquainted with the sales process. Consequently, it was easy for her to answer these questions. Before we consider her responses, however, you need to learn more about business processes and how they relate to information systems.

This could happen to you

Stefan, we need to do this!

Study Questions

Q1 How did this stuff get here?

Q2 What is a business process?

Q3 What are the components of a business process?

Q4 What is information?

Q5 What is the role of information in business processes?

Q6 How do information systems support business processes?

How does the knowledge in this chapter help Dee and you?

Q1 How Did This Stuff Get Here?

Suppose you've graduated, you've attained the exact job you'd hoped to get, and you have a year or two of experience. Maybe you're an auditor, a financial analyst, or a salesperson. . . . You can be whatever you want to be. One April day, your company asks you to travel to New York City for a meeting in Manhattan. Like any responsible business professional, you've arrived a bit early, so you decide to have a cup of coffee and a scone at the Europa Café on 53rd Street and 3rd Avenue.

Sitting there with your coffee and scone, you let your mind wander. As you look around the café, the question occurs to you, "How did this stuff get here? The milk? The coffee? The scone? How did it get here?"

You know that somewhere there must be a cow that produced the milk that's in your coffee. Where is that cow? Who owns that cow? Who milked that cow? Who decided to ship that particular milk to the Europa that morning? Who delivered the milk? On what truck? How was the truck routed to customers? Who trained the truck driver?

For that matter, how did the coffee get here? It was grown in Kenya, shipped to the United States, roasted in New Jersey, packaged by a vendor, and delivered to the Europa. How did all of that happen? Or the scone? Who baked it? When? How many scones did they bake? How did they make that decision?

What about the chair you're sitting on? The wood was grown in Brazil and shipped to China, where the chair was manufactured, and then it was delivered to an import/export business in San Francisco. How did it get here? Who bought it? For whom did they work? Who paid them? How?

The more you think about it, the more you realize that a near miracle occurred just to bring you to this experience. Hundreds, if not thousands, of different processes had successfully interacted just to bring together your scone and coffee and you. (Wait! How did you get here? You flew up from your office in Atlanta. . . . Think about the processes in that, too!)

It's truly amazing. And those processes had to do more than just work. They had to work in such a way that all of the economic entities involved obtained a payment to cover their costs and make a profit. How did that occur? Who set the prices? Who computed the quantity of milk to be shipped through the Lincoln Tunnel the night before? How does all of this come about? The more you think about this, the more amazing it is.

In truth, all of this activity comes about through the interaction of business processes. The Europa has a process for ordering, receiving, storing, and paying for ingredients like milk and coffee. The coffee roaster has a process for assessing demand, ordering its raw materials, and making deliveries. All of the other businesses have processes for conducting their affairs as well.

Q2 What Is a Business Process?

A **business process** is a network of activities, resources, facilities, and information that interact to achieve some business function. A business process is a system; sometimes business processes are referred to as **business systems**. In this text, we will use the term *business process.*

Examples of business processes are inventory management processes, manufacturing processes, sales and support processes, and so forth. Figure 2-1 shows a model of a portion of an inventory management business process that might be used at the Europa Café.

Purchasing (an activity) queries the Inventory Database (a facility) and obtains *QuantityOnHand* (information) for a particular product. If the quantity is below the reorder quantity, Purchasing generates and sends a *PurchaseOrder* (information) to a Supplier (a resource). Purchasing sends a copy of the *PurchaseOrder* to Receiving and Stocking (an activity). When the goods arrive, Receiving and Stocking places them in Inventory (a facility), and it then sends a record of *QuantityReceived* to both the Inventory Database and to Payment (an activity). When the Supplier sends a

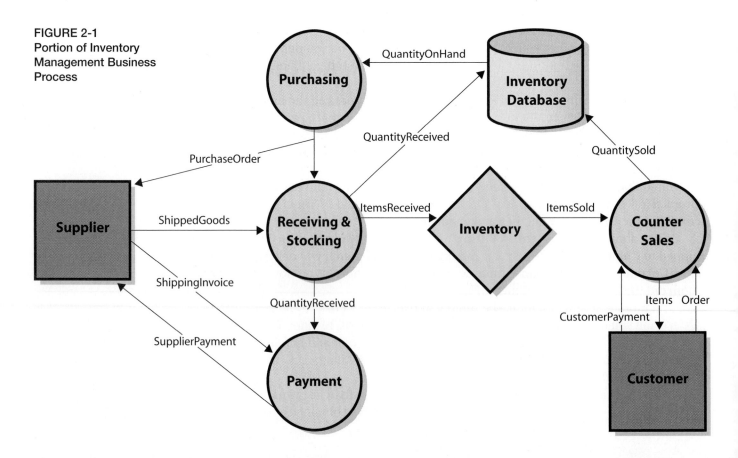

FIGURE 2-1
Portion of Inventory
Management Business
Process

ShippingInvoice (information) to Payment, the payment process compares the *ShippingInvoice* to the *QuantityReceived*, and it generates a *SupplierPayment* (a resource), as appropriate. *CounterSales* (an activity) interacts with the Customer (resource), Inventory, and the Inventory Database as shown in Figure 2-1.

Consider the diagram in Figure 2-1 as a snapshot of the system. It does not show logic; it does not show what causes what. It is just a picture of the elements of the business process and how they interact. Also, a business process can be represented in many different ways. Many vendors of business process software have their own documentation standards. Any clear and consistent representation will do.

Q3 What Are the Components of a Business Process?

As stated, a business process consists of activities, resources, facilities, and information. **Activities** transform resources and information of one type into resources and information of another type. The Payment activity transforms *QuantityReceived* and *ShippingInvoice* information into a *SupplierPayment* (resource). The Payment activity has rules and procedures that it follows for doing this.

An activity can be manual (people following procedures), it can be automated (hardware directed by software), or it can be a combination of manual and automated.

Resources are items of value. A case of milk is a resource, a check is a resource, and the customer's cash is a resource. In Figure 2-1, both Supplier and Customer are considered resources because they have value to this process. They are not considered activities, because they are external to the Europa and hence are not under the Europa's direction and control.

In business processes, **facilities** are structures used within the business process. Typical facilities are inventories and databases (as in Figure 2-1). Other examples of facilities are factories, pieces of equipment, trucks, file cabinets, and the like.

Information is the fourth element of a business process. Activities use information to determine how to transform the inputs they receive into the outputs they produce. Because this book is about *information* systems, understanding the nature of information and ways of defining it are crucial.

Q4 What Is Information?

Information is one of those fundamental terms that we use every day but that turns out to be surprisingly difficult to define. Defining *information* is like defining words such as *alive* and *truth*. We know what those words mean, we use them with each other without confusion, but they are nonetheless difficult to define.

In this text, we will avoid the technical issues of defining *information* and will use common, intuitive definitions instead. Probably the most common definition is that **information** is *knowledge derived from data*, where *data* is defined as recorded facts or figures. Thus, the facts that employee James Smith earns $17.50 per hour and that Mary Jones earns $25.00 per hour are *data*. The statement that the average hourly wage of all employees in the Garden Department is $22.37 per hour is *information*. *Average wage* is knowledge that is derived from the data of individual wages.

Another common definition is that *information is data presented in a meaningful context.* The fact that Jeff Parks earns $10.00 per hour is data.[1] The statement that Jeff Parks earns less than half the average hourly wage of the Garden Department, however, is information. It is data presented in a meaningful context.

---

[1]Actually, the word *data* is plural; to be correct, we should use the singular form *datum* and say, "The fact that Jeff Parks earns $10.00 per hour is a datum." The word *datum*, however, sounds pedantic and fussy, and we will avoid it in this text.

The *Guide* on pages 28–29 asks you to think about information from different people's perspectives and points of view. Demonstrating the ability to understand others' perspectives will increase your career success.

Another definition of *information* that you will hear is that *information is processed data*, or, sometimes, *information is data processed by summing, ordering, averaging, grouping, comparing, or other similar operations*. The fundamental idea of this definition is that we do something to data to produce information.

Yet a fourth definition of information is presented in the *Guide* on pages 28–29. There, information is defined as a *difference that makes a difference*.

For the purposes of this text, any of these definitions of information will do. Choose the definition of information that makes sense to you. The important point is that you discriminate between data and information. You also may find that different definitions work better in different situations.

Characteristics of Good Information

All information is not equal: Some information is better than other information. Figure 2-2 lists the characteristics of good information.

Accurate

First, good information is **accurate information**. Good information is based on correct and complete data, and it has been processed correctly as expected. Accuracy is crucial; managers must be able to rely on the results of their information systems. The IS function can develop a bad reputation in the organization if a system is known to produce inaccurate information. In such a case, the information system becomes a waste of time and money as users develop work-arounds to avoid the inaccurate data.

A corollary to this discussion is that you, a future user of information systems, ought not to rely on information just because it appears in the context of a Web page, a well-formatted report, or a fancy query. It is sometimes hard to be skeptical of information delivered with beautiful, active graphics. Do not be misled. When you begin to use an information system, be skeptical. Cross-check the information you are receiving. After weeks or months of using a system, you may relax. Begin, however, with skepticism.

Timely

Good information is **timely information**—produced in time for its intended use. A monthly report that arrives 6 weeks late is most likely useless. The information arrives long after the decisions have been made that needed that information. An information system that tells you not to extend credit to a customer after you have shipped the goods is unhelpful and frustrating. Notice that timeliness can be measured against a calendar (6 weeks late) or against events (before we ship).

When you participate in the development of an information system, timeliness will be part of the requirements you will request. You need to give appropriate and realistic timeliness needs. In some cases, developing systems that provide information in near real time is much more difficult and expensive than producing information a few hours later. If you can get by with information that is a few hours old, say so during the requirements specification phase.

Consider an example. Suppose you work in marketing and you need to be able to assess the effectiveness of new online ad programs. You want an information system that will not only deliver ads over the Web, but one that will also enable you to determine

FIGURE 2-2
Characteristics of Good Information

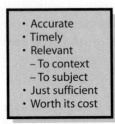

- Accurate
- Timely
- Relevant
  - To context
  - To subject
- Just sufficient
- Worth its cost

how frequently customers click on those ads. Determining click ratios in near real time will be very expensive; saving the data in a batch and processing it some hours later will be much easier and cheaper. If you can live with information that is a day or two old, the system will be easier and cheaper to implement.

Relevant

Information should be **relevant** both to the context and to the subject. Considering context, you, the CEO, need information that is summarized to an appropriate level for your job. A list of the hourly wage of every employee in the company is unlikely to be useful. More likely, you need average wage information by department or division. A list of all employee wages is irrelevant in your context.

Information should also be relevant to the subject at hand. If you want information about short-term interest rates for a possible line of credit, then a report that shows 15-year mortgage interest rates is irrelevant. Similarly, a report that buries the information you need in pages and pages of results is also irrelevant to your purposes.

Just Barely Sufficient

Information needs to be **sufficient** for the purpose for which it is generated, but **just barely so**. We live in an information age; one of the critical decisions that each of us has to make each day is what information to ignore. The higher you rise into management, the more information you will be given, and because there is only so much time, the more information you will need to ignore. So information should be sufficient, but just barely.

Worth Its Cost

Information is not free. There are costs for developing an information system, costs of operating and maintaining that system, and costs of your time and salary for reading and processing the information the system produces. For information to be **worth its cost**, an appropriate relationship must exist between the cost of information and its value.

Consider an example. What is the value of a daily report of the names of the occupants of a full graveyard? Zero, unless grave robbery is a problem for the cemetery. The report is not worth the time required to read it. It is easy to see the importance of information economics from this silly example. It will be more difficult, however, when someone proposes some new system to you. You need to be ready to ask, "What's the value of the information?" or "What is the cost?" or "Is there an appropriate relationship between value and cost?" Information systems should be subject to the same financial analyses to which other assets are subjected.

Q5 What Is the Role of Information in Business Processes?

The discussion about information may seem overly theoretical. What does it have to do with realistic business processes? How can Dee use the definitions of *information* to build a better blog?

Look again at the inventory management process in Figure 2-1. Consider the Payment process, which compares the *QuantityReceived* (from Receiving and Stocking) to the *ShippingInvoice* (from the Supplier). If the goods received match the goods billed, then Payment generates a *SupplierPayment*.

Now let's apply some of the definitions from the last section. Is *QuantityReceived* an example of *data* or is it *information*? By itself, it is just data, a recorded fact or figure: "We, Europa, received these items from that supplier on this date." Similarly, the *ShippingInvoice* could also be considered to be just data: "We, Supplier X, delivered these items to Europa on this date."

Understanding Perspectives and Points of View

Every human being speaks and acts from the perspective of a personal point of view. Everything we say or do is based on—or biased by—that point of view. Thus, everything you read in any textbook, including this one, is biased by the author's point of view. Authors may think that they are writing unbiased accounts of neutral subject material. But no one can write an unbiased account of anything, because we all write from a particular perspective.

Similarly, your professors speak to you from their points of view. They have experience, goals, objectives, hopes, and fears, and, like all of us, they use those elements to provide a framework from which they think and speak.

Sometimes, when you read or hear an editorial or opinion-oriented material, it is easy to recognize a strongly held point of view. It does not surprise you to think that such opinions might contain personal biases. But what about statements that do not appear to be opinions? For example, consider the following definition of *information*: "Information is a difference that makes a difference." By this definition, there are many differences, but only those that make a difference qualify as information.

This definition is obviously not an opinion, but it nevertheless was written from a biased perspective. The perspective is just less evident because the statement appears as a definition, not an opinion. But, in fact, it is the definition of information in the opinion of the well-known psychologist Gregory Bateson.

I find his definition informative and useful. It is imprecise, but it is a pretty good guideline, and I have used it to advantage when designing reports and queries for end users. I ask myself, "Does this report show people a difference that makes a difference to them?" So I find it to be a useful and helpful definition.

My colleagues who specialize in quantitative methods, however, find Bateson's definition vapid and useless. They ask, "What does it say?" or "How could I possibly use that definition to formalize anything?" or "A difference that makes a difference to what or whom?" Or they say, "I couldn't quantify anything about that definition; it's a waste of time."

And they are right, but so am I, and so was Gregory Bateson. The difference is a matter of perspective, and surprisingly, conflicting perspectives can all be true at the same time.

One last point: Whether it is apparent or not, authors write and professors teach not only from personal perspectives, but also with personal goals. I write this textbook in the hope that you will find the material useful and important and that you will tell your professor that it is a great book so that he or she will use it again. Whether you (or I) are aware of that fact, it and my other hopes and goals bias every sentence in this book.

Similarly, your professors have hopes and goals that influence what and how they teach. Your professors may want to see lightbulbs of recognition on your face, they may want to win the Professor of the Year award, or they may want to gain tenure status in order to be able to do some advanced research in the field. Whatever the case, they, too, have hopes and goals that bias everything they say.

So, as you read this book and as you listen to your professor, ask yourself, "What is her perspective?" and "What are his goals?" Then compare those perspectives and goals to your own. Learn to do this not just with your textbooks and your professors, but with your colleagues as well. When you enter the business world, being able to discern and adapt to the perspectives and goals of those with whom you work will make you much more effective.

DISCUSSION QUESTIONS

1. Consider the following statement: "The quality of your thinking is the most important component of an information system." Do you agree with this statement? Do you think it is even possible to say that one component is the most important one?

2. Although it does not appear to be so, the statement "There are five components of an information system: hardware, software, data, procedures, and people" is an opinion based on a perspective. Suppose you stated this opinion to a computer engineer who said, "Rubbish. That's not true at all. The only components that count are hardware and maybe software." Contrast the perspective of the engineer with that of your MIS professor. How do those perspectives influence their opinions about the five-component framework? Which is correct?

3. Consider Bateson's definition, "Information is a difference that makes a difference." How can this definition be used to advantage when designing a Web page? Explain why someone who specializes in quantitative methods might consider this definition to be useless. How can the same definition be both useful and useless?

4. Some students hate open-ended questions. They want questions that have one correct answer, like "7.3 miles per hour." When given a question like that in question 3, a question that has multiple, equally valid answers, some students get angry or frustrated. They want the book or the professor to give them the answer. How do you feel about this matter?

5. Do you think individuals can improve the quality of their thinking by learning to hold multiple, contradictory ideas in their minds at the same time? Or do you think that doing so just leads to indecisive and ineffective thinking? Discuss this question with some of your friends. What do they think? What are their perspectives?

When we bring these two items together, however, we generate information. Consider Bateson's definition of *information*: "Information is a difference that makes a difference." If the *QuantityReceived* says we received five cases of milk but the *ShippingInvoice* is billing us for eight cases (or three cases), we have a difference that makes a difference. By comparing records of the amount we received to records of the amount we were billed, we are presenting data in a meaningful context, which is another definition of information.

Thus, the business process generates information by bringing together important items of data in a given context. However, it also generates information at an even higher level. Over time, this process will generate information that will be useful for management and strategy decisions. For example, we could use the information produced by the process in Figure 2-1 to determine the cheapest, fastest, or most reliable suppliers. We could use the information in the Inventory Database to assess our inventory ordering strategy. We could also use it to estimate pilferage and theft losses.

Q6 How Do Information Systems Support Business Processes?

Information systems are used by the activities in a business process, but the particular relationship varies among business processes. In some processes, several activities use one information system. In other processes, each activity has its own information system, and in still other processes some activities use several different information systems.

During systems development, the systems designers determine the relationship of activities to information systems. You will learn more about this topic in Chapters 7, 8, and 10.

What Does It Mean to Automate a Process Activity?

We will consider the role of information systems for several of the activities in Figure 2-1, but before we do that, think about the five components of an information system. In Figure 2-3, notice the symmetry of components. The outermost components, hardware and people, are both *actors*; they can take actions. The software and procedure components are both sets of *instructions*: Software is instructions for hardware, and procedures are instructions for people. Finally, data is the bridge between the computer side on the left and the human side on the right.

When an activity in a business process is handled by an automated system, it means that work formerly done by people following procedures has been moved so that computers now do that work by following instructions in software. Thus, the

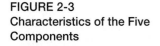

FIGURE 2-3
Characteristics of the Five
Components

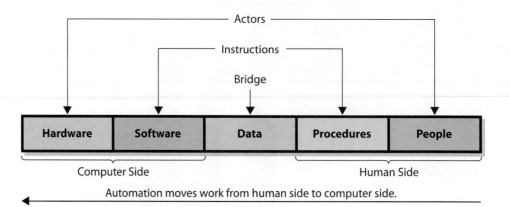

Hardware	Software	Data	Procedures	People
– Cash register computer – Database host computer	– Sales-recording program on cash register	– Sales data – Inventory database	– Operate cash register	– Cashier

FIGURE 2-4
Sales Recording Information System, Used by Counter Sales in Figure 2-1

Mostly an automated system.
Almost all work is done by computers and software.

automation of a process activity consists of moving work from the right-hand side of Figure 2-3 to the left.

An Information System to Support Counter Sales

According to Figure 2-1, the Counter Sales activity interacts with the customer. It receives the customer's order, takes the items from inventory, and receives the customer's payment. This is just a model of the familiar process of ordering coffee and a scone at a café.

Counter Sales uses the information system shown in Figure 2-4. This system is automated, however, and the cashiers do not even know they are using an information system. Each cash register contains a computer that communicates with another computer that hosts the inventory database. Programs in the cash register record sales and make appropriate changes to the inventory database whenever the cashier rings up a sale. The cashiers need to be trained only in how to use the cash register; they never need to work directly with the sales-recording programs on the computer.

The designers of this system decided to fully automate it because the cashier's job is a low-skill-level position with high turnover. The designers did not see a need for the cashiers to obtain training beyond learning to use the cash registers.

An Information System to Support Payment

Now consider the Payment activity in Figure 2-1. Payment receives the *QuantityReceived* and the *ShippingInvoice*, and it produces *SupplierPayment*. (In actuality, Payment does not generate the check to the supplier. Because of accounting controls, no single person should approve a payment and generate the check. Instead, Payment generates an authorization and sends it to someone else to cut the check. These details are omitted here for simplicity—they are important, however!)

As you can see in Figure 2-5, the information system that supports the Payment activity is a mostly **manual system**. The Accounts Payable clerk receives both the *QuantityReceived* and the *ShippingInvoice* as Adobe Acrobat PDF files (the same sort of PDF files that you receive over the Internet). He or she then reads those documents, compares the quantities, and issues the payment authorization as appropriate. If there is a discrepancy, the Accounts Payable clerk investigates and takes action as appropriate.

The designers of this system chose to leave it as a manual system because processing the exceptions is complicated. There are many different exceptions, and each requires a different response. The designers thought that programming all of those exceptions would be expensive and probably not very effective, so they decided it would be better to let humans deal with such varied situations. This means, by the way, that the Accounts Payable clerks will need much more training than the cashiers. Accounting management will need to ensure that Accounts Payable clerk turnover is low.

FIGURE 2-5
Payment System,
Used by Payment
Activity in
Figure 2-1

Hardware	Software	Data	Procedures	People
– Personal computer	– Adobe Acrobat Reader – Email	– *QuantityReceived* – *ShippingInvoice*	– Reconcile receipt document with invoice. – Issue payment authorization, if appropriate. – Process exceptions.	– Accounts payable

Mostly a manual system.
Little work is done by computers and software.
Most work is done by the Accounts Payable clerk.

An Information System to Support Purchasing

Now consider the information system that supports the Purchasing activity in Figure 2-1. This system, shown in Figure 2-6, balances the work between automation and manual activity. The Purchasing clerk has a personal computer that is connected to the computer that hosts the database. Her computer runs an Inventory application program that queries the database and identifies items that are low in stock and need to be ordered. That application produces a report that the Purchasing clerk reads.

The clerk decides which items to order and from which suppliers. In making this decision, she is guided by Europa's inventory management practices. When she does decide to order, she runs a Purchasing program on her computer. It is that program that generates the *PurchaseOrder* shown in Figure 2-1.

The designers of this information system decided to balance the work between the computer and the human. Searching the inventory database for items that are low in stock is a perfect application for a computer. It is a repetitive process that humans find tedious. However, selecting which supplier to use is a process that can require human judgment. The clerk needs to balance a number of factors: supplier quality, recent supplier experience, the need to have a variety of suppliers, and so forth. Such complicated balancing is better done by a human. Again, this means that the Purchasing clerks will need much more training than cashiers.

The three different information systems at the café support the needs of users in the company's various business processes—counter sales, payments, and purchasing. As *MIS in Use 2* discusses, though, even simple processes can be unexpectedly complicated.

FIGURE 2-6
Purchasing
Information
System, Used by
Purchasing
Activity in
Figure 2-1

Hardware	Software	Data	Procedures	People
– Personal computer – Database host computer	– Inventory application program – Purchasing program	– Inventory database	– Issue *PurchaseOrder* according to inventory management practices and guidelines.	– Purchasing clerk

Balance between computer and human work.

2 The Need for Business Processes

Many students, especially those with limited business experience, have difficulty understanding how important business processes are and how complex even simple processes can become. The following business situation (and related Collaboration Exercise) will help you understand the need for business processes, the importance of process design, and the role that information systems play in support of such processes.

Suppose you work for a supplier of electric and plumbing supplies, equipment, and tools. Your customers are home builders and construction companies that are accustomed to buying on credit. When you receive an order, you need to evaluate it and approve any special terms before you start removing items from inventory and packaging them for shipment. Accordingly, you have developed the order-approval process shown in Figure 1.

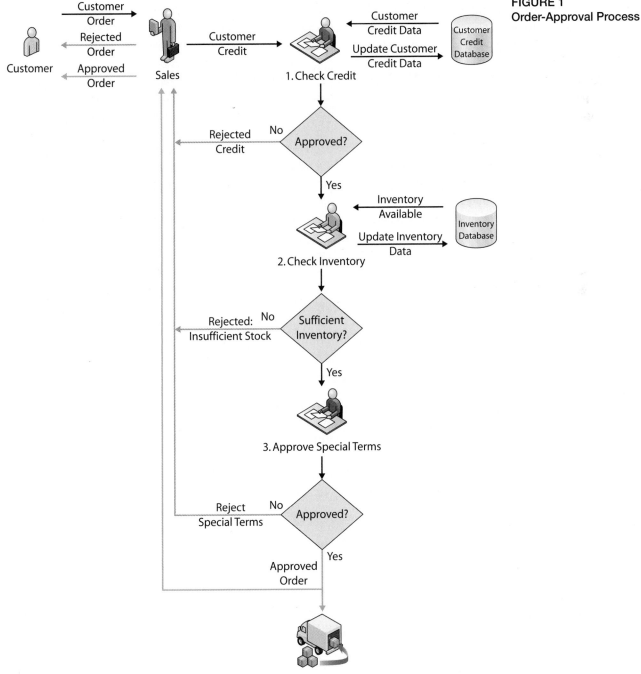

FIGURE 1
Order-Approval Process

(continued)

As you can see, your order-approval process consists of three stages: Check Credit, Check Inventory, and Approve Special Terms. You check credit and inventory on every order, but you need to approve special terms only if the customer asks for something special, such as free shipping, an extra discount, or unusually fast service and delivery.

As you will see, even a business process this simple has unexpected complexity. For one, are the checks in the proper order? This business process checks credit before it checks inventory levels. Does it make sense to take the time to evaluate credit if there is some possibility that you won't have the items in inventory? Should you check inventory before you check credit? And, if it turns out that you are going to reject the special terms of an order, would it make sense to check them first, before evaluating credit and inventory? (We will raise these questions here; you will have an opportunity to answer them with a group of your students in the Collaboration Exercise on page 39.)

Notice that the arrows between Check Credit and Customer Credit Database flow both ways. The arrow from Credit Check to the credit database means that once you have approved the credit for a customer, you update something about the customer's credit. Commonly, when an order is approved the amount of the order is removed from the total available credit for that customer.

Updating the customer credit database makes sense, but what if it turns out that you have insufficient inventory?

In that case, you will reject the order, but the credit has already been allocated. So you or one of your employees will need to remember to return the credit not used to the customer's credit record. Of course, you might have sufficient inventory to process part of the order, in which case you will need to return just part of the credit reserved to the customer.

Other problems occur because you are most likely processing many orders at the same time. Suppose two orders include one Kohler Supreme kitchen sink, but you have just one in inventory. You want to sell the sink to the first customer, but that means you must allocate that sink to it. Otherwise, both orders will be processed for the same sink. But suppose that the special terms of the order to which you've allocated the sink are disapproved. You would like to reassign the sink to the second order if it is still around to be processed. How can you accomplish that?

This scenario ignores another possibility. Suppose you have two order requests for the same sink; one is from a retail customer who wants it for her mountain home, and the second is from Big Sky Construction, a customer that buys 500 sinks a year from you. To which customer do you want to allocate that single sink? And how do you know how to do that?

Clearly, there is much to consider when designing business processes and information systems to support them. Collaboration Exercise 2 on page 39 will give you and your teammates a chance to do just that. ◎

Before we leave these five components, it is important for you to understand how *you* will relate to information systems. We consider that next.

What Is Your Role?

You are part of every information system that you use. When you consider the five components of an information system, the last component, *people*, includes you. Your mind and your thinking are not merely *a* component of the information systems you use; they are *the most important* component.

Consider an example. Suppose you have the perfect information system, one that can predict the future. No such information systems exist, but for this example let's assume that one does. Now suppose that on December 14, 1966, your perfect information system tells you that the next day, Walt Disney will die. Say you have $50,000 to invest; you can either buy Disney stock or you can short it (an investment technique that will net you a positive return if the stock value decreases). Given your perfect information system, how do you invest?

Before you read on, think about this question. If Walt Disney is going to die the next day, will the stock go up or down? Most students assume that the stock will go down, so they "short it" (sell borrowed securities) on the theory that the loss of a company's founder will mean a dramatic drop in the share price.

You cannot change the computer in your brain, so to speak, but you can change the way you have programmed that computer, your brain, to work. The *Ethics Guide* on pages 36–37 discusses one way of improving the quality of your thinking—that is, actively working to learn how others think in an activity called *empathic thinking*.

In fact, the day after Walt Disney's death the value of Disney stock increased substantially. Why? The market viewed Walt Disney as an artist; once he died he would no longer be able to create more art. Thus, the value of the existing art would increase because of scarcity, and the value of the corporation that owned that art would increase as well.

Here's the point: Even if you have the perfect information system, if you do not know what to do with the information that it produces, you are wasting your time and money. The *quality of your thinking* is a large part of the quality of the information system. Substantial cognitive research has shown that although you cannot increase your basic IQ, you can dramatically improve the quality of your thinking.

Dee needs to obtain a budget from her boss for her blog. When she asked him about the project, he wanted answers to the following three questions:

- "How will this blog impact the sales process?"
- "How will the salespeople use it?"
- "How will it help us gain sales?"

How does the knowledge in this chapter help Dee and you?

Stefan, we need to do this!

Dee can use the knowledge from this chapter to craft her responses. To answer the first question, she needs to diagram the sales *process* in a format like that in Figure 2-1. The diagram will show the sales reps, the doctors and pharmacists, and the various stages of the sales process. It also needs to show information that the sales reps need during this process.

To answer the second question, Dee can add the blog as a *facility* that the sales reps can access. She would then amend the first diagram to show how the *information* would be accessed from the Web.

Dee can structure her answer to the third question using Bateson's definition of information: a difference that makes a difference. For example, she can use the blog to publish successful sales strategies. When she does that, she will be publishing a difference (a new sales strategy) that makes a difference (it worked!). She can also publish other information (differences that make a difference) from herself, from sales management, and from doctors and pharmacists.

Her boss didn't ask for it, and it probably is beyond what Dee wants to do at this point, but she could also create diagrams like Figures 2-4, 2-5, and 2-6. In one figure, she could summarize the five components of the information system that the reps will use when they access the blog. In another figure, she could summarize the five components of the information system she will use when she (or others) publishes and creates blog entries.

Egocentric vs. Empathetic Thinking

According to one definition of the term, a *problem* is a perceived difference between what is and what ought to be. When developing information systems, it is critical for the development team to have a common definition and understanding of the problem. This common understanding, however, can be difficult to achieve.

Cognitive scientists distinguish between egocentric and empathetic thinking. Egocentric thinking centers on the self; someone who engages in egocentric thinking considers his or her view as "the real view" or "what really is." In contrast, those who engage in empathetic thinking consider their view as one possible interpretation of the situation and actively work to learn what other people are thinking.

Different experts recommend empathetic thinking for different reasons. Religious leaders say that such thinking is morally superior; psychologists say that empathetic thinking leads to richer, more fulfilling relationships. In business, empathetic thinking is recommended because it's smart. Business is a social endeavor, and those who can understand others' points of view are always more effective. Even if you do not agree with others' perspectives, you will be much better able to work with them if you understand their views.

Consider an example. Suppose you say to your MIS professor, "Professor Jones, I couldn't come to class last Monday. Did we do anything important?" Such a statement is a prime example of egocentric thinking. It takes no account of your professor's point of view and implies that your professor talked about nothing important. As a professor, it's tempting to say, "No, when I noticed you weren't there, I took out all the important material."

To engage in empathetic thinking, consider this situation from the professor's point of view. Students who do not come to class cause extra work for their professors. It doesn't matter how valid your reason for not coming to class was;

you may actually have been contagious with a fever of 102. But no matter what, your absence is more work for your professor. He or she must do something extra to help you recover from the lost class time.

Using empathetic thinking, you would do all you can to minimize the impact of your absence on your professor. For example, you could say, "I couldn't come to class, but I got the class notes from Mary. I read through them, and I have a question about business processes and how they relate to information. . . . Oh, by the way, I'm sorry to trouble you with my problem."

Before we go on, let's consider a corollary to this scenario: Never, ever, send an email to your boss that says, "I couldn't come to the staff meeting on Wednesday. Did we do anything important?" Avoid this for the same reasons as those for missing class. Instead, find a way to minimize the impact of your absence on your boss.

Now what does this have to do with MIS? Suppose that you buy a new laptop computer and within a few days, it fails. Repeated calls to customer support produce short-term fixes, but no one remembers who you are or what has been suggested to you in the past. Assume the keyboard continues to lock up every few days. In this scenario, there are a few views of the problem: (1) Customer support reps do not have data about prior customer contacts; (2) the customer support rep recommended a solution that did not work; and (3) the company is shipping too many defective laptops. The solution to each of these problem definitions requires a different information system.

Now imagine yourself in a meeting about this situation, and suppose that different people in the meeting hold the three problem views. If everyone engages in egocentric thinking, what will happen? The meeting will be argumentative and likely will end with nothing having been accomplished.

Suppose, instead, that the attendees think empathetically. In this case, people will make a concerted effort to understand the different points of view, and the outcome will be much more positive—possibly a definition of all three problems ranked in order of priority. In both scenarios, the attendees have the same information; the difference in outcomes results from the attendees' thinking style.

Empathetic thinking is an important skill in all business activities. Skilled negotiators always know what the other side wants; effective salespeople understand their customers' needs. Buyers who understand the problems of their vendors get better service. And students who understand the perspective of their professors get better. . . .

DISCUSSION QUESTIONS

1. In your own words, explain the difference between egocentric and empathetic thinking.

2. Suppose you and another person differ substantially on a problem definition. Suppose she says to you, "No, the real problem is that. . . ," followed by her definition of the problem. How do you respond?

3. Again, suppose you and another person differ substantially on a problem definition. Assume you understand his definition. How can you make that fact clear?

4. Explain the statement, "In business, empathetic thinking is smart." Do you agree?

Active Review

Use this Active Review to verify that you understand the material in the chapter. You can read the entire chapter and then perform the tasks in this review, or you can read the material for just one question and perform the tasks in this review for that question before moving on to the next one.

Q1 How did this stuff get here? Imagine yourself at a baseball or football game or at some other athletic event. What business processes are involved in producing that event? How did you buy a ticket? What processes were involved in that activity? What processes are needed to print the ticket? Who cleaned the stadium? What processes are involved in hiring, managing, and paying the cleaning staff? What processes must exist to support the coaches and athletes? What about the referees? Look up in the publicity booth. What processes exist to support the newscasters and their crews?

Q2 What is a business process? What is the definition of a *business process*? Consider one of the processes in your answer to Q1, and make a diagram similar to the one in Figure 2-1.

Q3 What are the components of a business process? List the components of a business process. Define each component. Identify each type of component on your diagram in your answer to Q2.

Q4 What is information? Give four definitions of *information*. Rank those definitions in order of usefulness in business. Justify your ranking.

Q5 What is the role of information in business processes? Explain how information is created in the Payment activity in Figure 2-1. Describe three different types of information that could be produced from the data in the inventory database.

Q6 How do information systems support business processes? Explain the meaning of each cell in Figures 2-4, 2-5, and 2-6. Explain the differences in the balance between automated and manual systems in these three information systems. Summarize the justification that the systems' designers used for constructing systems with the balance shown.

Summarize the ways in which Dee will use the knowledge in this chapter to answer the three questions her boss asked her. What do you think of this strategy? Is it likely to satisfy her boss? Can you think of other ways of responding to these questions that would be more effective?

Key Terms and Concepts

Using Your Knowledge

1. Consider the four definitions of *information* presented in this chapter. The problem with the first definition, "knowledge derived from data," is that it merely substitutes one word we don't know the meaning of (*information*) for a second word we don't know the meaning of (*knowledge*). The problem with the second definition, "data presented in a meaningful context," is that it is too subjective. Whose context? What makes a context meaningful? The third definition, "data processed by summing, ordering, averaging, etc.," is too mechanical. It tells us what to do, but it doesn't tell us what information is.

The fourth definition, "a difference that makes a difference," is vague and unhelpful.

Also, none of these definitions helps us to quantify the amount of information we receive. What is the information content of the statement that every human being has a navel? Zero—you already know that. However, the statement that someone has just deposited $50,000 into your checking account is chock-full of information. So, good information has an element of surprise.

Considering all of these points, answer the following questions:

a. What is information made of?
b. If you have more information, do you weigh more? Why or why not?
c. If you give a copy of your transcript to a prospective employer, is that information? If you show that same transcript to your dog, is it still information? Where is the information?
d. Give your own best definition of *information*.
e. Explain how you think it is possible that we have an industry called the *information technology industry*, but we have great difficulty defining the word *information*.

2. The text states that information should be worth its cost. Both cost and value can be broken into tangible and intangible factors. *Tangible* factors can be measured directly; *intangible* ones arise indirectly and are difficult to measure. For example, a tangible cost is the cost of a computer monitor; an intangible cost is the lost productivity of a poorly trained employee.

Give five important tangible and five important intangible costs of an information system. Give five important tangible and five important intangible measures of the value of an information system. If it helps to focus your thinking, use the example of the class scheduling system at your university or some other university information system. When determining whether an information system is worth its cost, how do you think the tangible and intangible factors should be considered?

3. Suppose you manage the Purchasing department for a chain of coffee shops like Europa Café. Assume that your company is in the process of developing the requirements for a new purchasing application. As you think about those requirements, you wonder how much autonomy you want your employees to have in selecting the supplier for each purchase. You can develop a system that will make the supplier selection automatically, or you can build one that allows employees to make that selection. Explain how this characteristic will impact:

a. The skill level required for your employees.
b. The number of employees you will need.
c. Your criteria for hiring employees.
d. Your management practices.
e. The degree of autonomy for your employees.
f. Your flexibility in managing your department.

Suppose management has left you out of the requirements-definition process. Explain how you could use the knowledge you developed in answering this question to justify your need to be involved in the requirements definition.

Collaboration Exercise 2 ◎

Before you start this exercise, read Chapter Extensions 1 and 2, which describe collaboration techniques and tools for managing collaboration tasks. In particular, consider using Google Docs & Spreadsheets, Google Groups, Microsoft Groove, Microsoft SharePoint, or some other collaboration tool.

To begin, reread *MIS in Use 2* on page 33. Then, collaborate with your team to answer the following questions.

1. Based on Figure 1 in *MIS in Use 2*, explain the business consequences if you debit customer credit in step 1, but then in steps 2 or 3 do not return credit for orders that you cannot process.

2. Recommend a process for adjusting credit for orders that are not approved. Who, in particular, should make the adjustment, and how do they receive the data they need to do so?

3. In Figure 1, explain why inventory must be allocated to orders in step 2. What is the business consequence if these allocations are not adjusted when special terms are not approved?

4. Recommend a process for adjusting inventory for orders for which the special terms are not approved. Who, in particular, should make the adjustment, and how to they receive the data they need to do so?

5. There are six different sequences for the three approval tasks in Figure 1. Name each and select what your team considers to be the most promising three.

6. Evaluate each of the three sequences that you selected in question 5. Identify which sequence you think is best.

7. State the criteria that you used for making your selections in questions 5 and 6.

8. So far, we haven't considered the impact of this process on the salesperson. What information do salespeople need to maintain good relationships with their customers?

9. *Optional extension.* Download the Visio diagram version of Figure 1 from this book's Web site, *www.pearsonhighered.com/kroenke*. Modify the diagram to illustrate the sequence of tasks you chose as best in your answer to question 6.

Case Study 2 Video

The Brose Group Integrates Its Processes—One Site at a Time

The Brose Group supplies windows, doors, seat adjusters, and related products for more than 40 auto brands. Major customers include General Motors, Ford, Chrysler, BMW, Porsche, Volkswagen, Toyota, and Honda. Founded as an auto and aircraft parts manufacturer in Berlin, Germany, in 1908, the company today has facilities at more than 30 locations in 20 different countries. Revenue for 2008 exceeded 3 billion euros. Every third vehicle produced includes at least one Brose product.

In the 1990s, Brose enjoyed rapid growth but found that its existing information systems were unable to support the company's emerging needs. Too many different information systems meant a lack of standardization, hampering communication among suppliers, plants, and customers. Brose decided to standardize operations using software that integrates different business processes. Rather than attempt to implement those processes on its own, Brose hired SAP Consulting to lead the project. (SAP is a vendor of enterprise-class software for supporting business processes. SAP Consulting is the consulting arm of that organization, which helps customers adapt and use SAP products.)

The SAP team provided process consulting and implementation support, and it trained end users. According to Christof Lutz, SAP project manager, "Our consultants and the Brose experts worked openly, flexibly, and constructively together. In this atmosphere of trust, we created an implementation module that the customer can use as a basis for the long term."

The Brose/SAP consulting team decided on a pilot approach. The first installation was conducted at a new plant in Curitiba, Brazil. The team constructed the implementation to be used as a prototype for installations at additional plants. Developing the first implementation was no small feat, because it involved information systems for sales and distribution, materials management, production planning, quality management, and financial accounting and control.

Once the initial system was operational at the Curitiba plant, the prototype was rolled out to additional facilities. The second implementation, in Puebla, Mexico, required just 6 months for first operational capability, and the next implementation in Meerane, Germany, was operational in just 19 weeks. By 2007, the system had been implemented in 22 plants in more than 10 countries.

The conversion to the integrated system has contributed to dramatically increased productivity. In 1994, Brose achieved sales of 541 million euros with 2,900 employees, or 186,000 euros per employee. By 2008, Brose attained sales of 3.1 billion euros with 14,700 employees, or 210,000 euros per employee, a gain of about 13 percent per employee.

Brose believes the key to its success was the development of a business-process master list. This master list is a collection of business processes created during the rollout of Brose systems across multiple sites and countries. Brose reuses these processes and functions to create new processes, when needed. Because Brose's interactions with customers have become more complex, the ability to develop and adapt processes has become more important.

Sources: www.brose.net/ww/en/pub/company/test.htm (accessed May 2008); www.sap.com/search/index.epx?q1=brose (accessed May 2008).

Questions

1. As you will learn in Chapter 7, the three types of business process are (1) processes within a single department, (2) processes that span several departments, and (3) processes that span different organizations. In the *MIS in Use 2* case, processing within a given activity, such as *Approve Credit,* represents processes within a single department. The process illustrated in Figure 1 in *MIS in Use 2* crosses multiple departments, and the processes described for Brose are processes that span different organizations (Brose to Toyota, for example). Compare and contrast these three process types according to:

   a. Size

   b. Capability

   c. Complexity of process

d. Need for information

e. Management control

2. Brose is a German company that has a factory in Brazil that sells to customers in the United States and Japan. Business processes span all of these countries. Do you think that different cultures and different languages might pose problems for cross-organizational processes? How do you think different languages and cultures may pose difficulties for the development of new business processes?

3. Access the SAP article cited in the *Sources* line on the previous page, and read the description of the use of the business-process master list. The article, which was written on behalf of SAP as part of its marketing efforts, implies that the inventory of business processes was of substantial value when implementing SAP in the various facilities.

a. Explain why such an inventory might be necessary.

b. In what ways do you think such an inventory would be valuable? How would it save costs? Result in faster implementations? Create better systems?

c. In what ways would such an inventory be of limited value? Would knowledge of a process developed to interface with Toyota in Japan be of use when developing a process to interface with Ford in Detroit?

d. In what ways would the development of a business process concerning the ordering and delivery of auto components between Brose and Ford be more difficult than the development of a similar business process between two Brose facilities?

Organizational Strategy, Information Systems, and Competitive Advantage

When Dee asked her boss for a budget to create her blog, he responded by asking the questions at the start of Chapter 2 (page 22). Using the knowledge in that chapter, she was able to respond, and he tentatively approved her budget request. Before he did so, however, he said that he wanted a memo from her on how her blog would provide a competitive advantage. He wanted that memo so that he could include it in the documentation he would use to justify the expense to his manager. The knowledge presented in this chapter will help her write that memo.

This could happen to you

It's really easy! They just log on, enter a password, and take care of business.

Study Questions

Q1 How does organizational strategy determine information systems structure?

Q2 What five forces determine industry structure?

Q3 What is competitive strategy?

Q4 What is a value chain?

Q5 How do value chains determine business processes and information systems?

Q6 How do information systems provide competitive advantages?

How does the knowledge in this chapter help Dee and you?

Q1 How Does Organizational Strategy Determine Information Systems Structure?

Recall from the definition of *MIS* that information systems exist to help organizations achieve their goals and objectives. As you will learn in your business strategy class, an organization's goals and objectives are determined by its *competitive strategy*. Thus, ultimately, competitive strategy determines the structure, features, and functions of every information system.

Figure 3-1 summarizes this situation. In short, organizations examine the structure of their industry and determine a competitive strategy. That strategy determines value chains, which in turn determine business processes like those we discussed in Chapter 2. As you saw in that chapter, the nature of business processes determines the structure of an information system.

Michael Porter, one of the key researchers and thinkers in competitive analysis, developed three different models that help one understand the elements of Figure 3-1. We begin with his five forces model.

FIGURE 3-1
Organizational Strategy Determines Information Systems

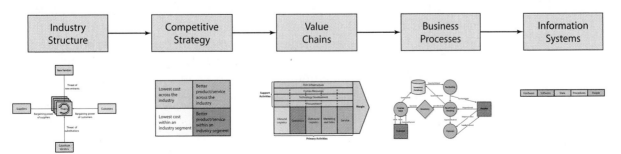

FIGURE 3-2
Porter's Model of Industry Structure

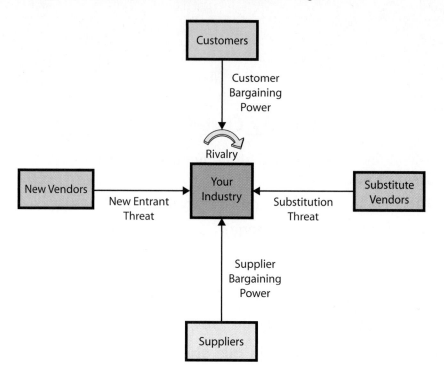

 ## Q2 What Five Forces Determine Industry Structure?

Organizational strategy begins with an assessment of the fundamental characteristics and structure of an industry. One model used to assess an industry structure is Porter's **five forces model**,[1] shown in Figure 3-2. According to this model, five competitive forces determine industry profitability: bargaining power of customers, threat of substitutions, bargaining power of suppliers, threat of new entrants, and rivalry among existing firms. The intensity of each of the five forces determines the characteristics of the industry, how profitable it is, and how sustainable that profitability will be.

To understand this model, consider the strong and weak examples for each of the forces in Figure 3-3. A good check of your understanding is to see if you can think of different forces of each category in Figure 3-3. Also, take a particular industry—say, auto repair—and consider how these five forces determine the competitive landscape of that industry.

Organizations examine these five forces and determine how they intend to respond to them. That examination leads to competitive strategy.

Q3 What Is Competitive Strategy?

An organization responds to the structure of its industry by choosing a **competitive strategy**. Porter followed his five forces model with the model of four competitive strategies shown in Figure 3-4.[2] According to Porter, a firm can engage in one of these four fundamental competitive strategies. An organization can focus on being the cost leader, or it can focus on differentiating its products from those of the competition. Further, the organization can employ the cost or differentiation strategy across an industry or it can focus its strategy on a particular industry segment.

---

[1]Michael Porter, *Competitive Strategy: Techniques for Analyzing Industries and Competitors* (New York: Free Press, 1980).
[2]Michael Porter, *Competitive Strategy* (New York: Free Press, 1980).

Force	Example of Strong Force	Example of Weak Force
Bargaining power of customers	Toyota's purchase of auto paint	Your power over the procedures and policies of your university
Threat of substitutions	Frequent-traveler's choice of auto rental	Patients using the only drug effective for their type of cancer
Bargaining power of suppliers	Students purchasing gasoline	Grain farmers in a surplus year
Threat of new entrants	Corner latte stand	Professional football team
Rivalry	Used car dealers	Internal Revenue Service

FIGURE 3-3
Examples of Five Forces

Consider the car rental industry, for example. According to the first column of Figure 3-4, a car rental company can strive to provide the lowest-cost car rentals across the industry, or it can seek to provide the lowest-cost car rentals to a "focused" industry segment—say, U.S. domestic business travelers.

As shown in the second column, a car rental company can seek to differentiate its products from the competition. It can do so in various ways—for example, by providing a wide range of high-quality cars, by providing the best reservation system, by having the cleanest cars or the fastest check-in, or by some other means. The company can strive to provide product differentiation across the industry or within particular segments of the industry, such as U.S. domestic business travelers.

According to Porter, to be effective the organization's goals, objectives, culture, and activities must be consistent with the organization's strategy. To those in the MIS field, this means that all information systems in the organization must facilitate the organization's competitive strategy.

Before leaving the topic of competitive strategy, consider the issues raised in the *Ethics Guide* on page 46. This guide discusses a company's decision to change its competitive strategy and its possible impact on employees.

Q4 What Is a Value Chain?

Organizations analyze the structure of their industry, and, using that analysis, they then formulate a competitive strategy. They then need to organize and structure the organization to implement that strategy. If, for example, the competitive strategy is to be *cost leader*, then business activities need to be developed to be as economically advantageous as possible.

However, a business that selects a *differentiation* strategy would not necessarily structure itself around least-cost activities. Instead, such a business might choose to

	Cost	Differentiation
Industry-wide	Lowest cost across the industry	Better product/service across the industry
Focus	Lowest cost within an industry segment	Better product/service within an industry segment

FIGURE 3-4
Porter's Four Competitive Strategies

Yikes! Bikes

Suppose you are an operations manager for Yikes! Bikes, a manufacturer of high-end mountain bicycles with $20 million in annual sales. Yikes! has been in business over 25 years, and the founder and sole owner recently sold the business to an investment group, Major Capital. You know nothing about the sale until your boss introduces you to Andrea Parks, a partner at Major Capital, who is in charge of the acquisition. Parks explains to you that Yikes! has been sold to Major Capital and that she will be the temporary general manager. She explains that the new owners see great potential in you, and they want to enlist your cooperation during the transition. She hints that if your potential is what she thinks it is, you will be made general manager of Yikes!

Parks explains that the new owners decided there are too many players in the high-end mountain bike business, and they plan to change the competitive strategy of Yikes! from high-end differentiation to lowest-cost vendor. Accordingly, they will eliminate local manufacturing, fire most of the manufacturing department, and import bikes from China. Further, Major Capital sees a need to reduce expenses and plans a 10 percent across-the-board staff reduction and a cut of two-thirds of the customer support department. The new bikes will be of lesser quality than current Yikes! bikes, but the price will be substantially less. The new ownership group believes it will take a few years for the market to realize that Yikes! bikes are not the same quality

as they were. Finally, Parks asks you to attend an all-employee meeting with the founder and her.

At the meeting, the founder explains that due to his age and personal situation, he decided to sell Yikes! to Major Capital and that starting today Andrea Parks is the general manager. He thanks the employees for their many years of service, wishes them well, and leaves the building. Parks introduces herself to the employees and states that Major Capital is very excited to own such a great company with a strong, quality brand. She says she will take a few weeks to orient herself to the business and its environment and plans no major changes to the company.

You are reeling from all this news when Parks calls you into her office and explains that she needs you to prepare two reports. In one, she wants a list of all the employees in the manufacturing department, sorted by their salary (or wage for hourly employees). She explains that she intends to cut the most costly employees first. "I don't want to be inflexible about this, though," she says. "If there is someone whom you think we should keep, let me know, and we can talk about it."

She also wants a list of the employees in the customer support department, sorted by the average amount of time each support rep spends with customers. She explains, "I'm not so concerned with payroll expense in customer support. It's not how much we're paying someone; it's how much time they're wasting with customers. We're going to have a bare-bones support department, and we want to get rid of the gabby chatters first."

You are, understandably, shocked and surprised . . . not only at the speed with which the transaction has occurred, but also because you wouldn't think the founder would do this to the employees. You call him at home and tell him what is going on.

"Look," he explains, "when I sold the company, I asked them to be sure to take care of the employees. They said they would. I'll call Andrea, but there's really nothing I can do at this point; they own the show."

In a black mood of depression, you realize you don't want to work for Yikes! anymore, but your wife is 6 months pregnant with your first child. You need medical insurance for her at least until the baby is born. But what miserable tasks are you going to be asked to do before then? And you suspect that if you balk at any task, Parks won't hesitate to fire you, too.

As you leave that night you run into Lori, the most popular customer support representative and one of your favorite employees. "Hey," Lori asks you, "what did you think of that meeting? Do you believe Andrea? Do you think they'll let us continue to make great bikes?"

Discussion Questions

1. In your opinion, did the new owners take any illegal action? Is there evidence of crime in this scenario?

2. Was the statement that Parks made to all of the employees unethical? Why or why not? If you questioned her about the ethics of her statement, how do you think she would justify herself?

3. What do you think Parks will tell the founder if he calls as a result of your conversation with him? Does he have any legal recourse? Is Major Capital's behavior toward him unethical? Why or why not?

4. Parks is going to use information to perform staff cuts. What do you think about her rationale? Ethically, should she consider other factors, such as number of years of service, past employee reviews, or other criteria?

5. How do you respond to Lori? What are the consequences if you tell her what you know? What are the consequences of lying to her? What are the consequences of saying something noncommittal?

6. If you actually were in this situation, would you leave the company? Why or why not?

7. In business school, we talk of principles like competitive strategy as interesting academic topics. But, as you can see from the Yikes! case, competitive strategy decisions have human consequences. How do you plan to resolve conflicts between human needs and tough business decisions?

8. How do you define job security?

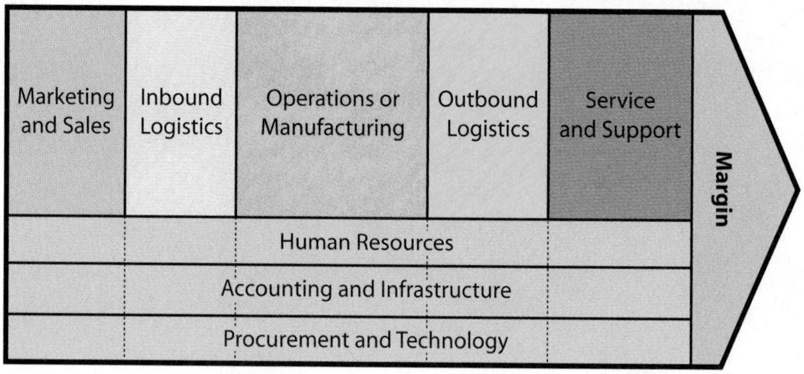

FIGURE 3-5
Porter's Value Chain Model

Source: Adapted with the permission of The Free Press, a Division of Simon & Schuster Adult Publishing Group, from *Competitive Advantage: Creating and Sustaining Superior Performance* by Michael E. Porter. Copyright © 1985, 1998 by Michael E. Porter. All rights reserved.

develop more costly systems, but it would do so only if those systems provided a net benefit, or **margin**, to the differentiation strategy. This line of thinking leads to Porter's definition of a third model, that of value chains.

Porter defined value as the amount of money that a customer is willing to pay for a resource, product, or service. A **value chain** is a network of value-creating activities. Figure 3-5 shows the generic value chain model as developed by Porter. That generic chain consists of five **primary activities** and three **support activities**.

Primary Activities in the Value Chain

To understand the essence of the value chain, consider a small manufacturer—say, a bicycle maker. First, to acquire customers and orders, the company must market and sell. Then, to manufacture its products, it needs to acquire raw materials using the inbound logistics activity. This activity involves the receiving and handling of raw materials and other inputs. The accumulation of those materials adds value in the sense that even a pile of unassembled parts is worth something to some customer. A collection of the parts needed to build a bicycle is worth more than an empty space on a shelf. The value is not only the parts themselves, but also the time required to contact vendors for those parts, to maintain business relationships with those vendors, to order the parts, to receive the shipment, and so forth.

In the operations activity, the bicycle maker transforms raw materials into a finished bicycle, a process that adds more value. Next, the company uses the outbound logistics activity to deliver the finished bicycle to a customer. Finally, the service activity provides customer support to the bicycle users.

Each stage of this generic chain accumulates costs and adds value to the product. The net result is the total margin of the chain, which is the difference between the total value added and the total costs incurred. Figure 3-6 summarizes the primary activities of the value chain.

FIGURE 3-6
Task Descriptions for Primary Activities of the Value Chain

Source: Adapted with the permission of The Free Press, a Division of Simon & Schuster Adult Publishing Group, from *Competitive Advantage: Creating and Sustaining Superior Performance* by Michael E. Porter. Copyright © 1985, 1998 by Michael E. Porter. All rights reserved.

Primary Activity	Description
Marketing and sales	Inducing buyers to purchase the product and providing a means for them to do so
In-bound logistics	Receiving, storing, and disseminating inputs to the product
Operations	Transforming inputs into the final product
Out-bound logistics	Collecting, storing, and physically distributing the product to buyers
Service	Assisting customer's use of the product and thus maintaining and enhancing the product's value

Support Activities in the Value Chain

The support activities in the generic value chain contribute indirectly to the production, sale, and service of the product. They include human resources, which Porter defined as recruiting, compensation, evaluation, and training of full- and part-time employees. Next, the accounting and infrastructure activity includes accounting, finance, general management, and legal and government affairs.

The third support activity is procurement and technology. Procurement consists of the processes of finding vendors, setting up contractual arrangements, negotiating prices, and ordering products. (This differs from inbound logistics, which is concerned with receiving, storing, and disseminating the inputs to the product.) According to Porter's model, the procurement function is spread throughout the firm. Raw materials are purchased by the purchasing department, but other items are purchased by the departments and managers who need them. Porter defined *technology* broadly. It includes research and development, but it also includes other activities within the firm for developing new techniques, methods, and procedures.

Supporting functions add value, sometimes indirectly, and they also have costs. Hence, as shown in Figure 3-5, the supporting activities contribute to a margin. In the case of supporting activities, it would be difficult to calculate the margin, because the specific value added of, say, the manufacturer's lobbyists in Washington, D.C., is difficult to know. But there is a value added, there are costs, and there is a margin, even if it is only in concept.

Linkages in the Value Chain

Porter's model of business activities includes **linkages**, which are interactions across value activities. Linkages are important sources of efficiencies and are readily supported by information systems. For example, manufacturing systems use linkages to reduce inventory costs. Such a system uses sales forecasts to plan production; it then uses the production plan to determine raw material needs and then uses the material needs to schedule purchases. The end result is just-in-time inventory, which reduces inventory size and cost.

By describing value chains and their linkages, Porter started a movement to create integrated, cross-departmental business systems. Over time, Porter's work led to the creation of a new discipline called *business process design*. The central idea is that organizations should not automate or improve existing functional systems. Rather, they should create new, more efficient business processes that integrate the activities of all departments involved in a value chain. We will discuss business process design further in Chapter 7.

Q5 How Do Value Chains Determine Business Processes and Information Systems?

As you learned in the last chapter, a business process is a network of activities, resources, facilities, and information that accomplish a business function. Now we can be more specific and say that business processes implement value chains or portions of value chains. Thus, each value chain is supported by one or more business processes.

For example, Figure 3-7 shows a portion of a bike rental value chain for a bicycle rental company. The top part of this figure shows how a company having a competitive strategy of providing low-cost rentals to college students might implement this portion

Your Personal Competitive Advantage

Consider the following possibility: After working hard to earn your degree in business, you graduate, only to discover that you cannot find a job in your area of study. You look for 6 weeks or so, but then you run out of money. In desperation, you take a job waiting tables at a local restaurant. Two years go by, the economy picks up, and the jobs you had been looking for become available. Unfortunately, your degree is now 2 years old; you are competing with students who have just graduated with fresh degrees (and fresh knowledge). Two years of waiting tables, good as you are at it, does not appear to be good experience for the job you want. You're stuck in a nightmare that will be hard to get out of—and one that you cannot allow to happen.

Examine Figure 3-8 again, but this time consider those elements of competitive advantage as they apply to you personally. As an employee, the skills and abilities you offer are your personal product. Examine the first three items in the list, and ask yourself, "How can I use my time in school—and in this MIS class, in particular—to create new skills, to enhance those I already have, and to differentiate my skills from the competition?" (By the way, you will enter a national/international market. Your competition is not just the students in your class; it's also students in classes in Ohio, California,

British Columbia, Florida, New York, and everywhere else they're teaching MIS today.)

Suppose you are interested in a sales job. Perhaps, like Dee, you want to sell in the pharmaceutical industry. What skills can you learn from your MIS class that will make you more competitive as a future salesperson? Ask yourself, "How does the pharmaceutical industry use MIS to gain competitive advantage?" Use the Internet to find examples of the use of information systems in the pharmaceutical industry. How does Parke-Davis, for example, use a customer information system to sell to doctors? How can your knowledge of such systems differentiate you from your competition for a job there? How does Parke-Davis use a knowledge management system? How does the firm keep track of drugs that have an adverse effect on each other?

The fourth and fifth items in Figure 3-8 concern locking in customers, buyers, and suppliers. How can you interpret those elements in terms of your personal competitive advantage? Well, to lock in, you first have to have a relationship to lock in. So do you have an internship? If not, can you get one? And once you have an internship, how can you use your knowledge of MIS to lock in your job so that you get a job offer? Does the company you are interning for have an information systems for managing customers (or any other information system that is important to the company)? If users are happy with the system, what characteristics make it worthwhile? Can you lock in a job by becoming an expert user of this system? Becoming an expert user not only locks you into your job, but it also raises barriers to entry for others who might be competing for the job. Also, can you suggest ways to improve the system, thus using your knowledge of the company and the system to lock in an extension of your job?

Human resources personnel say that networking is one of the most effective ways of finding a job. How can you use this class to establish alliances with other students? Does your class have a Web site? Is there an email list server for the students in your class? How about a FaceBook group? How can you use these to develop job-seeking alliances with other students? Who in your class already has a job or an internship? Can any of those people provide hints or opportunities for finding a job?

Don't restrict your job search to your local area. Are there regions of your country where jobs are more plentiful? How can you find out about student organizations in those regions? Search the Web for MIS classes in other cities, and make contact with students there. Find out what the hot opportunities are in other cities.

Finally, as you study MIS, think about how the knowledge you gain can help you save costs for your employers. Even more, see if you can build a case that an employer would actually save money by hiring you. The line of reasoning might be that because of your knowledge of IS, you will be able to facilitate cost savings that more than compensate for your salary.

In truth, few of the ideas that you generate for a potential employer will be feasible or pragmatically useful. The fact that you are thinking creatively, however, will indicate to a potential employer that you have initiative and are grappling with the problems that real businesses have. As this course progresses, keep thinking about competitive advantage, and strive to understand how the topics you study can help you to accomplish, personally, one or more of the principles in Figure 3-8.

❓ DISCUSSION QUESTIONS

1. Summarize the efforts you have taken thus far to build an employment record that will lead to job offers after graduation.

2. Considering the first three principles in Figure 3-8, describe one way in which you have a competitive advantage over your classmates. If you do not have such competitive advantage, describe actions you can take to obtain one.

3. In order to build your network, you can use your status as a student to approach business professionals. Namely, you can contact them for help with an assignment or for career guidance. For example, suppose you want to work in banking and you know that your local bank has a customer information system. You could call the manager of that bank and ask him or her how that system creates a competitive advantage for the bank. You also could ask to interview other employees and go armed with the list in Figure 3-8. Describe two specific ways in which you can use your status as a student and the list in Figure 3-8 to build your network in this way.

4. Describe two ways that you can use student alliances to obtain a job. How can you use information systems to build, maintain, and operate such alliances?

FIGURE 3-10
ABC, Inc., Web Page to
Select a Recipient from the
Customer's Records

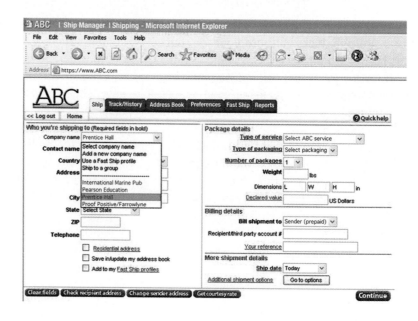

selects a Contact name, and the system inserts that contact's address and other data into the form using data from the database, as shown in Figure 3-11. Thus, the system saves customers from having to reenter data for people to whom they have shipped in the past. Providing the data in this way also reduces data-entry errors.

Figure 3-12 shows another feature of this system. On the right-hand side of this form, the customer can request that ABC send email messages to the sender (the customer), the recipient, and others as well. The customer can choose for ABC to send an email when the shipment is created and when it has been delivered. In Figure 3-12, the user has provided three email addresses. The customer wants all three addresses to receive delivery notification, but only the sender will receive shipment notification. The customer can add a personal message as well. By adding this capability to the shipment-scheduling system, ABC has extended its product from a package-delivery service to a package- *and* information-delivery service.

Figure 3-13 shows one other capability of this information system. It has generated a shipping label, complete with bar code, for the user to print. By doing this, the company not only reduces errors in the preparation of shipping labels, but it

FIGURE 3-11
ABC, Inc., Web Page to
Select a Contact from the
Customer's Records

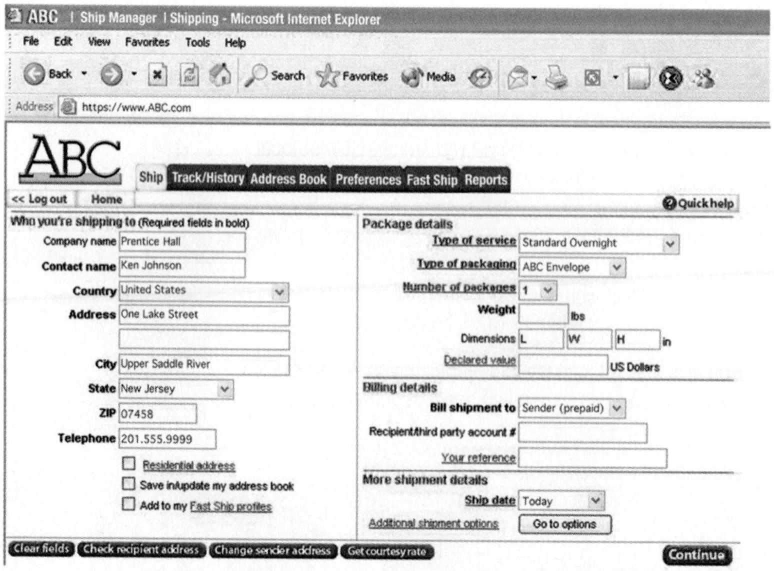

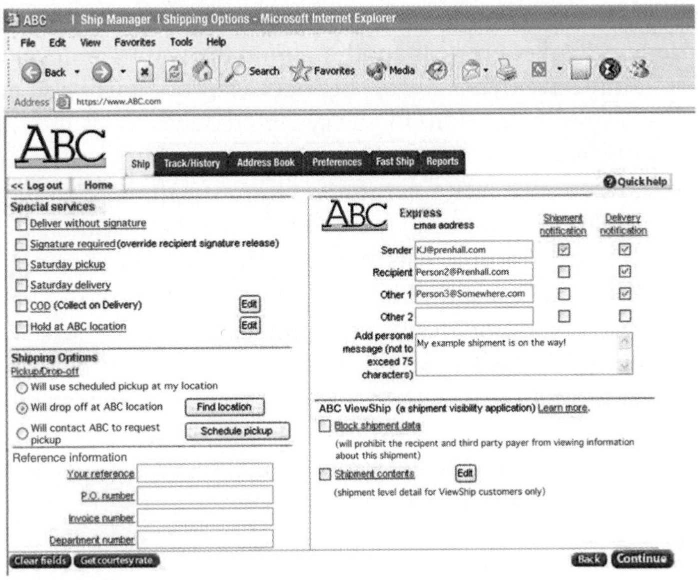

FIGURE 3-12
ABC, Inc., Web Page to
Specify Email Notification

also causes the customer to provide the paper and ink for document printing!
Millions of such documents are printed every day, resulting in a considerable savings to the company.

How Does This System Create a Competitive Advantage?

Now consider the ABC shipping information system in light of the competitive advantage factors in Figure 3-8. This information system *enhances* an existing product
because it eases the effort of creating a shipment to the customer while reducing
errors. The information system also helps to *differentiate* the ABC package delivery
product from competitors that do not have a similar system. Further, the generation
of email messages when ABC picks up and delivers a package could be considered to
be a *new* product.

Because this information system captures and stores data about recipients, it
reduces the amount of customer work when scheduling a shipment. Customers will
be *locked in* by this system: If a customer wants to change to a different shipper, he or
she will need to rekey recipient data for that new shipper. The disadvantage of rekeying data may well outweigh any advantage of switching to another shipper.

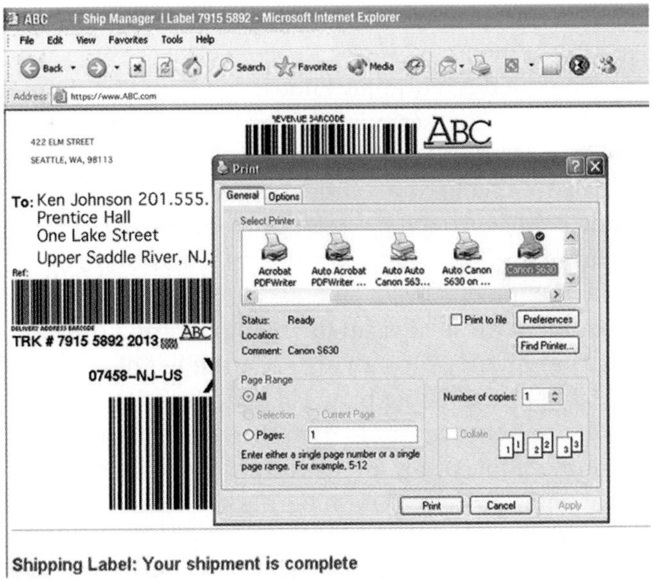

FIGURE 3-13
ABC, Inc., Web Page to
Print a Shipping Label

This system achieves a competitive advantage in two other ways as well: First, it raises the barriers to market entry. If another company wants to develop a shipping service, it will not only have to be able to ship packages, but it will also need to have a similar information system. In addition, the system reduces costs. It reduces errors in shipping documents, and it saves ABC paper, ink, and printing costs. (Of course, to determine if this system delivers a *net savings* in costs, the cost of developing and operating the information system will need to be offset against the gains in reduced errors and paper, ink, and printing costs. It may be that the system costs more than the savings. Even still, it may be a sound investment if the value of intangible benefits, such as locking in customers and raising entry barriers, exceeds the net cost.)

Before continuing, review Figure 3-8. Make sure that you understand each of the principles of competitive advantage and how information systems can help achieve them. In fact, the list in Figure 3-8 probably is important enough to memorize, because you can also use it for non-IS applications. You can consider any business project or initiative in light of competitive advantage.

Knowledge of industry structure gives Dee background and perspective that will make it easier for her to communicate with her senior management. At her level of management, she is unlikely to perform an analysis of industry structure and of the five competitive forces. Managers at a level much higher than Dee's perform that analysis.

Years ago, George Emerson (long deceased) must have considered these factors when he started the company. Today, Emerson is a multinational company, headquartered in London. Someone at Dee's level is unlikely to be deciding how to position the company within the worldwide pharmaceutical industry.

It's really easy! They just log on, enter a password, and take care of business.

This knowledge does enable her, however, to understand the company's competitive strategy and to translate that strategy into her project. For example, suppose that Emerson's competitive strategy is quality differentiation across the entire pharmaceutical market. Furthermore, suppose that Emerson defines quality as meaning that it produces and sells drugs based on the very latest medical research.

If this is the case, then all business systems in Emerson must facilitate that strategy. Drug developers must seek out the most current, leading-edge researchers; production must create processes that enable the drugs to flow through their medical-testing process as quickly as possible; and the sales team must be trained, reinforced, and financially rewarded for effectively presenting the "products based on the most current research" message to customers.

Here is where Dee can directly apply knowledge from this chapter. She can build her blog to provide the latest messages, examples, techniques, and success stories for delivering that message. When one salesperson succeeds with a technique, Dee can publish and broadcast that technique on the blog. With these features, she can state that her blog supports the competitive strategy by providing a cost-effective way of disseminating accurate and up-to-the-minute information to salespeople on how best to communicate the "most current" message.

Dee would document these ideas in the memo that her boss asked her to write. While she's writing that memo, she can also use the list of competitive advantage factors in Figure 3-8. In particular, her blog will help the sales team to differentiate its drugs from those of competitors and lock in their customers (help the sales force convince medical professionals they are gaining knowledge based on the most current research), and it will also help to raise barriers to market entry for new drugs or pharmaceutical companies (the need for other companies to commit resources to researching and producing the most current drugs).

Active Review

Use this Active Review to verify that you understand the material in the chapter. You can read the entire chapter and then perform the tasks in this review, or you can read the material for just one question and perform the tasks in this review for that question before moving on to the next one.

Q1 **How does organizational strategy determine information systems structure?** Diagram and explain the relationship among industry structure, competitive strategy, value chains, business systems, and information systems. Working from the bottom up, explain how the knowledge you've gained in these first three chapters pertains to that diagram.

Q2 **What five forces determine industry structure?** Name and briefly describe the five forces. Give your own examples of both strong and weak forces of each type, similar to those in Figure 3-3.

Q3 **What is competitive strategy?** Describe four different strategies, as defined by Porter. Give an example of four different companies that have implemented each of the strategies.

Q4 **What is a value chain?** How does the structure of a value chain relate to competitive strategy? Name and describe five primary value chain activities. Name and describe three support value chain activities. Explain value chain linkages.

Q5 **How do value chains determine business processes and information systems?** What is the relationship between a value chain and a business process? How do business processes relate to competitive strategy? How do information systems relate to competitive strategy? Justify the comments in the two rows labeled "Supporting business process" in Figure 3-7.

Q6 **How do information systems provide competitive advantages?** List and briefly describe eight principles of competitive advantage. Consider your college bookstore, and list one application of each of the eight principles. Strive to include examples that involve information systems.

Is Dee herself likely to perform an analysis of industry structure for Emerson? If not, how can Dee use knowledge of the five competitive forces in building her blog? How can she use knowledge of the competitive forces in writing the memo to her boss justifying the budget for her blog?

Key Terms and Concepts

Competitive strategy 44
Five forces model 44
Linkages 49

Margin 48
Primary activities 48
Support activities 48

Switching costs 52
Value chain 48

Using Your Knowledge

1. Apply the value chain model to a retailer such as Target (*www.target.com*). What is its competitive strategy? Describe the tasks Target must accomplish for each of the primary value chain activities. How does Target's competitive strategy and the nature of its business influence the general characteristics of Target's information systems?

2. Apply the value chain model to a mail-order company such as L.L.Bean (*www.llbean.com*). What is its

competitive strategy? Describe the tasks L.L.Bean must accomplish for each of the primary value chain activities. How does L.L.Bean's competitive strategy and the nature of its business influence the general characteristics of its information systems?

3. Suppose you decide to start a business that recruits students for summer jobs. You will match available students with available jobs. You need to learn what positions are available and what students are

available for filling those positions. In starting your business, you know you will be competing with local newspapers, Craig's List (*www.craigslist.org*), and with your college. You will probably have other local competitors as well.

a. Analyze the structure of this industry according to Porter's five forces model.

b. Given your analysis in part a, recommend a competitive strategy.

c. Describe the primary value chain activities as they apply to this business.

d. Describe a business process for recruiting students.

e. Describe information systems that could be used to support the business process in part d.

f. Explain how the process you described in part d and the system you described in part e reflect your competitive strategy.

4. Consider the two different bike rental companies in Figure 3-7. Think about the bikes that they rent. Clearly, the student bikes will be just about anything that can be ridden out of the shop. The bikes for the business executives, however, must be new, shiny, clean, and in tip-top shape.

a. Compare and contrast the operations value chains of these two businesses as they pertain to the management of bicycles.

b. Describe a business process for maintaining bicycles for both businesses.

c. Describe a business process for acquiring bicycles for both businesses.

d. Describe a business process for disposing of bicycles for both businesses.

e. What roles do you see for information systems in your answers to the earlier questions? The information systems can be those you develop within your company or they can be those developed by others, such as Craig's List.

5. Samantha Green owns and operates Twigs Tree Trimming Service. Samantha graduated from the forestry program of a nearby university and worked for a large landscape design firm, performing tree trimming and removal. After several years of experience, she bought her own truck, stump grinder, and other equipment and opened her own business in St. Louis, Missouri.

Although many of her jobs are one-time operations to remove a tree or stump, others are recurring, such as trimming a tree or groups of trees every year or every other year. When business is slow, she calls former clients to remind them of her services and of the need to trim their trees on a regular basis.

Samantha has never heard of Michael Porter or any of his theories. She operates her business "by the seat of her pants."

a. Explain how an analysis of the five competitive forces could help Samantha.

b. Do you think Samantha has a competitive strategy? What competitive strategy would seem to make sense for her?

c. How would knowledge of her competitive strategy help her sales and marketing efforts?

d. Describe, in general terms, the kind of information system that she needs to support sales and marketing efforts.

6. FiredUp, Inc., is a small business owned by Curt and Julie Robards. Based in Brisbane, Australia, FiredUp manufactures and sells a lightweight camping stove called the FiredNow. Curt, who previously worked as an aerospace engineer, invented and patented a burning nozzle that enables the stove to stay lit in very high winds—up to 90 miles per hour. Julie, an industrial designer by training, developed an elegant folding design that is small, lightweight, easy to set up, and very stable. Curt and Julie manufacture the stove in their garage, and they sell it directly to their customers over the Internet and via phone.

a. Explain how an analysis of the five competitive forces could help FiredUp.

b. What does FiredUp's competitive strategy seem to be?

c. Briefly summarize how the primary value chain activities pertain to FiredUp. How should the company design these value chains to conform to its competitive strategy?

d. Describe business processes that FiredUp needs in order to implement its marketing and sales and also its service value chain activities.

e. Describe, in general terms, information systems to support your answer to part d.

Collaboration Exercise 3 ☺

Before you start this exercise, read Chapter Extensions 1 and 2, which describe collaboration techniques and tools for managing collaboration tasks. In particular, consider using Google Docs & Spreadsheets, Google Groups, Microsoft Groove, Microsoft SharePoint, or some other collaboration tool.

To begin, reread *MIS in Use 3* on page 51. Then, collaborate with your team to answer the following questions.

1. Explain the relationship of value and cost according to the Porter model. When does it make sense to add cost to a business process?

2. Suppose you are told that the business process in Figure 1 in *MIS in Use 3* has a negative margin. Explain what that means. Suppose the margin of some business process is a negative $1 million. If costs are reduced by $1.2 million, will the margin necessarily be positive? Explain why or why not.

3. Consider the alternative of replacing the rental personnel from the business process in Figure 1.
   a. Describe changes that will need to be made to the process documented in Figure 1. One way to answer is to scan a copy of this diagram and annotate the changes on that copy. Or, if the annotations are too extensive, make another version of the diagram entirely.
   b. Would eliminating the rental personnel change the competitive strategy of this company? Is it possible to be a high-value company with no rental personnel? Explain why or why not.
   c. Would eliminating the rental personnel necessarily reduce costs? What costs would increase as a result of this change?

4. Consider the alternative of increasing the value delivered by existing rental personnel. The text suggests possibly renting more kinds of equipment or selling items of use to guests who are renting bicycles, but consider other options as well.
   a. Describe five ways that you think the existing personnel could increase the value of this business process.
   b. For the five alternatives you developed in part a, name and describe criteria for selecting among them.
   c. Using your criteria in part b, evaluate the alternative you identified in part a and select the best one. Explain your selection.
   d. Redraw Figure 1 for the alternative you selected in part c.

Case Study 3 Video

Bosu Balance Trainer

The Bosu balance trainer is a device for developing balance, strength, and aerobic conditioning. Bosu stands for "both sides utilized," because either side of the device can be used for training.

Invented in 1999, Bosu has become popular in health clubs, athletic departments, and homes.

Bosu reflects a philosophy in athletic conditioning that focuses on balance. According to the Bosu inventor, David Weck, "The Bosu Balance Trainer was born of passion to improve my balance. In my lifelong pursuit of enhanced athleticism, I have come to understand that balance is the foundation on which all other performance components are built." Bosu devices are sold at *www.bosu.com*.

Bosu devices have been successful enough that copycat products are undoubtedly on the way. For Bosu to be successful over the long term, it must transform its early market lead into a sustainable and durable market share. This means that Bosu must be used and recommended by coaches, personal trainers, and other significant purchase influencers. Bosu must develop a reputation among these market leaders as delivering significant benefits without risk of injury.

Source: Bosu, www.bosu.com (accessed November 2008).

Questions

1. Analyze the five competitive forces for Bosu's market.

2. Visit *www.bosu.com*. What appears to be Bosu's competitive strategy? Explain your answer.

3. Explain the nature of the five primary value chain activities for Bosu.

4. Review the principles of competitive advantage in Figure 3-8. What information systems can Bosu create to enhance its product or differentiate it from existing and emerging competition?

5. What information systems can Bosu develop to create barriers to entry to the competition?

6. What information system can Bosu develop to lock in customers?

7. What information systems can Bosu develop to establish alliances?

THE
International Dimension

The Global Economy

Q1 Why is the Global Economy Important Today?

Businesses compete today in a global market. International business has been sharply increasing since the middle of the twentieth century. After World War II, the Japanese and other Asian economies exploded when those countries began to manufacture and sell goods to the West. The rise of the Japanese auto industry and the semiconductor industry in southeastern Asia greatly expanded international trade. At the same time, the economies of North America and Europe became more closely integrated.

Since then, a number of other factors have caused international business to explode. The fall of the Soviet Union opened the economies of Russia and Eastern Europe to the world market. Even more important, the telecommunications boom during the dot-com heyday caused the world to be encircled many times over by optical fiber that can be used for data and voice communications.

After the dot-com bust, optical fiber was largely underutilized and could be purchased for pennies on the dollar. Plentiful, cheap telecommunications enabled people worldwide to participate in the global economy. Prior to the advent of the Internet, for a young Indian professional to participate in the Western economy, he or she had to migrate to the West—a process that was politicized and limited. Today, that same young Indian professional can sell his or her goods or services over the Internet without leaving home. During this same period, the Chinese economy became more open to the world, and it, too, benefits from plentiful, cheap telecommunications.

Author Thomas Friedman estimates that from 1991 until 2007, some 3 billion people have been added to the world economy.[1] Not all of those people speak English, and not all of them are well enough educated (or equipped) to participate in the world economy. But even if just 10 percent are, then 300 million people have been added to the world economy in the last 15 years!

Q2 How Does the Global Economy Change the Competitive Environment?

To understand the impact of globalization, consider each of the elements in Figure 3-1 (page 43), starting with industry structure. The changes have been so dramatic that the structure of seemingly every industry has changed. The enlarged and Internet-equipped world economy has altered every one of the five competitive forces. Suppliers have to reach a wider range of customers, and customers have to consider a wider range of vendors. As you will learn when we address e-commerce in Chapter 8, suppliers and customers benefit not just from the greater size of the economy, but also by the ease with which businesses can learn of each other using tools such as Google.

Because of the information available on the Internet, customers can more easily learn of substitutions. The Internet has made it easier for new market entrants, although not in all cases. Amazon.com, Yahoo!, and Google, for example, have garnered such a large market share that it would be difficult for any new entrant to challenge them. Still, in other industries, the global economy facilitates new entrants. Finally, the global economy has intensified rivalry by increasing product and vendor choices and by accelerating the flow of information about price, product, availability, and service.

Q3 How Does the Global Economy Change Competitive Strategy?

Today's global economy changes thinking about competitive strategies in two major ways. First, the sheer size and complexity of the global economy means that any organization that chooses a strategy allowing it to compete industrywide is taking a very big bite! Competing in many different countries, with products localized to the language and culture of those countries, is an enormous and expensive task.

For example, to promote its Windows monopoly, Microsoft must produce a version of Windows in dozens of different languages. Even in English, Microsoft produces a U.K. version, a U.S. version, an Australian version, and so forth. The problem for Microsoft is even greater, because different countries use different character sets. In some languages, writing flows from left to right. In other languages, it flows from right to left. When Microsoft set out to sell Windows worldwide, it embarked on an enormous project.

The second major way today's world economy changes competitive strategies is that its size, combined with the Internet, enables unprecedented product differentiation. If you choose to produce the world's highest quality and most exotic oatmeal—and

[1]Thomas L. Friedman, *The World Is Flat: A Brief History of the Twenty-First Century 3.0* (New York: Farrar, Strauss, and Giroux, 2007).

if your production costs require you to sell that oatmeal for $350 a pound—your target market might contain only 200 people worldwide. The Internet allows you to find them—and them to find you.

The decision involving a global competitive strategy requires the consideration of these two changing factors.

Q4 How Does the Global Economy Change Value Chains and Business Processes?

The growth in the world economy has major impacts on all activities in the value chain. An excellent example concerns the manufacture of the Boeing 787. Every primary activity for this airplane has an international component. Companies all over the world produce its parts and subassemblies. Major components of the airplane are constructed in worldwide locations and shipped for final assembly to Boeing's plant in Everett, Washington. *Outbound logistics* for Boeing refers not just to the delivery of an airplane, but also to the delivery of spare parts and supporting maintenance equipment. All of those items are produced at factories worldwide and delivered to customers worldwide. The global sales also change the marketing, sales, and service activities for the 787.

As you learned in Chapter 3, each value chain activity is supported by one or more business processes. These processes span the globe and need to address differences in language, culture, and economic environments. A process for servicing 787 customers in Egypt will be very different from the same service process in China, the United States, or India. For example, a business process organized around a central leader with strong authority may be expected in one culture and resisted in another. Global companies must design their business processes with these differences in mind.

Q5 How Does the Global Economy Change Information Systems?

To understand the impact of internationalization on information systems, consider the five components. Computer hardware is sold worldwide, and most vendors provide documentation in at least the major languages, so internationalization has little impact on that component. The remaining components of an information system, however, are markedly affected.

To begin, consider the user interface for an international information system. Does it include a localized version of Windows? What about the software application itself? Does an inventory system used worldwide by Boeing suppose that each user speaks English? If so, at what level of proficiency? If not, what languages must the user interface support? Most computer programs are written in computer languages that have an English base, but not all. Can an information system use a localized programming language?

Next, consider the data component. Suppose that the inventory database has a table for parts data and that table contains a column named Remarks. Suppose Boeing needs to integrate parts data from three different vendors: one in China, one in India, and one in Canada. What language is to be used for recording Remarks? Does someone need to translate all of the Remarks into one language? Into three languages?

The human components—procedures and people—are obviously affected by language and culture. As with business processes, information systems procedures need to reflect local cultural values and norms. For systems users, job descriptions and reporting relationships must be appropriate for the setting in which the system is used. We will say more about this in Part 4 of the book, when we discuss the development and management of information systems.

Active  Review

Use this Active Review to verify that you understand the material in the International Dimension. You can read the entire minichapter and then perform the tasks in this review, or you can read the material for just one question and perform the tasks in this review for that question before moving on to the next one.

Q1 **Why is the global economy important today?** Describe how the global economy has changed since the mid-twentieth century. Explain how the dot-com bust influenced the global economy and changed the number of workers worldwide.

Q2 **How does the global economy change the competitive environment?** Summarize the ways in which today's global economy influences the five competitive forces. Explain how the global economy changes the way organizations assess industry structure.

Q3 **How does the global economy change competitive strategy?** Explain how size and complexity change the costs of a competitive strategy. Describe what the size of the global economy means to differentiation.

Q4 **How does the global economy change value chains and business processes?** Describe, in general terms, how international business impacts value chains and business processes. Use the example of the Boeing 787 in your answer.

Q5 **How does the global economy change information systems?** Describe how international business impacts each of the five components of an information system. Identify the components that are most impacted by the need to support multiple cultures and languages.

Consider Your Net Worth

The ideas presented in the three chapters in this part can contribute substantially to your net worth as an employee as well as to your personal net worth. The key is to understand how to apply what you have learned here to your career goals. Here is one way to do that:

1. Write a description of what you want to do. Consider the following questions: Why do you want to work in business? What, specifically, do you want to do? Why did you choose your major? What would be the ideal first job for you?

2. Read the lists of questions that start each chapter. Think about each question in light of your answer in question 1. Select seven questions that seem particularly relevant to your career. Explain why each of them seems important to you.

3. Write a single paragraph answer to each one of the questions you selected in question 2.

4. Considering your answer to question 1, reflect on the experience of Dee, the marketing manager who wants to construct a blog. Even if you do not plan to work in marketing and even though you're unlikely to start a blog, what can you learn from Dee's experiences that might help you in your own career?

5. Assume you are about to be interviewed for the job you described in question 1. Using your answers to questions 3 and 4, prepare a list of notes that you could use to describe, in 5 minutes or so, how the knowledge you've gained from these three chapters will enable you to perform well in your new job.

Application Exercises

1. The spreadsheet in Microsoft Excel file **Ch1Ex1** contains records of employee activity on special projects. Open this workbook and examine the data that you find in the three spreadsheets it contains. Assess the accuracy, relevancy, and sufficiency of this data to the following people and problems.

a. You manage the Denver plant, and you want to know how much time your employees are spending on special projects.
b. You manage the Reno plant, and you want to know how much time your employees are spending on special projects.
c. You manage the Quota Computation project in Chicago, and you want to know how much time your employees have spent on that project.

d. You manage the Quota Computation project for all three plants, and you want to know the total time employees have spent on that project.

e. You manage the Quota Computation project for all three plants, and you want to know the total labor cost for all employees on that project.

f. You manage the Quota Computation project for all three plants, and you want to know how the labor hour total for that project compares to the labor hour totals for the other special projects.

g. What conclusions can you draw from this exercise?

2. The database in the Microsoft Access file **Ch1Ex2** contains the same records of employee activity on special projects as in Application Exercise 1. Before proceeding, open that database and view the records in the *EmployeeHours* table.

a. Seven queries have been created that process this data in different ways. Using the criteria of accuracy, relevancy, and sufficiency, select the single query that is most appropriate for the information requirements in Application Exercise 1, parts a–f. If no query meets the need, explain why not.

b. What conclusions can you draw from this exercise?

c. Comparing your experiences on these two projects, what are the advantages and disadvantages of spreadsheets and databases?

3. Figure 1 shows an Excel spreadsheet that the resort bicycle rental business uses to value and analyze its bicycle inventory. Examine this figure to understand the meaning of the data. Now use Excel to create the spreadsheet. Note the following:

- The top heading is in Calibri typeface, size 20 points. It is centered in the spreadsheet. Cells A1 through H1 all have been merged.
- The second heading, *Bicycle Inventory Valuation*, is in Calibri 18, italics. It is centered in Cells A2 through H2, which have been merged. The column headings are set in 11-point Calibri, bold. They are centered in their cells, and the text wraps in the cells.

a. Make the first two rows of your spreadsheet similar to that in Figure 1. Choose you own colors for background and type.

b. Place the current date centered in cells C3, C4, and C5, which must be merged.

c. Outline the cells as shown in the figure.

d. Note that Figure 1 uses the following formulas:

Cost of Current Inventory = Bike Cost × Number on Hand

Revenue per Bike = Total Rental Revenue / Number on Hand

Revenue as a percent of Cost of Inventory = Total Rental Revenue / Cost of Current Inventory

	Make of Bike	Bike Cost	Number on Hand	Cost of Current Inventory	Number of Rentals	Total Rental Revenue	Revenue per Bike	Revenue as percent of Cost of Inventory
	Resort Bicycle Rental							
	Bicycle Inventory Valuation							
			Monday, October 29, 2007					
5	Wonder Bike	$325	12	$3,900	85	$6,375	$531	163.5%
6	Wonder Bike II	$385	4	$1,540	34	$4,570	$1,143	296.8%
7	Wonder Bike Supreme	$475	8	$3,800	44	$5,200	$650	136.8%
8	LiteLift Pro	$655	8	$5,240	25	$2,480	$310	47.3%
9	LiteLift Ladies	$655	4	$2,620	40	$6,710	$1,678	256.1%
10	LiteLift Racer	$795	3	$2,385	37	$5,900	$1,967	247.4%

FIGURE 1
Resort Bicycle Rental Spreadsheet

Use these formulas in your spreadsheet, as shown in Figure 1. Format the cells in the columns as shown.

a. Give three examples of decisions that the management of the bike rental agency might make from this data.

b. What other calculation could you make from this data that would be useful to the bike rental management? Create a second version of this spreadsheet in your worksheet document that has this calculation.

4. In this exercise, you will learn how to create to create a query based on data that a user enters and how to use that query to create a data entry form.

a. Download the Microsoft Access file **Ch03Ex02**. Open the file and familiarize yourself with the data in the *Customer* table.

b. Click *Create* in the Access ribbon. On the far right, select *Query Design*. Select the *Customer* table as the basis for the query. Drag *CustomerName, CustomerEmail, DateOfLastRental, BikeLastRented, TotalNumberOfRentals, and TotalRentalRevenue* into the columns of the query results pane (the table at the bottom of the query design window).

c. In the *CustomerName* column, in the row labeled *Criteria,* place the following text:

[Enter Name of Customer:]

Type this entry exactly as shown, including the square brackets. This notation tells Access to ask you for a customer name to query.

d. In the ribbon, click the red exclamation mark labeled *Run*. Access will display a dialog box with the text "Enter Name of Customer:" (the text you entered in the query *Criteria* row). Enter the value *Scott, Rex* and click OK.

e. Save your query with the name *Parameter Query.*

f. Click the Home tab on the ribbon and click the Design View (upper left-hand button on the Home ribbon). Replace the text in the *Criteria* column of the *CustomerName* column with the following text. Type it exactly as shown:

Like "*" & [Enter part of Customer Name to search by:] & "*"

g. Run the query by clicking Run in the ribbon. Enter *Scott* when prompted *Enter part of Customer Name to search by*. Notice that the two customers who have the name Scott are displayed. If you have any problems, ensure that you have typed the phrase above **exactly** as shown into the *Criteria* row of the CustomerName column of your query.

h. Save your query again under the name *Parameter Query.* Close the query window.

i. Click *Create* in the Access ribbon. Under the *Forms* group, select the down arrow to the right of *More Forms*. Choose *Form Wizard*. In the dialog that opens, in the Tables/Queries box, click on the down arrow. Select *Parameter Query*. Click the double chevron >> symbol and all of the columns in the query will move to the Selected Fields area.

j. Click *Next* three times. In the box under *What title do you want for your form?,* enter *Customer Query Form* and click *Finish.*

k. Enter *Scott* in the dialog box that appears. Access will open a form with the values for Scott, Rex. At the bottom of the form, click the right facing arrow and the data for Scott, Bryan will appear.

l. Close the form. Select *Object Type* and *Forms* in the Access Navigation Pane. Double-click *Customer Query Form* and enter the value *James*. Access will display data for all six customers having the value *James* in their name.

Getty Images Serves Up Profit

Getty Images was founded in 1995 with the goal of consolidating the fragmented photography market by acquiring many small companies, applying business discipline to the merged entity, and developing modern information systems. The advent of the Web drove the company to e-commerce and in the process enabled Getty to change the work-flow and business practices of the professional visual content industry. Getty Images has grown from a start-up to become, by 2004, a global, $600 million plus, publicly traded (NYSE: GYI), very profitable company.

Getty Images obtains its imagery (both still and movie) from photographers under contract, and it owns the world's largest private archive of imagery. Getty also employs staff photographers to shoot the world's news, sports, and entertainment events. In the case of photography and film that it does not own, it provides a share of the revenue generated to the content owner. Getty Images is both a producer and a distributor of imagery, and all of its products are sold via e-commerce on the Web.

Getty Images employs three licensing models: The first is *subscription*, by which customers contract to use as many images as they want as often as they want (this applies to the news, sports, and entertainment imagery). The second model is *royalty-free*. In this model, customers pay a fee based on the file size of the image and can use the image any way they want and as many times as they want. However, under this model, customers have no exclusivity or ability to prevent a competitor from using the same image at the same time.

The third model, *rights managed*, also licenses creative imagery. In this model, which is the largest in revenue terms, users pay fees according to the rights that they wish to use—size, industry, geography, prominence, frequency, exclusivity, and so forth.

According to its Web site:

> Getty Images has been credited with the introduction of royalty-free photography and was the first company to license imagery via the Web, subsequently moving the entire industry online. The company was also the first to employ creative researchers to anticipate the visual content needs of the world's communicators, and Getty Images remains the first and only publicly traded imagery company in the world. (*http://www.gettyimages.com/Home. aspx*, accessed August 2008)

In 2003, Getty Images' Web site, *www.gettyimages.com*, received more than 51 million visits and served over 1.3 billion pages. Visitors to the site viewed more than 6.7 billion thumbnail-sized photos in the third quarter of 2004 alone.

Getty Images licenses photos in digital format, therefore its variable cost of production is essentially zero. Once the company has obtained a photo and placed it in the commerce server database, the cost of sending it to a customer is zero. Getty Images does have the overhead costs of setting up and operating the e-commerce site, and it does pay some costs for its images—either the costs of employing the photographer or the cost of setting up and maintaining the relationship with out-of-house photographers. For some images, it also pays a royalty to the owner. Once these costs are paid, however, the cost of producing a photo is nil. This means that Getty Images' profitability increases substantially with increased volume. Figure 1 shows a page that the Getty Images commerce server produced when the user selected creative, royalty-free photography and searched on the term *Boston*.

FIGURE 1
Getty Images' Search Results

Source: www.gettyimages.com (accessed December 2004).

When the user clicked "Calculate price" for the image named Photodisc Green, the commerce server produced the page shown in Figure 2. This Web page shows a default price. Users in different countries may have a different price depending on agreements, taxes, and local policies.

Questions

1. Visit *www.gettyimages.com*, and select "Creative/Search royalty-free." Search for an image of a city close to your campus. Select a photo and determine its default prices.

2. Explain how Getty Images' business model takes advantage of the nearly free data communications and data storage opportunities described in Chapter 1.

3. Evaluate the photography market using Porter's five forces. Do you think Getty Images' marginal cost is sustainable? Are its prices sustainable? What is the key to its continued success?

4. What seems to be Getty Images' competitive strategy?

5. Explain how Getty Images has used information systems to gain a competitive advantage.

6. Based on your answers to the previous questions, would you choose to buy Getty Images' stock?

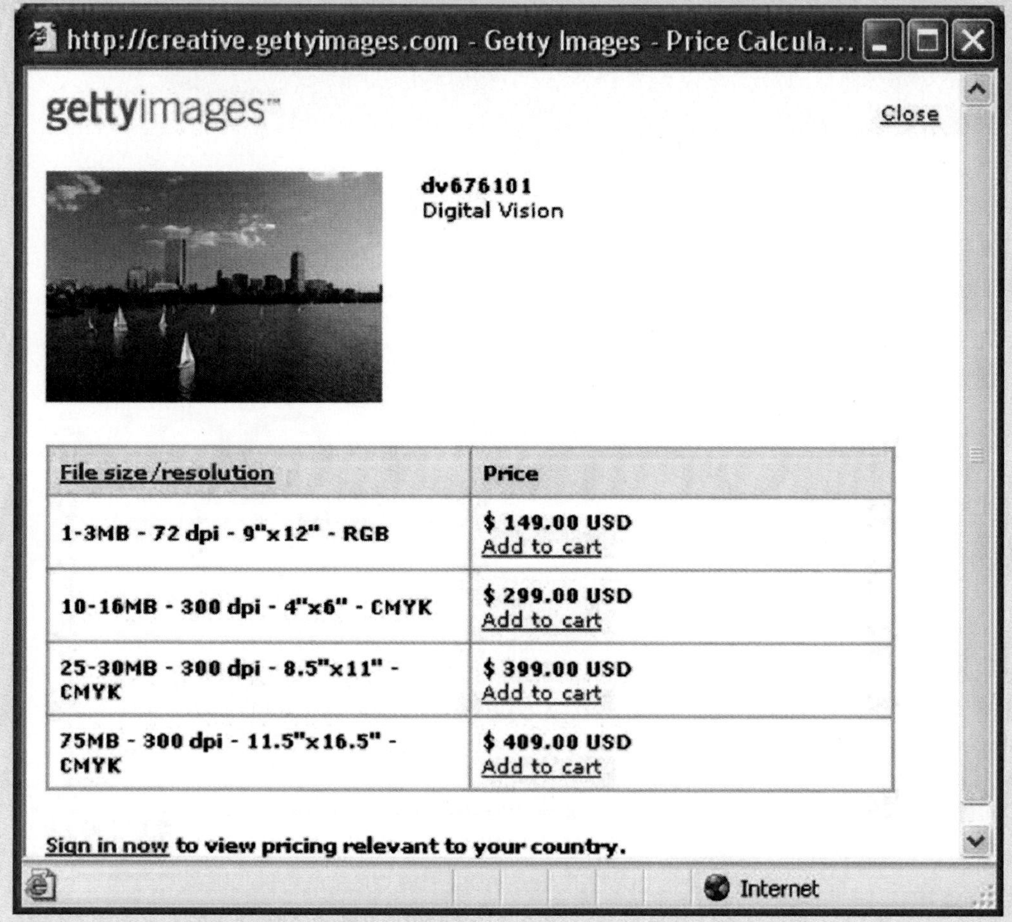

FIGURE 2
Price Calculation for an Image
of Boston

http://creative.gettyimages.com - Getty Images - Price Calcula...

gettyimages™   Close

dv676101
Digital Vision

File size/resolution	Price
1-3MB - 72 dpi - 9"x12" - RGB	$ 149.00 USD Add to cart
10-16MB - 300 dpi - 4"x6" - CMYK	$ 299.00 USD Add to cart
25-30MB - 300 dpi - 8.5"x11" - CMYK	$ 399.00 USD Add to cart
75MB - 300 dpi - 11.5"x16.5" - CMYK	$ 409.00 USD Add to cart

Sign in now to view pricing relevant to your country.

Internet

Source: www.gettyimages.com (accessed December 2004).

7. Getty Images has the enviable position of a near-zero variable cost of
production. Describe two other businesses that could use emerging IT to attain
the same advantage.

USING
INFORMATION
TECHNOLOGY

Dee knows that she needs an information system to support her blog. She knows that it has five components; she has justified it by explaining how it will positively impact the sales process and how it will give Emerson a competitive advantage. She's presented all of this to her boss, and he's endorsed the idea, but he wants to know how much it will cost before he'll give final approval.

How much will it cost? It depends. The cheapest solution would be to use one of the commercial sites that sponsor blogs, like MSN and Yahoo! She can't do that, however, because she needs to restrict access to Emerson employees. A public blog would be accessible by the competition.

So she needs to set up her own blog. But how? What's involved? She knows she has to think about hardware, software, data, procedures, and people. The people will be both the sales force and herself. The sales force will need procedures for accessing the blog and leaving comments; Dee will need procedures for posting entries to the blog. Although she's never done that before, she's confident that she can learn the procedures required.

The hardware, software, and data components, however, have her flummoxed. When she talked with her IT staff, she met a barrage of questions that she didn't understand, let alone know how to answer. Questions included, "Are you going to run on a Windows or Linux server? What blog software will you use? Are you going to put it on the Emerson network? If so, how are you going to get the software set up? Emerson uses Oracle, but what does your blog software require? Will you run it within the VPN, or will you use some private set of accounts and passwords?"

And finally: "You want it WHEN? By early January!?? You've got to be kidding! This is early December, and the holidays are coming up. There's no way."

Dee, however, is not easily put off. As a salesperson, she believes that the sale starts when the customer says, "No." She brought that same attitude to this project, and she wasn't about to quit.

This could happen to you

Through professional acquaintances, she learned about Don Gray, a consultant who specializes in setting up blogs and similar sites.

When she contacted him, Don responded more positively. Even he, however, asked her questions that she couldn't understand.

Dee needed the knowledge in the three chapters in this part. She needed a basic understanding of hardware; she needed to know the basics of database processing; and she needed to know about computer networks, firewalls, and something called a VPN. Had she possessed this knowledge, it would have taken her half as much time as it did—or even less time than that. She also would have had much less worry, anxiety, and stress.

Hardware and Software

Because of the short time available, Dee decided to hire Don Gray, a consultant who specializes in setting up systems like blogs. Don has many years of experience working with people like Dee, and he knew not to throw a barrage of technical questions at her. However, before he could help her develop a cost estimate, he needed answers to a few basic questions:

- "Will you run your blog on an internal Emerson site or contract with an outside hosting service?"

- "Either way, will your site use a Windows or Linux server?"

- "What blog software do you want to use?"

- "How do you want to code your entries? Are you going to use Dreamweaver, or do you want me to build an HTML editor into your blog software?"

- "What browsers do you want to support? Internet Explorer? Mozilla? Firefox? Others?"

- "Do you care if your blog doesn't render perfectly in all browsers?"

Dee was in a bind. She didn't know the answers to these questions. (She didn't even know what some of them meant—such as "render perfectly in all browsers.") She really had nowhere to turn. The people in her internal IT department had told her there was no way the project could be done on time, and they were dismissive of her requests for help—even just to answer Don's initial questions. She could ask Don to help her with the answers, but he had a potential conflict of interest: As a consultant, he might want to pad his bill with features she didn't need. Although Don's references indicated that this was unlikely, she was reluctant to ask him to answer the very questions he was asking. In short, Dee needed the knowledge in this chapter.

This isn't a NASA project.

As a future business professional, you may find yourself in the same spot. You may not be creating a blog, but you may be creating some other information system and need to answer questions similar to those Don posed to Dee. As you read this chapter, think about these kinds of questions, and focus on gaining a foundation in hardware and software terms and concepts. The discussion is not technical; it focuses on knowledge that a future manager will need.

Study Questions

Q1 What does a manager need to know about computer hardware?

Q2 What's the difference between a client and a server?

Q3 What does a manager need to know about software?

Q4 What buying decisions do you make?

Q5 What are viruses, Trojan horses, and worms?

How does the knowledge in this chapter help Dee and you?

Q1 What Does a Manager Need to Know About Computer Hardware?

As discussed in the five-component framework, **hardware** consists of electronic components and related gadgetry that input, process, output, and store data according to instructions encoded in computer programs or software. The essential knowledge that you need in order to be an effective manager and consumer of computer hardware is summarized in Figure 4-1.

Students vary in the knowledge of hardware they bring to this class. If you already know the terms in Figure 4-1, skip to the next question on page 82, "What's the difference between a client and a server?"

Input, Processing, Output, and Storage Hardware

To make sense of the rows in Figure 4-1, consider Figure 4-2, which shows the components of a generic computer. Notice that the basic hardware categories are input, process, output, and storage.

As shown in Figure 4-2, typical **input hardware** devices are the keyboard, mouse, document scanners, and bar-code (Universal Product Code) scanners, such as those used in grocery stores. Microphones also are input devices; with tablet PCs, human handwriting can be input as well. Older input devices include magnetic ink readers (used for reading the ink on the bottom of checks) and scanners such as the Scantron test scanner shown in Figure 4-3.

Processing devices include the **central processing unit (CPU)**, which is sometimes called "the brain" of the computer. Although the design of the CPU has nothing in common with the anatomy of animal brains, this description is helpful because the CPU does have the "smarts" of the machine. The CPU selects instructions, processes them, performs arithmetic and logical comparisons, and stores results of operations in memory.

Component	Performance Factors	Beneficial For	Example Application
CPU and data bus	• CPU speed • Cache memory • Data bus speed • Data bus width	• Fast processing of data once the data reside in main memory	• Repetitive calculations of formulas in a complicated spreadsheet • Manipulation of large picture images
Main memory	• Size • Speed	• Holding multiple programs at one time • Processing very large amounts of data	• Running Excel, Word, Paint Shop Pro, Adobe Acrobat, several Web sites, and email while processing large files in memory and viewing video clips • 3D games
Magnetic disk	• Size • Channel type and speed • Rotational speed • Seek time	• Storing many large programs • Storing many large files • Swapping files in and out of memory	• Store detailed maps of countries in the United States • Large data downloads from organizational servers • Partly compensate for too little main memory
Optical disk—CD	• Up to 700 MB • CD-ROM • CD-R (recordable) • CD-RW (rewritable)	• Reading CDs • Writable media can be used to back up files	• Install new programs • Play and record music • Back up data • CD being replaced by DVD
Optical disk—DVD	• Up to 4.7 GB • DVD-ROM • DVD-R (recordable) • DVD-RW (rewritable)	• Process both DVDs and CDs • Writable media can be used to back up files	• Install new programs • Play and record music • Play and record movies • Back up data
Monitor—CRT	• Viewing size • Dot pitch • Optimal resolution • Special memory?	• Limited budgets	• Nongraphic applications, such as word processing • Infrequently used computers
Monitor—LCD	• Viewing size • Pixel pitch • Optimal resolution • Special memory?	• Crowded workspaces • When brighter, sharper images are needed	• More than one monitor in use • Lots of graphics to be processed • Continual use

FIGURE 4-1
**What a Manager Needs
to Know About Hardware**

CPUs vary in speed, function, and cost. Hardware vendors such as Intel, Advanced Micro Devices, and National Semiconductor continually improve CPU speed and capabilities while reducing CPU costs (as discussed under Moore's Law in Chapter 1). Whether you or your department needs the latest, greatest CPU depends on the nature of your work.

FIGURE 4-2
**Input, Process, Output, and
Storage Hardware**

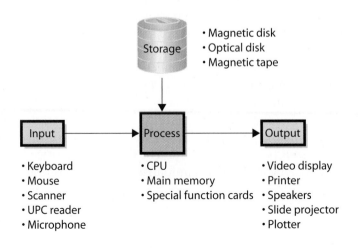

• Magnetic disk
• Optical disk
• Magnetic tape

Storage

Input → Process → Output

• Keyboard
• Mouse
• Scanner
• UPC reader
• Microphone

• CPU
• Main memory
• Special function cards

• Video display
• Printer
• Speakers
• Slide projector
• Plotter

FIGURE 4-3
Scantron Scanner
Scantron Corporation

The CPU works in conjunction with **main memory**. The CPU reads data and instructions from memory, and it stores results of computations in main memory. We will describe the relationship between the CPU and main memory later in the chapter. Main memory is sometimes called **RAM**, for random access memory.

Finally, computers also can have **special function cards** (see Figure 4-4) that can be added to the computer to augment the computer's basic capabilities. A common example is a video card, which enhances the clarity and refresh speed of the computer's video display.

Output hardware consists of video displays, printers, audio speakers, overhead projectors, and other special-purpose devices, such as large flatbed plotters.

Storage hardware saves data and programs. Magnetic disk is by far the most common storage device, although optical disks such as CDs and DVDs are also popular. In large corporate data centers, data are sometimes stored on magnetic tape.

Computer Data

Before we can further describe hardware, we need to define several important terms. We begin with binary digits.

Binary Digits

Computers represent data using **binary digits** called **bits**. A bit is either a zero or a one. Bits are used for computer data because they are easy to represent physically, as illustrated in Figure 4-5. A switch can be either closed or open. A computer can be designed so that an open switch represents zero and a closed switch represents one. Or, the orientation of a magnetic field can represent a bit; magnetism in one direction represents a zero, magnetism in the opposite direction represents a one. Or, for optical media, small pits are burned onto the surface of the disk so that they will reflect light. In a given spot, a reflection means a one; no reflection means a zero.

Sizing Computer Data

All computer data are represented by bits. The data can be numbers, characters, currency amounts, photos, recordings, or whatever. All are simply a string of bits.

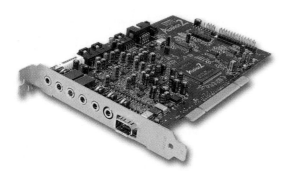

FIGURE 4-4
Special Function Card

Photo courtesy of Creative Labs, Inc. Sound Blaster and Audigy are registered trademarks of Creative Technology Ltd. in the United States and other countries.

FIGURE 4-5
Bits Are Easy to Represent
Physically

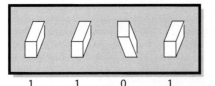

a. Light switches representing 1101

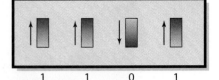

b. Direction of magnetism representing 1101

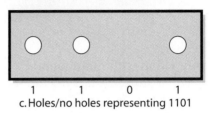

c. Holes/no holes representing 1101

For reasons that interest many but are irrelevant for future managers, bits are grouped into 8-bit chunks called **bytes**. For character data, such as the letters in a person's name, one character will fit into one byte. Thus, when you read a specification that a computing device has 100 million bytes of memory, you know that the device could hold up to 100 million characters.

Bytes are used to measure sizes of noncharacter data as well. Someone might say, for example, that a given picture is 100,000 bytes in size. This statement means that the length of the bit string that represents the picture is 100,000 bytes or 800,000 bits (because there are 8 bits per byte). The specifications for the size of main memory, disk, and other computer devices are expressed in bytes. Figure 4-6 shows the set of abbreviations that are used to represent data-storage capacity. A **kilobyte**, abbreviated **K**, is a collection of 1,024 bytes. A **megabyte**, or **MB**, is 1,024K bytes. A **gigabyte**, or **GB**, is 1,024MB bytes, and a **terabyte**, or **TB**, is 1,024GB.

Sometimes you will see these definitions simplified as 1K equals 1,000 bytes and 1MB equals 1,000K. Such simplifications are incorrect, but they do ease the math. Also, disk and computer manufacturers have an incentive to propagate this misconception. If a disk maker defines 1MB to be 1 million bytes—and not the correct 1,024K—the manufacturer can use its own definition of MB when specifying drive capacities. A buyer may think that a disk advertised as 100MB has space for 100 × 1,024K bytes, but, in truth, the drive will have space for only 100 × 1,000,000 bytes. Normally, the distinction is not too important, but be aware of the two possible interpretations of these abbreviations.

How a Computer Works, in Fewer Than 300 Words

Figure 4-7 shows a snapshot of a computer in use. The CPU (central processing unit) is the major actor. To run a program or process data, the CPU must first transfer the program or data from disk to *main memory*. Then, to execute an instruction, it moves the instruction from main memory into the CPU via the **data channel** or **bus**. The CPU has a small amount of very fast memory called a **cache**. The CPU keeps

FIGURE 4-6
Important Storage-Capacity
Terminology

Term	Definition	Abbreviation
Byte	Number of bits to represent one character	
Kilobyte	1,024 bytes	K
Megabyte	1,024 K = 1,048,576 bytes	MB
Gigabyte	1,024 MB = 1,073,741,824 bytes	GB
Terabyte	1,024 GB = 1,099,511,627,776 bytes	TB

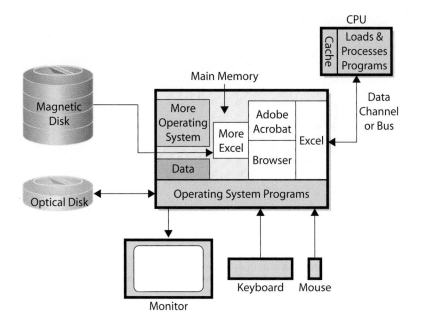

FIGURE 4-7
Computer Components

frequently used instructions in the cache. Having a large cache makes the computer faster, but cache is expensive.

Main memory of the computer in Figure 4-7 contains program instructions for Excel, Acrobat, and a browser (Internet Explorer or Firefox). It also contains instructions for the **operating system (OS)**, which is a program that controls the computer's resources as well as a block of data.

Main memory is too small to hold all of the programs and data that a user may want to process. For example, no personal computer has enough memory to hold all of the code in Microsoft Word, Excel, and Access. Consequently, the CPU loads programs into memory in chunks. In Figure 4-7, one portion of Excel was loaded into memory. When the user requested additional processing (say, to print the spreadsheet), the CPU loaded another piece of Excel.

If the user opens another program (say, Word) or needs to load more data (say, a picture), the operating system will direct the CPU to attempt to place the new program or data into unused memory. If there is not enough memory, it will remove something, perhaps the block of memory labeled More Excel, and then it will place the just-requested program or data into the vacated space. This process is called **memory swapping**.

Why Should a Manager Care How a Computer Works?

You can order computers with varying sizes of main memory. An employee who only runs one program at a time and who processes small amounts of data requires very little memory—512MB would be just fine. However, an employee who processes many programs at the same time (say, Word, Excel, Firefox, Access, Acrobat, and other programs) or an employee who processes very large files (pictures, movies, or sound files) needs lots of main memory, perhaps a gigabyte or more. If that employee's computer has too little memory, then the computer will constantly be swapping memory, and it will be slow. (This means, by the way, that if your computer is slow and if you have many programs open, you likely can improve performance by closing one or more programs.) Depending on your computer and the amount of memory it has, you might also be able to add more memory to it.

You can also order computers with CPUs of different speeds. CPU speed is expressed in cycles called *hertz*. In 2008, the CPU of a fast personal computer had a speed of 3.0 Gigahertz; a slow computer has a speed of less than 1 Gigahertz. As predicted by Moore's Law, CPU speeds continually increase.

The *Ethics Guide* on pages 80–81 poses questions about computer hardware and software that offer *more* than most users need.

Churn and Burn

An anonymous source, whom we'll call Mark, made the following statements about computing devices:

"I never upgrade my system. At least, I try not to. Look, I don't do anything at work but write memos and access email. I use Microsoft Word, but I don't use any features that weren't available in Word 3.0, 15 years ago. This whole industry is based on 'churn and burn': They churn their products so we'll burn our cash.

"All this hype about 3.0GHz processors and 500GB disks—who needs them? I'm sure I don't. And if Microsoft hadn't put so much junk into Windows, we could all be happy on an Intel 486 processor like the one I had in 1993. We're suckers for falling into the 'you gotta have this' trap.

"Frankly, I think there's a conspiracy between hardware and software vendors. They both want to sell new products, so the hardware people come up with these incredibly fast and huge computers. Then, given all that power, the software types develop monster products bloated with features and functions that nobody uses. It would take me months to learn all of the features in Word, only to find out that I don't need those features.

"To see what I mean, open Microsoft Word, click on View, then select Toolbars. In my version of Word, there are 19 toolbars to select, plus one more to customize my own toolbar. Now what in the world do I need with 19 toolbars? I write all the time, and

I have two selected: Standard and Formatting. Two out of 19! Could I pay Microsoft two-nineteenths of the price of Word because that's all I want or use?

"Here's how they get you, though. Because we live in a connected world, they don't have to get all of us to use those 19 toolbars, just one of us. Take Bridgette, over in legal, for example. Bridgette likes to use the redlining features, and she likes me to use them when I change draft contracts she sends me. So if I want to work on her documents, I have to turn on the Reviewing toolbar. You get the idea. Just get someone to use a feature and, because it is a connected world, then all of us have to have that feature.

"Viruses are one of their best ploys. They say you better buy the latest and greatest in software—and then apply all the patches that follow so that you'll be protected from the latest zinger from the computer 'bad guys.' Think about that for a minute. If vendors had built the products correctly the first time, then there would be no holes for the baddies to find, would there? So they have a defect in their products that they turn to a sales advantage. You see, they get us to focus on the virus and not on the hole in their product. In truth, they should be saying, 'Buy our latest product to protect yourself from the defective junk we sold you last year.' But truth in advertising hasn't come that far.

"Besides that, users are their own worst enemies as far as viruses are concerned. If I'm down on 17th Street at 4 in the morning, half drunk and with a bundle of cash hanging out of my pocket, what's likely to happen to me? I'm gonna get mugged. So if I'm out in some weirdo chat room—you know, out where you get pictures of . . . well . . . pictures that might not be in good taste and whatnot—and download and run a file, then of course I'm gonna get a virus. Viruses are brought on by user stupidity, that's all.

"One of these days, users are going to rise up and say, 'That's enough. I don't need any more. I'll stay with what I have, thank you very much.' In fact, maybe that's happening right now. Maybe that's why Vista sales aren't growing like they want. Maybe people have finally said, 'No more toolbars!'"

DISCUSSION QUESTIONS

1. Summarize Mark's view of the computer industry. Is there merit to his argument? Why or why not?

2. What holes do you see in the logic of his argument?

3. Someone could take the position that these statements are just empty rantings—that Mark can say all he wants, but the computer industry is going to keep on doing as it has been. Is there any point in Mark sharing his criticisms?

4. Read the section on viruses, Trojan horses, and worms that appears later in this chapter (pages 92–93). Comment on Mark's statement—"Viruses are brought on by user stupidity, that's all."

5. All software products ship with known problems. Microsoft, Adobe, and Apple all ship software that they know has failures. Is it unethical for them to do so? Do software vendors have an ethical responsibility to openly publish the problems in their software? How do these organizations protect themselves from lawsuits for damages caused by known problems in software?

6. Suppose a vendor licenses and ships a software product that has both known and unknown failures. As the vendor learns of the unknown failures, does it have an ethical responsibility to inform the users about them? Does the vendor have an ethical responsibility to fix the problems? Is it ethical for the vendor to require users to pay an upgrade fee for a new version of software that fixes problems in an existing version?

An employee who does only simple tasks, such as word processing, does not need a fast CPU; less than 1 Gigahertz will be fine. However, an employee who processes large, complicated spreadsheets or who manipulates large database files or edits large picture, sound, or movie files needs a very fast CPU—say, 3 Gigahertz or more.

In some cases, computer performance is improved not by making the CPU faster, but by installing more than one CPU. A **dual processor** computer has two CPUs and a **quad processor** has four. Dual processors are used in personal computers, and quad processors are generally used in servers (see next question).

One last comment: The cache and main memory are **volatile**, meaning their contents are lost when power is off. Magnetic disk and optical disk are **nonvolatile**, meaning their contents survive when power is off. If you suddenly lose power, the contents of unsaved memory—say, documents that have been altered—will be lost. Therefore, get into the habit of frequently (every few minutes or so) saving documents or files that you are changing. Save your documents before your roommate trips over the power cord.

Q2 What's the Difference Between a Client and a Server?

Before we can discuss computer software, you need to understand the difference between a client and a server. Figure 4-8 shows the environment of the typical computer user. Users employ **client** computers for word processing, spreadsheets, database access, and so forth. Most client computers also have software that enables them to connect to a network. It could be a private network at their company or school, or it could be the Internet, a public network. (We will discuss networks and related matters in Chapter 6. Just wait!)

Servers, as their name implies, provide some service. Dee will use a server to run her blog. Other servers publish Web sites, sell goods, host databases, and provide other functions.

As you might expect, server computers need to be faster, larger, and more powerful than client computers. Servers usually have very simple video displays. Many (even most) servers have no display at all, because they are only accessed from another computer via the network. For large commerce sites such as Amazon.com,

FIGURE 4-8
Client and Server Computers

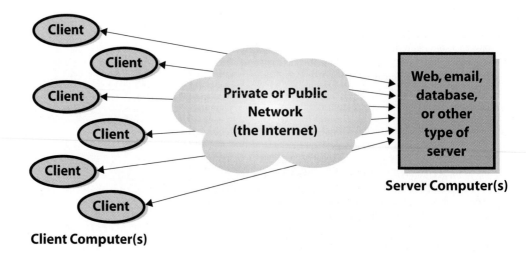

Private or Public Network (the Internet)

Web, email, database, or other type of server

Server Computer(s)

Client Computer(s)

the server is actually a large collection of computers (called a **server farm**) that coordinate all of their activities.

Actually, companies like Amazon.com and Google run dozens, even hundreds, of server farms. As of 2008, Google had 36 data centers around the world with several hundred thousand servers. The coordination of work among those computers is an incredibly sophisticated and fascinating technology dance. Google reports that an ordinary Google search may involve 700 to 1,000 servers.[1] Google's servers coordinate all that work, handing off partially completed searches or transactions, picking up the pieces when one computer fails—all in the blink of an eye. And the user does not need to know about the miracle that is underway. It's absolutely gorgeous engineering!

You may hear two new terms that have become popular with regard to server computers. A **grid** is a network of computers that operates as an integrated whole; the grid appears to be a single computer. The grid may operate to support a server farm, or it may support some other computing need. Organizations lease time on a grid from other organizations that create, support, and manage that grid. For example, IBM leases time on a grid for applications that require intensive arithmetic computing. It also leases time on a special-purpose grid that is used to archive medical records. (See *www-03.ibm.com/grid*.)

A second new term is **cloud**. The cloud refers to the computing network on the Internet. When you access a video from a site like Facebook, you are accessing computing services in the cloud. You don't know which server is processing your Facebook requests or which server is playing the video. You just know that somewhere in the cloud one or more servers are causing the video to be downloaded to your computer. You'll learn more about uses for clouds in Chapter 8.

MIS in Use 4 discusses a new device from Microsoft that consists of a cluster of computers working together. These computers are not servers, but they work together to provide sophisticated service on a single device.

A Server Farm

"Lucidio Studio, Inc."/The Stock Connection

[1]Stephen Shankland, "Google Spotlights Data Center Inner Workings," C/Net News, *http://news.cnet.com/8301-10784_3-9955184-7.html* (accessed June 2008).

4 Innovation in Practice: Microsoft Surface

In May 2007, Microsoft announced **Surface**, a new hardware–software product that enables people to interact with data on the surface of a table. Surface initiates a new product category, and the best way to understand it is to view one of Microsoft's promotional videos at *www.microsoft.com/surface*.

Surface paints the surface of the 30-inch table with invisible, near-infrared light to detect the presence of objects. It can respond to up to 52 different touches at the same time. According to Microsoft, this means that four people sitting around the Surface table could use all 10 of their fingers to manipulate up to 12 objects, simultaneously.

Surface uses wireless and other communications technologies to connect to devices that are placed on it, such as cameras or cell phones. When a camera is placed on Surface, pictures "spill" out of it, and users can manipulate those pictures with their hands. Products can be placed on Surface and product specifications displayed. Credit cards can be placed on Surface and items to be purchased can be dragged or dropped onto the credit card.

Currently Microsoft Surface is marketed and sold to large-scale leisure, entertainment, and retail companies in the United States. As of June 2008, Microsoft Surface is not available for individual purchase or for purchase by small to medium organizations. At present, Microsoft negotiates the price of Surface with each company.

As of June 2008, Surface has been implemented at select AT&T stores as well as the iBar lounge at Harrah's Rio All-Suite Hotel and Casino in Las Vegas, Nevada. The subtitle for the press release announcing iBar's system read,

"Harrah's reinvents flirting and offers new uninhibited fun and play to iBar patrons."[2]

The potential uses for Surface are staggering. Maps can display local events, and consumers can purchase tickets to those events by just using their fingers. Surface can be used for new computer games and gambling devices. Children can paint on the surface with virtual paintbrushes. Numerous other applications are possible. According to Steve Ballmer, CEO of Microsoft, "We see this as a multibillion dollar category, and we envision a time when surface computing technologies will be pervasive, from tabletops and counters to the hallway mirror. Surface is the first step in realizing that vision."[3]

As you can see at the Surface Web site, this product can be used for many different purposes in many different places, such as restaurants, retail kiosks, and eventually at home. Probably most of the eventual applications for Surface have not yet been envisioned. One clear application, however, is in the gambling and gaming industry. Imagine placing your credit card on a Surface gambling device and gambling the night away. Every time you lose, a charge is made against your credit card. Soon, before you know it, you've run up $15,000 in debt, which you learn when Surface tells you you've reached the maximum credit limit on your card.

You and a team of your fellow students will be given an opportunity to innovate with Surface in the Collaboration Exercise at the end of this chapter on page 96.

---

[2]"Harrah's Entertainment Launches Microsoft Surface at Rio iBar, Providing Guests with Innovative and Immersive New Entertainment Experiences." Microsoft Press Release, *www.microsoft.com/presspass/press/2008/jun08/06-11HETSurfacePR.mspx* (accessed June 2008).
[3]Microsoft Press Release, May 29, 2007.

Q3 What Does a Manager Need to Know About Software?

The essential knowledge that you need to know about computer software is summarized in Figure 4-9. If you already possess this knowledge, skip to the next question, "What buying decisions do you make?" on page 88.

Consider the two fundamental types of software. We have already spoken briefly about the *operating system*, which is a large and complicated program that controls the computer's resources, but there is also *application software*, which are programs that perform specific user tasks. An example of an operating system is Windows, and examples of applications are Microsoft Word and Oracle Customer Relationship Management.

Also, you need to understand two important software constraints. First, operating systems run only on particular types of hardware. Windows, for example, works only on processors from Intel and companies that make processors that conform to the Intel **instruction set** (the commands that a CPU can process). In other cases, such as Linux, numerous versions run on many different types of hardware and instruction sets.

Category	Operating System (OS)	Instruction Set	Common Applications	Typical User
Client	Windows	Intel	Microsoft Office: Word, Excel, Access, PowerPoint, many other applications	Business Home
	Mac OS (pre-2006)	Power PC	Macintosh applications plus Word and Excel	Graphic artists Arts community
	Mac OS (post-2006)	Intel	Macintosh applications plus Word and Excel Can also run Windows on Macintosh hardware	Graphic artists Arts community
	Unix	Sun and others	Engineering, computer-assisted design, architecture	Difficult for the typical client, but popular with some engineers and computer scientists
	Linux	Just about anything	Open Office (Microsoft Office look-alike)	Rare—used where budget is very limited
Server	Windows Server	Intel	Windows server applications	Business with commitment to Microsoft
	Unix	Sun and others	Unix server applications	Fading . . . Linux taking its market
	Linux	Just about anything	Linux & Unix server applications	Very popular—promulgated by IBM

FIGURE 4-9
What a Manager Needs to Know About Software

Second, application programs are written to use a particular operating system. Microsoft Access, for example, will run only on the Windows operating system. Some applications come in multiple versions. There are, for example, Windows and Macintosh versions of Microsoft Word. But unless informed otherwise, assume that a particular application runs on just one operating system.

What Are the Four Major Operating Systems?

The four major operating systems listed in Figure 4-9—Windows, Mac OS, Unix, and Linux—are very important. We describe them in the following sections.

Windows

For business users, the most important operating system is Microsoft **Windows**. Some version of Windows resides on more than 85 percent of the world's desktops, and considering just business users, the figure is more than 95 percent. Microsoft offers many different versions of Windows; Windows XP and Vista are current client versions. Windows Server 2008 is the current server version that supports Web sites, email, and other processes (discussed in Chapter 6). Windows runs the Intel instruction set.[4]

Mac OS

Apple Computer, Inc., developed its own operating system for the Macintosh, **Mac OS**. The current system is named Mac OS X. Macintosh computers are used primarily by graphic artists and workers in the arts community. Mac OS was designed originally to run the line of CPU processors from Motorola. In 1994, Mac OS switched to the PowerPC processor line from IBM. As of 2006, Macintosh computers are available for both PowerPC and Intel CPUs. A Macintosh with an Intel processor is able to run both Windows and Mac OS X.

---

[4]There are versions of Windows for other instruction sets, but they are unimportant for our purposes here.

Most people would agree that Apple has led the way in developing easy-to-use interfaces. Certainly, many innovative ideas have first appeared in a Macintosh and then later been added, in one form or another, to Windows.

Unix

Unix is an operating system that was developed at Bell Labs in the 1970s. It has been the workhorse of the scientific and engineering communities since then. Unix is generally regarded as being more difficult to use than either Windows or the Macintosh. Many Unix users know and employ an arcane language for manipulating files and data. However, once they surmount the rather steep learning curve, most Unix users swear by the system. Sun Microsystems and other vendors of computers for scientific and engineering applications are the major proponents of Unix. In general, Unix is not for the business user.

Linux

Linux is a version of Unix that was developed by the **open-source community**. This community is a loosely coupled group of programmers who mostly volunteer their time to contribute code to develop and maintain Linux. The open-source community owns Linux, and there is no fee to use it. Linux can run on client computers, but it is most frequently used on servers, particularly Web servers.

IBM is the primary proponent of Linux. Although IBM does not own Linux, IBM has developed many business systems solutions that use Linux. By using Linux, IBM does not have to pay a license fee to Microsoft or another vendor.

Own Versus License

When you buy a computer program, you are not actually buying that program. Instead, you are buying a **license** to use that program. For example, when you buy Windows, Microsoft is selling you the right to use Windows. Microsoft continues to own the Windows program.

In the case of Linux, no company can sell you a license to use it. It is owned by the open-source community, which states that Linux has no license fee (with certain reasonable restrictions). Companies such as IBM and smaller companies such as RedHat can make money by supporting Linux, but no company makes money selling Linux licenses.

What Types of Applications Exist, and How Do Organizations Obtain Them?

Application software consists of programs that perform a business function. Some application programs are general purpose, such as Excel or Word. Other application programs are specific. QuickBooks, for example, is an application program that provides general ledger and other accounting functions. We begin by describing categories of application programs and then move on to describe sources for them.

What Categories of Application Programs Exist?

Horizontal-market application software provides capabilities common across all organizations and industries. Word processors, graphics programs, spreadsheets, and presentation programs are all horizontal-market application software.

Examples of such software are Microsoft Word, Excel, and PowerPoint. Examples from other vendors are Adobe Acrobat, Photoshop, and PageMaker and Jasc Corporation's Paint Shop Pro. These applications are used in a wide variety of businesses, across all industries. They are purchased off-the-shelf, and little customization of features is necessary (or possible).

Vertical-market application software serves the needs of a specific industry. Examples of such programs are those used by dental offices to schedule appointments and bill patients, those used by auto mechanics to keep track of customer data and customers' automobile repairs, and those used by parts warehouses to track inventory, purchases, and sales.

Vertical applications usually can be altered or customized. Typically, the company that sells the application software provides such services or offers referrals to qualified consultants who can provide this service.

One-of-a-kind application software is developed for a specific, unique need. The IRS develops such software, for example, because it has needs that no other organization has.

Some application software does not neatly fit into the horizontal or vertical category. For example, customer relationship management (CRM) software is a horizontal application because every business has customers. But it usually needs to be customized to the requirements of businesses in a particular industry, and so it is also akin to vertical market software.

You will learn about other examples of such dual-category software in Chapter 7 when we discuss materials requirements planning (MRP), enterprise resource planning (ERP), and other such applications. In this book, we will consider such applications to be vertical market applications, even though they do not fit perfectly into this category.

How Do Organizations Acquire Application Software?

You can acquire application software in exactly the same ways that you can buy a new suit. The quickest and least risky option is to buy your suit off-the-rack. With this method, you get your suit immediately, and you know exactly what it will cost. You may not, however, get a good fit. Alternately, you can buy your suit off-the-rack and have it altered. This will take more time, it may cost more, and there's some possibility that the alteration will result in a poor fit. Most likely, however, an altered suit will fit better than an off-the-rack one.

Finally, you can hire a tailor to make a custom suit. In this case, you'll have to describe what you want, be available for multiple fittings, and be willing to pay considerably more. Although there is an excellent chance of a great fit, there is also the possibility of a disaster. Still, if you want a yellow and orange polka-dot silk suit with a hissing rattlesnake on the back, tailor-made is the only way to go.

You can buy computer software in the same three ways: **off-the-shelf**, **off-the-shelf with alterations**, or tailor-made. Tailor-made software is called **custom-developed software**.

Organizations develop custom application software themselves or hire a development vendor. Like buying the yellow and orange polka-dot suit, such development is done in situations in which the needs of the organization are so unique that no horizontal or vertical applications are available. By developing custom software, the organization can tailor its application to fit its requirements.

Custom development is difficult and risky. Staffing and managing teams of software developers is challenging. Managing software projects can be daunting. Many organizations have embarked on application development projects only to find that the projects take twice as long—or longer—to finish as planned. As we will discuss in Chapter 10, cost overruns of 200 and 300 percent are not uncommon.

In addition, every application program needs to be adapted to changing needs and changing technologies. The adaptation costs of horizontal and vertical software are amortized over all of the users of that software, perhaps thousands or millions of customers. For custom software developed in-house, however, the developing company must pay all of the adaptation costs itself. Over time, this can be a heavy burden.

Because of the risk and expense, in-house development is the last-choice alternative and is used only when there is no other option. Figure 4-10 summarizes software sources and types.

Over the course of your career, application software, hardware, and firmware will change, sometimes rapidly. The *Guide* on pages 90–91 challenges you to *choose* a strategy for addressing this change.

FIGURE 4-10
Software Sources and Types

Software Source

Software Type	Off-the-shelf	Off-the-shelf and then customized	Custom-developed
Horizontal applications			
Vertical applications			
One-of-a-kind applications			

What Is Firmware?

Firmware is computer software that is installed into devices such as printers, print servers, and various types of communication devices. The software is coded just like other software, but it is installed into special, read-only memory of the printer or other device. In this way, the program becomes part of the device's memory; it is as if the program's logic is designed into the device's circuitry. Users do not need to load firmware into the device's memory.

Firmware can be changed or upgraded, but this is normally a task for IS professionals. The task is easy, but it requires knowledge of special programs and techniques that most business users choose not to learn.

What Is the Difference Between a Thin and Thick Client?

When you use applications such as Word, Excel, or Acrobat, those programs run only on your computer. They do not require any service from a server, and you need not be connected to the Internet or other network for them to run.

Other applications, however, require processing on both the client and the server. Email is a good example. When you send email, you run a client program such as Microsoft Outlook on your computer, and it connects over the Internet or a private network to mail server software on a server. Similarly, when you access a Web site, you run a browser (client software) on your computer that connects over a network to Web server software on a server.

An application that requires nothing more than a browser is called a **thin client**. An application such as Microsoft Outlook that requires programs other than a browser on the user's computer is called a **thick client**. The terms *thin* and *thick* refer to the amount of code that must run on the client computer. All other things being equal, thin client applications are preferred to thick client applications because they do not require the installation and administration of client software. However, the thick client application may provide features and functions that more than compensate for the expense and administration of their installation.

Client and server computers can run different operating systems. Many organizations have standardized on Windows for their clients and Linux for their servers. Figure 4-11 shows an example. Two thin clients are connecting via browsers to a Web server that is running Windows. Two thick clients are connecting via an email client to an email server that is running Linux. Those two clients are thick because they have client email software installed.

Q4 What Buying Decisions Do You Make?

In general, most business professionals have some role in the specification of the client hardware and software they use. Business managers also play a role in the specification of client hardware and software for employees whom they manage. The

FIGURE 4-11
Thin and Thick
Clients

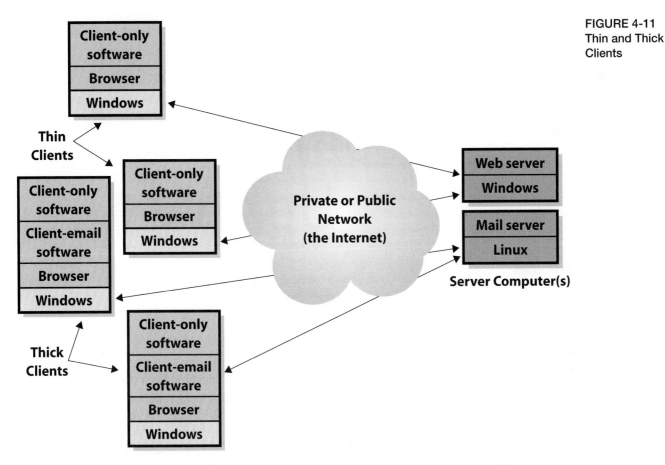

particular role depends on the policy manager's organization. Large organizations will have an IS department that is likely to set firm standards for client hardware and software. You will learn more about such standards and the need for them in Chapter 11.

In medium to small organizations, policies are often less formal, and managers will need to take an active role in setting the specifications for their own and their employees' computers. Figure 4-12 lists the major criteria for both hardware and software.

Except in rare circumstances, medium-to-small organizations will usually standardize on a single client operating system because the costs of supporting more than one are unjustifiable. Most organizations choose Windows clients. Some arts and design businesses standardize on the Macintosh, and some engineering firms standardize on Unix. Organizations with limited budgets might choose to use Linux on the clients, but this is rare.

Category	Hardware	Software
Client	Specify: • CPU speed • Size of main memory • Size of magnetic disk • CD or DVD and type • Monitor type and size	Specify: • Windows, Mac, or Linux OS. May be dictated by organizational standard. • PC applications such as Microsoft Office Adobe Acrobat, Photoshop, Paint Shop Pro may be dictated by organizational standard. • Browser such as Internet Explorer, FireFox, or Netscape Navigator. • Requirements for the client side of client-server applications. • Need for thin or thick client.
Server	In most cases, a business manager has no role in the specification of server hardware (except possibly a budgetary one).	• Specify requirements for the server side of client-server applications. • Work with technical personnel to test and accept software and hardware.

Keeping Up to Speed

Have you ever been to a cafeteria where you put your lunch tray on a conveyor belt that carries the dirty dishes into the kitchen? That conveyor belt reminds me of technology. Like the conveyor, technology just moves along, and all of us run on top of the technology conveyor, trying to keep up. We hope to keep up with the relentless change of technology for an entire career without ending up in the techno-trash.

Technology change is a fact, and the only appropriate question is, "What am I going to do about it?" One strategy you can take is to bury your head in the sand: "Look, I'm not a technology person. I'll leave it to the pros. As long as I can send email and use the Internet, I'm happy. If I have a problem, I'll call someone to fix it."

That strategy is fine, as far as it goes, and many businesspeople use it. Following that strategy won't give you a competitive advantage over anyone, and it will give someone else a competitive advantage over you, but as long as you develop your advantage elsewhere, you'll be OK—at least for yourself.

What about your department, though? If an expert says, "Every computer needs a 250GB disk," are you going to nod your head and say, "Great. Sell 'em to me!" Or are you going to know enough to realize that's a big disk (by 2008 standards, anyway) and ask why everyone needs such a large amount of

storage. Maybe then you'll be told, "Well, it's only another $150 per machine from the 80GB disk." At that point, you can make a decision, using your own decision-making skills, and not rely solely on the IS expert. The prudent business professional in the twenty-first century has a number of reasons not to bury his or her head in the technology sand.

At the other end of the spectrum are those who love technology. You'll find them everywhere—they may be accountants, marketing professionals, or production-line supervisors who not only know their field, but also enjoy information technology. Maybe they were IS majors or had double majors that combined IS with another area of expertise (for example., IS with accounting). These people read C/NET News and CIO.com most days, and they can tell you the latest on cloud computing offerings from Amazon and Microsoft. Those people are sprinting along the technology conveyor belt. They will never end up in the techno-trash, and they will use their knowledge of IT to gain competitive advantage throughout their careers.

Many business professionals are in between these extremes. They don't want to bury their heads, but they don't have the desire or interest to become technophiles (lovers of technology) either. What to do? There are a couple of strategies. For one, don't allow yourself to ignore technology. When you see a technology article in the *Wall Street Journal*, read it. Don't just skip it because it's about technology. Read the technology ads, too. Many vendors invest heavily in ads that instruct without seeming to. Another option is to take a seminar or pay attention to professional events that combine your specialty with technology. For example, when you go to the banker's convention, attend a session or two on "Technology Trends for Bankers." There are always sessions like that, and you might make a contact in another company with similar problems and concerns.

Probably the best option, if you have the time for it, is to get involved as a user representative in technology committees in your organization. If your company is doing a review of its CRM system, for instance, see if you can get on the review committee. When there's a need for a representative from your department to discuss needs for the next-generation help-line system, sign up. Or, later in your career, become a member of the business practice technology committee, or whatever they call it at your organization.

Just working with such groups will add to your knowledge of technology. Presentations made to such groups, discussions about uses of technology, and ideas about using IT for competitive advantage will all add to your IT knowledge. You'll gain important contacts and exposure to leaders in your organization as well.

It's up to you. You get to choose how you relate to technology. But be sure you choose; don't let your head fall into the sand without thinking about it.

DISCUSSION QUESTIONS

1. Do you agree that the changes in technology are relentless? What do you think that means to most business professionals? To most organizations?

2. Think about the three postures toward technology presented here. Which camp will you join? Why?

3. Write a two-paragraph memo to yourself justifying your choice in question 2. If you chose to ignore technology, explain how you will compensate for the loss of competitive advantage. If you're going to join one of the other two groups, explain why, and describe how you're going to accomplish your goal.

4. Given your answer to question 2, assume that you're in a job interview and the interviewer asks about your knowledge of technology. Write a three-sentence response to the interviewer's question.

Managers and their employees may have a role in specifying horizontal application software such as Microsoft Office or other software appropriate for their operating systems. They will also have an important role in specifying requirements for vertical market or custom applications. We will say more about this role in Chapter 10.

Concerning the server, a business manager typically has no role in the specification of server hardware, other than possibly approving the budget. Instead, technical personnel make such decisions. A business manager and those who will be the clients of a client-server application specify the requirements for vertical and custom-server software. They will also work with technical personnel to test and accept that software.

Q5 What Are Viruses, Trojan Horses, and Worms?

A **virus** is a computer program that replicates itself. Unchecked replication is like computer cancer; ultimately, the virus consumes the computer's resources. Furthermore, many viruses also take unwanted and harmful actions.

The program code that causes unwanted activity is called the **payload**. The payload can delete programs or data—or, even worse, modify data in undetected ways. Imagine the impact of a virus that changed the credit rating of all customers. Some viruses publish data in harmful ways—for example, sending out files of credit card data to unauthorized sites.

There are many different types of viruses. **Trojan horses** are viruses that masquerade as useful programs or files. The name refers to the gigantic mock-up of a horse that was filled with soldiers and moved into Troy during the Trojan War. A typical Trojan horse appears to be a computer game, an mp3 music file, or some other useful, innocuous program.

Macro viruses attach themselves to Word, Excel, or other types of documents. When the infected document is opened, the virus places itself in the startup files of the application. After that, the virus infects every file that the application creates or processes.

A **worm** is a virus that propagates using the Internet or other computer network. Worms spread faster than other virus types because they are specifically programmed to spread. Unlike nonworm viruses, which must wait for the user to share a file with a second computer, worms actively use the network to spread. Sometimes, worms so choke a network that it becomes unusable.

In 2003, the Slammer worm clogged the Internet and caused Bank of America ATM machines and the information systems of hundreds of other organizations to fail. Slammer operated so fast that 90 percent of the vulnerable machines were infected within 10 minutes.

You can take several measures to prevent viruses. First, most viruses take advantage of security holes in computer programs. As vendors find these holes, they create program modifications, called **patches**, that fix the problem. To keep from getting a virus, sign up for automatic updates from Microsoft and other vendor sites. Apply suggested patches immediately. A patch for the Slammer worm was available from Microsoft several months before Slammer occurred. The worm did not infect any site that had applied the patch.

When you think about it, it is not surprising that the problem occurred some time after the patch appeared. As soon as a vendor publishes the problem and the patch, every computer criminal in the world can learn about the hole. Virus developers can then write code to exploit that hole, and any machine that does not apply the patch is then doubly vulnerable. Therefore, the first rule in preventing viruses is to find and apply patches to the operating system and to applications.

Other prevention steps are:

- Never download files, programs, or attachments from unknown Web sites.
- Do not open attachments to emails from strangers.

- Do not open unexpected attachments to emails, even from known sources.
- Do not rely on file extensions. A file marked *MyPicture.jpg* is normally a picture (because of the *jpg* file extension). For a variety of reasons, however, this file may be something else—a virus.
- Companies such as Symantec, Sophos, McAfee, Norton, AVG, and others license products that detect and possibly eliminate viruses. Such products can operate in proactive mode by checking attachments as you receive them. They can also operate retroactively by checking memory and disk drives for the presence of viral code. You should run a retroactive antivirus program at regular intervals—at least once a week.

Such **antivirus programs** search the computer's memory and disk for known viruses. Obviously, if a virus is unknown to the antivirus software, then that virus will remain undetected. You should periodically obtain updates for the latest virus patterns from the vendor who produces the antivirus product. Additionally, realize that even though you use antivirus software, you are still vulnerable to viruses that are unknown to the virus detection company.

Now for the ugly news: What do you do if you have a virus? Most antivirus products include programs for removing viruses. If you have a virus, you can follow the instructions provided by that software to remove it. However, it is possible that the virus may have mutated into a different form. If so, then the antivirus product will not see the mutated version, and it will remain on your computer.

Unfortunately, the only sure way to eliminate a virus is to delete everything on your magnetic disk by reformatting it. Then you must reinstall the operating system and all applications from known, clean sources (e.g., the original CD from the vendor). Finally, one by one, you must reload data files that you know are free of the virus. This laborious and time-consuming process assumes that you have all of your data files backed up. If not, you're out of luck. Because of the time and expense involved, few organizations go through this process. However, reformatting the disk is the only sure way of removing a virus.

Viruses are expensive. C/Net estimated that the Slammer worm caused between $950 million and $1.2 billion in lost productivity during the first 5 days of its existence.[5] To protect your organization, you should ensure that procedures exist to install patches as soon as possible. Also, every computer should have and use a copy of an antivirus program. You and your organization cannot afford not to take these precautions. We will discuss other problematic programs, such as spyware, in more detail in Chapter 12.

Although this chapter does not help Dee answer all of the questions her consultant asked, the knowledge in this chapter would have

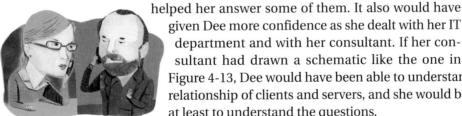

This isn't a NASA project.

helped her answer some of them. It also would have given Dee more confidence as she dealt with her IT department and with her consultant. If her consultant had drawn a schematic like the one in Figure 4-13, Dee would have been able to understand the relationship of clients and servers, and she would be able at least to understand the questions.

Also, with the knowledge in this chapter, she would have reduced the work (and fee) of her consultant by stating:

1. "No new client hardware. The sales reps need to use the hardware they have."
2. "Only a thin client on the sales reps computers. Sales reps must not be required to install any special software on their computers."
3. "I would prefer a thin client on my computer, but I would install software for creating blog entries on my computer if I have to."

[5]*http://news.cnet.com/2100-1001-982955.html*.

CHAPTER 5

Database Processing

Working with her consultant, Dee selected an application program called Movable Type for her blog. Although it was a bit more difficult to use than other programs, it had certain advanced features that gave her greater control over the look and feel of the blog. Her consultant said it was a professional-grade product.

Shortly after selecting the product, Don, the consultant, mentioned that she would need to install MySQL as well. "You need a DBMS to store your blog entries," he explained.

"A what?" asked Dee. "Oh, right," explained Don, "a database management system—a DBMS."

Dee had decided that her blog needed to run within the Emerson network (you'll learn why in the next chapter), and Don told her to check with her IT department to see if they already had MySQL. When she asked her IT department, she was told, "No, we've standardized on Oracle. We don't run any other DBMS products."

When Dee reported this news to Don, he said that this would be a problem. He told her that Oracle is difficult to work with, even though it generates terrific performance on large databases. He would have to revise his labor estimates for the project if they were going to use Oracle. Also, he said he'd have to determine if there was an Oracle version of Movable Type. If not, they'd have to pick another application. That meant backing up to reconsider the decisions they'd already made.

We are NOT about to change DBMS products.

Meanwhile, time was ticking away. It was now the second week in December, and Dee needed the blog up and running by the first week in January.

"Look," Don advised, "talk to them again. Installing MySQL isn't that hard. We're not talking about running the business on it; we're just going to run your blog. I can install it, and you can work out the license issues yourself. It won't be that expensive or hard."

When Dee called the IT department back, she was met with strong resistance and a barrage of terminology that she didn't understand. She needed the knowledge in this chapter.

Q1 What is the purpose of a database?

Q2 What does a database contain?

Q3 What is a DBMS, and what does it do?

Q4 What is a database application?

Q5 What is the difference between an enterprise DBMS
and a personal DBMS?

How does the knowledge in this chapter help Dee and you?

Q1 What Is the Purpose of a Database?

The purpose of a database is to keep track of things. When most students learn that, they wonder why we need a special technology for such a simple task. Why not just use a list? If the list is long, they think, put it into a spreadsheet.

Many professionals do keep track of things using spreadsheets. If the structure of the list is simple enough, there is no need to use database technology. The list of student grades in Figure 5-1, for example, works perfectly well in a spreadsheet.

Suppose, however, that the professor wants to track more than just grades. The professor may want to record email messages as well. Or perhaps the professor wants to record both email messages and office visits. There is no place in Figure 5-1 to record that additional data. Of course, the professor could set up a separate spreadsheet for email messages and another one for office visits, but that awkward solution would be difficult to use because it does not provide all of the data in one place.

Instead, the professor wants a form like that in Figure 5-2. With it, the professor can record student grades, emails, and office visits all in one place. A form like the one in Figure 5-2 is difficult, if not impossible, to produce from a spreadsheet. Such a form is easily produced, however, from a database.

The key distinction between Figures 5-1 and 5-2 is that the list in Figure 5-1 is about a single theme or concept. It is about student grades only. The list in Figure 5-2 has multiple themes; it shows student grades, student emails, and student office visits. We can make a general rule from these examples: Lists that involve a single theme can be stored in a spreadsheet;[1] lists that involve multiple themes require a database. We will learn more about this general rule as this chapter proceeds.

To summarize, the purpose of a database is to keep track of things that involve more than one theme.

---

[1]This doesn't mean, however, that any list with a single theme *should* be stored in a spreadsheet. If there is a lot of data, and if you want to query, sort, and filter that data, you probably should use a database, even for data having just one theme.

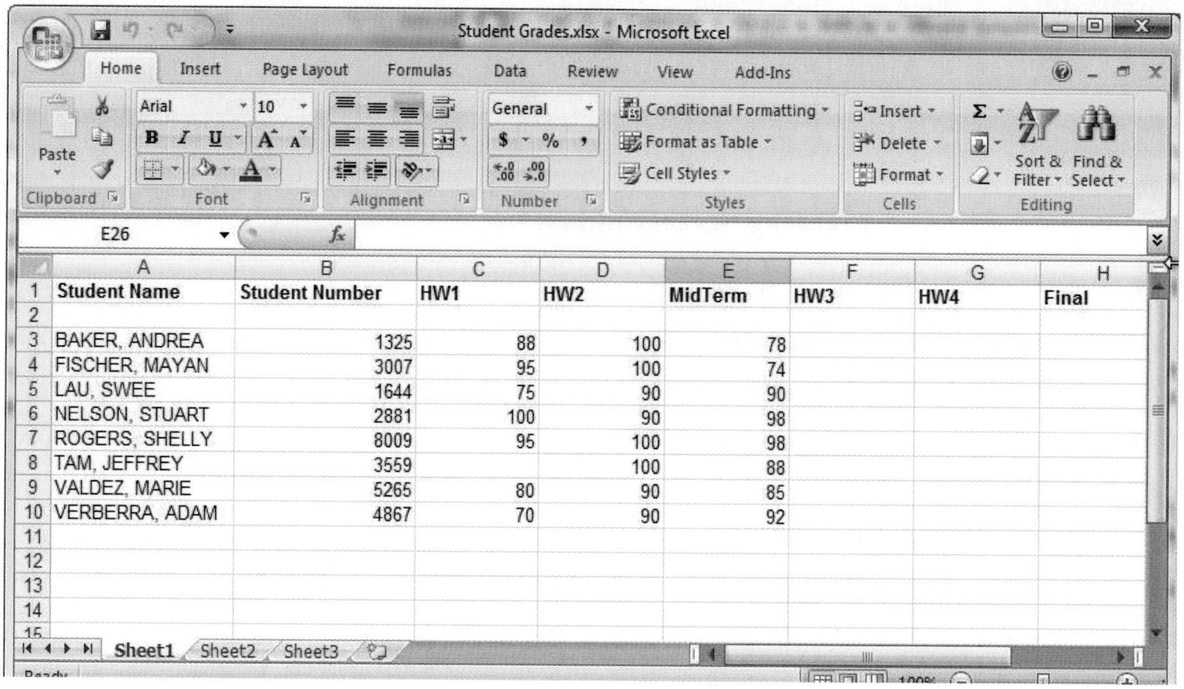

FIGURE 5-1
A List of Student Grades

Q2 What Does a Database Contain?

A **database** is a self-describing collection of integrated records. To understand this definition, you first need to understand the terms illustrated in Figure 5-3. As you learned in Chapter 4, a **byte** is a character of data. Bytes are grouped into **columns**, such as *Student Number* and *Student Name*. Columns are also called **fields**. Columns or fields, in turn, are grouped into **rows**, which are also called **records**. In Figure 5-3, the collection of data for all columns (*Student Name, Student Number, HW1, HW2,* and *MidTerm*) is called a row or a record. Finally, a group of similar rows or records is called

FIGURE 5-2
Student Data Shown in Form

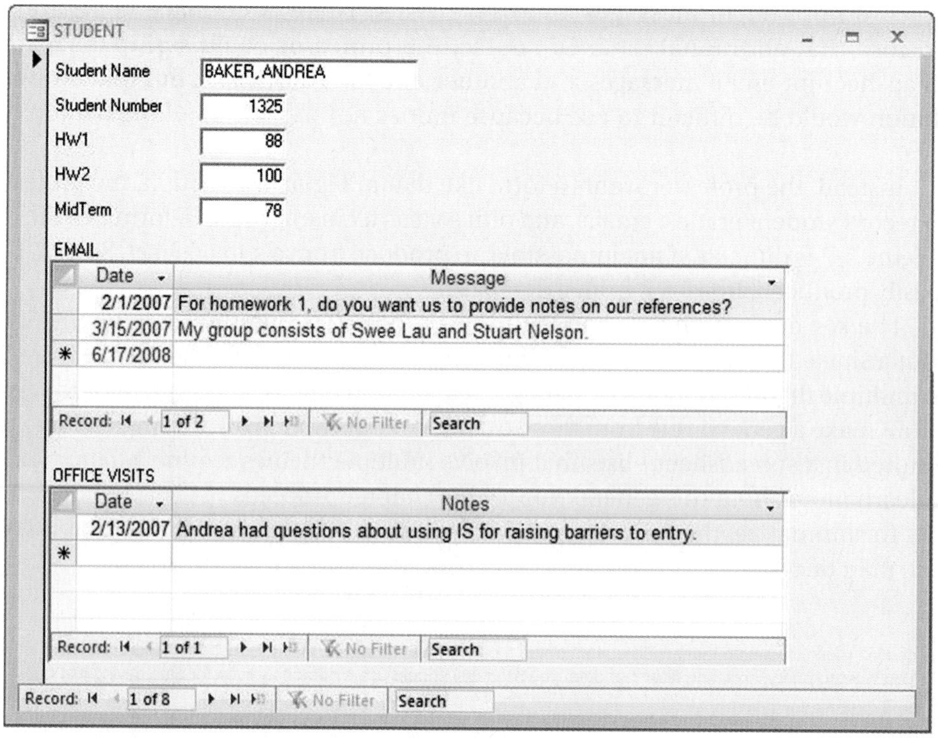

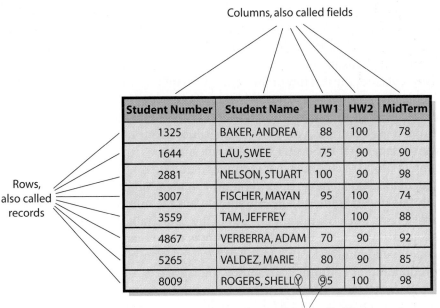

FIGURE 5-3
Student Table (also Called
a File)

Columns, also called fields

Student Number	Student Name	HW1	HW2	MidTerm
1325	BAKER, ANDREA	88	100	78
1644	LAU, SWEE	75	90	90
2881	NELSON, STUART	100	90	98
3007	FISCHER, MAYAN	95	100	74
3559	TAM, JEFFREY		100	88
4867	VERBERRA, ADAM	70	90	92
5265	VALDEZ, MARIE	80	90	85
8009	ROGERS, SHELLY	95	100	98

Rows, also called records

Characters, also called bytes

a **table** or a **file**. From these definitions, you can see that there is a hierarchy of data elements, as shown in Figure 5-4.

It is tempting to continue this grouping process by saying that a database is a group of tables or files. This statement, although true, does not go far enough. As shown in Figure 5-5, a database is a collection of tables *plus* relationships among the rows in those tables, *plus* special data, called *metadata*, that describes the structure of the database. By the way, the cylindrical symbol ▯ represents a computer disk drive. It is used in diagrams like that in Figure 5-5 because databases are normally stored on magnetic disks.

Relationships Among Records

Consider the terms on the left-hand side of Figure 5-5. You know what tables are. To understand what is meant by *relationships among rows in tables*, examine Figure 5-6. It shows sample data from the three tables *Email, Student,* and *Office_Visit.* Notice the column named *Student Number* in the *Email* table. That column indicates the row in *Student* to which a row of *Email* is connected. In the first row of *Email,* the *Student*

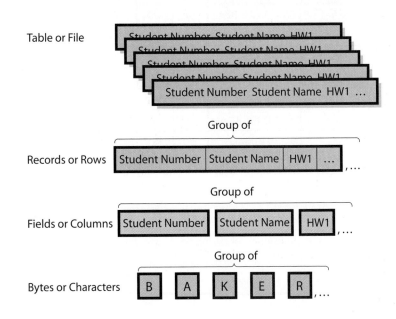

FIGURE 5-4
Hierarchy of Data Elements

Table or File

Student Number Student Name HW1

Group of

Records or Rows

| Student Number | Student Name | HW1 | ... | , ... |

Group of

Fields or Columns

| Student Number | Student Name | HW1 | , ... |

Group of

Bytes or Characters   B   A   K   E   R   , ...

Tables or Files
+
Relationships
Among   = Database
Rows in Tables
+
Metadata

FIGURE 5-5
Components of a Database

Number value is 1325. This indicates that this particular email was received from the student whose *Student Number* is 1325. If you examine the *Student* table, you will see that the row for Andrea Baker has this value. Thus, the first row of the *Email* table is related to Andrea Baker.

Now consider the last row of the *Office_Visit* table at the bottom of the figure. The value of *Student Number* in that row is 4867. This value indicates that the last row in *Office_Visit* belongs to Adam Verberra.

From these examples, you can see that values in one table relate rows of that table to rows in a second table. Several special terms are used to express these ideas. A **key** is a column or group of columns that identifies a unique row in a table. *Student Number* is the key of the *Student* table. Given a value of *Student Number*, you can determine one and only one row in *Student*. Only one student has the number 1325, for example.

Every table must have a key. The key of the *Email* table is *EmailNum*, and the key of the *Student_Visit* table is *VisitID*. Sometimes more than one column is needed to form a unique identifier. In a table called *City*, for example, the key would consist of the combination of columns (*City*, *State*), because a given city name can appear in more than one state.

Student Number is not the key of the *Email* or the *Office_Visit* tables. We know that about *Email*, because there are two rows in *Email* that have the *Student Number* value 1325. The value 1325 does not identify a unique row; therefore, *Student Number* is not the key of *Email*.

Nor is *Student Number* a key of *Office_Visit*, although you cannot tell that from the data in Figure 5-6. If you think about it, however, there is nothing to prevent a student from visiting a professor more than once. If that were to happen, there would be two rows in *Office_Visit* with the same value of *Student Number*. It just happens that no student has visited twice in the limited data in Figure 5-6.

FIGURE 5-6
Example of Relationships
Among Rows

Email Table

EmailNum	Date	Message	Student Number
1	2/1/2008	For homework 1, do you want us to provide notes on our references?	1325
2	3/15/2008	My group consists of Swee Lau and Stuart Nelson.	1325
3	3/15/2008	Could you please assign me to a group?	1644

Student Table

Student Number	Student Name	HW1	HW2	MidTerm
1325	BAKER, ANDREA	88	100	78
1644	LAU, SWEE	75	90	90
2881	NELSON, STUART	100	90	98
3007	FISCHER, MAYAN	95	100	74
3559	TAM, JEFFREY		100	88
4867	VERBERRA, ADAM	70	90	92
5265	VALDEZ, MARIE	80	90	85
8009	ROGERS, SHELLY	95	100	98

Office_Visit Table

VisitID	Date	Notes	Student Number
2	2/13/2008	Andrea had questions about using IS for raising barriers to entry.	1325
3	2/17/2008	Jeffrey is considering an IS major. Wanted to talk about career opportunities.	3559
4	2/17/2008	Will miss class Friday due to job conflict.	4867

Columns that fulfill a role like that of *Student Number* in the *Email* and *Office_Visit* tables are called **foreign keys**. This term is used because such columns are keys, but they are keys of a different (foreign) table than the one in which they reside.

Before we go on, databases that carry their data in the form of tables and that represent relationships using foreign keys are called **relational databases**. (The term *relational* is used because another, more formal name for a table is **relation**.) In the past, there were databases that were not relational in format, but such databases have nearly disappeared. Chances are you will never encounter one, and we will not consider them further.[2]

Metadata

Recall the definition of database again: A database is a self-describing collection of integrated records. The records are integrated because, as you just learned, relationships among rows are represented in the database. But what does *self-describing* mean?

It means that a database contains, within itself, a description of its contents. Think of a library. A library is a self-describing collection of books and other materials. It is self-describing because the library contains a catalog that describes the library's contents. The same idea also pertains to a database. Databases are self-describing because they contain not only data, but also data about the data in the database.

Metadata are data that describe data. Figure 5-7 shows metadata for the *Email* table. The format of metadata depends on the software product that is processing the database. Figure 5-7 shows the metadata as they appear in Microsoft Access 2007. Each row of the top part of this form describes a column of the *Email* table. The columns of these descriptions are *Field Name*, *Data Type*, and *Description*. *Field Name* contains the name of the column, *Data Type* shows the type of data the column may hold, and *Description* contains notes that explain the source or use of the column. As you can see, there is one row of metadata for each of the four columns of the *Email* table: *EmailNum*, *Date*, *Message*, and *Student Number*.

The bottom part of this form provides more metadata, which Access calls *Field Properties*, for each column. In Figure 5-7, the focus is on the *Date* column (the row surrounded by a tan line). Because the focus is on *Date* in the top pane, the details in the bottom pane pertain to the *Date* column. The *Field Properties* describe formats, a

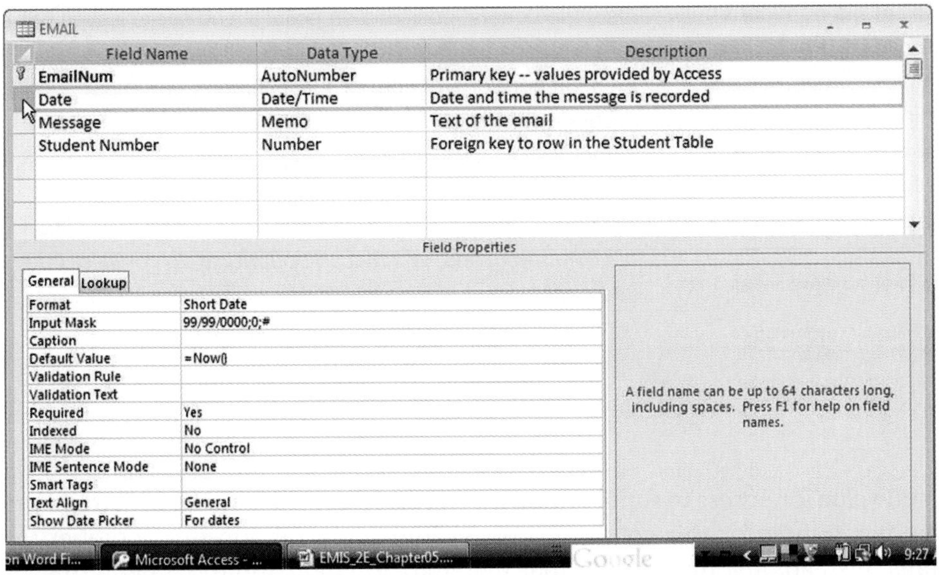

FIGURE 5-7
Example of Metadata (in Access)

---

[2]Another type of database, the **object-relational database**, is rarely used in commercial applications. Search the Web if you are interested in learning more about object-relational databases. In this book, we will consider only relational databases.

MIS in use

5 How Much Is a Database Worth?

Neil Miyamoto is a partner and the chief operations officer at The Firm, a popular, hip, and very successful workout studio in Minneapolis (*www.thefirmmpls.com*). The Firm provides clients a high-energy and positive workout environment and offers classes taught by fun, interesting, and skilled trainers and coaches. Each month, The Firm realizes over 15,000 person-visits, an average of 500 visits per day!

In a recent interview, Mr. Miyamoto stated,

> Our database is our biggest asset. Take away anything else—the building, the equipment, the inventory—anything else, and we'd be back in business 6 months or less. Take away our customer database, however, and we'd have to start all over. It would take us another 8 years to get back where we are.[3]

Why is the database so crucial? It records everything the company's customers do. If The Firm decides to offer an early morning kickboxing class featuring a particular trainer, it can use its database to offer that class to everyone who ever took an early morning class, a kickboxing class, or a class by that trainer. Customers receive targeted solicitations for offerings they care about and, maybe equally important, they *don't* receive solicitations for those they don't care about.

Speaking of solicitations, Barack Obama used the Internet and a Facebook-like Web site to raise more than $200 million from 1.4 million people early in the campaign (by June of 2008). Because of this funding, he was able to outspend Hillary Clinton, a key factor in his nomination victory, according to Clinton advisor Mark Penn. That $200 million is, of course, a powerful asset, but it may not be the biggest asset. In the long run, the database of donors, their contact data, and their positions on political and social matters will be far more valuable. Laura Quinn, CEO of Catalist, speaking of Obama's database, said, "It's

gigantic. The list is as transformational as the advent of political advertising."[4]

Why? Because Obama can use the database not only for his own benefit, but also to benefit others' fundraising efforts. According to Tad Devine, former political strategist for John Kerry, when Obama's staff "sends out a letter saying give money to someone, suddenly a House candidate can have a half a million dollars in a day. That may be what the House candidate was hoping to raise in a quarter."[5] The database asset belongs to Obama and represents an advantage that extends beyond his presidential victory. Having that database will give him additional clout in dealing with members of Congress, even in years after his presidency.

The value of Obama's database is not just its size, but its accuracy. Political organizations have been purchasing electoral data for years. The problem with such data is that it is often inaccurate and much of it is based on statistical conjecture.

If you own three Hummers and are married to a Republican governer, then it would be reasonable to conclude that you are a Republican. That conjecture will not work for Maria Shriver, lifelong Democrat (niece of President John F. Kennedy) and wife of California governor Arnold Schwarzenegger, however, and sometimes it is the outliers like her who are the most important people to reach.

At the Web site *my.barackobama.com* supporters can enter their own data; consequently, the data is very accurate. Also, the donors' positions on political and social issues will reflect their true interests. Similarly, when you order from Amazon.com or REI.com or LLBean.com, you must enter accurate contact data for your items to arrive. You also leave a track record of purchases that indicates your true product preferences.

In Collaboration Exercise 5 (page 117), you and a team of your classmates will have an opportunity to consider how you might develop databases of similar value during your business career.

---

[3]David Kroenke, *Using MIS*, 2d ed. (Upper Saddle River, NJ: Prentice Hall, 2008), p. 62.
[4]Christopher Stern, "Obama's 'Gigantic' Database May Make Him Party's Power Broker," *www.bloomberg.com*, June 19, 2008. http://www.bloomberg.com/apps/newshttp://www.bloomberg.com/apps/news?pid=washingtonstory&sid=aW_Qty8aiVTo (accessed June 2008).

[5]Ibid.

---

default value for Access to supply when a new row is created, and the constraint that a value is required for this column. It is not important for you to remember these details. Instead, just understand that metadata are data about data and that such metadata are always a part of a database.

The presence of metadata makes databases much more useful than spreadsheets or data in other lists. Because of metadata, no one needs to guess, remember, or even record what is in the database. To find out what a database contains, we just look at the metadata inside the database.

This section discussed the contents of a database from a technical viewpoint. But as a business person, you will find it also worthwhile to think about a database as an asset having value, as discussed in *MIS in Use 5*.

Q3 What Is a DBMS, and What Does It Do?

A database, all by itself, is not very useful. The tables in Figure 5-6 have all of the data the professor wants, but the format is unwieldy. The professor wants to see the data in a form like that in Figure 5-2 and also as a formatted report. Pure database data are correct, but in raw form they are not pertinent or useful.

Figure 5-8 shows the components of a **database application system**. Such applications make database data more accessible and useful. Users employ a database application that consists of forms (like that in Figure 5-2), formatted reports, queries, and application programs. Each of these, in turn, calls on the database management system (DBMS) to process the database tables. We will first describe DBMS characteristics and then discuss database application components.

Database Management Systems

A **database management system (DBMS)** is a program used to create, process, and administer a database. As with operating systems, almost no organization develops its own DBMS. Instead, companies license DBMS products from vendors such as IBM, Microsoft, Oracle, and others. Popular DBMS products are **DB2** from IBM, **Access** and **SQL Server** from Microsoft, and **Oracle** from the Oracle Corporation. Another popular DBMS is **MySQL**, an open-source DBMS product that is free for most applications. Other DBMS products are available, but these five process the great bulk of databases today.

Note that a DBMS and a database are two different things. For some reason, the trade press and even some books confuse the two. A DBMS is a software program; a database is a collection of tables, relationships, and metadata. The two are very different concepts.

Creating the Database and Its Structures

Database developers use the DBMS to create tables, relationships, and other structures in the database. The form in Figure 5-7 can be used to define a new table or to modify an existing one. To create a new table, the developer just fills out a new form like the one in Figure 5-7.

To modify an existing table—for example, to add a new column—the developer opens the metadata form for that table and adds a new row of metadata. For example, in Figure 5-9 the developer has added a new column called *Response?* This new column has the data type *Yes/No*, which means that the column can contain only one of the values—Yes or No. The professor will use this column to indicate whether he has responded to the student's email. Other database structures are defined in similar ways.

Metadata make databases easy to use—for both authorized and unauthorized purposes, as described in the *Ethics Guide* on pages 106–107.

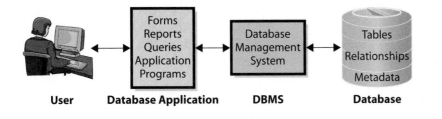

User   Database Application   DBMS   Database

FIGURE 5-8
Components of a Database Application System

Nobody Said I Shouldn't

"**M**y name is Kelly, and I do systems support for our group. I configure the new computers, set up the network, make sure the servers are operating, and so forth. I also do all of the database backups. I've always liked computers. After high school, I worked odd jobs to make some money, then I got an associate degree in information technology from our local community college.

"Anyway, as I said, I make backup copies of our databases. One weekend, I didn't have much going on, so I copied one of the database backups to a CD and took it home. I had taken a class on database processing as part of my associate degree, and we used SQL Server (our database management system) in my class. In fact, I suppose that's part of the reason I got the job. Anyway, it was easy to restore the database on my computer at home, and I did.

"Of course, as they'll tell you in your database class, one of the big advantages of database processing is that databases have metadata, or data that describe the content of the database. So, although I didn't know what tables were in our database, I did know how to access the SQL Server metadata. I just queried a table called *sysTables* to learn the names of our tables. From there it was easy to find out what columns each table had.

"I found tables with data about orders, customers, salespeople, and so forth, and just to amuse myself and to see how much of the query language SQL that I could remember, I started playing around with the data. I was curious to know which order entry clerk was the best, so I started querying each clerk's order data, the total number of orders, total order amounts, things like that. It was easy to do and fun.

"I know one of the order-entry clerks, Jason, pretty well, so I started looking at the data for his orders. I was just curious, and it was very simple SQL. I was just playing around with the data when I noticed something odd. All of his biggest orders were with one company, Valley Appliances, and even stranger, every one of its orders had a huge discount. I thought, well, maybe that's typical. Out of curiosity, I started looking at data for the other clerks, and very few of them had an order with Valley Appliances. But, when they did, Valley didn't get a big discount. Then I looked at the rest of Jason's orders, and none of them had much in the way of discounts, either.

"The next Friday, a bunch of us went out for a beer after work. I happened to see Jason, so I asked him about Valley Appliances and made a joke about the discounts. He asked me what I meant, and then I told him that I'd been looking at the data for fun and that I saw this odd pattern. He just laughed, said he just 'did his job,' and then changed the subject.

"Well, to make a long story short, when I got to work on Monday morning, my office was cleaned out. There was nothing there except a note telling me to go see my boss. The bottom line was, I was fired. The company also threatened that if I didn't return all of its data, I'd be in court for the next 5 years . . . things like that. I was so mad I didn't even tell them about Jason. Now my problem is that I'm out of a job, and I can't exactly use my last company for a reference."

DISCUSSION QUESTIONS

1. Where did Kelly go wrong?

2. Do you think it was illegal, unethical, or neither for Kelly to take the database home and query the data?

3. Does the company share culpability with Kelly?

4. What do you think Kelly should have done upon discovering the odd pattern in Jason's orders?

5. What should the company have done before firing Kelly?

6. Is it possible that someone other than Jason is involved in the arrangement with Valley Appliances? What should Kelly have done in light of that possibility?

7. What should Kelly do now?

8. "Metadata make databases easy to use—for both authorized and unauthorized purposes." Explain what organizations should do in light of this fact.

Processing the Database

The second function of the DBMS is to process the database. Applications use the DBMS for four operations: to *read, insert, modify,* or *delete* data. The applications call upon the DBMS in different ways. From a form, when the user enters new or changed data, a computer program that processes the form calls the DBMS to make the necessary database changes. From an application program, the program calls the DBMS directly to make the change.

Structured Query Language (SQL) is an international standard language for processing a database. All five of the DBMS products mentioned earlier accept and process SQL (pronounced "see-quell") statements. As an example, the following SQL statement inserts a new row into the *Student* table:

```
INSERT INTO Student
  ([Student Number], [Student Name], HW1, HW2,
  MidTerm)
  VALUES
  (1000, 'Franklin, Benjamin', 90, 95, 100)
```

Statements like this one are issued "behind the scenes" by programs that process forms. Alternatively, they can also be issued directly to the DBMS by an application program.

You do not need to understand or remember SQL language syntax. Instead, just realize that SQL is an international standard for processing a database. Also, SQL can be used to create databases and database structures. You will learn more about SQL if you take a database management class.

Administering the Database

A third DBMS function is to provide tools to assist in the administration of the database. Database administration involves a wide variety of activities. For example, the DBMS can be used to set up a security system involving user accounts, passwords, permissions, and limits for processing the database. To provide database security, a user must sign on using a valid user account before she can process the database.

Permissions can be limited in very specific ways. In the *Student* database example, it is possible to limit a particular user to reading only *Student Name* from the *Student* table. A different user could be given permission to read all of the *Student* table, but only be able to update the *HW1, HW2,* and *MidTerm* columns. Other users can be given still other permissions.

In addition to security, DBMS administrative functions include backing up database data, adding structures to improve the performance of database applications, removing data that are no longer wanted or needed, and similar tasks.

Q4 What Is a Database Application?

A **database application** is a collection of forms, reports, queries, and application programs that process a database. A database may have one or more applications, and each application may have one or more users. Figure 5-10 shows three applications; the top two have multiple users. These applications have different purposes, features, and functions, but they all process the same inventory data stored in a common database.

Forms, Reports, and Queries

Figure 5-2 (page 100) shows a typical database application data entry **form**, and Figure 5-11 shows a typical **report**. Data entry forms are used to read, insert, modify, and delete data. Reports show data in a structured context.

Some reports, like the one in Figure 5-11, also compute values as they present the data. An example is the computation of *Total weighted points* in Figure 5-11. Recall from Chapter 1 that one of the definitions of information is "data presented in a meaningful context." The structure of this report creates information because it shows the student data in a context that will be meaningful to the professor.

DBMS programs provide comprehensive and robust features for querying database data. For example, suppose the professor who uses the Student database remembers that one of the students referred to the topic "barriers to entry" in an office visit, but cannot remember which student or when. If there are hundreds of students and visits recorded in the database, it will take some effort and time for the professor to search through all office visit records to find that event. The DBMS, however, can find any such record quickly. Figure 5-12(a) (page 110) shows a **query** form in which the professor types in the keyword for which she is looking. Figure 5-12(b) shows the results of the query.

FIGURE 5-10
Use of Multiple Database Applications

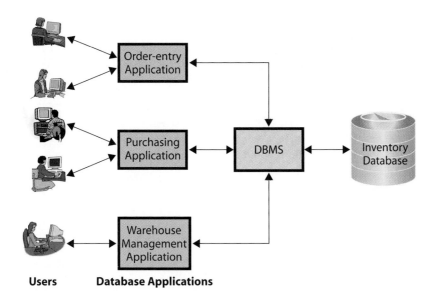

Users   **Database Applications**

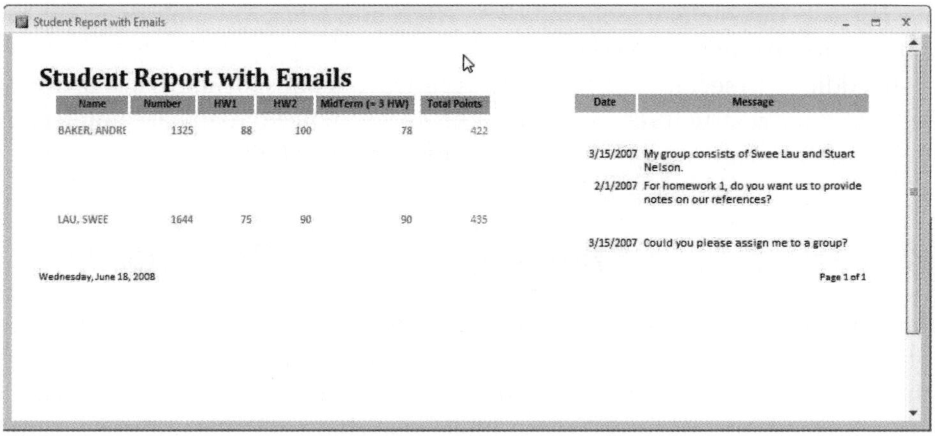

FIGURE 5-11
Example of a Student Report

Database Application Programs

Forms, reports, and queries work well for standard functions. However, most applications have unique requirements that a simple form, report, or query cannot meet. For example, in the order entry application in Figure 5-10, what should be done if only a portion of a customer's request can be met? If someone wants 10 widgets and only three are in stock, should a back order for seven more be generated automatically? Or should some other action be taken?

Application programs process logic that is specific to a given business need. In the Student database, an example application is one that assigns grades at the end of the term. If the professor grades on a curve, the application reads the break points for each grade from a form, and then processes each row in the *Student* table, allocating a grade based on the break points and the total number of points earned.

Another important use of application programs is to enable database processing over the Internet. For this use, the application program serves as an intermediary between the Web server and the database. The application program responds to events, such as when a user presses a submit button; it also reads, inserts, modifies, and deletes database data.

For a contrarian's view of databases, see the *Guide* on pages 112–113.

FIGURE 5-12
Example of a Query

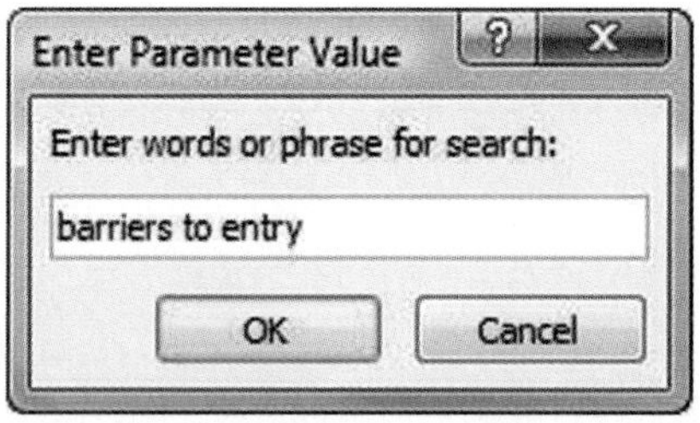

a. Form used to enter phrase for search

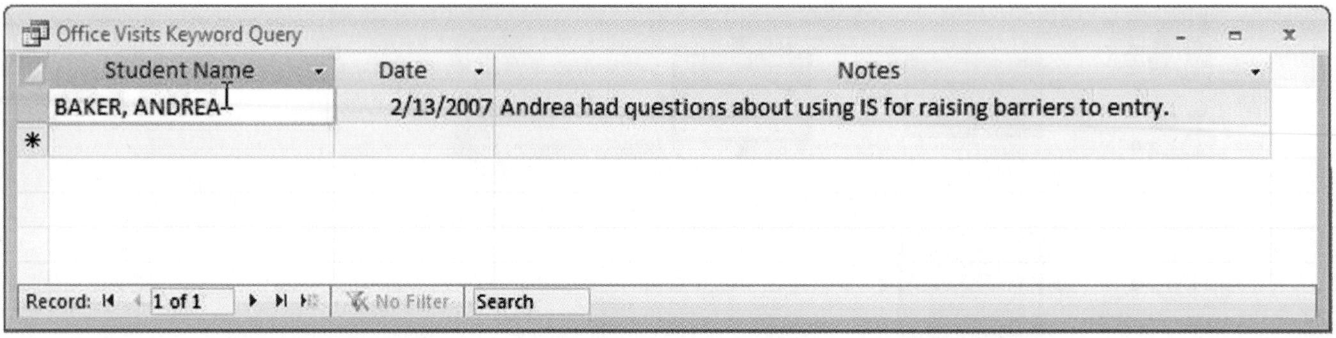

b. Results of query operation

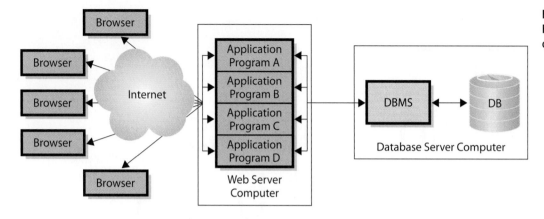

FIGURE 5-13
Four Application Programs
on a Web Server Computer

Figure 5-13 shows four different database application programs running on a Web server computer. Users with browsers connect to the Web server via the Internet. The Web server directs user requests to the appropriate application program. Each program then processes the database as necessary. You will learn more about Web-enabled databases in Chapter 8.

Multiuser Processing Considerations

Figures 5-10 and 5-13 show multiple users processing the database. Such **multiuser processing** is common, but it does pose unique problems that you, as a future manager, should know about. To understand the nature of those problems, consider the following scenario.

Two users, Andrea and Jeffrey, are clerks using the order entry application in Figure 5-10. Andrea is on the phone with her customer, who wants to purchase five widgets. At the same time, Jeffrey is talking with his customer, who wants to purchase three widgets. Andrea reads the database to determine how many widgets are in inventory. (She unknowingly invokes the order entry application when she types in her data entry form.) The DBMS returns a row showing 10 widgets in inventory.

Meanwhile, just after Andrea accesses the database, Jeffrey's customer says she wants widgets, and so he also reads the database (via the order entry application program) to determine how many widgets are in inventory. The DBMS returns the same row to him, indicating that 10 widgets are available.

Andrea's customer now says that he'll take five widgets, and Andrea records this fact in her form. The application rewrites the widget row back to the database, indicating that there are five widgets in inventory.

Meanwhile, Jeffrey's customer says that he'll take three widgets. Jeffrey records this fact in his form, and the application rewrites the widget row back to the database. However, Jeffrey's application knows nothing about Andrea's work and subtracts three from the original count of 10, thus storing an incorrect count of seven widgets in inventory. Clearly, there is a problem. We began with 10 widgets, Andrea took five and Jeffrey took three, but the database says there are seven widgets in inventory. It should show two, not seven.

This problem, known as the **lost-update problem**, exemplifies one of the special characteristics of multiuser database processing. To prevent this problem, some type of locking must be used to coordinate the activities of users who know nothing about one another. Locking brings its own set of problems, however, and those problems must be addressed as well. We will not delve further into this topic here, however.

Realize from this example that converting a single-user database to a multiuser database requires more than simply connecting another user's computer. The logic of the underlying application processing needs to be adjusted as well.

No, Thanks, I'll Use a Spreadsheet

"I'm not buying all this stuff about databases. I've tried them and they're a pain—way too complicated to set up, and most of the time, a spreadsheet works just as well. We had one project at the car dealership that seemed pretty simple to me: We wanted to keep track of customers and the models of used cars they were interested in. Then, when we got a car on the lot, we could query the database to see who wanted a car of that type and generate a letter to them.

"It took forever to build that system, and it never did work right. We hired three different consultants, and the last one finally did get it to work. But it was so complicated to produce the letters. You had to query the data in Access to generate some kind of file, then open Word, then go through some mumbo jumbo using mail/merge to cause Word to find the letter and put all the Access data in the right spot. I once printed over 200 letters and had the name in the address spot and the address in the name spot and no date. And it took me over an hour to do even that. I just wanted to do the query and push a button to get my letters generated. I gave up. Some of the salespeople are still trying to use it, but not me.

"No, unless you are General Motors or Toyota, I wouldn't mess with a database. You have to have professional IS people to create it and keep it running. Besides, I don't really want to share my data with anyone. I work pretty hard to develop my client list. Why would I want to give it away?

"My motto is, 'Keep it simple.' I use an Excel spreadsheet with four columns: Name, Phone Number, Car Interests, and Notes. When I get a new customer, I enter the name and phone number, and then I put the make and model of cars they like in the Car Interests column. Anything else that I think is important I put in the Notes column—extra phone numbers, address data if I have it, email addresses, spouse names, last time I called them, etc. The system isn't fancy, but it works fine.

"When I want to find something, I use Excel's Data Filter. I can usually get what I need. Of course, I still can't send form letters, but it really doesn't matter. I get most of my sales using the phone, anyway."

DISCUSSION QUESTIONS

1. To what extent do you agree with the opinions presented here? To what extent are the concerns expressed here justified? To what extent might they be due to other factors?

2. What problems do you see with the way that the car salesperson stores address data? What will he have to do if he ever does want to send a letter or an email to all of his customers?

3. From his comments, how many different themes are there in his data? What does this imply about his ability to keep his data in a spreadsheet?

4. Does the concern about not sharing data relate to whether he uses a database?

5. Apparently, management at the car dealership allows the salespeople to keep their contact data in whatever format they want. If you were management, how would you justify this policy? What disadvantages are there to this policy?

6. Suppose you manage the sales representatives, and you decide to require all of them to use a database to keep track of customers and customer car interest data. How would you sell your decision to this salesperson?

7. Given the limited information in this scenario, do you think a database or a spreadsheet is a better solution?

Be aware of possible data conflicts when you manage business activities that involve multiuser processing. If you find inaccurate results that seem not to have a cause, you may be experiencing multiuser data conflicts. Contact your MIS department for assistance.

Q5 What Is the Difference Between an Enterprise DBMS and a Personal DBMS?

DBMS products fall into two broad categories. **Enterprise DBMS** products process large organizational and workgroup databases. These products support many (perhaps thousands) of users and many different database applications. Such DBMS products support 24/7 operations and can manage databases that span dozens of different magnetic disks with hundreds of gigabytes or more of data. IBM's DB2, Microsoft's SQL Server, and Oracle's Oracle are examples of enterprise DBMS products.

Personal DBMS products are designed for smaller, simpler database applications. Such products are used for personal or small workgroup applications that involve fewer than 100 users, and normally fewer than 15. In fact, the great bulk of databases in this category have only a single user. The professor's Student database is an example of a database that is processed by a personal DBMS product.

In the past, there were many personal DBMS products—Paradox, dBase, R:base, and FoxPro. Microsoft put these products out of business when it developed Access and included it in the Microsoft Office suite. Today, the only remaining personal DBMS of significance is Microsoft Access.

To avoid one point of confusion for you in the future, the separation of application programs and the DBMS shown in Figure 5-10 is true only for enterprise DBMS products. Microsoft Access includes features and functions for application processing along with the DBMS itself. For example, Access has a form generator and a report generator. Thus, as shown in Figure 5-14, Access is both a DBMS and an application development product.

The knowledge in this chapter would have helped Dee to know what a DBMS is and what role it plays. She would have been able to understand the diagram in Figure 5-15 (and perhaps even draw it herself). This is the same diagram as you saw in Figure 4-13, page 94, except now we have filled in the software that runs on the server computer. The application is Movable Type, and it calls the DBMS MySQL, which processes the database. Of course, like every computer, the server also has an operating system, such as Windows or Linux.

We are NOT about to change DBMS products.

Although this system does run a DBMS, it is completely isolated from the rest of the Emerson databases and really should not be of concern to the IT department. Dee is not proposing to replace Oracle with MySQL for

FIGURE 5-14
Personal Database System

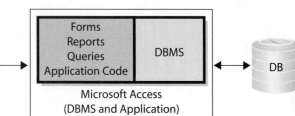

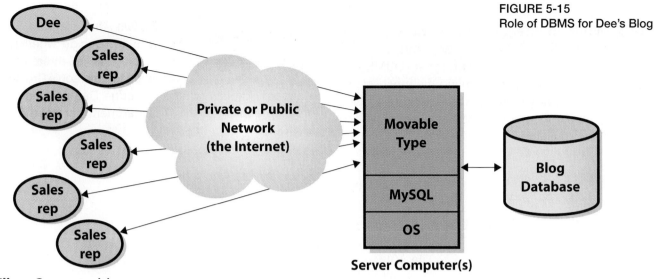

FIGURE 5-15
Role of DBMS for Dee's Blog

the processing of orders or the paying of salespeople. She just wants to include MySQL, as part of the functionality of her application, on the server.

With this knowledge, Dee could explain what she wants to do and that her project is no threat or exception to the Oracle standard. It is an isolated system that needs MySQL to run.

Ultimately, Don made that exact argument to the IT department. Once the department understood Dee's plan, they had no problem with Dee's use of MySQL—as long as she paid any required license fees for it out of her own budget. Unfortunately, without knowledge of database concepts, Dee was unable to make that argument herself, so she was forced to hire her consultant to make that argument for her. Doing this meant a delay of another few days as well as an additional expense. Still, she had passed another hurdle on the way to developing her system.

Active Review

Use this Active Review to verify that you understand the material in the chapter. You can read the entire chapter and then perform the tasks in this review, or you can read the material for just one question and perform the tasks in this review for that question before moving on to the next one.

Q1 What is the purpose of a database? Describe the purpose of a database. Explain when to use a spreadsheet and when to use a database.

Q2 What does a database contain? Explain the hierarchy of data from bytes to tables. Show how a database stores the relationships among rows. Define *key* and *foreign key*. Define *metadata*,

and explain how metadata makes databases more useful.

Q3 What is a DBMS, and what does it do? Describe a database application system. Define *DBMS*. Name three prominent DBMS products. Describe the difference between a database and a DBMS. Explain the three major functions of a DBMS. What is SQL used for?

Q4 What is a database application? Name and describe the components of a database application. Describe the circumstances that require a special logic for database applications. Describe the lost-update problem. Explain, in general terms, how this problem is prevented.

Q5 What is the difference between an enterprise DBMS and a personal DBMS? Explain the function of an enterprise DBMS and describe its characteristics. Explain the function of a personal DBMS and describe its characteristics. Name the only surviving personal DBMS. Explain the differences between Figure 5-10 and Figure 5-15.

How does the knowledge in this chapter help Dee and you?

Explain the diagram in Figure 5-15. Decide whether Dee's blog is a threat or exception to Emerson's Oracle standard. Explain what knowledge Dee needed in order to explain to the IT department her need for MySQL.

Key Terms and Concepts

Access 105	File 101	Personal DBMS 114
Byte 100	Foreign key 103	Record 100
Column 100	Form 109	Relation 103
Database 100	Key 102	Relational database 103
Database application 109	Lost-update problem 111	Report 109
Database application system 105	Metadata 103	Row 100
Database management system	Multiuser processing 111	SQL Server 105
(DBMS) 105	MySQL 105	Structured Query Language
DB2 105	Object-relational database 103	(SQL) 108
Enterprise DBMS 114	Oracle 105	Table 101
Field 100	Query 109	

Using Your Knowledge

1. Suppose you are a marketing assistant for a consumer electronics company and are in charge of setting up your company's booth at trade shows. Weeks before the shows, you meet with the marketing managers and determine what displays and equipment they want to display. Then, you identify each of the components that need to be shipped and schedule a shipper to deliver them to the trade-show site. You then supervise convention personnel as they set up the booths and equipment. Once the show is over, you supervise the packing of the booth and all equipment as well as schedule its shipment back to your home office. When the equipment arrives, you check it into your warehouse to ensure that all pieces of the booth and all equipment are returned. If there are problems due to shipping damage or loss, you handle those problems. Your job is important; at a typical show, you are responsible for more than a quarter of a million dollars of equipment.

   a. You will need to track data about booth components, equipment, shippers, and shipments. List typical fields for each type of data.

   b. Could you use a spreadsheet to keep track of this data? What would be the advantages and disadvantages of doing so?

   c. Using your answer to question a, give an example of two relationships that you need to track. Show the keys and foreign keys for each.

   d. Which of the following components of a database application are you likely to need: data entry forms, reports, queries, or application program? Explain one use for each that you will need.

   e. Will your application be for one user or for multiple users? Will you need a personal DBMS or an enterprise DBMS? If a personal DBMS, which product will you use?

2. Samantha Green (the same Samantha we met at the end of Chapter 3, p. 60) owns and operates Twigs Tree Trimming Service. Recall that Samantha has a degree from a forestry program and recently opened her business in St. Louis, Missouri. Her business consists of many one-time operations (e.g., remove a tree or stump), as well as recurring services (e.g., trimming customers' trees every year or two).

When business is slow, Samantha calls former clients to remind them of her services and of the need to trim their trees on a regular basis.

a. Name and describe tables of data that Samantha will need to run her business. Indicate possible fields for each table.

b. Could Samantha use a spreadsheet to keep track of this data? What would be the advantages and disadvantages of doing so?

c. Using your answer to question a, give an example of two relationships that Samantha needs to track. Show the keys and foreign keys for each.

d. Which of the following components of a database application is Samantha likely to need: data entry forms, reports, queries, or application program? Explain one use for each that she needs.

e. Will this application be for one user or for multiple users? Will she need a personal DBMS or an enterprise DBMS? If a personal DBMS, which product will she use?

3. FiredUp, Inc., (the same FiredUp we met at the end of Chapter 3, p. 60) is a small business owned by Curt and Julie Robards. Based in Brisbane, Australia, FiredUp manufactures and sells FiredNow, a lightweight camping stove. Recall that Curt used his previous experience as an aerospace engineer to invent a burning nozzle that enables the stove to stay lit in very high winds. Using her industrial design training, Julie designed the stove so that it is small, lightweight, easy to set up, and very stable. Curt and Julie sell the stove directly to their customers over the Internet and via phone. The warranty on the stove covers 5 years of cost-free repair for stoves used for recreational purposes.

FiredUp wants to track every stove and the customer who purchased it. They want to know which customers own which stoves in case they need to notify customers of safety problems or need to order a stove recall. Curt and Julie also want to keep track of any repairs they have performed.

a. Name and describe tables of data that FiredUp will need. Indicate possible fields for each table.

b. Could FiredUp use a spreadsheet to keep track of this data? What would be the advantages and disadvantages of doing so?

c. Using your answer to question a, give an example of two relationships that FiredUp needs to track. Show the keys and foreign keys for each.

d. Which of the following components of a database application is FiredUp likely to need: data entry forms, reports, queries, or application program? Explain one use for each needed component.

e. Will this application be for one user or for multiple users? Will FiredUp need a personal DBMS or an enterprise DBMS? If a personal DBMS, which product will it use? If an enterprise DBMS, which product can they obtain license-free?

Collaboration Exercise 5 ◎

Before you start this exercise, read Chapter Extensions 1 and 2, which describe collaboration techniques as well as tools for managing collaboration tasks. In particular, consider using Google Docs & Spreadsheets, Google Groups, Microsoft Groove, Microsoft SharePoint, or some other collaboration tool.

Reread *MIS in Use 5* on page 104. Then, collaborate with your team to answer the following questions.

1. Many small business owners have found it financially advantageous to purchase their own building. As one owner remarked upon his retirement, "We did well with the business, but we made our real money by buying the building." Explain why this might be so.

2. To what extent does the dynamic you identified in your answer to question 1 pertain to databases? Do you think it likely that, in 2050, some small business people will retire and make statements like, "We did well with the business, but we made our real money from the database we generated?" Why or why not?

3. Suppose you had a national database of student data. Assume your database includes the name, email address, university, grade level, and major for each student. Name five companies that would find that data valuable, and explain how they might use it. (For example, Pizza Hut could solicit orders from students during finals week.)

4. Describe a product or service that you could develop that would induce students to provide the data in question 3.

5. Considering your answers to questions 1 through 4, identify three organizations in your community that could generate a database that would potentially be more valuable than the organization itself. Consider

businesses, but also think about social organizations and government offices.

For each organization, describe the content of the database and the inducements that exist or that you could provide to cause customers or clients to provide that data. Also, explain why the data would be valuable and who might use it.

Case Study 5

Benchmarking, Bench Marketing, or Bench Baloney?

Which DBMS product is the fastest? Which product yields the lowest price/performance ratio? What computer equipment works best for each DBMS product? These reasonable questions should be easy to answer. They are not.

In fact, the deeper you dig, the more problems you find. To begin with, which product is fastest doing what? To have a valid comparison, all compared products must do the same work. So, vendors and third parties have defined *benchmarks*, which are descriptions of work to be done along with the data to be processed. To compare performance, analysts run competing DBMS products on the same benchmark and measure the results. Typical measures are number of transactions processed per second, number of Web pages served per second, and average response time per user.

At first, DBMS vendors set up their own benchmark tests and published those results. Of course, when vendor A used its own benchmark to claim that its product was superior to all others, no one believed the results. Clearly, vendor A had an incentive to set up the benchmark to play to its product strengths. So, third parties defined standard benchmarks. Even that led to problems, however. According to *The Benchmark Handbook* (at *benchmarkresources.com/handbook*, accessed August 2006):

> When comparative numbers were published by third parties or competitors, the losers generally cried foul and tried to discredit the benchmark. Such events often caused benchmark wars. Benchmark wars start if someone loses an important or visible benchmark evaluation. The loser reruns it using regional specialists and gets new and winning numbers. Then the opponent reruns it using his regional specialists, and of course gets even better numbers. The loser then reruns it using some one-star gurus. This progression can continue all the way to five-star gurus.

For example, in July 2002, *PC Magazine* ran a benchmark using a standard benchmark called the *Nile benchmark*. This particular test has a mixture of database tasks that are processed via Web pages. The faster the DBMS, the more pages that can be served.

The test compared five DBMS products: DB2 (from IBM), MySQL (a free, open-source DBMS product from MySQL.com), Oracle (from Oracle Corporation), SQL Server (from Microsoft), and ASE (from Sybase Corporation). SQL Server's performance was the worst. In the magazine review, the authors stated that they believed SQL Server scored poorly because the test used a new version of a non-Microsoft driver (a program that sends requests and returns results to and from the DBMS).

As you might imagine, no sooner was this test published than the phones and email server at *PC Magazine* were inundated by objections from Microsoft. *PC Magazine* reran the tests, replacing the suspect driver with a full panoply of Microsoft products. The article doesn't say, but one can imagine the five-star Microsoft gurus who chartered the next airplane to PC Labs, where the testing was done. (You can read about both phases of the benchmark at *www.eweek.com/article2/0,4149,293,00.asp.*)

Not surprisingly when the tests were rerun with Microsoft-supporting software, SQL Server performed better than all of the other products in the first test. But that second test compares apples and oranges. The first test used standard software, and the second test used Microsoft-specific software.

When the five-star gurus from Oracle or MySQL use *their* favorite supporting products and "tune" to this particular benchmark, their re-rerun results will be superior to those for SQL Server. And round and round it will go.

Questions

1. Suppose you manage a business activity that needs a new IS with a database. The development team is divided on which DBMS you should use. One faction wants to use Oracle, a second wants to use MySQL, and a third wants to use SQL Server. They cannot decide among themselves, and so they schedule a meeting with you. The team presents all of the benchmarks shown in the article at *www.eweek.com/article2/0,4149,293,00.asp*. How do you respond?

2. Performance is just one criterion for selecting a DBMS. Other criteria are the cost of the DBMS, hardware costs, staff knowledge, ease of use, ability to tune for extra performance, and backup and recovery capabilities. How does consideration of these other factors change your answer to question 1?

3. The Transaction Processing Council (TPC) is a not-for-profit corporation that defines transaction processing and database benchmarks and publishes vendor-neutral, verifiable performance data. Visit its Web site at *tpc.org*.

   a. What are TPC-C, TPC-R, and TPC-W?

   b. Suppose you work in the marketing department at Oracle Corporation. How would you use the TPC results in the TPC-C benchmark?

   c. What are the dangers to Oracle in your answer to part b?

   d. Suppose you work in the marketing department for DB2 at IBM. How would you use the TPC results in the TPC-C benchmark?

   e. Do the results for TPC-C change your answer to question 1?

   f. If you are a DBMS vendor, can you ignore benchmarks?

4. Reflect on your answers to questions 1 through 3. On balance, what good are benchmarks? Are they just footballs to be kicked around by vendors? Are advertisers and publishers the only true beneficiaries? Do DBMS customers benefit from the efforts of TPC and like groups? How should customers use benchmarks?

When Dee first proposed the idea of her blog, one of the first questions she was asked was, "Are you going to run it inside the Emerson network?" This question was crucial to the development of her blog, and she did not understand why. She wanted to say, "I don't know. What difference does it make?" but sensed that it would be unwise to reveal that much lack of knowledge.

This could happen to you

In order to provide a competitive advantage, the information on Dee's blog needs to be kept private. She wants the sales reps to have easy access to the blog, but she wants to keep it from the competition. Many sales reps work from home, and many travel extensively, using their computers from hotels. She knows that they can access the Internet from either home or hotel, but if she makes her blog publicly available on the Internet, the competition could access it, too.

An alternative is for Dee to require that the salespeople provide a user ID and password to access the blog. That, however, is just one more thing for them to remember to do, and, in the busy sales season, they are likely to forget their ID or password or leave it at home. Still, it could be done.

Emerson supports a private network that is protected from outside

How well do you know this Don Gray?

access by a firewall (discussed in this chapter). Employees can access that network from the Internet using a VPN (also discussed in this chapter). So, if she places the blog server within the Emerson network, it will be protected from unauthorized access, and the salespeople can access it using the same password they use to access the VPN. Placing the blog within the network requires the permission and support of the internal IT department. As you will see, Dee could have used the knowledge from this chapter to enlist (or leverage) the support of that department.

❓ Study Questions

Q1 What is a computer network?

Q2 What are the components of a LAN?

Q3 What are the alternatives for a WAN?

Q4 How does encryption work?

Q5 What is the purpose of a firewall?

Q6 What is a VPN, and why is it important?

How does the knowledge in this chapter help Dee and you?

Q1 What Is a Computer Network?

A computer **network** is a collection of computers that communicate with one another over transmission lines. As shown in Figure 6-1, the three basic types of networks are local area networks, wide area networks, and internets.

A **local area network (LAN)** connects computers that reside in a single geographic location on the premises of the company that operates the LAN. The number of connected computers can range from two to several hundred. The distinguishing characteristic of a LAN is *a single location*. **Wide area networks (WANs)** connect computers at different geographic locations. The computers in two separated company sites must be connected using a WAN. To illustrate, the computers for a College of Business located on a single campus can be connected via a LAN. The computers for a College of Business located on multiple campuses must be connected via a WAN.

The single versus multiple site distinction is important. With a LAN, an organization can place communications lines wherever it wants, because all lines reside on its premises. The same is not true for a WAN. A company with offices in Chicago and Atlanta cannot run a wire to connect computers in the two cities. Instead, the company must contract with a communications vendor that is licensed by the government and already has lines or has the authority to run new lines between the two cities.

An **internet** is a network of networks. Internets connect LANs, WANs, and other internets. The most famous internet is "**the Internet**" (with an upper-case letter *I*), the collection of networks that you use when you send email or access a Web site. In addition to the Internet, private networks of networks, called internets, also exist.

The networks that comprise an internet use a large variety of communication methods and conventions, and data must flow seamlessly across them. To provide seamless flow, an elaborate scheme called a *layered protocol* is used. A **protocol** is a set of rules that two communicating devices follow. There are many different protocols; some are used for LANs, some are used for WANs, some are used for internets and the

FIGURE 6-1
Major Network Types

Type	Characteristic
Local Area Network (LAN)	Computers connected at a single physical site
Wide Area Network (WAN)	Computers connected between two or more separated sites
The Internet and internets	Networks of networks

Internet, and some are used for all of these. The important point is that for two devices to communicate they must both use the same protocol.

Q2 What Are the Components of a LAN?

A LAN is a group of computers connected together on a single company site. Usually the computers are located within a half mile or so of each other, although longer distances are possible. The key distinction, however, is that all of the computers are located on property controlled by the company that operates the LAN. This means that the company can run cables wherever needed to connect the computers.

Consider the LAN in Figure 6-2. Here, five computers and two printers connect via a **switch**, which is a special-purpose computer that receives and transmits messages on the LAN. In Figure 6-2, when Computer 1 accesses Printer 1, it does so by sending the print job to the switch, which then redirects that data to Printer 1.

Each device on a LAN (computer, printer, etc.) has a hardware component called a **network interface card (NIC)** that connects the device's circuitry to the cable. The NIC works with programs in each device to implement the protocols necessary for communication. On desktops and older laptops, the NIC is a card that fits into an expansion slot. Most of today's laptops and many desktops have an **onboard NIC**, which is an NIC built into the computer.

Figure 6-3 shows an NIC card device. Each NIC has a unique identifier called the **MAC (media access control) address**. The computers, printers, switches, and other devices on a LAN are connected using one of two media. Most connections are made using **unshielded twisted pair (UTP) cable**. Figure 6-4 shows a section of UTP cable that contains four pairs of twisted wire. A device called an RJ-45 connector is used to connect the UTP cable into NIC devices on the LAN.

FIGURE 6-2
Local Area Network (LAN)

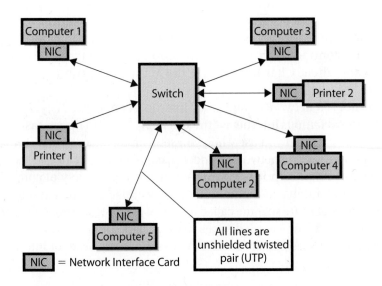

NIC = Network Interface Card

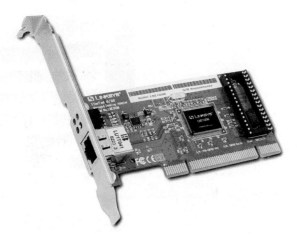

FIGURE 6-3
Network Interface Card (NIC)
Courtesy of Linksys

By the way, wires are twisted for reasons beyond aesthetics and style. Twisting the wires substantially reduces the cross-wire signal interference that occurs when wires run parallel over long distances.

Some LANs, usually those larger than the one in Figure 6-2, use more than one switch. Typically, in a building with several floors a switch is placed on each floor, and the computers on that floor are connected to the switch with UTP cable. The switches on each floor are connected together by a main switch, which is often located in the basement.

The connections between switches can use UTP cable, but if they carry a lot of traffic or are far apart UTP cable may be replaced by **optical fiber cables**. The signals on such cables are light rays, and they are reflected inside the glass core of the optical fiber cable. The core is surrounded by a *cladding* to contain the light signals, and the cladding, in turn, is wrapped with an outer protective layer. Optical fiber cable uses special connectors called ST and SC connectors, which are shown as the blue plugs in Figure 6-5. The meaning of the abbreviations ST and SC are unimportant; they are just the two most common optical connectors.

The IEEE 802.3, or Ethernet, Protocol

For a LAN to work, all devices on the LAN must use the same protocol. The Institute for Electrical and Electronics Engineers (IEEE, pronounced "I triple E") sponsors committees that create and publish protocols and other standards. The committee that addresses LAN standards is called the *IEEE 802 Committee*. Thus, IEEE LAN protocols always start with the numbers 802.

Today, the world's most popular protocol for LANs is the **IEEE 802.3 protocol**. This protocol standard, also called **Ethernet**, specifies hardware characteristics, such as which wire carries which signals. It also describes how messages are to be packaged and processed for transmission over the LAN.

Most personal computers today are equipped with an onboard NIC that supports what is called **10/100/1000 Ethernet**. These products conform to the 802.3 specification and allow for transmission at a rate of 10, 100, or 1,000 Mbps (megabits per second). Switches detect the speed that a given device can handle and communicate with it at that speed. If you check computer listings at Dell, HP, Toshiba, and other manufacturers, you will see PCs advertised as having 10/100/1000 Ethernet.

By the way, the abbreviations used for communication speeds differ from those used for computer memory. For communications equipment, *k* stands for 1,000, not

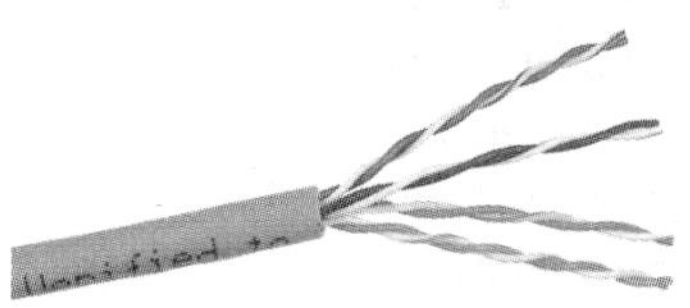

FIGURE 6-4
Unshielded Twisted Pair (UTP) Cable
Courtesy of Belkin Corporation

FIGURE 6-5
Optical Fiber Cable

Getty Images, Inc.–Photodisc   Getty Images, Inc.

1,024, as it does for memory. Similarly, *M* stands for 1,000,000, not 1,024 × 1,024; *G* stands for 1,000,000,000, not 1,024 × 1,024 × 1,024. Thus, 100 Mbps is 100,000,000 bits per second. Also note that communications speed is expressed in *bits*, whereas memory size is expressed in *bytes*.

LANs with Wireless Connections

In recent years, wireless LAN connections have become popular. Figure 6-6 shows a LAN in which two of the computers and one printer have wireless connections. Notice that in wireless devices the NIC has been replaced by a **wireless NIC (WNIC)**. Such devices can be cards that slide into an expansion slot or, more frequently, built-in devices.

FIGURE 6-6
Local Area Network with Wireless

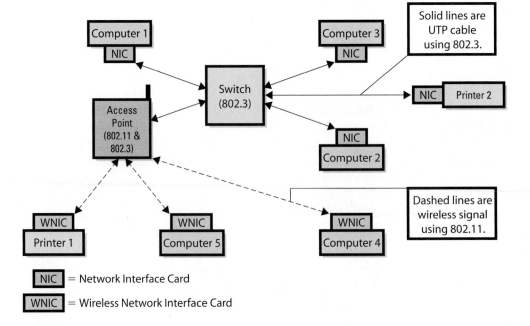

Several different wireless protocols exist. As of 2008, the most popular is **IEEE 802.11g.** The differences among the variations are beyond the scope of this discussion. Just note that the current standard, 802.11g, allows speeds of up to 54 Mbps.

Observe that the LAN in Figure 6-6 uses both the 802.3 and 802.11 protocols. The NICs operate according to the 802.3 protocol and connect directly to the switch, which also operates on the 802.3 standard. The WNICs operate according to the 802.11 protocol and connect to an **access point (AP)**. The AP must be able to process messages according to both the 802.3 and 802.11 standards, because it sends and receives wireless traffic using the 802.11 protocol and then communicates with the switch using the 802.3 protocol. Characteristics of LANs are summarized in the top part of Figure 6-7.

Wireless data communications technology is changing rapidly. *MIS in Use 6* describes emerging technology, not shown in Figure 6-7, that allows wireless at a distance.

FIGURE 6-7
Summary of LAN and WAN Networks

Type	Topology	Transmission Line	Transmission Speed	Equipment Used	Protocol Commonly Used	Remarks
Local Area Network	Local area network	UTP or optical fiber	10, 100, or 1,000 Mbps	Switch NIC UTP or optical	IEEE 802.3 (Ethernet)	Switches connect devices, multiple switches on all but small LANs.
	Local area network with wireless	UTP or optical for non-wireless connections	Up to 54 Mbps	Wireless access point Wireless NIC	IEEE 802.11g	Access point transforms wired LAN (802.3) to wireless LAN (802.11).
Wide Area Network	Dial-up modem to Internet service provider (ISP)	Regular telephone	Up to 55 kbps	Modem Telephone line	Modulation standards (V.32, V90, V92), PPP	Modulation required for first part of telephone line. Computer use blocks telephone use.
	DSL modem to ISP	DSL telephone	Personal: Upstream to 256 kbps, downstream to 768 kbps Business: to 1.544 Mbps	DSL modem DSL-capable telephone line	DSL	Can have computer and phone use simultaneously. Always connected.
	Cable modem to ISP	Cable TV lines to optical cable	Upstream to 256 kbps Downstream 300–600 kbps (10 Mbps in theory)	Cable modem Cable TV cable	Cable	Capacity is shared with other sites; performance varies depending on others' use.
	Point to point lines	Network of leased lines	T1–1.5 Mbps T3– 44.7Mbps OC48–2.5 Gbps OC768–40 Gbps	Access devices Optical cable Satellite	PPP	Span geographically distributed sites using lines provided by licensed communications vendors. Expensive to set up and manage.
	PSDN	Lease usage of private network	56 Kbps–40 Mbps+	Leased line to PSDN POP	Frame-relay ATM 10 Gbps and 40 Gbps Ethernet	Lease time on a public switched data network–operated by independent party. Ineffective for intercompany communication.
	Virtual private network (VPN)	Use the Internet to provide private network	Varies with speed of connection to Internet	VPN client software VPN server hardware and software	PPTP IPSec	Secure, private connection provides a tunnel through the Internet. Can support intercompany communication.

6 Keeping Up with Wireless

Data communications technology is one of the fastest changing technologies, if not *the* fastest changing, in all of IT. Consider the example of wireless technology. Craig McCaw built one of the world's first cellular networks in the early 1980s, making cell phone communication available to the masses. In the 1990s, he sold his company to AT&T for $11.5 billion. In 2003, McCaw started a new venture, Clearwire, that uses an emerging technology called **WiMax** to address the **last-mile problem**. When someone with McCaw's knowledge, experience, and wealth starts a new venture based on new technology, we should pay attention.

To begin, what is the last-mile problem? The bottleneck on data communications into homes and into smaller businesses is the last mile. Fast optical fiber transmission lines lie in the street in front of your apartment or office. The problem is getting that capacity into the building and to your computer or TV. Digging up the street and backyard of every residence and small business to install optical fiber is not an affordable proposition. Even if that could be done, such infrastructure isn't mobile. You cannot watch a downloaded movie on a commuter train using an optical fiber line.

Existing wireless technology does not solve the problem. Cell phones do not have the capacity to transmit video, and wireless technology based on the IEEE 802.11 standard is limited to devices within a few hundred feet of each other. WiMax, the technology chosen by Clearwire, solves both of these problems; it's fast, and its range is measured in miles.

According to the WiMax Forum,

WiMax is a standards-based technology enabling the delivery of last-mile wireless broadband access as an alternative to wired broadband like cable and DSL. WiMax provides fixed, nomadic, portable and, soon, mobile wireless broadband connectivity without the need for direct line-of-sight with a base station. In a

typical cell radius deployment of three to ten kilometers, WiMax Forum Certified™ systems can be expected to deliver capacity of up to 40 Mbps per channel, for fixed and portable access applications.[1]

What do the terms *fixed, nomadic, portable,* and *mobile* mean? The WiMax Forum published a white paper with the table shown in Figure 1.

Using knowledge from this chapter, you can guess the meaning of the last two columns. They must refer to IEEE standards: 802.3 is Ethernet and 802.11 is standard wireless, so **802.16** is a new IEEE WiMax standard. CPE stands for *customer premises equipment* (meaning a device, such as a computer chip or access device). PCMCIA cards are older technology. Think instead of onboard devices that Intel will make for new-generation laptops.

With these definitions, you can interpret this table. *Nomadic use* allows a user to sign in from sites at home and at work, but not to be connected in transit. *Portable use* allows the user to walk to work while connected. *Simple mobility* supports connection while driving on city streets, and *full mobility* allows access on the freeway or a commuter train.

Now, bring this back to Craig McCaw. He made cell phones accessible to the public in the 1980s, and he now intends to make portable, wireless, broadband accessible with WiMax.

With McCaw's track record, with recent investors like Comcast and Intel, something is clearly afoot. The question is, what opportunities does this create for you? That's the upside of all this change. It continually creates new opportunities for those who look for them.

You and a team of classmates will have an opportunity to explore WiMax opportunities for yourselves in Collaboration Exercise 6 (on page 143).

[1] *www.wimaxforum.org/technology*, accessed August, 2007.

FIGURE 1
Types of Access to a WiMax Network

Source: Table 1, "Types of Access to a WiMax Network," from *Fixed, Nomadic, Portable, and Mobile Applications for 802.16–2004 and 802.16e WiMax Networks,* prepared by Senza Fili Consulting on behalf of the WiMax Forum. © 2005 WiMax Forum, *www.wimaxforum.org/technology/downloads* (accessed June 2008).

Definition	Devices	Locations/Speed	Handoffs	802.16–2004	802.16e
Fixed access	Outdoor and indoor CPEs	Single/stationary	No	Yes	Yes
Nomadic access	Indoor CPEs, PCMCIA cards	Multiple/stationary	No	Yes	Yes
Portability	Laptop PCMCIA or mini cards	Multiple/walking speed	Hard handoffs	No	Yes
Simple mobility	Laptop PCMCIA or mini cards, PDAs or smartphones	Multiple/low vehicular speed	Hard handoffs	No	Yes
Full mobility	Laptop PCMCIA or mini cards, PDAs or smartphones	Multiple/high vehicular speed	Soft handoffs	No	Yes

Q3 What Are the Alternatives for a WAN?

A WAN connects computers located at physically separated sites. A company with offices in Detroit and Atlanta must use a WAN to connect the computers together. Because the sites are physically separated, the company cannot string wire from one site to another. Rather, it must obtain connection capabilities from another company (or companies) licensed by the government to provide communications.

Although you may not have realized it, when you connect your personal computer to the Internet, you are using a WAN. You are connecting to computers owned and operated by your **Internet service provider (ISP)** that are not located physically at your site.

An ISP has three important functions. First, it provides you with a legitimate Internet address. Second, it serves as your gateway to the Internet. The ISP receives the communications from your computer and passes them on to the Internet, and it receives communications from the Internet and passes them on to you. Finally, ISPs pay for the Internet. They collect money from their customers and pay access fees and other charges on your behalf.

We begin our discussion of WANs by considering modem connections to ISPs.

Connecting the Personal Computer to an ISP: Modems

Home computers and those of small businesses are commonly connected to an ISP in one of four ways: using a regular telephone line, using a special telephone line called a DSL line, using a cable TV line, or wireless.

All of these alternatives require that the *digital data* in the computer be converted to an **analog**, or wavy, signal. A device called a **modem**, or modulator/demodulator, performs this conversion. Figure 6-8 shows one way of converting the digital byte 01000001 to an analog signal.

As shown in Figure 6-9, once the modem converts your computer's digital data to analog, that analog signal is then sent over the telephone line or TV cable. If sent by telephone line, the first telephone switch that your signal reaches converts the signal into the form used by the international telephone system.

In the future, many computers will be connected to WANs using wireless technology as described in MIS in Use 6 on page 126.

Dial-Up Modems

A **dial-up modem** performs the conversion between analog and digital in such a way that the signal can be carried on a regular telephone line. As the name implies, you dial the phone number for your ISP and connect. The maximum transmission speed for a switch is 56 kbps (in practice, the limit is 53 kbps). By the way, when two devices connected by modems use different speeds, the slower speed is the one at which they operate.

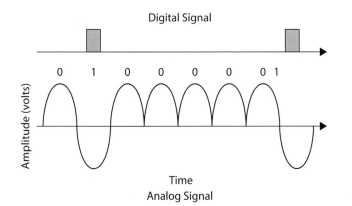

FIGURE 6-8
Analog Versus Digital Signals

FIGURE 6-9
Personal Computer (PC)
Internet Access

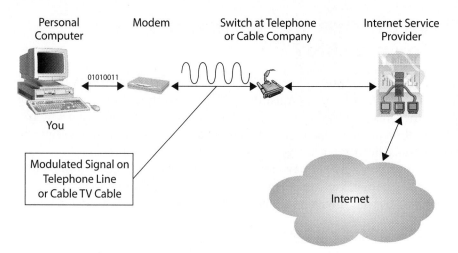

Modulation is governed by one of three standards: V.34, V.90, and V.92. These standards specify how digital signals will be transformed into analog. The way in which messages are packaged and handled between your modem and the ISP is governed by a protocol known as the **Point-to-Point Protocol (PPP)**. With a dial-up modem, voice and data communications cannot proceed simultaneously. Today, dial-up transmission is quite rare and has been replaced by DSL or cable.

DSL Modems

A **DSL modem** is the second modem type. DSL stands for **digital subscriber line**. DSL modems operate on the same lines as voice telephones and dial-up modems, but they operate so that their signals do not interfere with voice telephone service. DSL modems provide much faster data transmission speeds than dial-up modems. Additionally, DSL modems always maintain a connection, so there is no need to dial up; the Internet connection is available immediately. DSL modems use their own protocols for data transmission.

There are gradations of DSL service and speed. Most home DSL lines can download data at speeds ranging from 256 kbps to 768 kbps and can upload data at slower speeds—for example, 256 kbps. DSL lines that have different upload and download speeds are called **asymmetric digital subscriber lines (ADSL)**. Most homes and small businesses can use ADSL because they receive more data than they transmit (e.g., pictures in news stories), and hence they do not need to transmit as fast as they receive.

Some users and larger businesses, however, need DSL lines that have the same receiving and transmitting speeds. They also need performance-level guarantees. **Symmetrical digital subscriber lines (SDSL)** meet this need by offering the same fast speed in both directions. As much as 1.544 Mbps can be guaranteed.

Cable Modems

A **cable modem** is the third modem type. Cable modems provide high-speed data transmission using cable television lines. The cable company installs a fast, high-capacity optical fiber cable to a distribution center in each neighborhood that it serves. At the distribution center, the optical fiber cable connects to regular cable-television cables that run to subscribers' homes or businesses. Cable modems modulate in such a way that their signals do not interfere with TV signals. Like DSL lines, they are always on.

Because up to 500 user sites can share these facilities, performance varies depending on how many other users are sending and receiving data. At the maximum, users can download data up to 10 Mbps and can upload data at 256 kbps. Typically, performance is much lower than this. In most cases, the speed of cable modems and

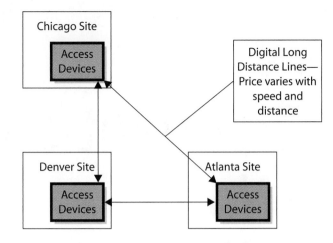

FIGURE 6-10
WAN Using Leased Lines

DSL modems is about the same. Cable modems use their own protocols. Figure 6-7 (page 125) summarized these alternatives.

You will sometimes hear the terms *narrowband* and *broadband* with regard to communications speeds. **Narrowband** lines typically have transmissions speeds less than 56 kbps. **Broadband** lines have speeds in excess of 256 kbps. Thus, a dial-up modem provides narrowband access, and DSL and cable modems provide broadband access.

The variety of LAN and WAN connections have resulted in the almost unbelievable growth of personal and business computing in the past 10 years. The *Guide* on pages 130–131 discusses possible responses to such exponential growth.

Networks of Leased Lines

As Figure 6-7 showed, a second WAN alternative is to create a **network of leased lines** between company sites. Figure 6-10 shows a WAN that connects computers located at three geographically distributed company sites. The lines that connect these sites are leased from telecommunications companies that are licensed to provide them.

A variety of **access devices** connect each site to the transmission lines. These devices are typically special-purpose computers; the particular devices required depend on the line used and other factors. Sometimes switches are used, and in other cases a device called a router is used. A **router** is a special-purpose computer that moves network traffic from one node on a network to another.

Several leased-line alternatives exist. As shown in Figure 6-11, lines are classified by their use and speed. A T1 line can support up to 1.544 Mbps; a T3 line can support up to 44.736 Mbps. Using optical fiber cable, even faster lines are possible; an OC-768

FIGURE 6-11
Transmission Line Types, Uses, and Speeds

Line Type	Use	Maximum Speed
Telephone line (twisted pair copper lines)	Dial-up modem	56 Kbps
	DSL modem	1.544 Mbps
	WAN—T1—using a pair of telephone lines	1.544 Mbps
Coaxial cable	Cable modem	Upstream to 256 Kbps Downstream to 10 Mbps (usually much less, however)
Unshielded twisted pair (UTP)	LAN	100 Mbps
Optical fiber cable	LAN and WAN—T3, OC-768, etc.	40 Gbps or more
Satellite	WAN—OC-768, etc.	40 Gbps or more

Thinking Exponentially Is Not Possible, but . . .

Nathan Myhrvold, the chief scientist at Microsoft during the 1990s, once said that humans are incapable of thinking exponentially. Instead, when something changes exponentially, we think of the fastest linear change we can imagine and extrapolate from there, as illustrated in the figure. Myhrvold was writing about the exponential growth of magnetic storage. His point was that no one could then imagine how much growth there would be in magnetic storage and what we would do with it.

This limitation pertains equally well to the growth of computer network phenomena. We have witnessed exponential growth in a number of areas: the number of Internet connections, the number of Web pages, and the amount of data accessible on the Internet. And all signs are that this exponential growth isn't over.

What, you might ask, does this have to do with *me*? Well, suppose you are a product manager for home appliances. Now that most homes have a wireless network, it would be cheap and easy for appliances to talk to one another. If that begins to happen, what impact will that have on your existing product line? Will the competition's talking appliances take away your market share? Or perhaps talking appliances will not satisfy a real need. If a toaster and a coffee pot have nothing to say to each other, you'll be wasting money to create them.

Every business, every organization needs to be thinking about the cheap connectivity that is growing exponentially. What are the new opportunities? What are the new threats? How will our competition react? How should we position ourselves? How should we respond? As you consider these questions, keep in mind that because humans cannot think exponentially, we're all just guessing.

So what can we do to better anticipate changes brought by exponential phenomena? For one, understand that technology does not drive people to do things they've never done before, no matter how much the technologists suggest it might. (Just because we *can* do something does not mean anyone will *want* to do that something.)

Social progress occurs in small, evolutionary, adaptive steps. A few years ago, millions of people drove to stores to rent a movie. When they arrived, they often did not find the movie they wanted, they often waited in a long line—or they never even found a parking spot. Netflix (among others) understood that someday there would be sufficient bandwidth to rent movies online. In 2008, that bandwidth is beginning to be available, and Netflix has started streaming movies directly to home televisions. This initial capability will become increasingly popular in the years to come. Thus, Netflix moved in steps from stores, to online rental, to online delivery. Because online rental and delivery are extensions of what people are already doing and solve a problem that people already have, they are successful and likely will continue to be successful.

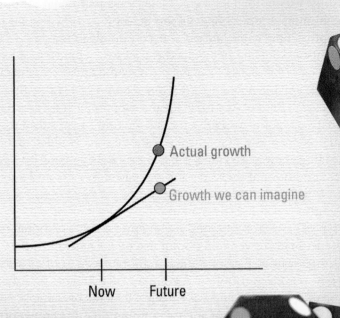

Actual growth

Growth we can imagine

Now   Future

Emerging network technology also enables my dry cleaner to notify me the minute my clothes are ready. Do I want to know? How much do I care to know that my clothes are ready Monday at 1:45 pm rather than sometime after 4:00 pm on Tuesday? In truth, I don't care. Such technology does not solve a problem that I have.

So even if technology enables a capability, that possibility doesn't mean anyone wants that capability. People want to do what they're already doing, but more easily; they want to solve problems that they already have.

Another response to exponential growth is to hedge your bets. If you can't know the outcome of an exponential phenomenon, don't commit to one direction. Position yourself to move as soon as the direction is clear. Develop a few talking appliances, position your organization to develop more, but wait for a clear sign of market acceptance before going all out.

Finally, notice in the exponential curve that the larger the distance between Now and the Future, the larger the error. In fact, the error increases exponentially with the length of the prediction. So if you read in this textbook that WiMax will replace 802.3 wireless in 2 years, assign that statement a certain level of doubt. If you read that it will replace 802.3 LANs in 5 years, assign that statement an exponentially greater level of doubt.

DISCUSSION QUESTIONS

1. In your own words, explain the meaning of the claim that no one can think exponentially. Do you agree with this claim?

2. Describe a phenomenon besides connectivity or magnetic memory that you believe is increasing exponentially. Explain why it is difficult to predict the consequences of this phenomenon in 5 years.

3. To what extent do you think technology is responsible for the growth in the number of news sources? On balance, do you think having many news sources of varying quality is better than having a few with high quality control?

4. List three products or services, like movie rental, that could dramatically change because of increased connectivity. Do not include movie rental.

5. Rate your answers to question 4 in terms of how closely they fit with problems that people have today.

line supports 40 Gbps. Except for T1 speeds, faster lines require either optical fiber cable or satellite communication. T1 speeds can be supported by regular telephone wires as well as by optical fiber cable and satellite communication.

Setting up a point-to-point line, once it has been leased, requires considerable work by highly trained, expensive specialists. Connecting the company's LANs and other facilities is a challenging task, and maintaining those connections is expensive. In some cases, organizations contract with third parties to set up and support the lines they have leased.

Notice, too, that with point-to-point lines, as the number of sites increases, the number of lines required increases dramatically. If another site is added to the network in Figure 6-11, up to three new leased lines will be needed. In general, if a network has n sites, as many as n additional lines need to be leased, set up, and supported to connect a new site to all the other sites.

Furthermore, only predefined sites can use the leased lines. It is not possible for an employee working at a temporary, remote location, such as a hotel, to use this network. Similarly, customers or vendors cannot use such a network, either.

However, if an organization has substantial traffic between fixed sites, leased lines can provide a low cost per bit transmitted. A company like Boeing, for example, with major facilities in Seattle, St. Louis, and Los Angeles, benefits by using leased lines to connect these sites. The operations of such a company require transmitting huge amounts of data between those fixed sites. Further, such a company knows how to hire and manage the technical personnel required to support such a network.

Public Switched Data Network

Yet another WAN alternative is a **public switched data network (PSDN)**, a network of computers and leased lines that is developed and maintained by a vendor that leases time on the network to other organizations. A PSDN is a utility that supplies a network for other companies to lease. Figure 6-12 shows the PSDN as a cloud of capability. What happens within that cloud is of no concern to the lessees. As long as they get the availability and speed they expect, the PSDN could consist of strings of spaghetti connected by meatballs. (This is not likely to be the case, however.)

When using a PSDN, each site must lease a line to connect to the PSDN network. The location at which this occurs is called a **point of presence (POP)**; it is the access point into the PSDN. Think of the POP as the phone number that one dials to connect to the PSDN. Once a site has connected to the PSDN POP, the site obtains access to all other sites connected to the PSDN.

FIGURE 6-12
WAN Using PSDN

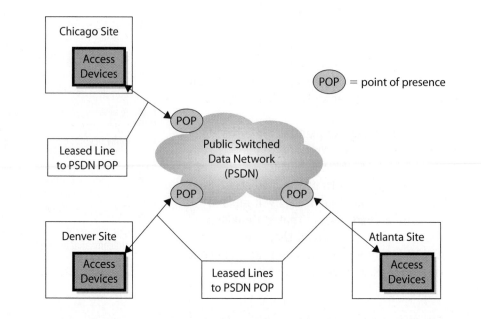

PSDNs save the setup and maintenance activities required when using leased lines. They also save costs because a company does not have to pay for the entire network; the company can pay just for the traffic that it sends. Further, using a PSDN requires much less management involvement than using leased lines. Another advantage of PSDNs is that only one line is required to connect a new site to all other sites.

Three protocols are used with PSDNs: frame relay, ATM (asynchronous transfer mode), and Ethernet. **Frame relay** can process traffic in the range of 56 kbps to 40 Mbps. **Asynchronous transfer mode (ATM)** can process speeds from 1 to 156 Mbps. Frame relay, although slower, is simpler and easier to support than ATM, and PSDNs can offer it at lower cost than ATM. However, some organizations need ATM's faster speed. Also, ATM can support both voice and data communication.

Often, PSDNs offer both frame relay and ATM on their network. Customers can choose whichever technique best fits their needs. Some companies use a PSDN network in lieu of a long-distance telephone carrier.

Ethernet, the protocol developed for LANs, also is used as a PSDN protocol. Newer versions of Ethernet can operate at speeds of 10 and 40 Gpbs.

Criteria for Comparing WANs

As you have learned, many different computer networking alternatives are available, each with different characteristics. Choosing among them can be a complicated task. Figure 6-13 lists three categories of criteria you can use to compare alternatives.

Criteria Category	Criteria	Description
Cost	Initial setup	Transmission line; equipment setup fees, including labor and training costs
	Operational	Fees for leases of lines and equipment; ISP and other service fees; ongoing training
	Maintenance	Periodic maintenance costs; problem diagnosis and repair costs; mandatory upgrade costs
Performance	Speed	Line and equipment speed
	Latency	Delays during busy periods
	Availability	Frequency of service outage
	Loss rate	Frequency retransmission required
	Transparency	User involvement in operation
	Performance guarantees	Vendors agree to cost penalties if levels of service not met
Other	Growth potential	How difficult to upgrade when service needs or capacity increase?
	Commitment periods	Length of leases and other agreements
	Management time	How much management activity is required?
	Risk, financial	How much is at stake if system not effective?
	Technical	If using new technology, what is the likelihood of failure?

FIGURE 6-13
Criteria for Comparing Networking Alternatives

As shown, managers need to consider three types of costs. *Setup costs* include the costs of acquiring transmission lines and equipment, such as switches, routers, and access devices. If lines or equipment are leased, setup fees also may be involved. Additionally, if your company is performing some of the setup work itself, labor costs need to be included. Finally, there are training costs. *Operational costs* include lease fees for lines and equipment, charges of the ISP, and the cost of ongoing training. *Maintenance costs* include those for periodic maintenance, for problem diagnosis and repair, and for mandatory upgrades.

Figure 6-13 shows six considerations with regard to performance: Line and equipment *speed* are self-explanatory. *Latency* is the transmission delay that occurs due to network congestion during busy periods. *Availability* refers to the frequency and length of service outages. *Loss rate* is the frequency of problems in the communications network that necessitate data retransmission. *Transparency* is the degree to which the user is unaware of the underlying communications system. For example, a DSL modem that is always connected is more transparent than a dial-up modem, which must find a phone line that is not in use and then dial the ISP number. The greater the transparency, the greater the ease of network use. Finally, many vendors of communications equipment and services are willing to make *performance guarantees* that commit them to levels of service quality. When a performance guarantee is in place, the vendor agrees to monetary penalties if agreed-on levels are not met.

Other criteria to consider when comparing network alternatives include the growth potential (greater capacity) and the length of contract commitment periods. Shorter periods allow for greater flexibility and usually are preferred. Also, how much management time is required? An alternative that requires in-house technical staff will require more management time than one that does not. The final two criteria consider financial and technical risk.

Q4 How Does Encryption Work?

Computer networks, as you have just seen, can offer substantial value to organizations. Unfortunately, networks also open the door to malicious activity. In this and the next study questions, we will consider two data communication threats and responses to those threats. In this question, we consider snooping and the use of encryption to protect data from snooping. In the last question, we will consider threats to organizational network resources and the use of firewalls to protect them.

Encryption is the process of transforming clear text into coded, unintelligible text for secure storage or communication. Considerable research has gone into developing **encryption algorithms** that are difficult to break. Commonly used methods are DES, 3DES, and AES; search the Web for these terms if you want to know more about them.

A **key** is a number used to encrypt the data. The encryption algorithm applies the key to the original message to produce the coded message. Decoding (decrypting) a message is similar; a key is applied to the coded message to recover the original text. In **symmetric encryption**, the same key is used to encode and to decode. With **asymmetric encryption**, different keys are used; one key encodes the message, and the other key decodes the message. Symmetric encryption is simpler and much faster than asymmetric encryption.

A special version of asymmetric encryption, **public key/private key**, is used on the Internet. With this method, each site has a public key for encoding messages and a private key for decoding them. (For now, suppose we have two generic computers, A and B.) To exchange secure messages, A and B send each other their public keys as uncoded text. Thus, A receives B's public key and B receives A's public key, all as uncoded text. Now, when A sends a message to B, it encrypts the message using B's public key and sends the encrypted message to B. Computer B receives the encrypted

1. Your computer obtains public key of Web site.

Web Site Public Key

2. Your computer generates key for symmetric encryption.

You

3. Your computer encrypts symmetric key using Web site's public key.

Symmetric Key Encrypted Using Web Site's Public Key

Web Site

4. Web site decodes your message using its private key. Obtains key for symmetric encryption.

Communications Using Symmetric Encryption

5. All communications between you and Web site use symmetric encryption.

FIGURE 6-14
The Essence of HTTPS
(SSL or TLS)

message from A and decodes it using its private key. Similarly, when B wants to send an encrypted message to A, it encodes its message with A's public key and sends the encrypted message to A. Computer A then decodes B's message with its own private key. The private keys are never communicated.

Most secure communication over the Internet uses a protocol called **HTTPS**. With HTTPS, data are encrypted using a protocol called the **Secure Socket Layer (SSL)**, also known as **Transport Layer Security (TLS)**. SSL/TLS uses a combination of public key/private key and symmetric encryption. The basic idea is this: Symmetric encryption is fast and is preferred. But, the two parties (say you and a Web site) don't share a symmetric key. How can one be generated and shared? One of the parties generates a symmetric key and uses public/private key encryption to send it securely to the other party. The flow is summarized in Figure 6-14. It works as follows:

1. Your computer obtains the public key of the Web site to which it will connect.
2. Your computer generates a key for symmetric encryption.
3. Your computer encodes that key using the Web site's public key. It sends the encrypted symmetric key to the Web site.
4. The Web site then decodes the symmetric key using its private key.
5. From that point forward, your computer and the Web site communicate using symmetric encryption.

At the end of the session, your computer and the secure site discard the keys. Using this strategy, the bulk of the secure communication occurs using the faster symmetric encryption. Also, because keys are used for short intervals, there is less likelihood they can be discovered.

Use of SSL/TLS makes it safe to send sensitive data such as credit card numbers and bank balances. Just be certain that you see https//: in your browser and not just http://. *Warning:* Under normal circumstances, neither email nor instant messaging (IM) uses encryption. It would be quite easy for one of your classmates or your professor to read any email or IM that you send over a wireless network in your classroom, in the student lounge, at a coffee shop, or in any other wireless setting. Let the sender beware!

Q5 What Is the Purpose of a Firewall?

A **firewall** is a computing device that prevents unauthorized network access. A firewall can be a special-purpose computer or it can be a program on a general-purpose computer or on a router.

FIGURE 6-15
Use of Multiple Firewalls

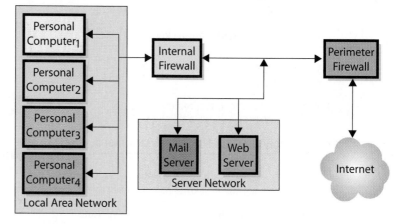

Organizations normally use multiple firewalls. A **perimeter firewall** sits outside the organizational network; it is the first device that Internet traffic encounters. In addition to perimeter firewalls, some organizations employ **internal firewalls** inside the organizational network. Figure 6-15 shows the use of a perimeter firewall that protects all of an organization's computers and a second internal firewall that protects a LAN.

A **packet-filtering firewall** examines each part of a message and determines whether to let that part pass. To make this decision, it examines the source address, the destination address(es), and other data.

Packet-filtering firewalls can prohibit outsiders from starting a session with any user behind the firewall. They can also disallow traffic from particular sites, such as known hacker addresses. They also can prohibit traffic from legitimate, but unwanted addresses, such as competitors' computers. Firewalls can filter outbound traffic as well. They can keep employees from accessing specific sites, such as competitors' sites, sites with pornographic material, or popular news sites.

A firewall has an **access control list (ACL)**, which encodes the rules stating which addresses are to be allowed and which are to be prohibited. As a future manager, if you have particular sites with which you do not want your employees to communicate, you can ask your IS department to enforce that limit via the ACL in one or more routers. Most likely, your IS organization has a procedure for making such requests.

Packet-filtering firewalls are the simplest type of firewall. Other firewalls filter on a more sophisticated basis. If you take a data communications class, you will learn about them. For now, just understand that firewalls help to protect organizational computers from unauthorized network access.

No computer should connect to the Internet without firewall protection. Many ISPs provide firewalls for their customers. By nature, these firewalls are generic. Large organizations supplement such generic firewalls with their own. Most home routers include firewalls, and Microsoft Vista has a built-in firewall as well. Third parties also license firewall products.

Q6 What Is a VPN, and Why Is It Important?

The **virtual private network (VPN)** is the last WAN alternative shown in Figure 6-7 (page 125). A VPN uses the Internet or a private internet to create the appearance of private point-to-point connections. In the IT world, the term *virtual* means something that appears to exist that does not in fact exist. Here, a VPN uses the public Internet to create the appearance of a private connection.

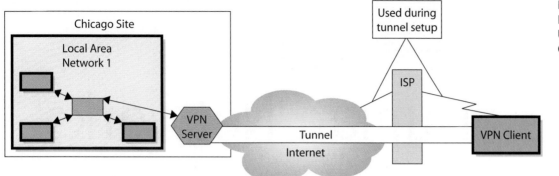

FIGURE 6-16
Remote Access
Using VPN: Actual
Connections

A Typical VPN

Figure 6-16 shows one way to create a VPN to connect a remote computer, perhaps an employee working at a hotel in Miami, to a LAN at the Chicago site. The remote user is the VPN client. That client first establishes a connection to the Internet. The connection can be obtained by accessing a local ISP, as shown in the figure, or, in most hotels, the hotel itself provides a direct Internet connection.

In either case, once the Internet connection is made, VPN software on the remote user's computer establishes a connection with the VPN server in Chicago. The VPN client and the VPN server then have a point-to-point connection. That connection, called a **tunnel**, is a virtual, private pathway over a public or shared network from the VPN client to the VPN server. Figure 6-17 illustrates the connection as it appears to the remote user.

VPN communications are secure, even though they are transmitted over the public Internet. To ensure security, VPN client software *encrypts*, or codes, the original message so that its contents are hidden. Then the VPN client appends the Internet address of the VPN server to the message and sends that package over the Internet to the VPN server. When the VPN server receives the message, it strips its address off the front of the message, *decrypts* the coded message, and sends the plain text message to the original address on the LAN. In this way, secure private messages are delivered over the public Internet.

VPNs offer the benefit of point-to-point leased lines, and they enable remote access, both by employees and by any others who have been registered with the VPN server. For example, if customers or vendors are registered with the VPN server, they can use the VPN from their own sites. Figure 6-18 on page 140 shows three tunnels; one supports a point-to-point connection between the Atlanta and Chicago sites and the other two support remote connections.

Microsoft has fostered the popularity of VPNs by including VPN support in Windows. All versions of Microsoft Windows have the capability of working as VPN clients. Windows server products can operate as VPN servers.

In this chapter, you've learned (a lot, we hope) about computer networks. Read the *Ethics Guide* on pages 138–139 for insights into the importance of your *human* networks as well.

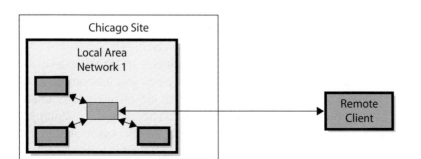

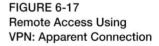

FIGURE 6-17
Remote Access Using
VPN: Apparent Connection

ETHICS
GUIDE

Human Networks Matter More

In case you missed it, *Six Degrees of Separation* is a play by John Guare that was made into a movie starring Stockard Channing and Donald Sutherland. The title is related to the idea, originated by the Hungarian writer Frigyes Karinthy, that everyone on earth is connected to everyone else by five (Karinthy) or six (Guare) people.[2] For example, according to the theory, you are connected to Angelina Jolie by no more than five or six people. By the same theory, you are also connected to a Siberian seal hunter. Today, in fact, with Facebook and Linked In, the number may be closer to three people than to five or six, but in any case, the theory points out the importance of human networks.

Suppose you want to meet your university's president. The president has a secretary who acts as a gatekeeper. If you walk up to that secretary and say, "I'd like a half an hour with President Jones," you're likely to be palmed off to some other university administrator. What else can you do?

If you are connected to everyone on the planet by no more than six degrees, then surely you are connected to your president in fewer steps. Perhaps you play on the tennis team, and you know that the president plays tennis. In that case, it is likely that

○ People in Accounting
○ People in Your Department

the tennis coach knows the president. So arrange a tennis match with your coach and the president. Voilà! You have your meeting.

The problem with the six-degree theory, as Stockard Channing said so eloquently, is that even though those six people do exist, we don't know who they are. Even worse, we often don't know who the person is with whom we want to connect. For example, there is someone, right now who knows someone who has a job for which you are perfectly suited. Unfortunately, you don't know the name of that person.

It doesn't stop when you get your job, either. When you have a problem at work, like setting up a blog within the corporate network, there is someone who knows exactly how to help you. You, however, don't know who that is.

Accordingly, most successful professionals consistently build personal human networks and they keep building them. They meet people at professional and social situations, collect and pass out cards, and engage in pleasant conversation (all part of a social protocol) to expand their networks.

Assume that each line represents a relationship between two people. Notice that the people in your department tend to know each other, and the people in the accounting department also tend to know each other. That's typical.

Now suppose you are at the weekly employee after-hours party and you have an opportunity to introduce yourself either to Linda or Eileen. Setting aside personal considerations, thinking just about network building, which person should you meet?

[2]See "The Third Link" in Albert Laszlo Barabasi's book *Linked* (New York: Perseus Publishing, 2002) for background on this theory.

If you introduce yourself to Linda, you shorten your pathway to her from two steps to one and your pathway to Shawna from three to two. You do not open up any new channels because you already have them to the people in your floor.

However, if you introduce yourself to Eileen, you open up an entirely new network of acquaintances. So, considering just network building, you use your time better by meeting Eileen and other people who are not part of your current circle. It opens up many more possibilities.

The connection from you to Eileen is called a *weak tie* in social network theory,[3] and such links are crucial in connecting you to everyone in six degrees. *In general, the people you know the least contribute the most to your network.*

This concept is simple, but you'd be surprised by how few people pay attention to it. At most company events, everyone talks with the people they know, and if the purpose of the function is to have fun, then that behavior makes sense. In truth, however, no business social function exists for having fun, regardless of what people say. Business functions exist for business reasons, and you can use them to create and expand networks. Given that time is always limited, you may as well use such functions efficiently.

[3]See Terry Granovetter, "The Strength of Weak Ties," *American Journal of Sociology*, May 1973.

DISCUSSION QUESTIONS

1. Determine the shortest path from you to your university's president. How many links does it have?

2. Give an example of a network to which you belong that is like the floor in the figure. Sketch a diagram of who knows whom for six or so members of that group.

3. Recall a recent social situation and identify two people, one of whom could have played the role of Linda (someone in your group whom you do not know) and one of whom could have played the role of Eileen (someone in a different group whom you do not know). How could you have introduced yourself to either person?

4. Does it seem too contrived and calculating to think about your social relationships in this way? Even if you do not approach relationships like this, are you surprised to think that others do? Under what circumstances does this kind of analysis seem appropriate, and when does it seem inappropriate? Are you using people?

5. Consider the phrase, "It's not what you know, it's whom you know that matters." Relate this phrase to the diagram. Under what circumstances is this likely to be true? When is it false? When is it ethical?

6. Describe how you can apply the principle, "The people you know the least contribute the most to your network" to the process of a job search. Are you abusing your relationships for personal gain?

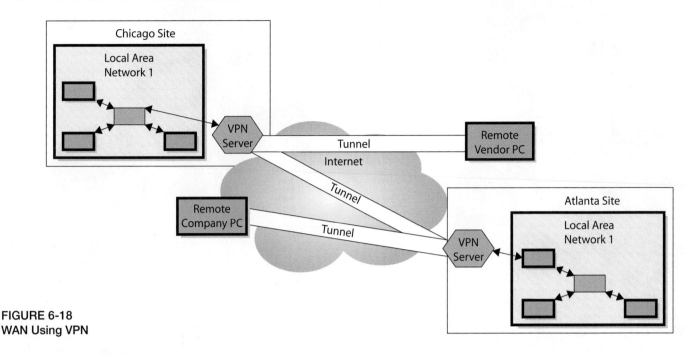

FIGURE 6-18
WAN Using VPN

How well do you know this Don Gray?

How does
the knowledge
in this chapter
help
Dee and **you?**

The knowledge in this and the prior two chapters enables Dee to understand a diagram of the IS that supports her blog, like the one shown in Figure 6-19. On the left are two types of client computers: Dee's and the computers used by the salespeople. Both types are thin clients; Dee uses Web pages provided by Movable Type that enable her to create blog entries, and the salespeople use pages of blog content that are also served by Movable Type.

The client computers contain VPN client software. That software interacts with the VPN server via the Internet. By using the VPN, both Dee and the salespeople have a secure, private connection over the Internet. On the server side, a firewall stops any traffic that is not addressed to the VPN server; only snoopers or viruses would attempt to access this network without using the VPN. Once authenticated by user ID and password, the VPN server will allow access to the servers within the network, including the blog server.

The salespeople already know how to access the VPN, so Dee wants them to use this system. Because of the short time frame, however, the Emerson IT department says that they are unable to schedule the resources necessary to set up the blog server. Dee's consultant Don has the time and skill to set up that server, but the Emerson IT department will not allow an outside person to access their network. Once inside, anyone with technical skills and a desire to cause mischief could easily do so.

Dee is at an impasse. She understands why Emerson doesn't want a stranger installing programs on her computer. Meanwhile, her boss is asking her daily whether her blog will be ready for the national sales meeting.

In desperation, she calls Don, who suggests the following compromise: If Emerson will make an unprotected, test server available to him, one that is outside its network, he can set up all of the blog software exactly as it will need to exist on the operational server. He, Dee, and the IT department can test that server. Once it is working, he can write instructions for the IT personnel to copy the test-server

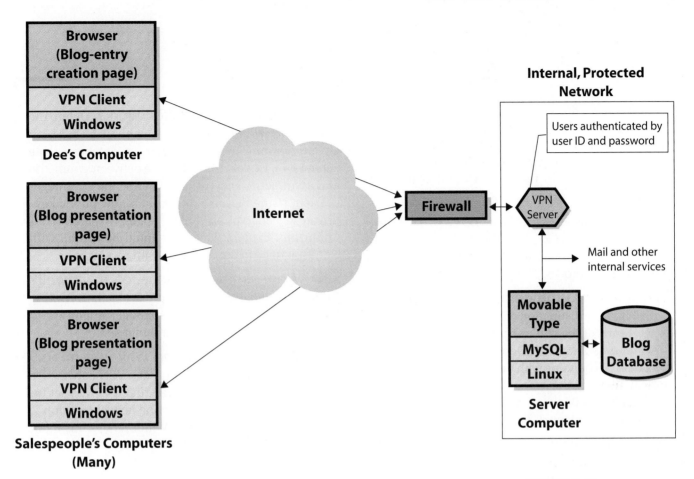

FIGURE 6-19
Using a Firewall and the VPN for Dee's Blog

software onto a server within the network, and the production blog will be up and running.

This is not a perfect solution. It does require some internal IT department labor. Also, were Don a criminal, it would be possible for him to include a Trojan horse virus in his code. To avoid this possibility, Don creates the instructions so that the IT department will be installing only public software from known sources; they can obtain Movable Type from its vendor, MySQL from its vendor, and Linux from its vendor. Then they copy the blog database from the test server. In this way, the IT department will be installing software from known sources, and none of Don's code will ever reside on any production server.

Ultimately, this is exactly what happened. However, it was not easy for Dee. She had to get an email from her boss's boss to a high-level IT manager in order to get the approval. Also, she used the knowledge she'd gained from Don and her negotiating skills to force the IT department's hand. She threatened that if they didn't cooperate, she would set up her own system of user IDs and passwords and place her blog on a public server on which she would rent time. She hoped it would not come to that, but she knew that the IT department knew that such a duplicate set of user IDs and passwords would confuse the salespeople. Ultimately, it would be the IT department who would have to straighten out the mess. She wanted them to view her proposal as the lesser of two evils. That's not exactly fair play, as we learn when we view this situation from the IT department's perspective in Chapter 11, but it worked for Dee in this instance.

You are the ultimate beneficiary of this story, however. Dee had to pay in blood, sweat, tears, lost sleep, and money to learn what she needed to know. All you had to do was read six chapters.

Active  Review

Use this Active Review to verify that you understand the material in the chapter. You can read the entire chapter and then perform the tasks in this review, or you can read the material for just one question and perform the tasks in this review for that question before moving on to the next one.

Q1 **What is a computer network?** Define *computer network*. Explain the differences among LANs, WANs, internets, and the Internet. Describe the purpose of a protocol.

Q2 **What are the components of a LAN?** Explain the key distinction of a LAN. Describe the purpose of each of the components of Figure 6-2. Define *MAC address* and *UTP*. Describe the placement of switches on a building with many floors. Explain when optical fiber cables are used for a LAN. Explain Ethernet. Describe the purpose of each of the wireless components in Figure 6-6.

Q3 **What are the alternatives for a WAN?** Explain why your connection to an ISP is a WAN and not a LAN. Describe the purpose of a modem. Explain three ways you can connect to the Internet. Describe the difference between DSL and cable modems. Explain the advantages and disadvantages of leased lines. Explain each cell of Figure 6-7. Explain each cell of Figure 6-11. Explain each cell of Figure 6-13.

Q4 **How does encryption work?** Define the terms *encryption* and *key*. Distinguish between an encryption key and a key of a database table (Chapter 5). Explain the difference between symmetric and asymmetric encryption. Describe the advantages of each. Using Figure 6-14, explain how public key/private key encryption works. Explain why SSL/TLS is important. Explain why you should be careful with what you write in emails and instant messages.

Q5 **What is the purpose of a firewall?** Define *firewall*. Explain the role for each firewall in Figure 6-15. Describe how a manager might ask to shut off access to or from a particular site.

Q6 **What is a VPN, and why is it important?** Describe the problem that a VPN solves. Use Figure 6-16 to explain one way that a VPN is set up and used. Define *tunnel*. Describe how encryption is used in a VPN. Explain why a Windows user need not license nor install other software to use a VPN.

 Explain why, in Figure 6-19, the client computers in Dee's blog can be thin clients. Describe what kind of software will be used on the client computers for the blog. Explain the benefit of the VPN to Dee's blog.

Key Terms and Concepts

Access control list (ACL) 136
Access device 129
Access point (AP) 125
Analog signal 127
Asymmetric digital subscriber line (ADSL) 128
Asymmetric encryption 134
Asynchronous transfer mode (ATM) 133
Broadband 129
Cable modem 128
Dial-up modem 127
DSL (digital subscriber line) modem 128
Encryption 134
Encryption algorithms 134

Ethernet 123
Firewall 135
Frame relay 133
HTTPS 135
IEEE 802.3 protocol 123
IEEE 802.11 protocol 125
IEEE 802.16 protocol 126
Internal firewall 136
internet 121
Internet 121
Internet service provider (ISP) 127
Key 134
Last-mile problem 126
Local area network (LAN) 121
MAC address 122
Modem 127

Narrowband 129
Network 121
Network interface card (NIC) 122
Network of leased lines 129
Onboard NIC 122
Optical fiber cable 123
Packet-filtering firewall 136
Perimeter firewall 136
Point-to-Point Protocol (PPP) 128
Point of presence (POP) 132
Protocol 121
Public key/private key 134
Public switched data network (PSDN) 132
Router 129

Using Your Knowledge

1. Suppose you manage a group of seven employees in a small business. Each of your employees wants to be connected to the Internet. Consider two alternatives:
   - Alternative A: Each employee has his own modem and connects individually to the Internet
   - Alternative B: The employees' computers are connected using a LAN and the network uses a single modem to connect.

   a. Sketch the equipment and lines required for each alternative.
   b. Explain the actions you need to take to create each alternative.
   c. Compare the alternatives using the criteria in Figure 6-13.
   d. Which of these two alternatives do you recommend?

2. Consider the situation of a company that has two offices at physically separated sites. Suppose each office has a group of 15 computers.
   a. If the two offices are retail art galleries, what is likely to be the most common type of interoffice communication? Given your answer, what type of WAN do you think is most appropriate?
   b. Suppose the two offices are manufacturing sites that communicate via email and that regularly exchange large drawings and plans. What are the advantages and disadvantages of each of the four WAN types for these offices? Under what circumstances would you recommend a leased-line WAN?
   c. Suppose the two offices are the same as described in part b, but that in addition each has salespeople on the road who need to connect to the office computers. How would your answer to part b change?
   d. Would you change your answer to part c if both offices are located in the same building? Why or why not?
   e. What additional factors would you need to consider if one of the offices in part c was in Los Angeles and the other was located in Singapore?

Collaboration Exercise 6 ◎

Before you start this exercise, read Chapter Extensions 1 and 2, which describe collaboration techniques as well as tools for managing collaboration tasks. In particular, consider using Google Docs & Spreadsheets, Google Groups, Microsoft Groove, Microsoft SharePoint, or some other collaboration tool.

Reread *MIS in Use 6* on page 126. Clearwire has not implemented full WiMax, and in fact the company is simulating it using existing wireless and wired telephone technology. In May 2007, Clearwire did conduct a successful test of limited portability using the 802.16e standard (*http://investors.clearwire.com/phoenix.zhtml?c=198722&p=irolnewsArticle&ID=1004778*) in Portland, Oregon, but as of June 2008, Clearwire is providing what is, in essence, a very large wireless hotspot. Instead of wireless in a coffee shop, it is wireless over a several-mile or larger region. True portability is yet to come.

Clearly, this is a complex situation. With people like McCaw, with Clearwire's partners, and with the promise of the technology, there is some major promise here. But

what? What technology works today? What is Clearwire's true capability? How do its products and capabilities compare to, say, iPhone connectivity? Why did the venture need $3.2 billion? How much more will it need? Would Clearwire be a good investment today? You and your team can find out in this assignment as you answer the following questions.

1. What is the current situation?
   a. What technology is operational today?
   b. What products are being offered?
   c. How many customers does Clearwire have? Where are they?
   d. What is Clearwire's current revenue and profitability? (You can find out because Clearwire is a public company.)

2. What is Clearwire's near term (2- to 3-year) opportunity?
   a. What does the company plan to do with the $3.2 billion raised in May 2008?

b. What new WiMax technologies does it expect to develop in the next 2 to 3 years?

c. What new products will it offer?

d. What are its projections for the number of customers, revenue, and earnings in the near term?

3. Who is Clearwire's competition?

a. Compare and contrast Clearwire's capability with that of the iPhone.

b. Besides the iPhone, who else is in competition with Clearwire?

c. How will the competitive landscape change in the next few years?

4. Assume that Clearwire is successful. Identify five opportunities that its success will create for you. Use the example of Larry Jones in Case Study 6 to stimulate your thinking, but do not constrain yourself to the campus market that he considered.

Case Study 6

Larry Jones Network Services

In 2003, Larry Jones was an entering freshman at Big State University. (This case is real; however, to protect privacy, the student and university names are fictional.) Larry had always been interested in technology and as a high school student had won a scholarship from Cisco Corporation (a maker of communications hardware). As part of his scholarship, Larry had attended several Cisco training classes on setting up LANs, switches, and other devices.

Larry pledged a fraternity at Big State, and when the fraternity leadership learned of his expertise, they asked him to set up a LAN with an Internet connection for the fraternity house. It was a simple job for Larry, and his fraternity brothers were quite satisfied with his solution. He did it for free, as a volunteer, and appreciated the introductions the project gave him to senior leaders of the fraternity. The project enabled him to build his network of personal contacts.

Over the summer of 2003, however, it dawned on Larry that his fraternity was not the only one on the Big State campus that had the need for a LAN with access to the Internet. Accordingly, that summer he developed marketing materials describing the need and the services he could provide. That fall he called on fraternities and sororities and made presentations of his skills and of the network he had built for the fraternity. Within a year, he had a dozen or so fraternities and sororities as customers.

Larry quickly realized that he couldn't just set up a LAN and Internet connection, charge his fee, and walk away. His customers had continuing problems that required him to return to resolve problems, add new computers, add printer servers, and so forth. At first, he provided such support as part of his installation package price. He soon learned that he could charge a support fee for regular support, and even add extra charges for

support beyond normal wear and tear. By the end of 2004, the support fees were meeting all of Larry's college expenses, and then some.

When I last saw him, Larry had formed a partnership with several other students to expand his services to local apartment houses and condominiums.

It is probably too late for you to do something like Larry did for wireless LAN communications, but there are other opportunities that you might explore as suggested in the following questions:

Questions

1. Consider the information technology skills and needs of your parents, relatives, family friends, and others in the Baby Boomer generation. Though you may not know it, you possess many skills that that generation wants but does not have. You know how to text chat, how to download music from iTunes, how to buy and sell items on eBay, how to use Craigslist, and how to use a PDA, an iPhone, and so forth. You probably can even run the navigation system in your parents' car.

   Thinking about Baby Boomers whom you know, identify skills that you possess that they do not. Consider the ideas just described and as well as others that come to mind. List those skills.

2. Interview, survey, or informally discuss the items on your list in question 1 with your parents and other Baby Boomers. Determine what you think are the five most frustrating and important skills that these people do not possess.

3. The Baby Boomer market has both money and time, but not as much information technology capability as they need, and they do not like that situation. Brainstorm products that you could sell

to this market that would address the Baby Boomers' techno-ignorance. For example, you might create a video of necessary skills, or you might provide a consulting service setting up Microsoft Home Server computers. Consider other ideas and describe them as specifically as you can.

You should consider at least five different product concepts.

4. How viable are your concepts? Do you think you can make money with these products? If so, summarize an implementation plan. If not, explain why not.

THE
International
Dimension

Global Communication

? Study Questions

Q1 What does it mean to localize software?

Q2 What are the problems and issues of localizing and distributing databases worldwide?

Q3 What are the consequences of global data communication?

The International Dimension

Q1 What Does It Mean to Localize Software?

The process of making a computer program work in a second language is called **localizing**. It turns out to be surprisingly hard to do. To localize a document or a Web page, all you need to do is hire a translator to convert your document or page from one language to another. The situation is much more difficult for a computer program, however.

Suppose, for example, that your company has developed its own inventory control database application and that your firm has just acquired a company in Mexico. You want to use that same inventory control program for your Mexican operations. As a new manager, suppose you haven't even considered this matter during the acquisition process. After the acquisition is done, you ask your technical people to give you a time estimate for converting your inventory application into Spanish. Unless that program was designed from the beginning to be localized, you will be shocked at the effort and cost required.

Why is it so difficult to localize a software program? Consider a program you use frequently—say, Microsoft Word—and ask what would need to be done to translate it to a different language. The entire user interface will need to be translated. The menu bar and the commands on the menu bar will need to be translated. It is possible that some of the icons (the small graphics on a menu bar) will need to be changed, because some graphic symbols that are harmless in one culture are confusing or offensive in another.

The inventory control application is a database application, so it will have forms, reports, and queries. The labels on each of these will need to be translated. Of course, not all labels translate into words of the same length, and so the forms and reports may need to be redesigned. The questions and prompts for queries, such as "Enter part number for back order," must also be translated.

All of the documentation will need to be translated. That should be just a matter of hiring a translator, except that all of the illustrations in the documentation will need to be redrawn in the second language.

Think, too, about error messages. When someone attempts to order more items than there are in inventory, your application produces an error message. All of those messages will need to be translated. There are other issues as well. Sorting order is one. Spanish uses accents on certain letters, and it turns out that an accented $ó$ will sort after z when you use the computer's default sort ordering. Your programmers will have to deal with this issue as well.

Figure 1 presents a short list of issues that will emerge when localizing a computer program.

Programming techniques can be used to simplify and reduce the cost of localization. However, those

FIGURE 1
Issues to Address When Localizing a Computer Program

- Translate the user interface, including menu bars and commands.
- Translate, and possibly redesign, labels in forms, reports, and query prompts.
- Translate all documentation and help text.
- Redraw and translate diagrams and examples in help text.
- Translate all error messages.
- Translate text in all message boxes.
- Adjust sorting order for different character set.
- Fix special problems in Asian character sets and in languages that read and write from right to left.

techniques must be used in the beginning. For example, suppose that when a certain condition occurs, the program is to display the message "Insufficient quantity in stock." If the programmer codes all such messages into the computer program, then, to localize that program, the programmer will have to find every such message in the code and then ask a translator to change that code. A preferred technique is to give every error message a number and to place the number and text of the error message into a separate file. Then, the code is written to display a particular error number from

that file. During localization, translators simply translate the file of error messages into the second language.

The bottom line for you, as a future manager, is to understand two points: (1) Localizing computer programs is much more difficult, expensive, and time-consuming than translating documents. (2) If a computer program is likely to be localized, then plan for that localization from the beginning. In addition, when considering the acquisition of a company in a foreign country, be sure to budget time and expense for the localization of information systems.

Q2 What Are the Problems and Issues of Localizing and Distributing Databases Worldwide?

Consider the acquisition of the Mexican company just described. You have decided to localize your inventory control application. The next question is, "Do you want to localize your inventory database?"

Assume you have a centralized inventory database in the United States. Do you want the inventory control programs that will run in Mexico to access that same database? With modern data communications, that is entirely possible.

However, your business requirements may dictate that you need to create a second database in Mexico. In that case, there are two issues. First, you will need to localize it. Second, you will need to determine the relationship between the two databases. Do the contents of those two databases refer to a single centralized inventory, or do they refer to two different inventories? If, for example, the two databases both indicate that there are 10 widgets in inventory, is that a single centralized inventory or are there two separate inventories, one in the United States and one in Mexico, and do they both happen to have 10 widgets in stock?

Consider database localization first. In most cases, when companies localize databases, they choose to translate the data, but not the metadata. Thus, the contents of the *Remarks* field or the *Description* files are translated. However, the names of tables, the names of fields, the description of the meaning of the fields, and other such metadata are left in English (or whatever the original language was). As stated in the previous section, forms, reports, queries, and database application programs will also need to be localized.

Now consider the relationship between the two databases. If they refer to two separate inventories, then there is no problem. Each database can be processed and administered as an independent entity. If the two databases refer to the *same* inventory, however, then they contain duplicated records. Such databases are said to be **replicated**. In this case, if it is possible to partition the workload so that the inventory application running on a server in Mexico updates different records than the inventory application running on a server in the United States, then the situation can be managed.

If, however, the two inventory applications running on the two servers can update the *same items at the same time*, serious problems occur. Considerable time, expense, and sophisticated programming are necessary to develop and support such databases. Because of the expense, difficulty, and risk, most organizations define their business processes to avoid this situation.

This problem, by the way, is not strictly an international problem. The two separate servers could be running in the same country, and the problem will be the same. The situation arises more frequently, however, in international situations.

Q3 What Are the Consequences of Global Data Communication?

We discussed the impact of modern data communications on the development of the global economy in the International Dimension for Part 1 (page 62). In brief, data communications have expanded tremendously the size of the global economy and the global workforce.

In this section, consider the impact of data communications on less-developed countries. One of the most positive aspects of IT is that technology users can skip generations: People can benefit from the most modern technology without having to use the earlier technology. When Microsoft introduces a new version of Word, you can receive the benefit of that new version without having to learn Word 1.0, then Word 2.0, then Word 3.0, and so forth. Similarly, you can buy a cell phone and use it without ever having used a wired phone. You can do instant messaging with your friends without ever having sent an email.

What are the consequences? In many developing countries, cell or satellite phones are the first phones that most people use. There are parts of the world that do not have telephone wires and that will never have them. In some countries, the first weather forecast someone sees will be presented on a Web page that is delivered via a cell phone.

The economic, social, and political consequences of this phenomenon are staggering. A coffee farmer in Kenya, someone who has never sold his or her beans to anyone but a local trader, can suddenly sell them to Starbucks in Seattle. A basket weaver in Cameroon, who has sold her wares only at the local market, can suddenly sell her baskets to collectors in Tokyo. People whose world horizon has been restricted to villages, neighborhoods, or streets in their city suddenly find themselves connected to the rest of the world. Local laws and customs become outmoded, even irrelevant.

Furthermore, existing companies, organizations, and governments are seriously challenged. The public telephone utility in many countries has been a profitable monopoly and medium of control. Cell and satellite phones threaten this monopoly and reduce the power of individuals and cartels. In some countries, the government has restricted the spread of technology. Such measures only delay the inevitable. How can a country with serious penalties for using a copy machine for political purposes maintain control in the face of email, instant messaging, and the Web?

During your career, these countries will see unprecedented change. This change will create many opportunities for interesting jobs, careers, and new businesses.

Active  Review

Use this Active Review to verify that you understand the material in the International Dimension. You can read the entire minichapter and then perform the tasks in this review, or you can read the material for just one question and perform the tasks in this review for that question before moving on to the next one.

Q1 What does it mean to localize software? Explain why information systems, and in particular, software, should be considered during the merger and acquisition process. Summarize the work required to localize a computer program. In your own words, explain why it is better to design a program to be localized rather than attempt to adapt an existing single-language program to a second language.

Q2 What are the problems and issues of localizing and distributing databases worldwide? Explain what is required to localize a database. Explain possible relationships of two databases. Define *replicated databases*. Explain the conditions for which replicated databases are not a problem. Explain the conditions for which replicated databases are a problem. How do most organizations deal with this problem?

Q3 What are the consequences of global data communication? Explain the statement, "Technology users can skip generations." Illustrate this principle with an example from your own life. Describe the economic consequences of this principle on developing countries. Describe the social and political consequences of this principle. Give an example of a job, career, or business opportunity that these changes will present.

Key Terms and Concepts

Localizing 146
Replicated databases 148

review

Consider Your Net Worth

Examine the questions addressed in each chapter and think about how those ideas will pertain to you as a future manager and professional businessperson. How can you use the knowledge you've gained to increase your net worth both to your employer and yourself?

1. Considering your future goals (use your answer to question 1, "Consider Your Net Worth," page 66), describe how the knowledge you've gained about computer hardware and software helps you. How will it help you specify equipment that you need? How will it help you specify equipment for your employees? How can you use the knowledge about buying decisions? What does the information about viruses tell you to do for yourself and for your employees?

2. As a business professional, when would you choose to use a database? When would you use a spreadsheet? Describe the kind of problem for which you would use a personal DBMS. What kind of problem needs an enterprise-class DBMS? Under what conditions could you get by with just forms, reports, and queries, and under what other conditions would you need to hire someone to develop database application programs?

3. Suppose you manage a department. Under what conditions can the needs of your department be satisfied by a LAN? Besides Internet access, under what conditions would your group need a WAN? When would a network of leased lines be appropriate? Under what conditions would you want your employees to ensure they have the *https://* characters in their browser address line? When would a VPN be appropriate? What steps could you take to prevent your employees from accessing a particular Web site? Under what conditions are email and instant messaging protected by encryption?

4. Reflect on Dee's experiences as discussed in Chapters 4 through 6. Even though you are unlikely to start a blog within a corporate network, what can you learn from her? How does knowledge of IT and IS help you better work with the IT department? How does it help you be a better negotiator with personnel? How can you use knowledge of hardware and software, databases, and data communications to be a better advocate for your needs and the needs of your department? How does such knowledge give you a competitive advantage over other professionals and managers who do not have it?

Application Exercises

1. Suppose that you work in a sales office and your boss asks you to create a "computer file" to keep track of product prices offered to customers. Suppose you decide to use a spreadsheet for this purpose as follows.

   a. Create a spreadsheet with the following columns: *CustomerName, CustomerLocation, MeetingDate, ProductName, UnitPrice, Salesperson*, and *Salesperson_Email*.

   b. Suppose you have three customers: Ajax, Baker, and Champion. Suppose Ajax is located in New York City, Baker is located in Toronto, and Champion is located in New York City. Assume you have two salespeople: Johnson and Jackson. (Make up email addresses for each.)

      Assume you have three products: P1, P2, and P3. Periodically, your salespeople meet with customers, and during these meetings, they agree on product prices. The salespeople pitch one, two, or three products in each of these meetings. Some customers negotiate better prices than others, so the price varies by customer.

      Using this information, fill your spreadsheet with at least 20 rows of sample data. Make up the price data. Assume that prices increase and decrease over time. Enter data for some meetings in 2008 and for some meetings in 2009.

   c. Copy your spreadsheet to a new worksheet. Suppose that you made a mistake and Champion is based in San Francisco, not New York City. Using this second worksheet, make the necessary changes to correct your mistake.

   d. Suppose that you learn that the product P1 was renamed P1-Turbo in 2008. Explain the steps you need to take to correct this mistake.

   e. A real sales-tracking application would have hundreds of customers, many salespeople, hundreds of products, and possibly thousands of meetings. For such a spreadsheet, how would you correct the problems in parts c and d? Comment on the appropriateness of using a spreadsheet for such an application.

2. Consider the same problem as in question 1, except use a database to keep track of the price quotations.

   a. Create a new database using Microsoft Access and create the following three tables:

      CUSTOMER *(CustomerName, Location)*
      SALESPERSON *(SalespersonName, Saleperson_Email)*
      PRICE_QUOTE *(Date, Product, Price, CustomerName, SalespersonName)*

      Assume the following: *CustomerName* is the key of CUSTOMER; *SalespersonName* is the key of SALESPERSON; and the three columns (*Date, Product*, and *CustomerName*) are the key of PRICE_QUOTE. Make appropriate assumptions about the data types for each table column.

   b. Use Access to create a 1:N relationship between CUSTOMER and PRICE_QUOTE. Create a 1:N relationship between SALESPERSON and PRICE_QUOTE. Check Enforce Referential Integrity for both relationships.

c. Fill your tables using the same data that you used in question 1.

d. Make the changes necessary to record the fact that customer Champion is based in San Francisco rather than in New York City. How many items do you need to change?

e. Make the changes necessary to change the name of product P1 to P1-Turbo for all quotes after 2008.

f. Using the Access Help system, learn about update action queries. Create an update action query to make the change in part e.

g. Compare spreadsheets and databases for this application. Which is better? Why? What are the characteristics of an application that would cause you to choose a database over a spreadsheet? A spreadsheet over a database?

 3. Read the *Guide* on page 112. Suppose you are given the task of converting the salesperson's data into a database. Because his data is so poorly structured, it will be a challenge, as you will see.

a. Download the Excel file named **Ch05Ex02** from *www.pearsonhighered. com/kroenke*. This spreadsheet contains data that fits the salesperson's description in the *Guide*. Open the spreadsheet and view the data.

b. Download the Access file with the same name, **Ch05Ex02**. Open the database, select *Database Tools*, and click *Relationships*. Examine the four tables and their relationships.

c. Somehow, you have to transform the data in the spreadsheet into the table structure in the database. Because so little discipline was shown when creating the spreadsheet, this will be a labor-intensive task. To begin, import the spreadsheet data into a new table in the database; call that table *Sheet1* or some other name.

d. Copy the *Name* data in *Sheet1* onto the clipboard. Then, open the *Customer* table and paste the column of name data into that table.

e. Unfortunately, the task becomes messy at this point. You can copy the *Car Interests* column into *Make or Model of Auto*, but then you will need to straighten out the values by hand. Phone numbers will need to be copied one at a time.

f. Open the *Customer* form and manually add any remaining data from the spreadsheet into each customer record. Connect the customer to his or her auto interests.

4. Numerous Web sites are available that will test your Internet data communications speed. You can find a good one at Speakeasy (*www.speakeasy.net/speedtest*). (If that site is no longer active, perform a search for "What is my Internet speed?" to find another speed-testing site. Use it.)

a. While connected to your university's network, go to Speakeasy and test your speed against servers in Seattle, New York City, and Atlanta. Compute your average upload and download speeds. Compare your speed to the speeds listed in Figure 6-11.

b. Go home, or to a public wireless site, and run the Speakeasy test again. Compute your average upload and download speeds. Compare your speed to those listed in Figure 6-11. If you are performing this test at home, are you getting the performance you are paying for?

c. Contact a friend or relative in another state. Ask him or her to run the Speakeasy test against those same three cities.

d. Compare the results in parts a, b, and c. What conclusion, if any, can you make from these tests?

FIGURE 7-1
Sample E-Commerce Site

Source: Used with permission of REI.

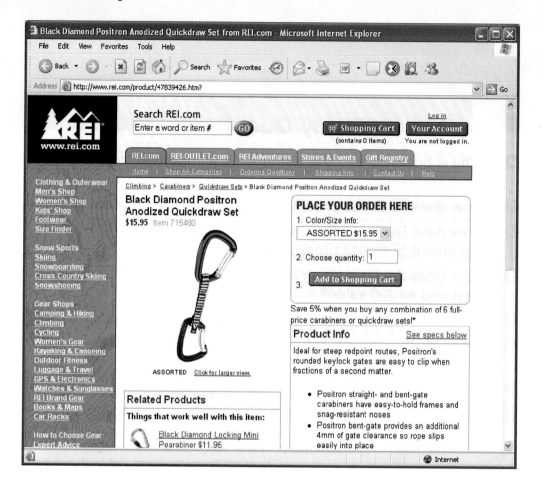

Now, consider what has to happen at REI to process your transaction. As listed in Figure 7-2, the Web site has to be sufficiently rich to capture your intent. What items are you buying? What size? Color? Quantity? Then, how are you going to pay? Where do you want the goods to be sent? How fast do you want them delivered, and are there special terms, such as gift cards? Once you've provided that data, information systems then verify your credit, remove items from inventory, charge your credit card, cause your items to be packed and shipped, and record all of this for accounting, marketing, and service purposes. Also, information systems need to

FIGURE 7-2
Tasks for Processing an Order

1. **Learn customer intent:**
   • Buy what? (product, size, color, quantity)
   • Pay how?
   • Send where?
   • Ship how?
   • Special terms?
2. **Verify credit.**
3. **Remove from inventory:**
   • Verify quantity
   • Pick items from inventory
   • Process purchase order, and reorder as necessary
4. **Charge credit.**
5. **Pack and ship:**
   • Pack item(s)
   • Schedule shipment
   • Process special terms as needed
6. **Record transaction for accounting, marketing, and service.**
7. **Provide customer service as needed.**

store sufficient data about this order so that REI can provide you customer support in case of a problem.

That's quite a bit of work, but there's more to it than you might imagine. For one, suppose that you do not provide all the necessary data, or that you provide inconsistent data, or that you make a keying mistake. Maybe you intend to order 10 pairs of shoes for you and your 9 best friends, but accidentally key 100. Should the Web site just accept that number? Or should the site be smart enough to realize that ordering 100 pairs of the same shoes is highly unusual and ask someone to verify your order?

Further, what happens if the items you want are not available in inventory? Or what if only some of them are? Also, should the information system reorder to restock the inventory if the quantity left after your order falls below a certain level? In spring, the company may want to reorder summer shoe, but by fall it may not. How is all of that to be handled?

Notice that this information system crosses departmental boundaries. It involves all the primary value chain activities, as well as accounting. Each of those functions has different goals and objectives. Accounting worries about complying with accounting rules, for example, whereas operations worries about inventory turnover, and marketing worries about sales trends.

In addition, this system not only crosses department boundaries at REI, it extends to include other companies. A financial institution handles the credit card operations: REI's information system contacts information systems at the credit card company to verify your credit and to charge your account. It also interacts with the information systems at the shipper to schedule your shipment. Finally, if there is a problem, customer service will need data about both REI processing and that of the credit card company and the shipper.

We've described considerable complexity, but there is another factor that redoubles the problems: *Nothing stays the same*. REI may buy another business, open new warehouses (maybe internationally), change its inventory-management policy, set up special accounts and credit cards, add more shipping choices, and so on. The business processes that underlie your transaction, and the information systems that support them, must evolve with the business. They must change while never shutting down. It's like performing heart surgery on someone who is running a 100-yard dash.

Because business processes are critical, complex, and dynamic in structure, well-managed organizations practice **business process management (BPM)**. BPM is the systematic process of creating, assessing, and altering business processes. It has the four stages, as shown in Figure 7-3. The process begins by creating a model of the business process. The business users who have expertise and are involved in the

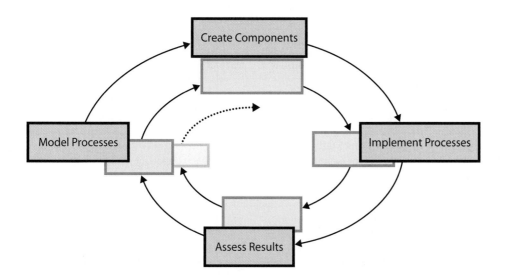

FIGURE 7-3
Stages of the BPM Cycle

particular process (this could be you!) adjust and evaluate that model. Usually teams build an **as-is model** that documents the current situation and then change that model to make adjustments necessary to solve process problems.

Given the model, the next stop is to create system components. Those components have the five elements of every information system, although some are entirely automated (no people and procedures) and some are entirely manual (no hardware or software). The organizations involved then implement the business processes needed. Well-managed organizations don't stop there. Instead, they create policy, procedures, and committees to continually assess business process effectiveness. When a need for change arises, the company models a new, adjusted business process, and the cycle repeats.

No business can avoid these activities. Every business needs business processes, and those processes will change, whether the organization wants them to or not. Thus, organizations can either plan to develop and modify business processes using BPM, or they can wait and let the need for change just happen to them. In the latter case, the business will continually be in crisis, dealing with one process failure after another. Majestic River Ventures is an example of such a company. As you might guess from the dialog at the beginning of the chapter, Majestic has never thought about business processes *per se*; it just let them evolve. The company has no program for assessing its business processes, and failures frequently occur. Mr. Butterworth's missing tent is one such failure.

Q2 How Does BPM Vary in Scope?

The nature and difficulty of business process management varies with the scope of the business process. As summarized in Figure 7-4, some processes reside entirely within a single business function. Some cross departmental boundaries, and some cross organizational boundaries. Consider each.

Functional Processes

Functional processes involve activities within a single department or function. Examples are accounting, human resources, sales forecasting, and other processes that are contained in a single department. BPM is easier to accomplish with functional processes: A single department manager has authority over all of the activities and the resources assigned to them. If the department decides to change a business process, the change and attendant problems are localized within that manager's authority.

FIGURE 7-4
Scope of Business Process
Management

Scope	Description	Example	BPM Role
Functional	Business process resides within a single business function.	Accounts payable	BPM authority belongs to a single departmental manager who has authority to resolve BPM issues.
Cross-functional	Business process crosses into multiple departments within a single company.	Customer relationship management (CRM) Enterprise resource management (ERP)	BPM authority shared across several or many departments. Problem resolution via committee and policy.
Interorganizational	Business process crosses into multiple companies.	Supply chain management (SCM)	BPM authority shared by multiple companies. Problem resolution via negotiation and contract.

The problem with functional processes is their isolation. Functional processes lead to **islands of automation** because they work independently of one another. Unfortunately, independent, isolated processes cannot produce the productivity and efficiency necessary for many businesses. Purchasing influences inventory, which influences production, which influences customer satisfaction, which influences future sales. Decisions that are appropriate when considering only a single function like purchasing may create inefficiencies when the entire process is considered.

Cross-Functional Processes

As the name implies, **cross-functional processes** involve activities among several, or even many, business departments. A classic example is the **customer relationship management (CRM)** process, which involves the activities of various departments, such as sales, marketing, operations, and customer support. Cross-functional processes eliminate or at least drastically reduce the problems of isolated systems and data. For example, before an important sales call, salespeople can use a CRM system to learn if the customer has any outstanding issues or problems in customer support. Or, customer support can know which customers have high volume and thus justify high levels of support. Such integration is not possible with functional processes.

Process management is more difficult for cross-functional systems because no manager has authority over all of the activities and the resources assigned to them. (OK, the CEO or president has authority over all the activities, but it would be silly to tie up the CEO's time with most process management decisions. The CEO is likely to say, "That's what we pay you to do.") So, BPM for cross-functional processes is shared across several departments that most frequently need to resolve conflict via committee and policy.

Interorganizational Processes

Some business processes cross not only departmental boundaries, but organizational boundaries as well. The order-processing example at REI is an **interorganizational process**. It includes activities at REI of course, but it also includes activities at the company that processes your credit card transactions and activities at the shipper. Supply chain management (SCM) processes involve even greater organizational integration. In some cases, the SCM company will have information systems that directly access processes in your own company.

As you might imagine, BPM for interorganizational processes is much more difficult than for functional or cross-functional systems. Not only are different managers involved, but different owners are involved as well. Problem resolution occurs via negotiation, contracts, and (shudder) even litigation.

By the way, do not assume that business process management applies only to commercial, profit-making organizations. Nonprofit and government organizations have all three types of processes, but most are service-oriented, rather than revenue-oriented. Your state's Department of Labor, for example, has a need to manage its processes, as does the Girl Scouts of America. BPM applies to all types of organizations.

Sometimes interorganizational processes and information systems can result in deceptive practices, as described in the *Ethics Guide* on pages 166–167.

Q3 How Does Business Process Modeling Notation (BPMN) Document Business Processes?

A key task for business process management is to document models of business processes. Both the as-is model and the models that incorporate business change need to be documented. In this section, you will learn standard notation for creating

Dialing for Dollars

Suppose you are a salesperson, and your company's sales forecasting system predicts that your quarterly sales will be substantially under quota. You call your best customers to increase sales, but no one is willing to buy more.

Your boss says that it has been a bad quarter for all of the salespeople. It's so bad, in fact, that the vice president of sales has authorized a 20-percent discount on new orders. The only stipulation is that customers must take delivery prior to the end of the quarter so that accounting can book the order. "Start dialing for dollars," she says, "and get what you can. Be creative."

Using your customer management system, you identify your top customers and present the discount offer to them. The first customer balks at increasing her inventory, "I just don't think we can sell that much."

"Well," you respond, "how about if we agree to take back any inventory you don't sell next quarter?" (By doing this, you increase your current sales and commission, and you also help your company make its quarterly sales projections. The additional product is likely to come back next quarter, but you think, "Hey, that's then and this is now.")

"OK," she says, "but I want you to stipulate the return option on the purchase order."

You know that you cannot write that on the purchase order because accounting won't book all of the order if you do. So you tell her that you'll send her an email with that stipulation. She increases her order, and accounting books the full amount.

With another customer, you try a second strategy. Instead of offering the discount, you offer the product at full price, but agree to pay a 20-percent credit in the next quarter. That way you can book the full price now. You pitch this offer as follows: "Our marketing department analyzed past sales using our fancy new computer system, and we know that increasing advertising will cause additional sales. So, if you order more product now, next quarter we'll give you 20 percent of the order back to pay for advertising."

In truth, you doubt the customer will spend the money on advertising. Instead, they'll just take the credit and sit on a bigger inventory. That will kill your sales to them next quarter, but you'll solve that problem then.

Even with these additional orders, you're still under quota. In desperation, you decide to sell product to a fictitious company that is "owned" by your brother-in-law. You set up a new account, and when accounting calls your brother-in-law for a credit check, he cooperates with your scheme. You then sell $40,000 of product to the fictitious company and ship the product to your brother-in-law's garage. Accounting books the revenue in the quarter, and you have finally made quota. A week into the next quarter, your brother-in-law returns the merchandise.

Meanwhile, unknown to you, your company's manufacturing system is scheduling production. The program that creates the production schedule reads the sales from your activities (and those of the other salespeople) and finds a sharp increase in product demand. Accordingly, it generates a schedule that calls for substantial production increases and schedules workers for the production runs. The production system, in turn, schedules the material requirements with the inventory application, which increases raw materials purchases to meet the increased production schedule.

DISCUSSION QUESTIONS

1. Is it ethical for you to write the email agreeing to take the product back? If that email comes to light later, what do you think your boss will say?

2. Is it ethical for you to offer the "advertising" discount? What effect does that discount have on your company's balance sheet?

3. Is it ethical for you to ship to the fictitious company? Is it legal?

4. Describe the impact of your activities on next quarter's inventories.

process documentation. However, the interorganizational process at REI is far too complex for our purposes. We could devote this entire book to describing that business process and still not discuss all of it. Instead, we will focus on the simpler, more easily understood example of Majestic River Ventures.

Need for Standard for Business Processing Notation

In Chapter 2, you learned that a business process is a network of activities, resources, facilities, and data that interact to achieve a function or purpose. To recap, an activity is a task to be performed; resources are people or equipment that can be assigned to activities; facilities are collections of resources. For example, a database is a facility that collects data (and more, as explained in Chapter 5), and a warehouse is a facility that collects inventory items. Finally, data is recorded facts and figures. Data can be simple, like the name of an employee, or structured, like a customer order document.

This definition of business process is commonly accepted, but unfortunately dozens of other definitions are used by other authors, industry analysts, and software products. For example, IBM, a key leader in business process management, has a product called WebSphere Business Modeler that uses a different set of terms. It has activities and resources, but it uses the term *repository* for *facility* and the term *business item* for *data.* Other business-modeling software products use other definitions and terms. These differences and inconsistencies can be problematic, especially when two different organizations with two different sets of definitions must work together.

Accordingly, a software-industry standards organization called the **Object Management Group (OMG)** created a standard set of terms and graphical notations for documenting business processes. That standard, called **Business Process Modeling Notation (BPMN)**, is documented at *www.bpmn.org.* A complete description of BPMN is beyond the scope of this text. However, the basic symbols are easy to understand, and they work naturally with our definition of business process. Hence, we will use the BPMN symbols in the illustrations in the chapter. Be aware, however, that the companies you work for may use a different set of terms and symbols. The essence of the ideas you learn here will help you, however, regardless of the tools, symbols, and terms your company uses.

Documenting the As-Is Business Processes at MRV

Figure 7-5 shows a BPMN process diagram of the top-level business process at the river rafting company. Each of the rectangles with rounded corners represents an activity. The plus sign at the bottom of the *Assemble and Ship Equipment* activity

FIGURE 7-5
Top-Level Business Processes for Majestic River Ventures

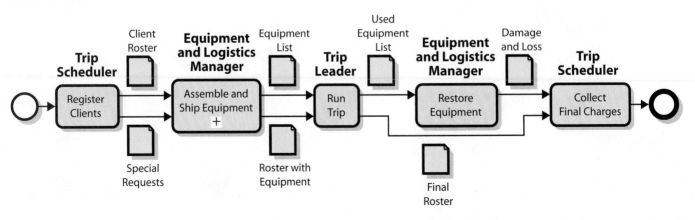

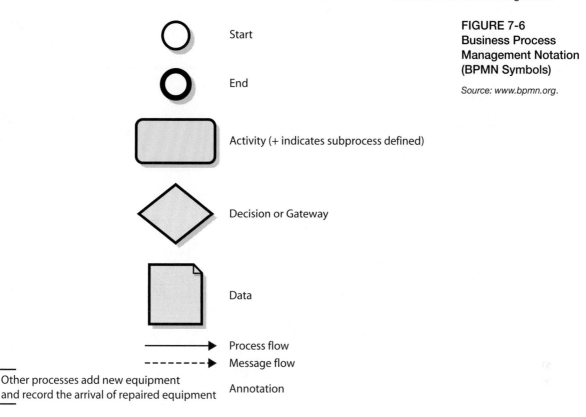

FIGURE 7-6
Business Process
Management Notation
(BPMN Symbols)

Source: www.bpmn.org.

indicates that it contains a subprocess (discussed next). The rectangles with the right top corner cut off represent data. The solid arrows document process flow; data often accompanies process flows, but this is not required. The thin-lined circle represents the start of the process, and the heavy-lined circle represents the end. The labels on the top of each activity are resources. The Trip Scheduler resource is assigned to the Register Clients activity, for example.

Figure 7-6 summarizes the BPMN process symbols that we will use in this text.

We can interpret Figure 7-5 as follows: The river-rafting process begins with the *Trip Scheduler* resource performing the *Register Clients* activity. That process generates *Client Roster* and *Special Requests* data. Those data items flow to a second activity called *Assemble & Ship Equipment* (with a subprocess indicated by the + in the activity symbol). *Assemble & Ship* generates the *Equip List* and *Roster & Equip* data as output, and so forth. Notice that the *Final Roster* data, created by *Run Trip,* skips *Restore Equipment* and is sent directly to the *Collect Final Charges* activity.

At Majestic, the first and last processes are performed by someone acting as the trip scheduler. The second and fourth processes are performed by someone acting as the equipment and logistics manager, and the *Run Trip* process is managed by a trip leader. We can show these assignments by depicting the diagram in what is called a **swim-lane layout**, as illustrated in Figure 7-7. Like swim lanes in a swimming pool, each role is shown in its own horizontal rectangle. Swim-lane layout can be used to simplify process diagrams and to draw attention to interactions among components of the diagram.

The *Assemble & Ship Equipment* Process

Figure 7-8 shows the subprocess within the *Assemble & Ship Equipment* process. Notice that the inputs to this process (*Client Roster* and *Special Requests*) and the outputs from this process (*Equip List* and *Roster w/Equip*) are the same as the inputs and outputs for the *Assemble & Ship Equipment* activity in the higher-level diagrams in Figures 7-5 and 7-7. Also, the resources assigned are the same.

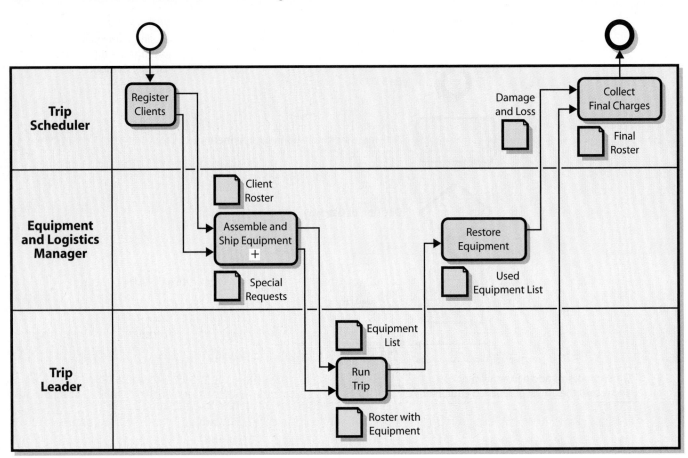

FIGURE 7-7
Business Process with
Three Swim Lanes

This process consists of two parallel flows. Either of the parallel flows can be done before the other, they can be done simultaneously, or some other arrangement can be used (say, do part of one and then do part of another). The diagram does not stipulate any order. The top flow concerns the picking of regular trip equipment from inventory, and the bottom one concerns the picking of special equipment. Notice that if there is a problem with regular equipment (missing an oar, for example), the trip leader is to be contacted. He or she can decide how to deal with the problem. However, if there is a problem with special requests, the trip scheduler is contacted. (He or she may contact the client; we cannot tell that from Figure 7-8, however.) As indicated in Figure 7-6, the dashed-line arrow represents the flow of messages and not of process.

The diagrams shown in Figures 7-5, 7-7, and 7-8 are examples of as-is diagrams. They represent the modelers' best representation of the current processes used by Majestic. If you examine these diagrams, especially that in Figure 7-8, you can begin to see what may have caused the missing-tent problem at the start of the chapter. The diagram indicates that if there is missing special equipment, the logistics manager is to notify the trip scheduler, but take no other action. According to the diagram, the logistics manager makes the notification and then proceeds to *Ship*.

We do not know what the trip scheduler does with the notification. In fact, in this diagram, we do not even know *if* the trip scheduler received the notification. This particular pattern is sometimes called **fire-and-forget**. That is, the activity sends the message ("fires" it) and then forgets about it. Such a pattern is appropriate in some circumstances, but probably not in this one. You will have a chance to think about this matter in the Using Your Knowledge exercises.

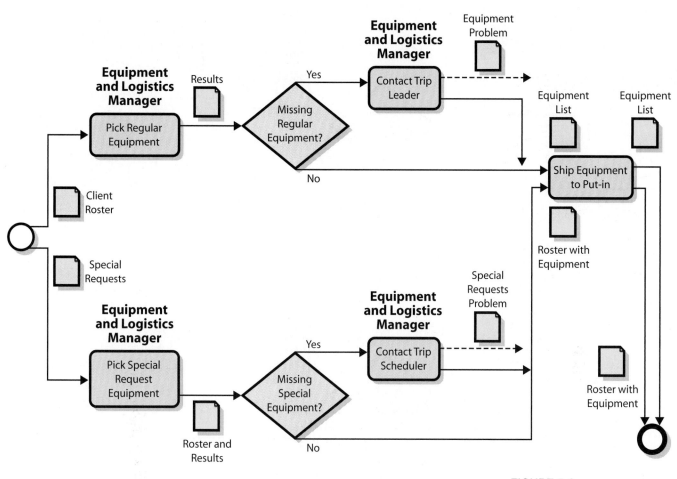

FIGURE 7-8
Business Process Within the
Assemble & Ship Equipment
Process

Q4 How Does the Interaction of Business Process Elements Affect Cost and Added Value?

Process designers can increase the performance of a business process in three fundamental ways. First, they can add more resources to a given process without changing its structure. This is the *brute-force approach:* add more people or equipment to the existing way of doing business. Second, designers can change the *structure* of a process without changing resource allocations. If the change is particularly effective, it can result in greater performance at no additional cost. It does require people to change the way they do things, which can be a difficult transition to make, however. Finally, designers can do both.

Changing a Process by Adding Resources

Figure 7-9 illustrates the first response. Here, a specialist as been added to each of the activities in the process. It is possible that one person would perform all four roles, but in that case the process is essentially unchanged from that in Figure 7-8. Assume instead that Majestic hires someone to perform each of the roles for the activities in Figure 7-9. This change will result in substantially increased cost. Is it worthwhile? According to Porter's model, one should add cost to a value chain (here, the business process) *if the change generates value greater than its cost.* That is clear and sensible, but it's a bit like the investment advice to "buy low and sell high." Great, but how do you do it? Some businesses use computer simulations to assess the impact of resource-allocation changes. Other businesses perform other types of financial analysis to determine if the changes are worth the cost.

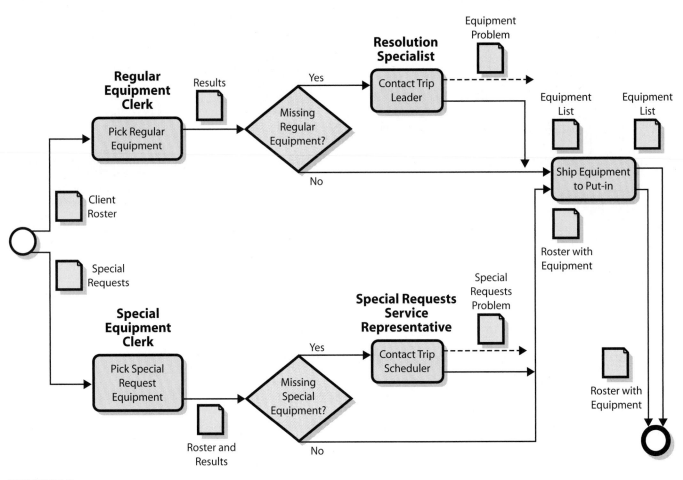

FIGURE 7-9
Modified Allocations in the
Assemble & Ship Equipment
Process

The resources that are added to a process need not necessarily be humans. Information systems can play a role as well. In Figure 7-9, the contact trip leader or contact trip scheduler activities could be automated. We will explore such possibilities further in Q5.

Changing a Process by Altering Process Structure

A second way of altering a business process is to change its structure. Suppose the equipment and logistics manager at Majestic River Ventures notices that he is wasting time repeating steps when he picks the regular equipment and then picks the special equipment. He goes to an upper floor of the warehouse, finds regular equipment, and then later goes back to that same floor to pick special equipment. Given this inefficiency, process designers could decide to alter the process, as shown in Figure 7-10. Here, the equipment and logistics manager first creates an *integrated* picking list. He organizes the list so as to minimize his travel through the warehouse. This change enables him to pick equipment more quickly and allows him more time to follow up on problem messages that he sends to trip leaders and trip schedulers. In fact, such a change could be one way to eliminate problems like the missing tent. As with resource changes, businesses can investigate the impact of process-structure changes using simulation or other types of analyses.

Also, as stated, a third alternative is a combination of adding (or reducing) resources and changing the process. In fact, the goal of some business process

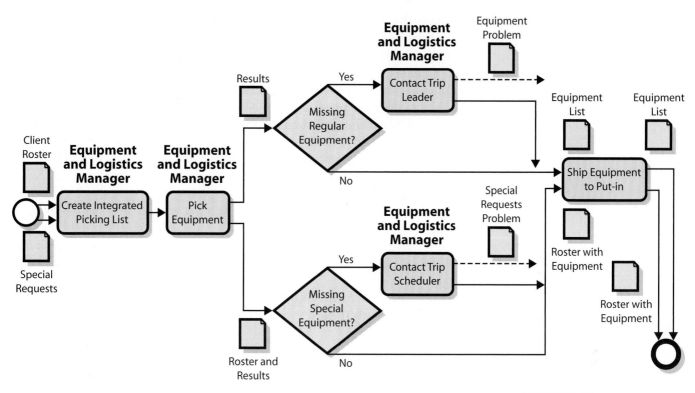

FIGURE 7-10
Modified Activities in the
Assemble & Ship Equipment
Process

changes is to enable the organization to reduce resources required to obtain the same result. Changing both resources and process structure is obviously more complicated and has greater potential, but will cause the organization more turmoil, and hence will be more difficult to implement.

Q5 What Role Do Information Systems Play in Business Processes?

As you can tell, business processes are important to organizations, and you will devote considerable time to such processes in your operations management courses. You might be wondering why we are addressing such processes here, in your MIS class. Today, information systems are playing an increasingly important role in the implementation of business processes. Think again about the tasks that need to be performed just to sell you equipment from REI (Figure 7-2), and you will realize that most of those tasks have an IS component. In December 2005, Amazon.com processed over 41 order items per second for 24 hours, an impossible feat without information systems.

What role do information systems play in business processes? They implement business process activities. Some of those information systems are entirely manual (they have data, procedures, and people components); some are entirely automated (they have hardware, software, and data components); and some are a mixture, having all five components of an information system—hardware, software, data, procedures, and people. Consider the following two examples.

IS Alternatives for Implementing the *Register Clients* Activity

Consider the first task in the raft-trip business process, *Register Clients*. It is possible to accomplish this activity entirely with human resources, with a system that is a balance of human and computer resources, or with a system that is totally computer-based.

In the first case, the trip scheduler (one or more humans) collects data from clients, determines trip availability, and collects reservation deposits and payments. When it is time to assemble and ship the equipment, the trip scheduler uses a word processing program to prepare documents detailing the client roster and special requests lists.

Another alternative is to use a spreadsheet or database application to record clients and their special requests and prepare the client roster and special requests lists. For this alternative, the trip scheduler manually collects data from clients, determines trip availability, and collects reservation deposits and trip payments. Once the roster is set, the spreadsheet or database application produces the roster and special equipment outputs. Having the automated system create those outputs will save considerable labor and reduce errors.

Finally, it is possible to create an entirely automated *Register Client* system. In this case, clients contact Majestic via the Internet and use a Web site to register for a trip. They enter credit card information for deposits and trip payments on that site and record any special requests. The automated system prepares the client roster and special requests outputs.

In all three alternatives, the *Register Clients* activity is performed by an information system. However, only the last two are computer-based information systems.

Information Systems for Facilitating Linkages Among Activities

Information systems, and database information systems in particular, can play an important role in implementing activities that link other activities. To see why, consider the missing-tent problem. Mr. Butterworth requested and paid for a private tent. His request and payment were processed by the *Register Clients* activity. However, no such tent was available in inventory, and the equipment and logistics manager was supposed to notify the trip scheduler, who was supposed to notify the client. However, this did not happen. It turns out that the tent did exist, but it had been

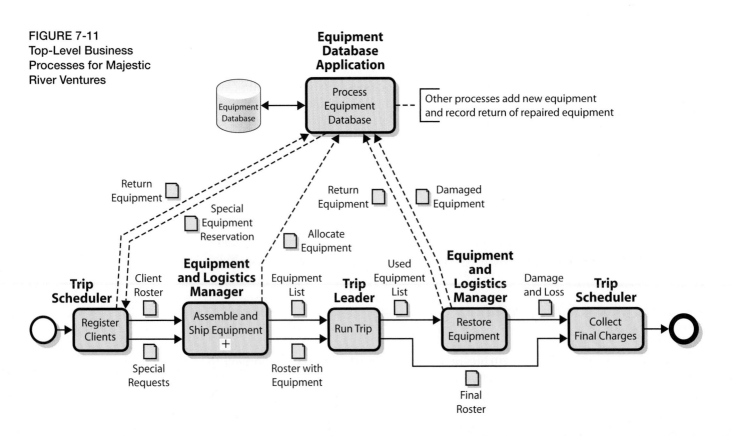

FIGURE 7-11
Top-Level Business
Processes for Majestic
River Ventures

damaged in a prior trip and was sent out for repair. The trip scheduler did not know it was under repair and allocated it to Mr. Butterworth. Notice the linkages about equipment among the *Register Clients, Assemble & Ship Equipment,* and *Restore Equipment* activities.

One solution to this problem is to create a database application to track equipment, its location, and its status. Figure 7-11 shows a new activity, *Process Equipment Database,* which processes updates to the database from *Register Clients, Assemble & Ship Equipment,* and *Restore Equipment* activities. The trip scheduler can use this activity to reserve special equipment and be notified when such equipment is not available. Such an information system implements an activity that provides linkages among several other business process activities. In Figure 7-11, the resource named *Equipment Database Application* is assigned to the *Process Equipment Database* activity. This resource is a computer program running on a server and is entirely automated.

These two examples show some of the possibilities for implementing business activities with information systems. As the price performance ratio of computers, storage, and communications continues to plummet, you can expect greater and greater use of information systems in business processes. During your career, you will also see more and more business processes redesigned to take advantage of information systems and cheaper, more powerful computer networks and communications.

Q6 What Are the Advantages of the Service-Oriented Architecture (SOA)?

There are many ways of implementing information systems that support business process activities. Some ways are easier, some are cheaper, some are easier to maintain. Over time, information systems developers studied best-of-practice techniques and from these developed a design philosophy known as **service-oriented architecture (SOA)**. SOA was originally used to design interacting computer programs. More recently, systems designers have applied SOA principles to business process activities, whether those activities are manual, partly automated, or fully automated.

A **service** is a repeatable task that a business needs to perform. At Majestic, the following are examples of services:

- Check space available on a river trip.
- Enroll client on a river trip.
- Bill client's credit card.

In service-oriented architecture, each activity is modeled as a service and the interactions among the services are governed by standard techniques. Consider the two parts of this definition.

Activities Modeled as Services

The examples so far in this chapter have been based on SOA, so it may be hard to understand why SOA is advantageous. Consider the process in Figure 7-12, which is definitely not designed with SOA principles. The client requests a private tent, and the trip scheduler then attempts to compute how many tents there are, how many are needed, and how many are in repair. Given that computation, the trip scheduler responds "Yes" or "No."

Consider some of the problems of this process. First, the circles are people (resources), not services. From the diagram, we must guess or infer what it is the trip

FIGURE 7-12
Non–SOA Business
Process

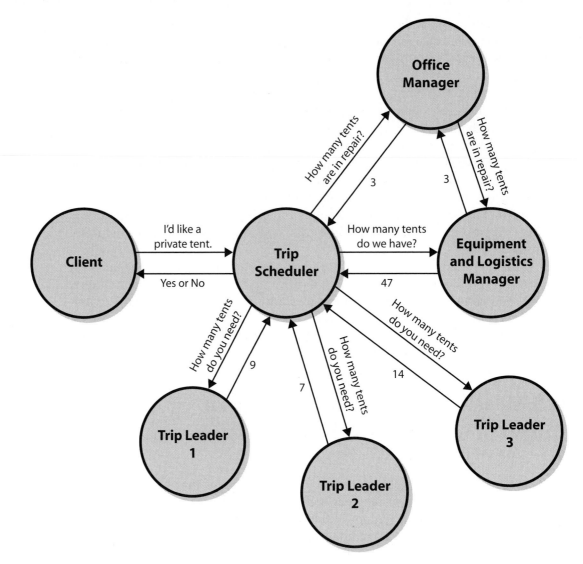

FIGURE 7-12
Non–SOA Business
Process

scheduler is trying to do. Also, if it turns out that Majestic wants to add more resources to answer tent-availability questions, how would it do so? Add another set of symbols for a second trip scheduler? That would be awkward, at best.

Additionally, data about the tent requirements is spread all over the company. In fact, the trip scheduler doesn't know where some of the data is located. He asks the office manager how many tents are out for repair, and the office manager, in turn, asks the equipment and logistics manager. This process is inefficient and error-prone. The design has many other problems as well. What happens when Majestic hires more trip leaders? Or what if one of the trip leaders wants to know if she can borrow a tent for personal use for the weekend? Majestic allows employees to borrow certain equipment, but only if it is not needed. That trip leader will have to duplicate this process to find out if a tent is available.

If Majestic decides to create an information system for this process, what does that information system do? It certainly does not replace any of the blue circles. In fact, to proceed, the designers of the information system must interpret this diagram to infer that there is some computation going on and somehow develop an information system to make that computation. Behind the scenes, or in the creases of this diagram, there is an inventory-management service. But that service is inferred, not modeled. Furthermore, what happens if Majestic changes inventory policy? Suppose it decides to lease tents when necessary. Such a change will have an impact in many places in this diagram and an impact on any information system developed in an attempt to support this process.

Contrast the impact of a change in policy on the SOA business process shown in Figure 7-11. If Majestic decides to lease equipment, all that is needed is to add a new activity (service) *Lease Equipment*. That activity would use the *Process Equipment Database* service to indicate the availability of leased equipment. No other service is affected. Also, if a trip leader wants to know if he or she can borrow a tent for the weekend, he or she can get the availability data directly from the *Process Equipment Database* service.

So, now you understand the first part of the definition of SOA: All activities must be modeled as services (repeatable business tasks). Because all activities are services, we can use the terms *activity* and *service* interchangeably.

BPMN and the idea of modeling activity as services can be applied to the design of business processes, regardless of whether those processes will be supported by information systems. To learn more and to practice these ideas, read *MIS in Use 7*.

Service Interactions Governed by Standards

Now consider the second requirement for SOA: All interactions among services must be governed by standards. Consider Figure 7-13, which shows the interactions of two services. The *Process Credit Order* service is part of a business process called *Ordering Process*. *Authorize Credit* is a second service that is part of a different business process called *Credit Authorization Process*. Each process (and service) is independent; neither is aware of how the other does its work, and neither needs to know. Instead, these services need only to agree on how they will exchange data and what that exchange means.

Process Credit Order sends customer credit data to the *Authorize Credit* service. It receives back a credit authorization that contains an approval or rejection and other data. The *Credit Authorization Process* could involve flipping a coin, throwing darts, or performing some sophisticated data mining analysis on the customer's data. *Process Credit Order* does not know, nor does it need to know, how that authorization is made.

When the logic for some service is isolated in this way, the logic is said to be **encapsulated** in the service. **Encapsulation** places the logic in one place, which is desirable; all other services go to that one place for that service. Even more important, if the managers of the credit department decide to change how they make credit authorizations, the *Process Credit Order* activity is not affected. As long as the structure and meaning of customer credit data and credit authorization data do not change, *Process Credit Order* is completely isolated from changes in *Authorize Credit* or any other service in the *Credit Authorization Process*.

Because of encapsulation, it does not matter who performs the services or where they are performed. They could be done by the same department on the same computer. Or, they could be located on computers in different companies and in different parts of the world.

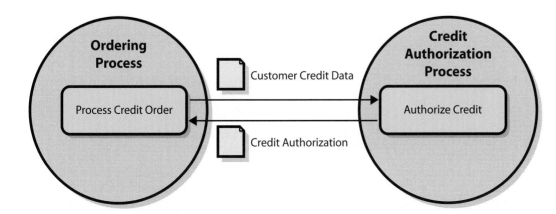

FIGURE 7-13
Example of Two Independent, Encapsulated Services

7 The County Planning Office

The county planning office issues building permits, septic system permits, and county road access permits for all building projects county in an eastern state. The planning office issues permits to homeowners and builders for the construction of new homes and buildings and for any remodeling projects that involve electrical, gas, plumbing, and other utilities, as well as the conversion of unoccupied spaces such as garages into living or working space. The office also issues permits for new or upgraded septic systems and permits to provide driveway entrances to county roads.

Figure 1 shows the permit process that the county used for many years. Contractors and homeowners found this process to be slow and very frustrating. For one, they did not like its sequential nature. Only after a permit had been approved or rejected by engineering review process would they find out that a health or highway review was also needed. Because each of these reviews could take 3 or 4 weeks, applicants requesting permits wanted the review processes to be concurrent rather than serial. Also, both the permit applicants and county personnel were

FIGURE 1
Sequential Permit-Review Process

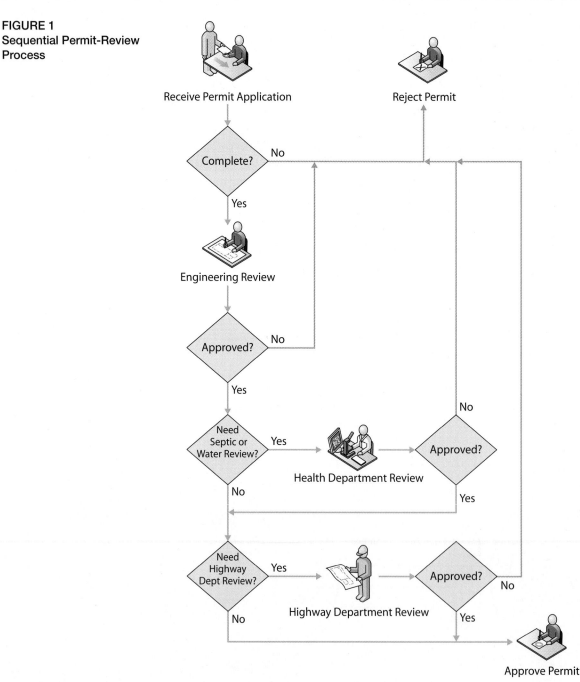

frustrated because they never knew where a particular application was in the permit process. A contractor would call to ask how much longer, and it might take an hour or more just to find which desk the permits were on.

Accordingly, the county changed the permit process to that shown in Figure 2. In this second process, the permit office made three copies of the permit and distributed one to each department. The departments reviewed the permits in parallel; a clerk would analyze the results and, if there were no rejections, approve the permit.

Unfortunately, this process had a number of problems, too. For one, some of the permit applications were lengthy; some included as many as 40 to 50 pages of large architectural drawings. The labor and copy expense to the county was considerable.

Second, in some cases departments reviewed documents unnecessarily. If, for example, the highway department rejected an application, then neither the engineering nor health departments needed to continue their reviews. At first, the county responded to this problem by

having the clerk who analyzed results cancel the reviews of other departments when he or she received a rejection. However, that policy was exceedingly unpopular with the permit applicants, because once an application was rejected and the problem corrected, the permit had to go back through the other departments. The permit would go to the end of the line and work its way back into the departments from which it had been pulled. Sometimes this resulted in a delay of 5 or 6 weeks.

Canceling reviews was unpopular with the departments as well, because permit-review work had to be repeated. An application might have been nearly completed when it was cancelled due to a rejection in another department. When the application came through again, the partial work results from the earlier review were lost.

These diagrams are not shown using the BPMN standard nor do they use SOA. *You and a group of students will have a chance to convert them to BPMN in SOA in Collaboration Exercise 7, on page 186. You will also have a chance there to propose a process solution.*

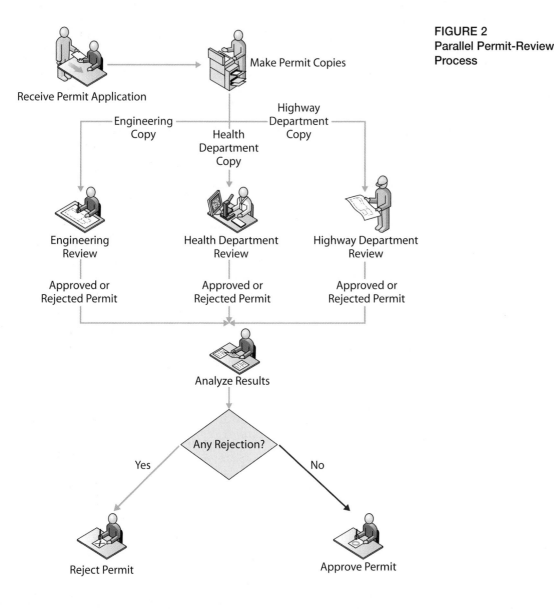

FIGURE 2
Parallel Permit-Review Process

To communicate, the two services must agree on the structure of the data that they will exchange and on a protocol for making that data exchange. In the past, the programmers of the *Process Credit Order* program would meet with the programmers of the *Authorize Credit* program and design a unique, proprietary means for exchanging data via this interface. Such a design is expensive and time-consuming. Consequently, the computer industry developed standard ways for describing services and data and developed protocols for managing the exchanges among services. Those standards dramatically reduced the need for proprietary designs and in the process greatly expanded the scope and importance of SOA. We consider three of those standards next.

Q7 Why Are XML and Other SOA Standards Important?

Quite a number of standards have been developed for SOA, but the most important of them, and the ones you should be able to recognize, are XML, SOAP, and WSDL. In fact, XML is important for many reasons beyond SOA; Bill Gates once called XML "the *lingua franca*" of the Internet. Here we will discuss just a few of the important features of XML.

eXtensible Markup Language (XML)

XML, which stands for the eXtensible Markup Language, is used to model and structure data. Consider, for example, the customer credit data in Figure 7-13. XML can provide structure to that data so that the *Process Credit Order* and *Authorize Credit* services can use the data without confusion. For example, suppose that the data is to contain a customer name, an account number, and the amount of credit that is requested. Such data can be encoded in XML as follows:

```
<CustomerCreditData>
<CustomerName>Ajax Landscaping</CustomerName>
<AccountNumber>124345</AccountNumber>
<AmountRequested>$1588</AmountRequested>
</CustomerCreditData>
```

XML includes **tags**, which are metadata that name and identify data items. Tags are enclosed in matching chevrons < >. For example, the tag <CustomerName> specifies that a value for customer name is about to be provided. The end of the *Customer Name* data is signified by a closing tag that starts with the virgule /. Hence, </CustomerName> closes the *CustomerName* data. Notice in this XML coding that *CustomerCreditData* starts in the first line and is closed in the last. This signifies that *CustomerCreditData* consists of the entire group of items. A set of XML tags and data is referred to as an **XML document**.

XML has many important features, most of which are beyond the scope of this text. You should know, however, that the purpose of some XML documents is to describe the structure of other XML documents. In particular, an **XML schema** is an XML document whose content describes the structure of other XML documents. An XML schema document for the *CustomerCreditData* above would indicate that the *CustomerCreditData* consists of *CustomerName, AccountNumber,* and *AmountRequested* data, in that order.

The importance of a schema document is that any program (or human, for that matter) can read the schema to determine the structure of an XML document for processing. For example, the services in Figure 7-13 would read the *CustomerCreditData* schema before creating, reading, or modifying any of the *CustomerCreditData*. The schema document tells those programs how to structure and interpret the data.

XML is important for SOA because it enables programs to share data in a standardized way. As long as all services create and maintain XML data in conformance with that data's schema, XML data can be passed from one service to another without problem.

The SOAP and WSDL Standards

Two other standards are important for service-oriented architecture. **SOAP** (which, oddly enough, is not an acronym) is a protocol for exchanging messages encoded in XML. When the ordering process in Figure 7-13 sends customer credit data to the *Authorize Credit* service, it formats the data in accordance with the XML schema for *Customer Credit Data* and then sends that data as a message using SOAP. SOAP sits on top of the transport protocol and can use any available protocol. SOAP messages can be exchanged using HTTP, HTTPS, FTP, or other transport protocol.

A SOAP message can include metadata that specifies how the message is to be routed, what services need to process it, how security and encryption are to be handled, and so forth. SOAP is independent of any device, network, vendor, or product. By the way, while SOAP is commonly used, other messaging protocols also exist.[1]

The last important SOA standard that you should know about is the **Web Services Description Language (WSDL)**. To understand the need for WSDL, suppose you are a computer programmer assigned the task of writing a program to implement the *Process Credit Order* service in Figure 7-13. You know that you want to use the *Authorize Credit* service, but you do not know how to do that. Suppose that *Authorize Credit* provides five different features about five different aspects of credit. As a computer programmer, how do you learn how to interface with those features?

The answer is WSDL. To expose a service or services to the world, the designer of the service creates a WSDL document that describes, in a standard way, the particular features that the service provides and the data that need to be sent or that will be returned from the service. Microsoft, IBM, and other interested companies create developer tools for creating SOA service programs. Those developer tools are created to read a service's WSDL and to provide seamless integration with that service to the programmer. Additionally, when you, as a programmer, create a service, those developer tools will write the WSDL for your service for you.

In short, WSDL is a language that services can use to describe what they do and how other computer programs can access their features. To understand this more deeply, you need to know quite a bit about computer programming.

The bottom line is that XML, SOAP, and WSDL eliminate the need for proprietary SOA services designs and make it much easier for programs to interact with one another, whether on the same machine, the same network, or just somewhere off in the cloud. Figure 7-14 summarizes the key features of these three important SOA standards.

SOA represents the latest thinking for business process design, although some might treat it as a passing fad, like the individual in the *Guide* on page 182–183.

FIGURE 7-14
Important SOA Standards

Standard	Purpose	Remarks
XML (eXtensible Markup Language)	Provide structure to data exchanges among SOA services. Schema documents used to ensure documents comply with defined data structures.	*Lingua franca* of the Internet. Very important. No significant challengers for SOA.
SOAP	A protocol for message exchange. Sits on top of transport protocols such a as HTTP, HTTPS, and FTP. Allows for description of message routing, processing, security, and encryption.	Other protocols, such as REST, are also used.
WSDL (Web Services Description Language)	Languages for describing the programmatic interface to a service. Makes service-to-service programming much easier.	Microsoft, IBM, and others build WSDL into their programming development tools.

[1]Another messaging protocol called *REST* (Representational State Transfer) is also very popular. We will not discuss REST here, however.

The Flavor-of-the-Month Club

"**O**h, come on. I've been here 30 years and I've heard it all. All these management programs. . . . Years ago, we had Zero Defects. Then it was Total Quality Management, and after that, Six Sigma. We've had all the pet theories from every consultant in the Western Hemisphere. No, wait, we had consultants from Asia, too.

"Do you know what flavor we're having now? We're redesigning ourselves to be 'customer-centric.' We are going to integrate our functional systems into a CRM system to transform the entire company to be 'customer-centric.'

"You know how these programs go? First, we have a pronouncement at a 'kick-off meeting' where the CEO tells us what the new flavor is going to be and why it's so important. Then a swarm of consultants and 'change management' experts tell us how they're going to 'empower' us. Then HR adds some new item to our annual review, such as, 'Measures taken to achieve customer-centric company.'

"So, we all figure out some lame thing to do so that we have something to put in that category of our annual review. Then we forget about it because we know the next new flavor of the month will be along soon. Or worse, if they actually force us to use the new system, we comply, but viciously. You know, go out of our way to show that the new system can't work, that it really screws things up.

"You think I sound bitter, but I've seen this so many times before. The consultants and rising stars

in our company get together and dream up one of these programs. Then they present it to the senior managers. That's when they make their first mistake: They think that if they can sell it to management, then it must be a good idea. They treat senior management like the customer. They should have to sell the idea to those of us who actually sell, support, or make things. Senior management is just the banker; the managers should let us decide if it's a good idea.

"If someone really wanted to empower me, she would listen rather than talk. Those of us who do the work have hundreds of ideas of how to do it better. Now it's customer-centric? As if we haven't been trying to do that for years!

"Anyway, after the CEO issues the pronouncements about the new system, he gets busy with other things and forgets about it for a while. Six months might go by, and then we're either told we're not doing enough to become customer-centric (or whatever the flavor is) or the company announces another new flavor.

"In manufacturing they talk about push versus pull. You know, with push style, you make things and push them onto the sales force and the customers. With pull style, you let the customers' demand pull the product out of manufacturing. You build when you have holes in inventory. Well, they should adapt those ideas to what they call 'change management.' I mean, does anybody need to manage real change? Did somebody have a 'Use the cell phone program'? Did some CEO announce, 'This year, we're all going to use the cell phone'? Did the HR department put a line into our annual evaluation form that asked how many times we'd used a cell phone? No, no, no, and no. Customers pulled the cell phone through. We wanted it, so we bought and used cell phones. Same with color printers, Palm Pilots, and wireless networks.

"That's pull. You get a group of workers to form a network, and you get things going among the people who do the work. Then you build on that to obtain true organizational change. Why don't they figure it out?

"Anyway, I've got to run. We've got the kick-off meeting of our new initiative—something called business process management. Now they're going to empower me to manage my own activities, I suppose. Like, after 30 years, I don't know how to do that. Oh, well, I plan to retire soon.

"Oh, wait. Here, take my T-shirt from the knowledge management program 2 years ago. I never wore it. It says, 'Empowering You through Knowledge Management.' That one didn't last long."

DISCUSSION QUESTIONS

1. Clearly, this person is bitter about new programs and new ideas. What do you think might have been the cause of her antagonism? What seems to be her principal concern?

2. What does she mean by "vicious" compliance? Give an example of an experience you've had that exemplifies such compliance.

3. Consider her point that the proponents of new programs treat senior managers as the customer. What does she mean? To a consultant, is senior management the customer? What do you think she's trying to say?

4. What does she mean when she says, "If someone wants to empower me, she would listen rather than talk"? How does listening to someone empower that person?

5. Her examples of "pull change" all involve the use of new products. To what extent do you think pull works for new management programs?

6. How do you think management could introduce new programs in a way that would cause them to be pulled through the organization? Consider the suggestion she makes, as well as your own ideas.

7. If you managed an employee who had an attitude like this, what could you do to make her more positive about organizational change and new programs and initiatives?

How does the knowledge in this chapter help MRV and you?

Majestic River Ventures needs business process management. It is too small a company to set up official committees, policies, and procedures for assessing its processes, but if situations like Mr. Butterworth's missing tent are common, Majestic should review its processes now. It should also be aware that process reviews will be needed again at various times in the future.

To review the processes, someone at Majestic needs to know to create as-is process documentation. Given the company's size, it may not need to strictly follow the BPMN standard, but using that standard is a good starting point. Also, an understanding of its processes will be better if Majestic creates each activity as a service.

Given the as-is documentation, the knowledge of this chapter would help Majestic pinpoint problem areas. We have seen one problem in the interaction between the equipment and logistics manager and the trip scheduler, but there might be more problems as well. MRV can examine its processes while reflecting on issues that have arisen when running past river trips.

Majestic could possibly create services that "call" other services. A good example could be services on the company's Web site that interact with social networking sites (see Chapter 8). MRV's management is not likely to create programs to implement those services, but they may hire consultants or other vendors to do it for them. Knowledge of the SOA standards will help them become better consumers of those vendors' services.

I am NOT a Happy camper.

You, of course, may work for a company that develops its own service-processing programs. Knowledge of SOA will help you be a better consumer of your company's software development staff. You also may be called upon to review process diagrams or even to help produce them.

Active ? Review

Use this Active Review to verify that you understand the material in the chapter. You can read the entire chapter and then perform the tasks in this review, or you can read the material for just one question and perform the tasks in this review for that question before moving on to the next one.

Q1 Why is business process management important to organizations? Explain the difference in perspective between your experience using computers and information systems and the experiences of a retailer like REI. Summarize each of the activities in Figure 7-2. Explain why the fact that nothing stays the same gives rise to the need for business process management. Define *BPM,* and name and briefly describe each of the four stages.

Q2 How does BPM vary in scope? Compare and contrast functional, cross-functional, and interorganizational processes. Use Figure 7-4 as a guide. Summarize the differences and challenges of BPM for each type of business process.

Q3 How does Business Process Modeling Notation (BPMN) document business processes? Define *business process,* and name the four components of a business process, according to this chapter. Explain how these definitions vary from those used by IBM's Business Process Modeler software. Describe the need for a standard. Define *BPMN.* Explain the meaning of each of the symbols in Figure 7-5. Explain the purpose and role of each of the symbols in Figure 7-6. Define swim-lane layout and explain its advantages in your own words. Explain the meaning of each of the symbols in Figure 7-8, and describe the relationship of this process diagram to that in Figure 7-5. Explain why the fire-and-forget pattern applies to Figure 7-8.

Q4 **How does the interaction of business process elements affect cost and added value?** Name three ways that process designers can increase the performance of a business process. Explain the advantages and disadvantages of each. State Porter's criterion for adding the cost of a process. Explain two ways that organizations can use to decide on whether to add the cost of a business process. Give an example, other than one in this book, of increasing process performance by changing its structure.

Q5 **What role do information systems play in business processes?** Explain why business processes are part of an MIS class. Describe the role that information systems play with regard to business processes. Using the five-component model, describe three different types of information system that are used in business processes. Use an example other than trip scheduling. Which of the three types is probably the most common at Majestic River Ventures? Explain how the process in Figure 7-11 facilitates process-activity linkages.

Q6 **What are the advantages of the service-oriented architecture (SOA)?** Define *service*, and give three examples not used in this chapter. Define *SOA*, and state and explain its two defining characteristics. Describe the problems with a process like that in Figure 7-12. Explain why Figure 7-12 does not follow SOA principles. Explain why the process in Figure 7-11 would be easier to change than that in Figure 7-12 if Majestic decides to lease equipment.

Q7 **Why are XML and other SOA standards important?** Name the three SOA standards described in this chapter and explain the purpose of each. Give an example of a four-line XML document different from the one in this chapter. If you do not know the meaning of the term *lingua franca*, learn it and explain what it means to say that XML is the *lingua franca* of the Internet. Explain the purpose and use of an XML schema document. Explain how SOAP and WSDL are used in an SOA system.

How does **the knowledge** in this chapter help **MRV** and **you?** Summarize the ways Majestic can use the knowledge from this chapter. Explain how you, too, can use this knowledge. Given your career goals, state the use that is most likely for you.

Key Terms and Concepts

Using Your Knowledge

1. In your own words, explain the characteristic of the business process in Figure 7-8 that most likely caused the missing-tent problem. Describe, in general terms, how you think Majestic's business processes should be changed to prevent such problems.

2. Modify the process shown in Figure 7-8 to conform to the process in Figure 7-11. You will need to cause the *Assemble and Ship Equipment* process to access the *Process Equipment Database* service. You can download PowerPoint diagrams of the processes in

this chapter from the book's Web site at *www.pearsonhighered.com/kroenke.*

3. Using your own experience and knowledge, create a process diagram for the *Register Clients* process shown in Figure 7-11. Your process diagram should show the next level of details of *Register Clients* in the same way that the process in Figure 7-8 shows the next level of details of *Assemble & Ship Equipment.*

4. Using your answers to questions 2 and 3, modify the process in Figure 7-8 to work with *Register Clients* so

that problems like the missing tent are either not possible or at least very unlikely. You will have to replace the fire-and-forget interaction in Figure 7-8 with some other type of interaction.

5. Describe potential management challenges when implementing the changes you propose in your answer to question 4. How would you, as a future manager, respond to those challenges?

Collaboration Exercise 7 ◎

Before you start this exercise, read Chapter Extensions 1 and 2, which describe collaboration techniques as well as tools for managing collaboration tasks. In particular, consider using Google Docs & Spreadsheets, Google Groups, Microsoft Groove, Microsoft SharePoint, or some other collaboration tool.

1. Reread *MIS in Use 7* on pages 178–179. Redraw Figure 1 so that all activities are services. Use the standard BPMN symbols.

2. Explain the problems in the business process in Figure 1.

3. Redraw Figure 2 so that all activities are services. Use the standard BPMN symbols.

4. Explain the problems in the business process in Figure 2.

5. Develop a process that solves the problems you identified in your answers to questions 2 and 4. Consider the use of information systems and information technology. Possible technologies to use are email, FTP, and Microsoft SharePoint, but you need not restrict your thinking to these technologies. Document your solution using BPMN symbols; ensure that each activity is a service.

Case Study 7

Process Cast in Stone

Bill Gates and Microsoft were exceedingly generous in the allocation of stock options to Microsoft employees, especially during Microsoft's first 20 years. Because of that generosity, Microsoft created 4 billionaires and an estimated 12,000 millionaires as Microsoft succeeded and the value of employee stock options soared. Not all of those millionaires stayed in the Seattle/Redmond/Bellevue, Washington, area, but thousands did. These thousands of millionaires were joined by a lesser number who made their millions at Amazon.com and, to a lesser extent, at RealNetworks, Visio (acquired by Microsoft), and Aldus (acquired by Adobe). Today, some Google employees who work at Google's Seattle office are joining these ranks.

The influx of this wealth had a strong impact on Seattle and the surrounding communities. One result has been the creation of a thriving industry in high-end, very expensive homes. These Microsoft and other millionaires are college educated; many were exposed to

fine arts at the university. They created homes that are not just large and situated on exceedingly valuable property, but that also are appointed with the highest-quality components.

Today, if you drive through a small area just south of central Seattle, you will find a half dozen vendors of premium granite, marble, limestone, soapstone, quartzite, and other types of stone slabs within a few blocks of each other. These materials cover counters, bathrooms, and other surfaces in the new and remodeled homes of this millionaire class. The stone is quarried in Brazil, India, Italy, Turkey, and other countries and either cut at its origin or sent to Italy for cutting. Huge cut slabs, 6 feet by 10 feet, arrive at the stone vendors in south Seattle, who stock them in their warehouses. The stone slabs vary not only in material, but also in color, veining pattern, and overall beauty. Choosing these slabs is like selecting fine art. (Visit *www.pentalonline.com* or *www.metamarble.com* to understand the premium quality of these vendors and products.)

Typically, the client (homeowner) hires an architect who either draws plans for the kitchen, bath, or other stone area as part of the overall house design or who hires a specialized kitchen architect who draws those plans. Most of these clients also hire interior decorators who help them select colors, fabrics, furniture, art, and other home furnishings. Because selecting a stone slab is like selecting art, clients usually visit the stone vendors' warehouses personally. They walk through the warehouses, often accompanied by their interior designer, and maybe also their kitchen architect, carrying little boxes into which stone vendor employees place chips of slabs in which the client expresses interest.

Usually, the team selects several stone slabs for consideration, and those are set aside for that client. The name of the client or the decorator is written in indelible ink on the side of the stone to reserve it. When the client or design team makes a final selection, the name is crossed out on the stone slabs they do not purchase. The purchased slabs are set aside for shipping.

During the construction process, the contractor will have selected a stone fabricator, who will cut the stone slab to fit the client's counters. The fabricator will also treat the stone's edges, possibly repolish the stone, and cut holes for sinks and faucets. Fabricators move the slabs from the stone vendor to their workshops, prepare the slab, and eventually install it in the client's home.

Questions

1. Identify the activities that are performed in the process of selecting and installing stone countertops. Ensure that each activity is a service.

2. Identify the resources that apply to these activities.

3. Identify the data that flows among activities.

4. Model the stone selection process using BPMN notation. Use PowerPoint to create your model and construct it in swim-lane format.

5. Suppose that you work for a stone vendor and you realize that there are many slabs of stone that are reserved that ought not to be. (The clients have selected other slabs.) Identify possible causes for this situation and suggest a process remedy.

6. Suppose that you work for a stone vendor and have just learned that seven slabs of rare and expensive stone were installed that the client did not purchase. The slabs that were installed had been selected as a possibility by the client, but the client had intended to purchase a different set of stone slabs. Identify possible causes for this situation. Explain why the interorganizational scope of this process will make problem-resolution difficult. Suggest changes to the process that would prevent this error from occurring again.

7. Explain how a knowledge of business process management could help you become a stone slab client rather than a stone chipper.

"This is lame, Mr. Butterworth. It really is."

"Look, kid, since we're sharing this tent, let's not be formal. Call me Franklin. What's so bad?"

"There's no girls on this trip. It's so boring."

Butterworth (to himself): "How will I survive 3 days of this?"

This could happen to you

"Kid, what's your name?"

"Graham."

"Nice name. Did I hear you're in college?"

"Right."

"How old are you?"

"15."

"Wow. Well, first, since you're in college, you ought to say women: 'There's no women on this trip.'"

"Women, girls, whatever, there aren't any."

"What about that woman with Crosby?"

"You mean Ringo? Oh, come on, she's ancient. I mean girls . . . women . . . my age."

"Why'd you come?"

"It's a PE credit. Because of my age, they can't put me into basketball or regular sports. I thought it would be better than bowling. Can you believe they give credit for bowling? I don't like putting my fingers in those creepy holes."

This is LAME, Mr. Buttterworth.

"I'm with you there. What are you doing now?"

"What? Oh, playing *Grand Theft Auto*."

"You got earplugs or something? I can hear the game over here."

"I *am* using my earplugs."

"I'm going out to look around. Don't play after 10, OK?"

"You sound like my parents."

Butterworth (to himself): "Three days of this? What a mistake!"

Graham and Butterworth are not realizing their hopes and expectations for their river trip. Of course, longer term, they don't have the problem; Majestic does. MRV differentiates itself on the basis of quality, and creating trips with people having similar perspectives and interests can be an important part of trip quality. Is there a way to use computer systems or the Internet to create better groups? Yes, as you will learn in this chapter.

Q1 How do companies use e-commerce?

Q2 How does e-commerce improve market efficiency?

Q3 What economic factors disfavor e-commerce?

Q4 What technology is needed for e-commerce?

Q5 What is Web 2.0?

Q6 How can businesses benefit from Web 2.0?

How does the knowledge in this chapter help MRV and you?

Q1 How Do Companies Use E-Commerce?

E-commerce is the buying and selling of goods and services over public and private computer networks. Notice that this definition restricts e-commerce to buying and selling transactions. Checking the weather at *http://yahoo.com* is not e-commerce; buying a weather-service subscription that is paid for and delivered over the Internet is.

Figure 8-1 lists categories of e-commerce companies. The U.S. Census Bureau, which publishes statistics on e-commerce activity, defines **merchant companies** as those that take title to the goods they sell. They buy goods and resell them. It defines **nonmerchant companies** as those that arrange for the purchase and sale of goods without ever owning or taking title to those goods. Regarding services, merchant companies sell services that they provide; nonmerchant companies sell services provided by others. We will consider merchants and nonmerchants separately in the following sections.

E-Commerce Merchant Companies

The three main types of merchant companies are those that sell directly to consumers, those that sell to companies, and those that sell to government. Each uses slightly different information systems in the course of doing business. **B2C**, or **business-to-consumer**, e-commerce concerns sales between a supplier and a retail customer (the consumer). A typical information system for B2C provides a Web-based

Merchant companies	Nonmerchant companies
– Business-to-consumer (B2C) – Business-to-business (B2B) – Business-to-government (B2G)	– Auctions – Clearinghouses – Exchanges

FIGURE 8-1
E-Commerce Categories

FIGURE 8-2
Example of Use of B2B,
B2G, and B2C

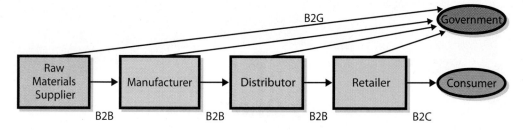

application or **Web storefront** by which customers enter and manage their orders. Amazon.com, REI.com, and LLBean.com are examples of companies that use B2C information systems.

The term **B2B**, or **business-to-business**, e-commerce refers to sales between companies. As Figure 8-2 shows, raw materials suppliers use B2B systems to sell to manufacturers, manufacturers use B2B systems to sell to distributors, and distributors uses B2B systems to sell to retailers.

B2G, or **business-to-government**, refers to sales between companies and government agencies. In Figure 8-2, the manufacturer that uses an e-commerce site to sell computer hardware to the U.S. Department of State is engaging in B2G commerce. Suppliers, distributors, and retailers sell to the government as well.

B2C applications first captured the attention of mail-order and related businesses. However, companies in all sectors of the economy soon realized the enormous potential of B2B and B2G. The number of companies engaged in B2B and B2G commerce now far exceeds those engaging in B2C commerce.

Furthermore, today's B2B and B2G applications implement just a small portion of their potential capability. Their full utilization is some years away. Although most experts agree that these applications will involve some sort of system integration using SOA and the service-oriented standards, the nature of that integration is not well understood and is still being developed. Consequently, you can expect further progress and development in B2B and B2G applications during your career.

Nonmerchant E-Commerce

The most common nonmerchant e-commerce companies are auctions and clearinghouses. E-commerce **auctions** match buyers and sellers by using an e-commerce version of a standard auction. This e-commerce application enables the auction company to offer goods for sale and to support a competitive-bidding process. The best-known auction company is eBay, but many other auction companies exist; many serve particular industries.

Clearinghouses provide goods and services at a stated price and arrange for the delivery of the goods, but they never take title. One division of Amazon.com, for example, operates as a nonmerchant clearinghouse and sells books owned by others. As a clearinghouse, Amazon.com matches the seller and the buyer and then takes payment from the buyer and transfers the payment to the seller, minus a commission. Figure 8-3 shows a typical Amazon.com listing for selling books that it does not own.

Another type of clearinghouse is an **electronic exchange** that matches buyers and sellers; the business process is similar to that of a stock exchange. Sellers offer goods at a given price through the electronic exchange, and buyers make offers to purchase over the same exchange. Price matches result in transactions from which the exchange takes a commission. Priceline.com is an example of an exchange used by consumers.

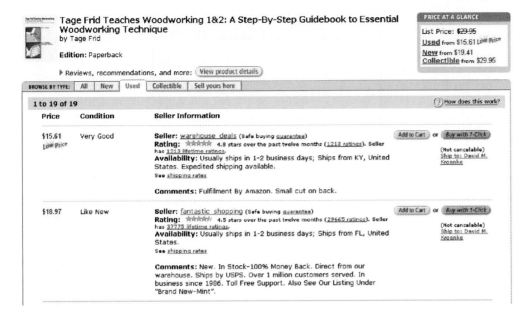

FIGURE 8-3
Amazon.com Clearinghouse Sales

Source: © 2006 Amazon.com, Inc., or its affiliates. All Rights Reserved.

Q2 How Does E-Commerce Improve Market Efficiency?

The debate continues among business observers as to whether e-commerce is something new or if it is just a technology extension to existing business practice. During the dot-com heyday of 1999–2000, some claimed that e-commerce was ushering in a new era and a "new economy." Although experts differ as to whether a "new economy" was created, all agree that e-commerce does lead to greater market efficiency.

For one, e-commerce leads to **disintermediation**, which is the elimination of middle layers in the supply chain. You can buy a flat-screen LCD HDTV from a typical "bricks-and-mortar" electronics store, or you can use e-commerce to buy it from the manufacturer. If you take the latter route, you eliminate the distributor, the retailer, and possibly more. The product is shipped directly from the manufacturer's finished goods inventory to you. You eliminate the distributor's and retailer's inventory carrying costs, and you eliminate shipping overhead and handling activity. Because the distributor and associated inventories have become unnecessary waste, disintermediation increases market efficiency.

E-commerce also improves the flow of price information. As a consumer, you can go to any number of Web sites that offer product price comparisons. You can search for the HDTV you want and sort the results by price and vendor reputation. You can find vendors that avoid your state sales tax or that omit or reduce shipping charges. The improved distribution of information about price and terms enables you to pay the lowest possible cost and serves ultimately to remove inefficient vendors. The market as a whole becomes more efficient.

From the seller's side, e-commerce produces information about **price elasticity** that has not been available before. Price elasticity measures the amount that demand rises or falls with changes in price. Using an auction, a company can learn not just what the top price for an item is, but also the second, third, and other prices from the losing bids. In this way, the company can determine the shape of the price elasticity curve.

Similarly, e-commerce companies can learn price elasticity directly from experiments on customers. For example, in one experiment, Amazon.com created three groups of similar books. It raised the price of one group 10 percent, lowered the price of the second group 10 percent, and left the price of the third group unchanged. Customers provided feedback to these changes by deciding whether to buy books at

FIGURE 8-4
E-Commerce Market
Efficiencies

Market Efficiencies

– Disintermediation
– Increased information on price and terms
– Knowledge of price elasticity
  • Losing-bidder auction prices
  • Price experimentation
  • More accurate information obtained
    directly from customer

the offered prices. Amazon.com measured the total revenue (quantity times price) of each group and took the action (raise, lower, or maintain prices) on all books that maximized revenue. Amazon.com repeated the process until it reached the point at which the indicated action was to maintain current prices.

Managing prices by direct interaction with the customer yields better information than managing prices by watching competitors' pricing. By experimenting with customers, companies learn how customers have internalized competitors' pricing, advertising, and messaging. It might be that customers do not know about a competitor's lower prices, in which case there is no need for a price reduction. Or, it may be that the competitor is using a price that, if lowered, would increase demand sufficiently to increase total revenue. Figure 8-4 summarizes the ways e-commerce generates market efficiencies.

Q3 What Economic Factors Disfavor E-Commerce?

Although there are tremendous advantages and opportunities for many organizations to engage in e-commerce, the economics of some industries may disfavor e-commerce activity. Companies need to consider the following economic factors:

• Channel conflict

• Price conflict

• Logistics expense

• Customer-service expense

Consider the example of the manufacturer selling directly to a government agency shown in Figure 8-2. Before engaging in such e-commerce, the manufacturer must consider the unfavorable economic factors just listed. First, what **channel conflict** will develop? Suppose the manufacturer is a computer maker that decides to sell directly, B2G, to the State Department. When the manufacturer begins to sell goods that State Department employees used to purchase from a retailer down the street, that retailer will resent the competition and might drop the manufacturer. If the value of the lost sales is greater than the value of the B2G sales, e-commerce is not a good solution, at least not on that basis.

Furthermore, when a business engages in e-commerce it may also cause **price conflict** with its traditional channels. Because of disintermediation, the manufacturer may be able to offer a lower price and still make a profit. However, as soon as the manufacturer offers the lower price, existing channels will object. Even if the manufacturer and the retailer are not competing for the same customers, the retailer still will not want a lower price to be readily known via the Web.

Also, the existing distribution and retailing partners do provide value; they are not just a cost. Without them, the manufacturer will have the increased *logistics expense* of entering and processing orders in small quantities. If the expense of processing a 1-unit order is the same as that for processing a 12-unit order (which it might be), the average logistics expense per item will be much higher for goods sold via e-commerce.

Similarly, *customer-service* expenses are likely to increase for manufacturers that use e-commerce to sell directly to consumers. The manufacturer will be required to provide service to less sophisticated users and on a one-by-one basis. For example, instead of explaining to a single sales professional that the recent shipment of 100 Gizmo 3.0s requires a new bracket, the manufacturer will need to explain that 100 times to less knowledgeable, frustrated customers. Such service requires more training and more expense.

All four economic factors are important for organizations to consider when they contemplate e-commerce sales.

Q4 What Technology Is Needed for E-Commerce?

In Chapter 7, we considered what happens from a business process standpoint when you buy something over the Internet. Here, let's consider the same problem, but this time from the perspective of the technology that is involved in the process of filling your order.

Consider that same REI Web page that you saw in Figure 7-1. You use it to navigate to the product(s) that you want to buy. When you find something you want, you add it to your shopping cart and keep shopping. At some point you check out by supplying credit card data.

Now, this time consider the technology that is necessary to support the underlying business process. Or, from another perspective, if you want to set up a Web storefront for your company, what facilities do you need?

Three-Tier Architecture

Almost all e-commerce applications use the **three-tier architecture** shown in Figure 8-5. The tiers refer to three different classes of computers. The **user tier** consists of computers that have browsers that request and process Web pages. The **server tier** consists of computers that run Web servers and process application programs. The **database tier** consists of computers that run a DBMS that processes SQL requests to retrieve and store

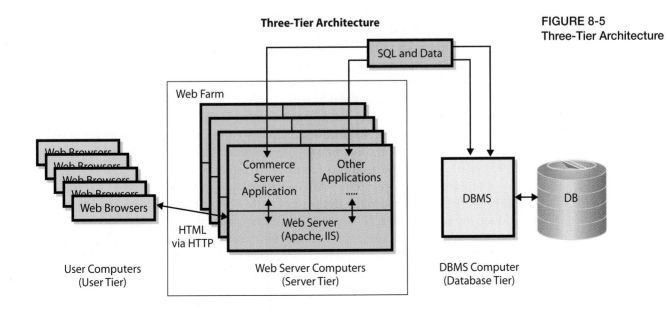

FIGURE 8-5
Three-Tier Architecture

Three-Tier Architecture

data. Figure 8-5 shows only one computer at the database tier. Some sites have multicomputer database tiers as well.

Communication between the user and server computers is governed by a protocol called **Hypertext Transfer Protocol (HTTP)**. This protocol is a set of rules for transferring documents and data over the Internet.

A **Web page** is a document, coded in one of the standard page markup languages, that is transmitted using HTTP. The most popular page markup language is the *Hypertext Markup Language (HTML)*, which is described later in this section.

Web servers are programs that run on a server tier computer and that manage HTTP traffic by sending and receiving Web pages to and from clients. A **browser** is a computer program on the client computer that processes Web pages. When you type *http://ibm.com*, your browser issues a request via HTTP for the Web server at the domain name ibm.com to send you its default Web page. The two most popular Web server programs are Apache, commonly used on Linux, and IIS (Internet Information Server), a component of Windows XP Professional, Windows Server, and Windows Vista. Common browsers are Microsoft's Internet Explorer and Mozilla's Firefox.

A **commerce server** is an application program that runs on a server tier computer. A commerce server receives requests from users via the Web server, takes some action, and returns a response to the users via the Web server. Typical commerce server functions are to obtain product data from a database, manage the items in a shopping cart, and coordinate the checkout process. In Figure 8-5, the server tier computers are running a Web server program, a commerce server application, and other applications having an unspecified purpose.

To ensure acceptable performance, commercial Web sites usually are supported by several or even many Web server computers in a facility called a **Web farm**. Work is distributed among the computers in a Web farm so as to minimize customer delays. The coordination among multiple Web server computers is a fantastic dance, but, alas, we do not have space to tell that story here. Just imagine the coordination that must occur as you add items to an online order when, to improve performance, different Web server computers receive and process each addition to your order.

Watch the Three Tiers in Action!

To see a three-tier example in action, go to your favorite Web storefront site, place something in a shopping cart, and consider Figure 8-5 as you do so. As stated earlier, when you enter an address into your browser, the browser sends a request for the default page to a server computer at that address. A Web server and possibly a commerce server process your request and send back the default page.

As you click Web pages to find products you want, the commerce server accesses the database to retrieve data about those products. It creates pages according to your selections and sends the results back to your browser via the Web server. Again, different computers on the server tier may process your series of requests and must constantly communicate about your activities. You can follow this process in Figure 8-6.

In Figure 8-6(a), the user has navigated through climbing equipment at REI.com to find a particular item. To produce this page, the commerce server accessed a database to obtain the product picture, price, special terms (a 5-percent discount for buying six or more), product information, and related products.

The user placed six items in her basket, and you can see the response in Figure 8-6(b). Again, trace the action in Figure 8-5 and imagine what occurred to produce the second page. Notice that the discount was applied correctly.

When the customer checks out, the commerce server program will be called to process payment, schedule inventory processing, and arrange for shipping. Most likely the commerce server interfaces with applications at other companies using SOA standards. Truly this is an amazing capability!

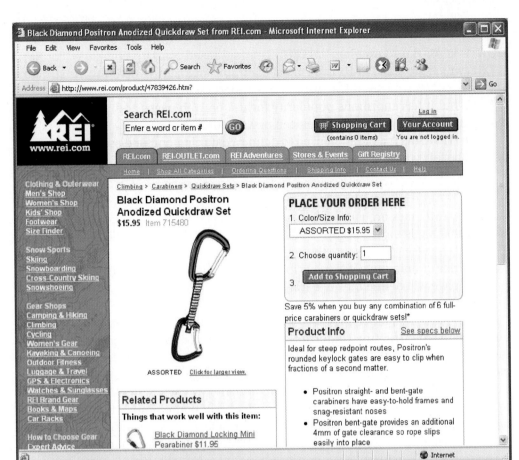

FIGURE 8-6a
Sample of Commerce Server Pages: Product-Offer Page

Source: Used with permission of REI.

FIGURE 8-6b
Shopping-Cart Page

Source: Used with permission of REI.

What Is Hypertext Markup Language (HTML)?

Hypertext Markup Language (HTML) is a tag-based markup language like XML. HTML, which preceded XML, is the most common language for defining the structure and layout of Web pages. HTML has several important disadvantages when compared to XML, but it has enormous popularity for use on Web pages and, in spite of those disadvantages, is unlikely to be replaced by XML for that purpose.

An HTML **tag** is a notation used to define a data element for display or other purposes. The following HTML is a typical heading tag:

```
<h2>Price of Item</h2>
```

Like XML, tags are enclosed in angle brackets < > and they occur in pairs. The start of this tag is indicated by <h2>, and the end of the tag is indicated by </h2>. The words between the tags are the value of the tag. This HTML tag means to place the words "Price of Item" on a Web page in the style of a level-two heading. The creator of the Web page will define the style (font size, color, and so forth) for h2 headings and the other tags to be used.

Web pages include **hyperlinks**, which are pointers to other Web pages. A hyperlink contains the URL (the Uniform Resource Locator) of the Web page to find when the user clicks the hyperlink. The URL can reference a page on the server that generated the page containing the hyperlink or it can reference a page on another server.

Figure 8-7(a) shows a sample HTML document. The document has a heading that provides metadata about the page and a body that contains the content. The tag <h1> means to format the indicated text as a level-one heading; <h2> means a level-two heading. The tag <a> defines a hyperlink. This tag has an **attribute**, which is a variable used to provide properties about a tag. Not all tags have attributes, but many do. Each attribute has a standard name. The attribute for a hyperlink is *href*, and its value indicates which Web page is to be displayed when the user clicks the link. Here, the page *www.prenhall.com/kroenke* is to be returned when the user clicks the hyperlink. Figure 8-7(b) shows this page as rendered by Internet Explorer.

FIGURE 8-7a
Sample HTML Document

```
<html>

<head>
<meta http-equiv="Content-Language" content="en-us">
<meta http-equiv="Content-Type" content="text/html; charset=windows-1252">
<title>Example HTML Document</title>
</head>

<body>
<h1 align="center"><font color="#FF00FF">Experiencing MIS</font></h1>
<h2> </h2>
<h2> </h2>
<h2 align="left"><font color="#0000FF"><i>Example HTML Document</h1></i></font></h2></i>

<p> </p>
<p>Click here for textbook Web site:  <a href="http://www.prenhall.com/kroenke">Web
Site Link</a></p>

</body>

</html>
```

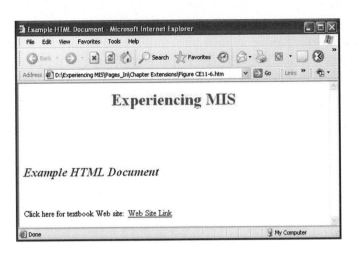

FIGURE 8-7b
HTML Document from
Figure 8-7(a) Rendered
Using Internet Explorer

Source: Microsoft product screen shot reprinted with permission from Microsoft Corporation.

Q5 What Is Web 2.0?

As you saw in the REI example, e-commerce sites duplicate the experience of shopping in a grocery store or other retail shop. The customer moves around the store, places items in a shopping cart, and then checks out. Shopping using a cart is a familiar scenario, but it does not take advantage of the Web's potential.

Amazon.com was one of the first companies to recognize other possibilities when it added the "Customers Who Bought This Book Also Bought" feature to its Web site. With that feature, e-commerce broke new ground. No grocery store could or would have a sign that announced, "Customers who bought this tomato soup, also bought. . . ." That idea was the first step toward what has come to be known as Web 2.0.

The term **Web 2.0** originated at a 2001 conference brainstorming session between O'Reilly Publications and MediaLive International.[1] Although the specific meaning of Web 2.0 is hard to pin down, it generally refers to a loose cloud of capabilities, technologies, business models, and philosophies. Figure 8-8 compares Web 2.0 to traditional processing. (By the way, the term *Web 1.0* is never used.)

Software as a (Free) Service

Google, Amazon.com, and eBay exemplify Web 2.0. These companies do not sell software licenses, because software is not their product. Instead, they provide **software as a service (SAAS)**. You can search Google, run Google Docs & Spreadsheets, use Google

Web 2.0 Processing	Traditional Processing
Major winners: Google, Amazon.com, eBay	Major winners: Microsoft, Oracle, SAP
Software as service	Software as product
Frequent releases of perpetual betas	Infrequent, controlled releases
Business model relies on advertising or other revenue-from-use	Business model relies on sale of software licenses
Viral marketing	Extensive advertising
Product value increases with use and users	Product value fixed
Organic interfaces, mashups encouraged	Controlled, fixed interface
Participation	Publishing
Some rights reserved	All rights reserved

FIGURE 8-8
Comparison of Web 2.0 with Traditional Processing

[1] *http://www.oreillynet.com/pub/a/oreilly/tim/news/2005/09/30/what-is-web-20.html*, accessed October, 2008.

Earth, process Gmail, and access Google maps—all from a thin-client browser, with the bulk of the processing occurring in the cloud, somewhere on the Internet. Like all Web 2.0 programs, Google releases new versions of its programs frequently. Instead of software license fees, the Web 2.0 business model relies on advertising or other revenue that results as users employ the software as a service.

Many Web 2.0 programs are perpetually classified as "beta." Traditionally, a **beta program** is a prerelease version of software that is used for testing; it becomes obsolete when the final version is released. In the Web 2.0 world, many programs are always beta. Figure 8-9 shows Gmail as a beta program. I have been using this "beta" program for more than 3 years. Features and functions are constantly changing; none of the functions listed in the *More* menu item existed 3 years ago. But, because the program remains classified as beta, with no license fee, no user can complain about the changing user interface.

Software as a service clashes with the software model used by traditional software vendors such as Microsoft, Oracle, and SAP. For such companies, software is their product. They release new versions and new products infrequently. For example, 4 years separated the release of Microsoft Office 2007 from 2003. Releases are made in a very controlled fashion, and extensive testing and true beta programs precede every release.

Traditional software vendors depend on software license fees. If many Office users switched to free word processing and spreadsheet applications, the hit on Microsoft revenue would be catastrophic. Because of the importance of software licensing revenue, substantial marketing efforts are made to convert users to new releases.

In the Web 2.0 world, no such marketing is done; new features are released and vendors wait for users to spread the news to one another, a process called **viral marketing**. Google has never announced any software in a formal marketing campaign. Users carry the message to one another. In fact, if a product requires advertising to be successful, then it is not a Web 2.0 product.

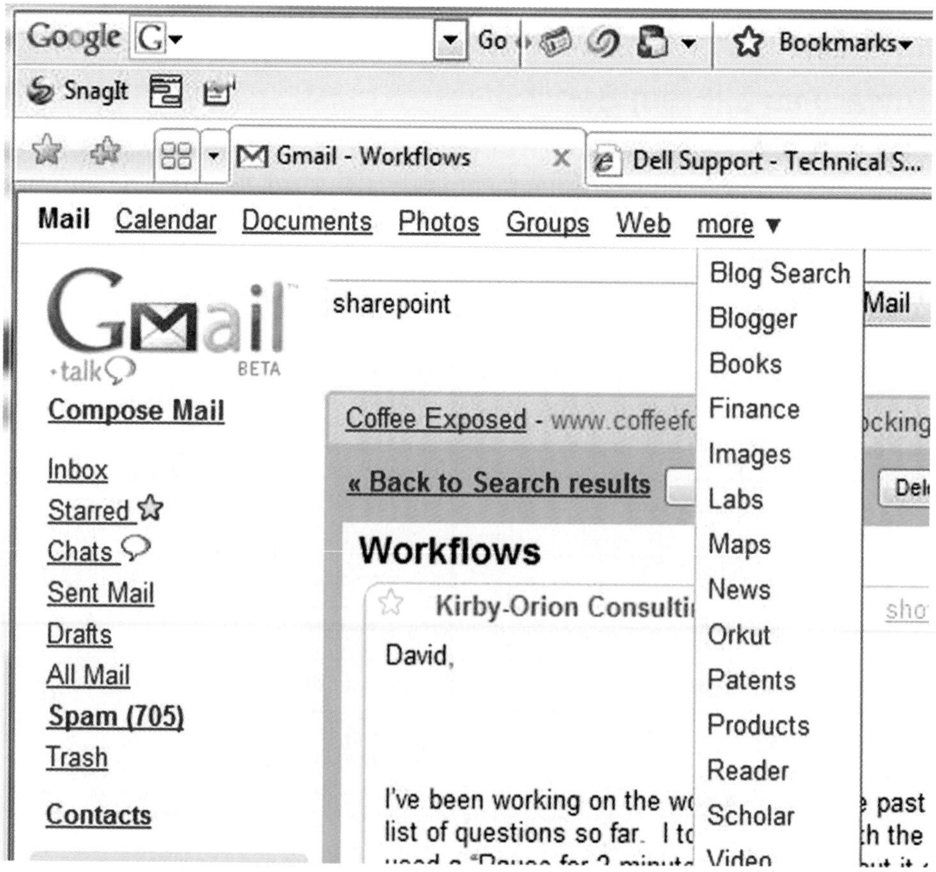

FIGURE 8-9
Sample Gmail Screen

Source: Gmail™. GOOGLE is a trademark of Google Inc.

By the way, traditional software companies do use the term *software as a service.* However, they use it only to mean that they will provide their software products via the cloud rather than having customers install that software on their computers. Software licenses for their products still carry a sometimes hefty license fee. So, perhaps we should say that in the Web 2.0 world software is provided as a *free* service.

Use Increases Value

Another characteristic of Web 2.0 is that the value of the site increases with users and use. Amazon.com gains more value as more users write more reviews. Amazon.com becomes *the* place to go for information about books or other products. Similarly, the more people who buy or sell on eBay, the more eBay gains value as a site.

Contrast this with traditional products where the value is fixed. Millions upon millions of Microsoft Word users may have created templates of potential use to others, but because Microsoft does not serve as a clearinghouse for sharing those templates, the value of Word does not grow with the number of Word users.

Organic User Interface and Mashups

The traditional software model carefully controls the users' experience. All Office programs share a common user interface; the ribbon (toolbar) in Word is similar to the ribbon in PowerPoint and in Excel. In contrast, Web 2.0 interfaces are organic. Users find their way around eBay and PayPal, and if the user interface changes from day to day, well, that is just the nature of Web 2.0. Further, Web 2.0 encourages **mashups**, which occur when the output from two or more Web sites is combined into a single user experience.

Google's **My Maps** is an excellent example of a mashup. Google publishes Google Maps (created, incidentally, by a vendor other than Google) and provides tools for users to make custom modifications to those maps. Thus, users mash the Google map product with their own knowledge. One user demonstrated the growth of gang activity to the local police by mapping new graffiti sites on Google maps. Other users share their experiences or photos of hiking trips or other travel.

In Web 2.0 fashion, Google provides users a means for sharing their mashed-up map over the Internet and then indexes that map for the Google search engine. For example, if you publish a mashup of a Google map with your knowledge of a hiking trip on Mt. Pugh, anyone who Googles "Mt. Pugh" will find your map. Again, the more users who create My Maps, the greater the value of the My Maps site.

Participation and Ownership Differences

Mashups lead to another key difference. Traditional sites are about publishing; Web 2.0 is about participation. Users provide reviews, map content, discussion responses, blog entries, and so forth. A final difference, listed in Figure 8-8, concerns *ownership.* Traditional vendors and Web sites lock down all the legal rights they can. For example, Oracle publishes content and demands that others obtain written permission before reusing it. Web 2.0 locks down only some rights. Google publishes maps and says, "Do what you want with them. We'll help you share them."

Q6 How Can Businesses Benefit from Web 2.0?

Amazon.com, Google, eBay and other Web 2.0 companies have pioneered Web 2.0 technologies and techniques to their benefit. A good question today, however, is how these techniques might be used by non–Internet companies. How might 3M, Alaska Airlines, Procter & Gamble, or even Majestic River Ventures use Web 2.0?

In the preparation of this text, a number of Pearson (this text's publisher) employees joined a private Facebook group, and we used it to discuss the issues raised in the *Guide* on pages 200–201.

Blending the Personal and the Professional

Many businesses are beginning to use social sites like Facebook and MySpace for professional purposes. It began with coworkers sharing their accounts with each other socially, just as they did in college. The first interactions concerned activities such as photos of the company softball team or photos at a cocktail party at a recent sales meeting. However, as stated in the networking guide in Chapter 6, every business social function is a *business* function, so even sharing photos and pages with the work softball team began to blur the personal–professional boundary.

The employees of Pearson, the publisher of this textbook, are no exception. When I began work on this chapter, I started a Facebook group called "Experiencing MIS." I then queried Facebook for Pearson employees I guessed might have Facebook accounts, and invited them to be "friends." Most accepted, and I asked them to join the Experiencing MIS group.

The first day I checked my account, I found an entry from Anne, one of my new friends, who stated that she had been out too late the prior night. That day she happened to be working on the sales plan for this book, and I realized that I didn't want to know her current condition. So, in the group, I asked whether the blending of the personal and the

professional is a good thing, and the following conversation resulted:

Anne: I think that for a lot of reasons it is a good thing . . . within reason. I think that people seeing a personal side of you can humanize you. For example, my "I was out too late last night" post didn't mean that I was not into work early and ready to go (which I was, just with a larger coffee than usual), just that I like to have a good time outside of my work life. Also, with all the time we spend at work, our social lives are intertwined with our work lives.

Also, 9–5 work hours are becoming more and more obsolete. I may be updating my Facebook page at noon on a Friday, but you will surely find me working at least part of my day on Saturday and Sunday.

Bob: I definitely see Anne's point of view. There is the temptation to believe that we are all family. I am too old to believe that, but corporate advancement is always going to be predicated to some degree on your willingness to surrender the personal for the professional and/or allow blur. Technology may give you the illusion that you can safely have it both ways.

I am skeptical of business applications for Facebook. My guess is most folks find them lame in the way that business blogs and Xmas cards from your insurance agent are.

Lisa: I actually think there is a place for Facebook in business . . . For example, think about how it's connected a team like ours—where everyone is located all over the country—to have a place where we actually get to know each other a little better. It's corny, perhaps, but reading people's status updates on my iPhone gives me a better sense of who they are in "real life," not just on the job. I'd get that if we all sat in the same office every day; given that we don't, it's a pretty decent substitute.

I totally agree with Anne's notion that, in many ways, the personal and the professional already do blur . . . but I think that's more to do with who we are and what we do, than any specific notion of "corporations." Our work is portable and always on—and judged by results, not hours logged (I think!). In a work universe like that, the lines sort of slowly and inevitably blur . . . PS: Anne, I was out too late too. :)

Clearly, I am the curmudgeon here. But, just as I was reflecting on these comments, I received a private email from another person who chose not to be identified:

Other person: A few weeks ago, Pearson started getting really into Facebook. I went from not really using it to getting tons of "friend requests" from coworkers. Then, I got a request from somebody in an executive position at Pearson. I was worried at first—I had heard so many stories of people who had lost their jobs due to social networking, blogging, or other information they posted on the Internet. When I received this request, I must have gone over my profile 10 times to ensure there was nothing that could any way be misconstrued as offensive or illegal. I think many people at the company already know a lot about me, but I . . . I think you would have to be more careful if you're in the introductory months of a new job.

DISCUSSION QUESTIONS

1. Do you think Anne's post that she was "Out too late last night" was inappropriate, given that she knew that her professional colleagues were reading her page? Explain your answer.

2. Anne and Lisa contend that Facebook allows employees to get to know each other better in "real life" and not just on the job. Both of these women are very successful business professionals, and they believe such knowledge is important. Do you? Why or why not?

3. Bob is skeptical that Facebook has potential business applications. He thinks social networking sites will become as lame and as uninteresting as business blogs and corporate holiday cards. Do you agree? Why or why not?

4. In the olden days before social networking, instant messaging, email, and "free" long-distance phone calls, social networking was restricted to the people in your department, or maybe those who worked on your floor. You knew the people to whom you revealed personal data, and they were close to you in the organizational hierarchy. You would have had almost no contact with your manager's manager's manager, and what contact you did have would have been in the context of a formal meeting. How do you think management is affected when personal data is readily shared far up and down the organizational hierarchy?

5. Do you think it was appropriate for the senior manager to invite distant subordinates in the organization to be friends? Why did this action put the junior employees in a tight spot? What advantages accrue to the senior manager of having very junior friends? What advantages accrue to the junior professional of having a senior friend?

6. All of the people in this dialog update Facebook using iPhones that they purchased with their own money. Because they are not using a corporate asset, managers at Pearson would be unable to stop these employees from using Facebook, if they wanted to. How does this fact change the power structure within an organization? Consider, for example, what would happen if senior management announced an unpopular change in employee benefits or some other program.

7. As the lawyers say, "You cannot un-ring the bell." Once you've revealed something about yourself, you cannot take it back. Knowing that, what criteria will you use to decide what you will post on a social networking site that is read by your professional colleagues? How do those criteria differ from the criteria you use at school?

Advertising

When Oracle runs an ad in the *Wall Street Journal*, it has no control over who reads that ad, nor does it know much about the people who do (just that they fit the general demographic of *Wall Street Journal* readers). On any particular day, 10,000 qualified buyers for Oracle products might happen to read the ad, or then again perhaps only 1,000 qualified buyers read it. Neither Oracle nor the *Wall Street Journal* knows the number, but Oracle pays the same amount for the ad, regardless of the number of readers or who they are.

In the Web 2.0 world, advertising is specific to user interests. Someone who Googles *enterprise database management* is likely an IT person (or a student) who has at least a strong interest in Oracle and its competing products. Oracle would like to advertise to that person.

Google pioneered Web 2.0 advertising with its **AdWords** product. Vendors agree to pay Google a certain amount for particular search words. For example, a fitness studio might agree to pay $2 for the word *workout*. When someone Googles that term, Google will display a link to the fitness studio's Web site. If the user clicks that link (and *only* if the user clicks that link), Google charges the studio's account $2. The studio pays nothing if the user does not click the link. If it chooses, the studio can agree to pay for clicks on the word that are made only by users in certain geographic areas.

The amount that a company pays per word can change from day to day, and even hour to hour. If the studio is about to start a new spinning class, it will pay more for the word *spinning* just before the class starts than it will afterwards. The value of a click on *spinning* is low when the start of the next spinning class is a month away.

AdSense is another advertising alternative. Google searches an organization's Web site and inserts ads that match content on that site. When users click those ads, Google pays the organization a fee. Other Web 2.0 vendors offer services similar to AdWords and AdSense.

With Web 2.0, the cost of reaching a particular, qualified person is much smaller than in the traditional advertising model. As a consequence, most advertisers have switched to this lower cost, more focused form of advertising, and newspapers and magazines are either changing their business models or going broke. Even the venerable *New York Times* is struggling. Profits in the second quarter of 2008 fell 82 percent, and the paper was forced to make two price increases in the year.[2]

Social Networking

Social networking is the interaction of people connected by interests, friendship, business associations, or some other common trait. Although sociologists used the term as far back as the early 1900s, most people today use it to refer to networks of people that are supported by Web 2.0 technology.

You are undoubtedly familiar with Facebook and MySpace, and you may be aware of efforts to use those sites for commercial purposes. For example, some businesses use Facebook to connect employees with similar professional interests.

A company such as Majestic could use Facebook to bring friends to its reservation site and possibly solve Graham's "lack of girls" problem mentioned at the start of the chapter. You will have a chance to investigate that possibility in the exercise on page 208.

---

[2]*http://www.breitbart.com/article.php?id=D923IUFO0&show_article=1*

8 *Fine Woodworking* Versus *Wooden Boat*

Fine Woodworking is a high-quality, bimonthly publication that addresses topics of interest to serious woodworking enthusiasts. Issues include woodworking techniques, project descriptions, tool reviews, classified ads, and considerable advertising. *Fine Woodworking* has been published for about 30 years. UGC includes user videos, tool reviews, and other topics as you can see at *www.FineWoodworking.com*.

Wooden Boat is also a high-quality, bimonthly publication; it focuses on the design and construction of wooden boats. Issues include boat-building techniques; project descriptions; reviews of tools, books, and boats; classified ads; and considerable advertising. It, too, has been published for about 30 years. UGC includes user demonstrations of building techniques, sailboat trials, and other topics. See *www.WoodenBoat.com*.

These two publications, which are very similar, are owned and published by different companies. In recent years, both publications have incorporated Web 2.0 techniques, but they have done so in two different ways.

Wooden Boat provides an online index to past issues at its Web site. Subscribers who have kept past issues frequently access this site to locate an article about some topic. While readers are at the site, *Wooden Boat* offers to sell them a number of products, as you can see when you visit the site. One of the products for sale is past issues of the magazine. Thus, using the online index, if you locate an article you want, and if you do not have that issue, you can buy it from the Web site.

Fine Woodworking has taken a different approach. It offers an online subscription to the magazine and its archives for an annual fee. You can find the current offer at its Web site. Anyone who has paid that fee can access the site, search for topics of interest, and download articles about that topic in PDF format. If you want to know how, for example, to sharpen a hand plane, you can search for that topic and download quite a number of articles from the magazine's archives.

You and a team of your classmates will have an opportunity to compare and evaluate these uses of e-commerce in Collaboration Exercise 8, on page 209.

Mashups

How can two non–Internet companies mash the content of their products? Suppose you are watching a movie and would like to buy the jewelry, dress, or watch worn by the leading actress. Suppose that Nordstrom's sells all of those items. With Web 2.0 technology, the movie's producer and Nordstrom's can mash their content together so that you, watching the movie at home, can click on the watch and be directed to a Nordstrom's e-commerce site that will sell it to you. Or, perhaps Nordstrom's is disintermediated out of the transaction, and you are taken to the e-commerce site of the watch's manufacturer. Such possibilities are on the leading edge of e-commerce today. Many will be developed during your business career.

User Generated Content

Another way businesses take advantage of Web 2.0 is to sponsor the development of **user generated content (UGC)**. Early examples of UGC include product recommendations and user reviews. Some travel sites extend that idea to enable users to post pictures of their trips along with recommendations for accommodations and restaurants.

Some companies and organizations allow users to share videos or other content on topics of interest to the company and its customers. For example, *Fine Woodworking* magazine sponsors GlueTube, a site where users can share videos of woodworking projects and techniques. In other cases, companies leverage UGC to enable products' users to support one another, thus reducing the company's support costs.

See *MIS in Use 8* to consider some other ways that companies might use UGC.

Of course, when people contribute UGC, they have personal interests and biases. To reflect on ethical issues involved when contributing UGC, see the Ethics Guide on pages 204–205.

Hiding the Truth?

No one is going to publish their ugliest picture on their Facebook page, but how far should you go to create a positive impression? If your hips and legs are not your best features, is it unethical to stand behind your sexy car in your photo? If you've been to one event with someone very popular in your crowd, is it unethical to publish photos that imply you meet as an everyday occurrence? Surely there is no obligation to publish pictures of yourself at boring events with unpopular people just to balance the scale for those photos in which you appear unrealistically attractive and overly popular.

As long as all of this occurs on a Facebook or MySpace account that you use for personal relationships, well, what goes around comes around. But consider social networking in the business arena.

a. Suppose that Majestic starts a group on a social networking site for a particular rafting trip. Graham, the 15-year-old college student who started this chapter, decides to use that group to attract women at his college to join the trip. He posts a picture of a handsome 22-year-old male as a picture of himself, and he writes witty and clever comments on the site photos. He also claims to play the guitar and be an accomplished masseuse. Are his actions unethical? Suppose someone decided to go on the rafting trip, in part because of Graham's postings, and was disappointed with the truth about Graham. Would Majestic have any responsibility to refund that person's fees?

b. Suppose you own and manage Majestic. Is it unethical for you to encourage your employees to write positive reviews about MRV? Does your assessment change if you ask your employees to use an email address other than the one they have at MRV?

c. Again, suppose you own and manage Majestic and that you pay your employees a bonus for every client they bring to a rafting trip. Without specifying any particular technique, you encourage your employees to be creative in how they obtain clients. One employee invites his MySpace friends to a party at which he shows photos of prior rafting trips. On the way to the party, one of the friends has an automobile accident and dies. His spouse sues Majestic. Should you be held accountable? Does it matter if you knew about the presentation? Would it matter if you had not encouraged your employees to be creative?

d. Suppose Majestic has a Web site for customer reviews. In spite of your best efforts at camp cleanliness, on one trip (out of dozens) your staff accidentally serves contaminated food and everyone becomes ill with food-poisoning. One of those clients writes a poor review because of that experience. Is it ethical for you to delete that review from your site?

have dozens of photos of her, some of which were taken at parties and are unflattering and revealing. You post those photos along with critical comments that she made about clients or employees. Most of the comments were made when she was tired or frustrated, and they are hurtful, but because of her wit, also humorous. You send friend invitations to people whom she knows, many of whom are the target of her biting and critical remarks. Are your actions unethical?

e. Assume you have a professor who has written a popular textbook. You are upset with the grade you received in his class, so you write a scandalously poor review of that professor's book on Amazon.com. Are your actions ethical?

f. Suppose you were at one time employed by Majestic and you were, undeservedly you think, terminated by the company. To get even, you use Facebook to spread rumors to your friends (many of whom are river guides) about the safety of MRV trips. Are your actions unethical? Are they illegal? Do you see any ethical distinctions between this situation and that in item d?

g. Again, suppose that you were at one time employed by Majestic and were undeservedly terminated. You notice that the owner of MRV has no Facebook account, so you create one for her. You've known her for many years and

DISCUSSION QUESTIONS

1. Read the situations in items a through g and answer the questions contained in each.

2. Based on your answers in question 1, formulate ethical principles for creating or using social networks for business purposes.

3. Based on your answers in question 1, formulate ethical principles for creating or using user-generated content for business purposes.

4. Summarize the risks that a business assumes when it chooses to sponsor user-generated content.

5. Summarize the risks that a business assumes when it uses social networks for business purposes.

FIGURE 8-10
Design by Crowdsourcing

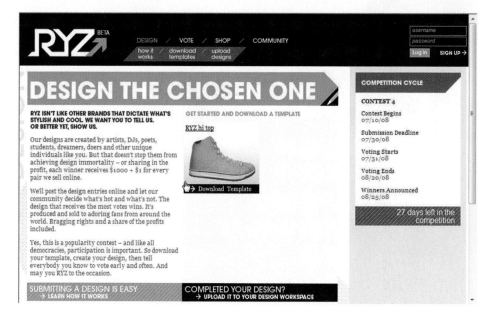

As another example, Zillow (*zillow.com*) offers free appraisals of homes and condominiums. The site is supported by advertising from lenders and other companies. In addition to appraisals, Zillow provides resources about the house-buying process and information on neighborhoods. It enables users to publish opinions regarding the lifestyle of a given neighborhood, interesting places and businesses, schools, transportation, noise, and other issues to consider when buying in that neighborhood. Zillow adds value to its site by enabling people with an interest in real estate to share their knowledge and experience.

Crowdsourcing is the process by which organizations involve their users in the design and marketing of their products. For example, as shown in Figure 8-10, the shoe startup company RYZ (*ryzwear.com*) sponsors shoe design contests to help it understand which shoes to create and how to market those designs. Crowdsourcing combines social networking, viral marketing, and open-source design, saving considerable cost while cultivating customers. With crowdsourcing, the crowd performs classic in-house market research and development and does so in such a way that customers are being set up to buy.

Who Is in Control?

Before we get too carried away with the potential for Web 2.0, note that not all business information systems benefit from flexibility and organic growth. Any information system that deals with assets, whether financial or material, requires, some level of control. You probably do not want to mash up your credit card transactions on My Map and share that mashup with the world. As CFO, you probably do not want your accounts payable or general ledger system to have an organic user interface; in fact, Sarbanes-Oxley prohibits that possibility.

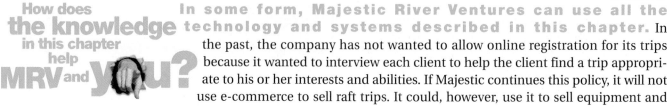

How does the knowledge in this chapter help MRV and you?

In some form, Majestic River Ventures can use all the technology and systems described in this chapter. In the past, the company has not wanted to allow online registration for its trips because it wanted to interview each client to help the client find a trip appropriate to his or her interests and abilities. If Majestic continues this policy, it will not use e-commerce to sell raft trips. It could, however, use it to sell equipment and memorabilia such as T-shirts and coffee mugs.

This is LAME, Mr. Buttterworth.

The application of Web 2.0 technology offers even more interesting and exciting possibilities. Majestic can use AdWords to advertise its trips, and it might want to allow AdSense on its site as well. Because the company's competitive strategy is to form quality relationships with quality people, it can make extensive use of social networking by connecting customers to each other via its site. Majestic can also use social networking to connect clients to raft guides. Additionally, it can add UGC content to its site, including customer reviews, user trip descriptions, user photos, and videos. It could also use crowdsourcing to allow past customers to design future river trips. It could ask their customers, "Where would you most like to go?" and then build trips around that feedback.

Web 2.0 is a boon to companies like Majestic, and they will gain significant benefit by developing Web 2.0 applications. Of more importance to you, though, is that Web 2.0 can be a boon to your career. You know more about Web 2.0 technologies (consider Facebook or MySpace) than many, possibly most, business professionals. Start thinking about how social networking or UGC might pertain to your business interests. Early in your work life, you will not know as much about accounting or marketing as someone who's been working 10 years. But, you might know as much or more about leading-edge Web 2.0 as they do. Think about using such technologies to gain a personal competitive edge.

Active Review

Use this Active Review to verify that you understand the material in the chapter. You can read the entire chapter and then perform the tasks in this review, or you can read the material for just one question and perform the tasks in this review for that question before moving on to the next one.

Q1 How do companies use e-commerce? Define *e-commerce*. Define *B2C, B2B,* and *B2G*. Distinguish among auctions, clearinghouses, and exchanges.

Q2 How does e-commerce improve market efficiency? Define and explain *disintermediation*, and give an example other than one in this text. Explain how e-commerce improves the flow of price information. Define *price elasticity*, and explain how e-commerce companies can estimate it.

Q3 What economic factors disfavor e-commerce? Name four factors that disfavor e-commerce. Explain the impact of each factor.

Q4 What technology supports e-commerce? Define *commerce servers, Web pages,* and *HTML*. Explain the purpose of SMTP, FTP, and HTTP. Define *tag, hyperlink, attribute,* and *Web server*.

Explain the purpose of a browser and cite two example products. Name the three tiers of the three-tier architecture and explain the purpose of each. Explain the term *Web farm*. Describe what happens behind the scenes when the user processes the Web pages shown in Figures 8-6a and 8-6b.

Q5 What is Web 2.0? How did Amazon.com usher in Web 2.0? Explain the term *software as a (free) service* and how it differs from traditional software licensing. Explain the difference in betas between Web 2.0 and traditional software publishing. Describe the difference in business models between Web 2.0 and traditional software companies. Explain the statement, "If a product requires advertising, then it is not Web 2.0." Explain how use increases value in Web 2.0. Define *mashup*. In what way are Web 2.0 interfaces organic? How does rights management differ between Web 2.0 and traditional software?

Q6 How can businesses benefit from Web 2.0? Describe the differences between Web 2.0 advertising and traditional advertising. Explain the difference between Google's AdWords and AdSense. Define *social networking*, and describe one business use of social networking sites. Explain one commercial application of mashups. Explain user-generated content, and give three examples not cited in this chapter. Define *crowdsourcing*, and explain why it both saves costs and facilitates sales.

How does **the knowledge** in this chapter help **MRV** and **you?** Summarize the ways that Majestic can use e-commerce and Web 2.0. Select what you think are the two most promising Web 2.0 opportunities for them, and explain your selection.

Key Terms and Concepts

Using Your Knowledge

1. Sue, the owner of Majestic River Ventures, decided some time ago that she or one of the senior trip leaders should interview each client to ensure that they have enrolled in the proper raft trip. She decided this when a man who could barely get in and out of the raft enrolled in a trip with numerous class IV and class V rapids (big, wild experiences). Suppose that Sue wants to revisit the decision not to use e-commerce. Prepare a one-page memo describing what would be required for Majestic to create an e-commerce site to enroll clients. Describe manual procedures that you could develop to prevent inappropriate enrollments.

2. Develop three different ways that Majestic could use social networking to facilitate its competitive strategy. Select what you think is the best alternative and justify your selection.

3. Develop three different ways that Majestic could use user-generated content (other than crowdsourcing) to facilitate its competitive strategy. Select what you think is the best alternative and justify your selection.

4. Develop three different ways that Majestic could use crowdsourcing to facilitate its competitive strategy. Select what you think is the best alternative and justify your selection.

5. At the start of this chapter, Graham complains because there are "no girls" on his trip. Take that complaint as a statement of a larger problem—namely, that trips are randomly composed of clients who happen to show up. Describe how Majestic could use a Facebook group to foster the creation of trips composed of like-minded individuals.

Collaboration Exercise 8 ◎

Before you start this exercise, read Chapter Extensions 1 and 2, which describe collaboration techniques as well as tools for managing collaboration tasks. In particular, consider using Google Docs & Spreadsheets, Google Groups, Microsoft Groove, Microsoft SharePoint, or some other collaboration tool.

Reread *MIS in Use 8* on page 203. In this exercise, you will compare and evaluate these two publications' strategies for using e-commerce.

1. These two very similar publications have taken two different approaches for using the Internet to gain revenue from their archives. Describe what you believe are the advantages and disadvantages of each approach.

2. Visit *http://woodenboat.com* and *http://finewoodworking.com*. Compare the ways that these two publications use social networking on their sites. For each, how does their use of social networking contribute to revenue? To what other goals does social networking contribute? Which publication uses social networking more effectively? Explain your answer.

3. Compare the ways that these two publications host UGC on their sites. For each, how does UGC contribute to revenue? To what other goals does UGC contribute? Which publication employs UGC more effectively? Explain your answer.

4. Choose one of the two publications and identify a new use for social networking. Write a one-page memo to the publisher of that magazine describing your idea and how it would contribute to the goals of the publication.

5. Choose one of the two publications and identify a new use for UGC. Write a one-page memo to the publisher of that magazine describing your idea and how it would contribute to the goals of the publication.

6. Is *Fine Woodworking* in danger of losing subscriptions to its paper magazine to the online magazine? Does it matter? Why or why not?

7. *Fine Woodworking* earns revenue from subscriptions to its online magazine. *Wooden Boat* earns no subscription revenue at all. Is it missing the boat? Why or why not?

Case Study 8

YOU, Inc.

Interorganizational information systems allow small businesses to avoid the time and expense of building infrastructure, thus reducing capital requirements and shortening time to market. In particular, they can help YOU. Consider the following business opportunity.

People often pay more for new items on eBay than they would pay if they shopped for bargains on the Internet. Either they do not like to e-shop, or perhaps they become entangled in the excitement of an auction, lose a bid, and decide to pay the *BuyItNow* price for a similar item in another auction. Whatever the reason, there is often an inefficiency in the flow of price information among eBay users.

Consider that inefficiency as a business opportunity for your own small business. Assume you are willing to invest no more than $700 in a computer, $49 per month for a DSL line, and a few hours of your time each day. How many of the value-chain activities can you outsource using interorganizational information systems?

Begin with market research. Using your Internet connection to the Web, you can investigate auctions, product categories, and related market segments. Doing this work saves hiring market research firms to produce this information for you. You do not need to conduct extensive and expensive market surveys; the information you need is on the Internet. Suppose you notice that there are opportunities on the sale of high-end motorcycle parts. The Baby Boomers are reliving their childhoods and now have considerable disposable income to spend. They cannot stand to lose an auction and will pay to get what they want, right now. You decide to focus on this opportunity.

Using the Internet, you find sources for motorcycle parts. Sourcing is a typical supply-chain activity; and again, by using the Internet, you have avoided hiring someone else to do this work for you. You search for sites that offer the products you want; that have free shipping; and, if possible, do not require payment of sales taxes.

When you find an item offered at a bargain price, you set up an auction for that item on eBay. You have not

Baby Boomer Bike Market

Bryan & Cherry
Alexander Photography

yet purchased the item; you just know where you can buy it. You set a price and the terms of the auction so that, at whatever price the item sells, you will make some profit (after deducting the cost of the auction). Avoiding the expense of hiring a photo team to take photos, you download pictures of the item from your vendor, and copy those photos into your auction. Your only financial exposure if the item does not sell is the cost of the auction.

Suppose the item sells. You then buy it from the vendor you've located, paying for it using PayPal or a credit card, and you request the vendor to ship the item directly to your customer, a process called *drop shipping*. If you pay with a credit card, it is possible you will receive payment from your customer before you pay for the item you sold. Because the item is new, and because you sell only high-quality items, all service and support are handled by the manufacturer.

Review this scenario in terms of Porter's value chain model. You did market research, but you outsourced all of the data-gathering activities to eBay, PriceGrabber, etc. You set up the auction on eBay and thus outsourced the sales infrastructure to eBay. You did the product-sourcing yourself, but again, you had considerable help from the Internet. Because you drop-shipped the item to your customer, you outsourced all inventory, operations, and shipping activities to that vendor. If the customer pays you before you pay your credit card, you can even earn interest on the customer's money. You outsourced service and support to the manufacturer.

Consider support activities: Because you avoided building infrastructure, you only have one part-time employee, yourself; you have no payroll or other compensation needs. You might want insurance, but if you sell enough using eBay, you can buy life and medical insurance from eBay at attractive terms, so you can outsource those functions as well.

Consider accounting: eBay, PayPal, your credit card company, and the vendor will do most of the work. All you need to do is maintain records to track your income for tax reporting. You can even pay your taxes online if you choose. All of this is possible only because of the prevalence of interorganizational information systems!

Questions

1. Investigate auctions on eBay and, for any category of product in which you have knowledge or interest, compare selling prices to prices of new goods from e-commerce sites. Attempt to find one or more products in which the item sold on eBay costs more than if it had been purchased from a vendor. State the price differential(s). If you find no such products, list the products' eBay prices and vendor prices for five of the products you investigated.

2. Go to *www.ebay.com* and learn how eBay charges for its auctions. You have many options to choose from; select the option(s) that you believe will be best for selling goods using this strategy. Explain why you think that option is the best.

3. Using price comparison sites (such as PriceGrabber, CNET, or Froogle), identify three sources for

products that you identified in question 1. If you did not find any qualifying products in that question, identify sources for some product in which you have an interest. Seek sources that provide free shipping and to which you do not need to pay taxes.

4. Either by yourself or with a group of classmates, find a product from your answer in question 3 that seems to you to be a good bargain. Set up an auction for that item on eBay with terms that will enable you to make some profit, even if the product sells at the lowest price.

5. Run the auction. If you make some profit, celebrate, and run it again. If not, state why and what you would do differently to earn some profit.

Business Intelligence and Information Systems for Decision Making

"Sue, I'm telling you, Trevor is a great guide. If we don't give him a decent bonus, he'll leave us."

"Well, maybe . . . but what makes you think he's a great guide?"

"He's terrific around the customers. He's personable, nobody can tell a funnier story, his rafting skills are good. Hey, he's just fun to have on the trips."

"Sure. All true. But what does he do for Majestic?"

"What do you mean?"

"What are we trying to do? Form quality relationships with quality customers. Right?"

"Yeah, you say that all the time."

"And why are we doing that? Repeat business. We want our customers to come back, and we want them to tell their friends."

"Well, Trevor does that."

"You think so? Tell me one of Trevor's customers who's come back."

"Well, I can't think of any names. But I'm sure there's a bunch of them."

"You are? Hmpf. Well, I looked through the data and I can't find one."

"That can't be right."

"I think Trevor is fun, I think he's decent on the river, but it's all about Trevor."

"If he finds out other guides got bigger bonuses, he'll leave."

"We may miss his humor and stories, but the business isn't going to miss him. Whatever he does doesn't translate into repeat business. We hand him the customers, and he doesn't develop our relationship with them."

"So, what are you going to do?"

"I want to align guide compensation with our strategy. I want to relate bonuses to repeat customers. Or, maybe give a commission on repeat customers. I was looking at our payroll. This season, we've employed 17 different guides; 14 of those people were here last year, and 11 have been with us 3 years or more."

"Yeah, so what?"

"Well, let's rank those people on the business they've generated. I started to do that, but it's a pain linking all the records together. We should use a computer, I guess . . . . "

Most companies, Majestic included, are awash in data. Submerged in this data is information that, if found and made available to the right people at the right time, can improve Majestic's decision making. Trevor, the rafting guide, is a good example.

This could happen to you

Trevor will leave us...

Study Questions

Q1 How big is an exabyte, and why does it matter?

Q2 How do business intelligence (BI) systems provide competitive advantages?

Q3 What problems do operational data pose for BI systems?

Q4 What are the purpose and components of a data warehouse?

Q5 What is a data mart, and how does it differ from a data warehouse?

Q6 What are the characteristics of data-mining systems?

How does the knowledge in this chapter help MRV and you?

Q1 How Big Is an Exabtye, and Why Does It Matter?

As stated in Chapter 1, today data communication and data storage costs are essentially zero. The result has been an explosion in the use and capacity of both. In 2007, Kevin Kelly estimated that 2 million emails, 31,000 text messages, and 162,000 instant messages are transmitted *every second.* He also estimated total online computer storage to be 246 exabytes and predicts it will grow to 600 exabytes by 2010.[1]

The size of such numbers is almost impossible to fathom. An **exabyte** equals 1,000 **petabytes**, which equals 1,000 terabytes. As shown in Figure 9-1, 200 petabytes is roughly the amount of all printed material ever written. So, one exabyte equals five times the amount of all printed material. Five exabytes equals all the words ever spoken by human beings, so 246 exabytes is roughly 50 times all the words ever spoken by humans. And 600 exabytes is, well, unfathomably large.

Not all of that storage is used for business. Much of it is used to store music, digital pictures, video, and phone conversations. However, much of that capacity is used to store the data from business information systems. For example, as of 2007 AT&T's customer database contained more than 312 terabytes of data.[2] If the data were published in books, a bookshelf 10,000 miles long would be required to hold them.

Why does this exponential growth in data matter to us? First, understand that the phenomenal data growth occurs inside organizations just as much as outside of them, even in a small company like Majestic. Every time it runs a rafting trip, it generates client data, supply data, inventory data, cost and revenue data, photos, videos, and so forth.

[1]Kevin Kelly, *The Technium,* November 2, 2007, *www.kk.org/thetechnium/archives/2007/11/dimensions_of_t.php* (accessed August 2008).
[2]*www.businessintelligencelowdown.com/2007/02/top_10_largest_.html* (accessed August 2008).

FIGURE 9-1
How Big Is an Exabyte?

*Source: http://sims.berkeley.edu/
research/projects/how-much-info/
datapowers.html*, accessed May 2005.
Used with the permission of Peter
Lyman and Hal R. Varian, University
of California at Berkeley.

Kilobyte (KB)	*1,000 bytes or 10^3 bytes* 2 Kilobytes: A typewritten page 100 Kilobytes: A low-resolution photograph
Megabyte (MB)	*1,000,000 bytes or 10^6 bytes* 1 Megabyte: A small novel or a 3.5-inch floppy disk 2 Megabytes: A high-resolution photograph 5 Megabytes: The complete works of Shakespeare 10 Megabytes: A minute of high-fidelity sound 100 Megabytes: One meter of shelved books 500 Megabytes: A CD-ROM
Gigabyte (GB)	*1,000,000,000 bytes or 10^9 bytes* 1 Gigabyte: A pickup truck filled with books 20 Gigabytes: A good collection of the works of Beethoven 100 Gigabytes: A library floor of academic journals
Terabyte (TB)	*1,000,000,000,000 bytes or 10^{12} bytes* 1 Terabyte: 50,000 trees made into paper and printed 2 Terabytes: An academic research library 10 Terabytes: The print collections of the U.S. Library of Congress 400 Terabytes: National Climactic Data Center (NOAA) database
Petabyte (PB)	*1,000,000,000,000,000 bytes or 10^{15} bytes* 1 Petabyte: Three years of EOS data (2001) 2 Petabytes: All U.S. academic research libraries 20 Petabytes: Production of hard-disk drives in 1995 200 Petabytes: All printed material
Exabyte (EB)	*1,000,000,000,000,000,000 bytes or 10^{18} bytes* 2 Exabytes: Total volume of information generated in 1999 5 Exabytes: All words ever spoken by human beings

Buried in all of this data is information that, if found and made available to the right people at the right time, can improve company decision making. Trevor, the rafting guide at the start of this chapter is a good example. Sue needs to make a decision about how to compensate Trevor and the other guides. The data she needs for this decision exists. How does she convert it into information for allocating bonuses or commissions?

The problem just mushrooms for larger companies. Consider the 300+ terabytes in Verizon's customer database. Buried in all of that data is a pattern that can help the company decide which customers are at risk of switching to another company. The same data can forecast the revenue impact of alternative cell phone prices and programs. Either analysis will improve Verizon's decisions, and by doing so, will increase Verizon's competitive strength.

Q2 How Do Business Intelligence (BI) Systems Provide Competitive Advantages?

A **business intelligence (BI) system** is an information system that provides information for improving decision making. BI systems vary in their characteristics and capabilities and in the way they foster competitive advantage.

Figure 9-2 summarizes the characteristics and competitive advantages of four categories of business intelligence systems. **Reporting systems** integrate data from multiple sources, and they process that data by sorting, grouping, summing, averaging, and comparing. Such systems format the results into reports and deliver those

Business Intelligence System	Characteristics	Competitive Advantage
Reporting systems	Integrate and process data by sorting, grouping, summing, and formatting. Produce, administer, and deliver reports.	Improve decisions by providing relevant, accurate, and timely information to the right person.
Data-mining systems	Use sophisticated statistical techniques to find patterns and relationships.	Improve decisions by discovering patterns and relationships in data to predict future outcomes.
Knowledge management systems	Share knowledge of products, product uses, best practices, etc., among employees, managers, customers, and others.	Improve decisions by publishing employee and others' knowledge. Create value from existing intellectual capital. Foster innovation, improve customer service, increase organizational responsiveness, and reduce costs.
Expert systems	Encode human knowledge in the form of If/Then rules and process those rules to make a diagnosis or recommendation.	Improve decision making by nonexperts by encoding, saving, and processing expert knowledge.

FIGURE 9-2
Characteristics and Competitive Advantage of BI Systems

reports to users. Reporting systems improve decision making by providing the right information to the right user at the right time.

Data-mining systems process data using sophisticated statistical techniques, such as regression analysis and decision tree analysis. Data-mining systems find patterns and relationships that cannot be found by simpler reporting operations, such as sorting, grouping, and averaging. Data-mining systems improve decision making by using the discovered patterns and relationships to *anticipate* events or to *predict* future outcomes. An example of a data-mining system is one that predicts the likelihood that a prospect will donate to a cause or political campaign based on the prospect's characteristics, such as age, sex, and home zip code. **Market-basket analysis** is another data-mining system, which computes correlations of items on past orders to determine items that are frequently purchased together. We will discuss data mining in more detail at the end of this chapter.

Knowledge-management (KM) systems create value from intellectual capital by collecting and sharing human knowledge of products, product uses, best practices, and other critical knowledge with employees, managers, customers, suppliers, and others who need it. Knowledge management is supported by the five components of an information system.

Expert systems are the fourth category of BI system in Figure 9-2. Expert systems encapsulate the knowledge of human experts in the form of *If/Then* rules. In a medical diagnosis system, for example, an expert system might have a rule such as:

If Patient_Temperature > 103, *Then* Initiate High_Fever_Procedure

Operational expert systems can have hundreds or even thousands of such rules. Although few expert systems have demonstrated a capability equivalent to a human expert, some are good enough to considerably improve the diagnosis and decision making of nonexperts.

As with all information systems, it is important to distinguish between business intelligence *tools* and business intelligence *systems.* Business Objects licenses the reporting tool Crystal Reports. SPSS licenses the data-mining suite Clementine, and Microsoft offers SharePoint Server as, in part, a knowledge-management system. All of these products are, however, just software. They represent just one of the five components.

To gain the promise of improved decision making, organizations must incorporate data-mining products into complete information systems. A reporting tool can generate a report that shows a customer has cancelled an important order. It takes a reporting *system*, however, to alert the customer's salesperson to this unwanted news in time for the salesperson to attempt to reverse the decision. Similarly, a data-mining tool can create an equation that computes the probability that a customer will default on a loan. A data-mining *system*, however, uses that equation to enable banking personnel to approve or reject a loan on the spot.

Q3 What Problems Do Operational Data Pose for BI Systems?

Data from transaction processing and other operational systems can be processed to create basic reports without problem. If we want to know, for example, current sales and how those sales relate to sales projections, we simply process data in the order-entry database.

However, raw operational data is seldom suitable for more sophisticated reporting or data mining. Figure 9-3 lists the major problem categories. First, although data that are critical for successful operations must be complete and accurate, data that are only marginally necessary do not need to be. For example, some systems gather demographic data in the ordering process. But because such data are not needed to fill, ship, and bill orders, their quality suffers.

Problematic data are termed **dirty data**. Examples are values of *B* for customer gender and of *213* for customer age. Other examples are a value of *999-999-9999* for a U.S. phone number, a part color of *gren*, and an email address of *WhyMe@GuessWhoIAM.org*. All of these values can be problematic for data-mining purposes.

Missing values are a second problem. A nonprofit organization can process a donation without knowing the donor's gender or age, but a data-mining application will suffer if there are many such missing values.

Inconsistent data, the third problem in Figure 9-3, are particularly common for data that have been gathered over time. When an area code changes, for example, the phone number for a given customer before the change will not match the customer's number after the change. Likewise, part codes can change, as can sales territories. Before such data can be used, they must be recoded for consistency over the period of the study.

Some data inconsistencies occur from the nature of the business activity. Consider a Web-based order-entry system used by customers worldwide. When the Web server records the time of order, which time zone does it use? The server's system clock time is irrelevant to an analysis of customer behavior. Coordinated Universal Time (formerly called Greenwich Mean Time) is also meaningless. Somehow, Web server time must be adjusted to the customer's time zone.

Another problem is nonintegrated data. Suppose, for example, that an organization wants to perform an analysis of customer purchase and payment behavior.

FIGURE 9-3
Problems of Using
Operational Data for BI
Systems

• Dirty data	• Wrong granularity
• Missing values	– Too fine
• Inconsistent data	– Not fine enough
• Data not integrated	• Too much data
	– Too many attributes
	– Too many data points

Unfortunately, the organization records payment data in an Oracle financial management database that is separate from the Microsoft CRM database that has the order data. Before the organization can perform the analysis, the data must be integrated.

Data can also be too fine or too coarse. Data **granularity** refers to the degree of summarization or detail. Coarse data is highly summarized; fine data express precise details. For example, suppose we want to analyze the placement of graphics and controls on an order-entry Web page. It is possible to capture the customers' clicking behavior in what is termed **clickstream data**. Those data are very fine, however, including everything the customer does at the Web site. In the middle of the order stream are data for clicks on the news, email, instant chat, and a weather check. Although all of that data is needed for a study of consumer computer behavior, such data will be overwhelming if all we want to know is how customers respond to ad locations. Because the data are too fine, the data analysts must throw away millions and millions of clicks.

Data can also be too coarse. For example, a file of order totals cannot be used for a market-basket analysis. For market-basket analysis, we need to know which items were purchased with which others. This doesn't mean the order-total data are useless. They can be adequate for other purposes; they just won't do for a market-basket analysis.

Generally, it is better to have too fine a granularity than too coarse. If the granularity is too fine, the data can be made coarser by summing and combining. Only analysts' labor and computer processing are required. If the granularity is too coarse, however, there is no way to separate the data into constituent parts.

The final problem listed in Figure 9-3 concerns too much data. As shown in the figure, we can have either too many attributes or too many data points. Think of the tables in Chapter 5. We can have too many columns or too many rows.

Consider the first problem: too many attributes. Suppose we want to know the factors that influence how customers respond to a promotion. If we combine internal customer data with customer data that we can purchase, we could have more than a hundred different attributes to consider. How do we select among them? Because of a phenomenon called the **curse of dimensionality**, the more attributes there are, the easier it is to build a model that fits the sample data but that is worthless as a predictor. There are other good reasons for reducing the number of attributes, and one of the major activities in data mining concerns efficient and effective ways of selecting attributes.

The second way to have too much data is to have too many data points—too many rows of data. Suppose we want to analyze clickstream data on *CNN.com*. How many clicks does that site receive per month? Millions upon millions! In order to meaningfully analyze such data, we need to reduce the amount of data. There is a good solution to this problem: statistical sampling. Organizations should not be reluctant to sample data in such situations.

The *Guide* on pages 218–219 discusses the uses of data sampling in more detail.

Q4 What Are the Purpose and Components of a Data Warehouse?

The purpose of a **data warehouse** is to extract and clean data from operational systems and other sources, and to store and catalog that data for processing by BI tools. Figure 9-4 shows the basic components of a data warehouse. Programs read operational data and extract, clean, and prepare that data for BI processing. The prepared data are stored in a data-warehouse database using a data-warehouse DBMS, which can be different from the organization's operational DBMS. For example, an organization might use Oracle for its operational processing, but use SQL Server for its data warehouse. Other organizations use SQL Server for operational processing, but use DBMSs from statistical package vendors, such as SAS or SPSS, in the data warehouse.

Counting and Counting and Counting

Not long ago, in a very large software company, a meeting occurred between a group of highly competent product managers and a group of equally competent data miners. The product managers wanted the data miners to analyze customer clicks on a Web page to determine customer preferences for particular product lines. The products were competing with one another for resources, and the results of the analysis were important in allocating those resources.

The meeting progressed well until one of the data miners started to explain the sampling scheme that they would use.

"Sampling?" asked the product managers in a chorus. "Sampling? No way. We want all the data. This is important, and we don't want a guess."

"But there are millions, literally, millions of ad clicks to analyze. If we don't sample, it will take hours, maybe even days, to perform the calculations. You won't see the results from each day's analysis until several days later if we don't sample." The data miners were squirming.

"We don't care," said the product managers. "We must have an accurate study. Don't sample!"

This leads us to a statistical concept you need to know: *There's nothing wrong with sampling.* Properly done, the results from a sample are just as accurate as results from the complete data set. Studies done from samples are also cheaper and faster. Sampling is a great way to save time and money.

Suppose you have a bag of randomly mixed blue and red balls. Let's say the bag is big enough to contain 100,000 balls. How many of those balls do you need to examine to calculate, accurately, the proportion of each color?

You go to the park on a sunny day, sit down with your bag, and start pulling balls out of the bag. After 100 balls, you conclude the ratio of blue to red is 4.1 to 5.9. After 1,000 balls, you conclude the ratio of blue to red balls is 4.02 to 5.98. After 5,000 balls, you conclude the ratio of blue to red balls is 4.002 to 5.998. After 10,000 balls, you conclude the ratio of blue to red balls is 4 to 6. Do you really need to sit there until next week, counting balls day and night, to examine every ball in the bag? And, if you're the manager who needs to know that ratio, do you really want to pay someone to count all those balls?

That's why the data miners were so depressed after their meeting with the product managers. They

knew they had to count Web clicks long, long after there was any more information to be gained from continuing to count. To add to the pain of their situation, they had to do it only because of the product managers' ignorance.

In truth, skill is required to develop a good sample. The product managers should have listened to the data miners' sampling plan and ensured that the sample would be appropriate, given the goals of the study. If they weren't competent to know if the sampling plan was correct, they should have employed a knowledgeable third party to assess it. Hiring the third party would have been far cheaper and faster than buying all the computers necessary to process all the data. Unfortunately, this company bought the computers!

Understanding just this concept will save you and your organization substantial money!

DISCUSSION QUESTIONS

1. In your own words, explain why a sample can give the same accuracy of results as the entire data set. Under what circumstances would it not give the same results?

2. Suppose you want to predict the demand for toothbrushes from past sales data. Suppose there are 5 colors and 10 styles. If you want to predict the sales for all types of toothbrushes, how should you sample? If you want to predict the sales for each color and style, would you sample differently? Why or why not?

3. The data miners tried to sell the idea of sampling based on the reduction of work. Suppose instead they had tried to sell the idea based on the idea of equal accuracy. Would the result have been different?

FIGURE 9-4
Components of a Data
Warehouse

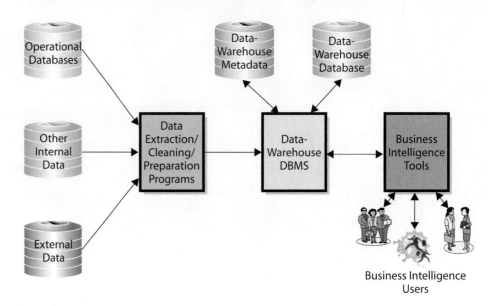

Data warehouses can include external data purchased from outside sources. A typical example is customer credit data. Figure 9-5 lists some of the consumer data than can be purchased from commercial vendors. An amazing (and from a privacy standpoint, frightening) amount of data is available.

Social networking and user-generated content applications generate potentially large amounts of data. Because the data comes directly from the source (prospect or client), it will likely be more accurate than purchased data. Social networking and user-generated content are just now coming into use in business, and organizations have not yet compiled large amounts of that data. In the years to come, however, such data will play a key role in data warehouse applications.

Metadata concerning the data—its source, its format, its assumptions and constraints, and other facts about the data—is kept in a data-warehouse metadata database. The data-warehouse DBMS extracts and provides data to business intelligence tools, such as data-mining programs.

By the way, do not interpret the term *warehouse* literally. It is a warehouse only in the sense that it is a facility for storing data for use by others. It is *not* a large building with shelves and forklifts buzzing through aisles loaded with pallets. Physically, a data warehouse consists of a few fast computers with very large storage devices. The data warehouse is usually staffed by a small department consisting of both technical personnel and business analysts. The technical personnel work to develop the best ways of storing and cataloging the data warehouse's contents. The business analysts work to ensure the contents are relevant and sufficient for the business needs of BI system users.

Data warehouses can have
enormous amounts of data.
Consider, for example, the
amount of data generated by
grocery stores, as described
in *MIS in Use 9.*

FIGURE 9-5
Consumer Data Available for
Purchase from Data Vendors

- Name, address, phone
- Age
- Gender
- Ethnicity
- Religion
- Income
- Education
- Voter registration
- Home ownership
- Vehicles
- Magazine subscriptions
- Hobbies
- Catalog orders
- Marital status, life stage
- Height, weight, hair and eye color
- Spouse name, birth date
- Children's names and birth dates

9 The Value of Grocery Store Data

Many grocery stores sponsor "card" programs that customers use to receive purchase discounts. Safeway, for example, sponsors the Safeway Club Card. The customer provides personal data, including his or her name, phone number, and address, and in return receives an identification card with a magnetic strip. When checking out, the customer gives the card to the cashier and receives small discounts on purchase prices. Ostensibly, the discount is a reward for being a frequent customer.

However, there must be more to the story. Unlike other frequent-buyer programs, the discount is not related to the number or size of previous purchases or to the total amount spent over time. Such programs are popular; many grocery chains have them, so they must provide value. The question is, what is that value?

Consider this question from a business intelligence perspective. What might Safeway or any other grocery chain do with data that correlates a particular customer to that customer's purchases over time? What information can such data provide? The data includes not only the customer's identity, purchases, and purchase items, it also includes the store location and the date and time of sale. The cards are valid at any Safeway store, so purchases at different stores can be associated with the same customer at a centralized data warehouse, somewhere.

You and a team of your fellow students will have an opportunity to answer the question about the value of grocery cards in Collaboration Exercise 9 on page 228.

Q5 What Is a Data Mart, and How Does It Differ from a Data Warehouse?

A **data mart** is a data collection that is created to address the needs of a particular business function, problem, or opportunity. An e-commerce company, for example, might create a data mart that stores clickstream data that is presampled and summarized in such a way as to enable the analysis of Web page design features.

That same company might have a second data mart for market-basket analysis. This second data mart would contain records of past sales data organized to facilitate the computation of item-purchase correlations. A third data mart could contain inventory data and be organized to support a BI system used to plan the layout of inventory.

So how is a data warehouse different from a data mart? In a way, you can think of a *data warehouse* as a distributor in a supply chain. The data warehouse takes data from the data manufacturers (operational systems, other internal systems, etc.), cleans and processes the data, and locates the data on its shelves, so to speak—that is, on the disks of the data warehouse computers. The people who work with a data warehouse are experts at data management, data cleaning, data transformation, metadata design, and the like. Data warehouse business analysts know the general needs of the business, but they are not experts in a given business function.

As stated, a *data mart* is a data collection, smaller than the data warehouse, that addresses a particular component or functional area of the business. If the data warehouse is the distributor in a supply chain, then a data mart is like a retail store in a supply chain. Users in the data mart obtain data that pertain to a particular business function from the data warehouse. Such users do not have the data management expertise that data warehouse employees have, but they are knowledgeable analysts for a given business function. Figure 9-6 illustrates these relationships.

As you can imagine, it is expensive to create, staff, and operate data warehouses and data marts. Only large organizations with deep pockets can afford to operate a system like that shown in Figure 9-6. Smaller organizations operate subsets of this system; they may have just a simple data mart for analyzing promotion data, for example.

FIGURE 9-6
Data Mart Examples

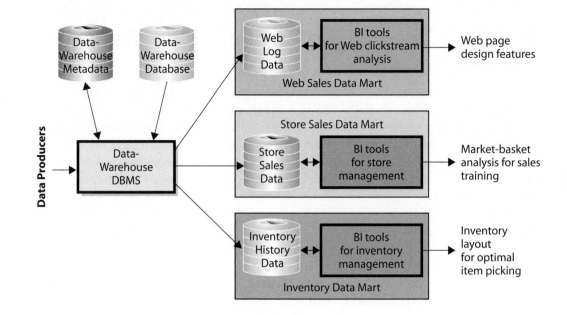

Q6 What Are the Characteristics of Data-Mining Systems?

We now return to the concept of data mining. **Data mining** is the application of statistical techniques to find patterns and relationships among data and to classify and predict. As shown in Figure 9-7, data mining represents a convergence of disciplines. Data-mining techniques emerged from statistics and mathematics and from artificial intelligence and machine-learning fields in computer science. As a result, data-mining terminology is an odd blend of terms from these different disciplines. Sometimes people use the term *knowledge discovery in databases (KDD)* as a synonym for *data mining*.

Data-mining techniques take advantage of developments in data management for processing the enormous databases that have emerged in the last 10 years. Of course, these data would not have been generated were it not for fast and cheap computers, and without such computers, the new techniques would be impossible to compute.

Most data-mining techniques are sophisticated, and many are difficult to use. Such techniques are valuable to organizations, however, and some business professionals, especially those in finance and marketing, have become expert in their use. Today, in fact,

FIGURE 9-7
Convergence Disciplines
for Data Mining

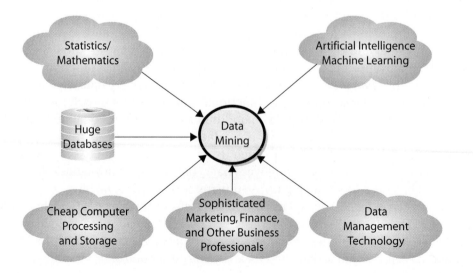

there are many interesting and rewarding careers for business professionals who are knowledgeable about data-mining techniques.

Data-mining techniques fall into two broad categories: unsupervised and supervised. We explain both types in the following sections.

Unsupervised Data Mining

With **unsupervised data mining**, analysts do not create a model or hypothesis before running the analysis. Instead, they apply the data-mining technique to the data and observe the results. With this method, analysts create hypotheses after the analysis to explain the patterns found.

One common unsupervised technique is **cluster analysis**. With it, statistical techniques identify groups of entities that have similar characteristics. A common use for cluster analysis is to find groups of similar customers from customer order and demographic data.

For example, suppose a cluster analysis finds two very different customer groups: One group has an average age of 33, owns at least one laptop and at least one PDA, drives an expensive SUV, and tends to buy expensive children's play equipment. The second group has an average age of 64, owns vacation property, plays golf, and buys expensive wines. Suppose the analysis also finds that both groups buy designer children's clothing.

These findings are obtained solely by data analysis. There is no prior model about the patterns and relationship that exist. It is up to the analyst to form hypotheses, after the fact, to explain why two such different groups are both buying designer children's clothes.

Supervised Data Mining

With **supervised data mining**, data miners develop a model prior to the analysis and apply statistical techniques to data to estimate parameters of the model. For example, suppose marketing experts in a communications company believe that cell phone usage on weekends is determined by the age of the customer and the number of months the customer has had the cell phone account. A data-mining analyst would then run an analysis that estimates the impact of customer and account age. One such analysis, which measures the impact of a set of variables on another variable, is called a **regression analysis**. A sample result for the cell phone example is:

```
CellPhoneWeekendMinutes = 12 + (17.5 × CustomerAge)
+ (23.7 × NumberMonthsOfAccount)
```

Using this equation, analysts can predict the number of minutes of weekend cell phone use by summing 12, plus 17.5 times the customer's age, plus 23.7 times the number of months of the account.

As you will learn in your statistics classes, considerable skill is required to interpret the quality of such a model. The regression tool will create an equation, such as the one shown. Whether that equation is a good predictor of future cell phone usage depends on statistical factors such as t values, confidence intervals, and related statistical techniques.

Neural networks are another popular supervised data-mining technique used to predict values and make classifications, such as "good prospect" or "poor prospect" customers. The term *neural networks* is deceiving, because it connotes a biological process similar to that in animal brains. In fact, although the original *idea* of neural nets may have come from the anatomy and physiology of neurons, a neural net is nothing more than a complicated set of possibly nonlinear equations. Explaining the techniques used for neural networks is beyond the scope of this text. If you want to learn more, search *kdnuggets.com* for the term *neural network*.

As useful as data mining and business intelligence can be for organizations, they are not without problems, as discussed in the *Ethics Guide* on pages 224–225.

Data Mining in the Real World

"I'm not really against data mining. I believe in it. After all, it's my career. But data mining in the real world is a lot different from the way it's described in textbooks.

"There are many reasons it's different. One is that the data are always dirty, with missing values, values way out of the range of possibility, and time values that make no sense. Here's an example: Somebody sets the server system clock incorrectly and runs the server for a while with the wrong time. When they notice the mistake, they set the clock to the correct time. But all of the transactions that were running during that interval have an ending time before the starting time. When we run the data analysis, and compute elapsed time, the results are negative for those transactions.

"Missing values are a similar problem. Consider the records of just 10 purchases. Suppose that two of the records are missing the customer number and one is missing the year part of the transaction date. So you throw out three records, which is 30 percent of the data. You then notice that two more records have dirty data, and so you throw them out, too. Now you've lost half your data.

"Another problem is that you know the least when you start the study. So you work for a few months and learn that if you had another variable, say the customer's zip code, or age, or something else, you could do a much better analysis. But those other data just aren't available. Or, maybe they are available, but to get the data you have to reprocess millions of transactions, and you don't have the time or budget to do that.

"Overfitting is another problem, a huge one. I can build a model to fit any set of data you have. Give me 100 data points and in a few minutes, I can give you 100 different equations that will predict those 100 data points. With neural networks, you can create a model of any level of complexity you want, except that none of those equations will predict new cases with any accuracy at all. When using neural nets, you have to be very careful not to overfit the data.

"Then, too, data mining is about probabilities, not certainty. Bad luck happens. Say I build a model that predicts the probability that a customer will make a purchase. Using the model on new-customer data, I find three customers who have a .7 probability of buying something. That's a good number, well over a 50-50 chance, but it's still possible that none of them will buy. In fact, the probability that none of them will buy is $.3 \times .3 \times .3$, or .027, which is 2.7 percent.

"Now suppose I give the names of the three customers to a salesperson who calls on them, and sure enough, we have a stream of bad luck and none of them buys. This bad result doesn't mean the model is wrong. But what does the salesperson think? He thinks that the model is worthless and that he can do better on his own. He tells his manager who tells her associate, who tells the northeast regional manager, and sure enough, the model has a bad reputation across the company.

"Seasonality is another problem. Say all your training data are from the summer. Will your model be valid for the winter? Maybe, but maybe not. You might even know that it won't be valid for predicting winter sales, but if you don't have winter data, what do you do?

"When you start a data-mining project, you never know how it will turn out. I worked on one project for six months, and when we finished, I didn't think our model was any good. We had too many problems with data: wrong, dirty, and missing. There was no way we could know ahead of time that it would happen, but it did.

"When the time came to present the results to senior management, what could we do? How could we say we took 6 months of our time and substantial computer resources to create a bad model? We had a model, but I just didn't think it would make accurate predictions. I was a junior member of the team, and it wasn't for me to decide. I kept my mouth shut, but I never felt good about it."

Discussion Questions

1. Did this employee have an ethical responsibility to speak up regarding his belief about the quality of the data-mining model? Why or why not?

2. If you were this employee, what would you have done?

3. The case doesn't indicate how the data-mining model was to be used. Suppose it was to be used at a hospital emergency room to predict the criticality of emergency cases. In this case, would you change your answers to questions 1 and 2? Why or why not?

4. Suppose the data-mining model was to be used to predict the likelihood that sales prospects respond to a promotional postal mailing. Say the cost of the mailing is $10,000 and will be paid by a marketing department having an annual budget of $25 million. Do your answers to questions 1 and 2 change for this situation? Why or why not?

5. If your answers are different for questions 3 and 4, explain why. If they are not different, explain why not.

6. Suppose you were this employee and you spoke to your direct boss about your misgivings. Your boss said, "Forget about it, junior." How would you respond?

7. Suppose your boss told you to forget about it, but in a meeting with your boss and your boss's boss, the senior manager asks you what you think of the predictive ability of this model. How do you respond?

How does the knowledge in this chapter help MRV and you?

By now you should know the error in Sue's last statement. Majestic doesn't need a computer—it needs an *information system*, having all five components. In the back of her mind, she may know that she needs procedures and trained people, but saying *information system* instead of *computer* will help her keep the time and cost of developing the system in mind.

Trevor will leave us...

Beyond that, how can Majestic use the knowledge of this chapter? Majestic is too small to have a data warehouse, or even a data mart. But, it could utilize the essence of the idea of a data warehouse. Sue and her managers can be thinking about how they might use the data that they generate in the course of business to enable decision making. They should create a plan for organizing the storage of that data. We can imagine that at the moment client data, equipment data, food-purchase data, and revenue data are spread over several different computers. Data about past years' operations might well be located on old computers that are sitting in someone's closet or worse, have been recycled. So, Majestic should analyze the data it creates, decide which data it wants to keep, and organize storage for it.

Consider some of the potential uses for Majestic's data. For one, as Sue indicates, she could use it to determine which guides generate the most repeat business. The company could also determine its highest-revenue customers as well as the customers who have generated the most referrals. It might also be able to assess possible lost customers and attempt to woo them back.

Other applications include analyzing the equipment inventory to determine seldom-used equipment that could be sold. Majestic could use equipment data to guide future purchases by determining which equipment lasts the longest and which equipment needs frequent repair. It could also use equipment data to detect pilferage, if any.

Majestic could use data about food purchases to determine which are the best vendors and the best recipes. Majestic asks customers to complete feedback forms at the end of the trips. It could correlate customers' assessments of food with food purchases to determine which food vendors and recipes deliver the most value for the dollar.

Majestic is a small business, but even so, it has numerous possibilities for using its operational data for decision making. Remember this example in your future; learn to look for management applications of data that your organization generates.

Active Review

Use this Active Review to verify that you understand the material in the chapter. You can read the entire chapter and then perform the tasks in this review, or you can read the material for just one question and perform the tasks in this review for that question before moving on to the next one.

Q1 How big is an exabyte, and why does it matter? State the total disk storage capacity as of 2007. Compare this storage capacity to the number of words ever spoken by human beings. Explain how this phenomenon impacts organizations today; use Majestic as an example, but expand your explanation to larger organizations as well.

Q2 How do business intelligence (BI) systems provide competitive advantages? Define *business intelligence systems*. Name four categories of BI systems, and describe the basic characteristics of each. Explain how systems in each category contribute to competitive advantage.

Q3 **What problems do operational data pose for BI systems?** List problems that occur when using operational data for BI systems. Briefly summarize each problem. Define *granularity*. Explain the problem posed by the curse of dimensionality.

Q4 **What are the purpose and components of a data warehouse?** State the purpose of a data warehouse. Explain the role of each component in Figure 9-4. Of the many different types of data that can be purchased, name five that you think are the most concerning from a privacy standpoint. State reasons why some businesses might want to purchase this data. Describe the impact that social networks and user-generated content will have on data warehouses. Explain why the term *warehouse* is misleading.

Q5 **What is a data mart, and how does it differ from a data warehouse?** Define *data mart*, and give an example of one not described in this chapter. Explain how data warehouses and data marts are like components of a supply chain. Under

what conditions does an organization staff a data warehouse with several data marts?

Q6 **What are the characteristics of data-mining systems?** State the purpose of data-mining systems. Explain how data mining emerged from the convergence of different disciplines. Describe the impact this history had on data-mining terminology. Explain the characteristics and uses of unsupervised data mining. Explain the characteristics and uses of supervised data mining. Explain why the term *neural network* is a misnomer.

Explain the error that Sue makes in the dialog that opens this chapter, and describe why it is important. Explain how Majestic can use the principles of data warehousing even though they are too small to have a formal data warehouse facility. Describe four different decision-making applications for Majestic's operational data.

Key Terms and Concepts

Using Your Knowledge

1. Explain why the knowledge that we are storing exabytes of data is important to decision making. Name and describe three decision-making applications of stored data not mentioned in this chapter. Use one example for each of the four types of BI system in Figure 9-2.

2. How does the data storage trend described in question 1 impact your university? What types of data do you think are growing the fastest? Of the fast-growing data, what percentage do you think is generated by students? By classroom activities? By administration? By research? Explain your answer.

3. Suppose you work for the university and have access to student, class, professor, department, and grade data. Suppose you want to determine whether grade inflation exists, and, if so, where it seems to be the greatest. Describe a reporting system that would produce evidence of grade inflation. How would you structure the reports to determine where it is the greatest?

4. Suppose you work for the university and have access to student, class, professor, department, and grade data. Assume the student data includes students' home address, high school, and prior college

performance (if any). Describe an unsupervised data-mining technique that could be used to predict college applicants who are likely to succeed academically. Is it responsible or irresponsible to use an unsupervised technique for such a problem?

5. Same as question 4, but describe a supervised data-mining technique that could be used to predict the success of applicants. Is using a supervised technique more justifiable than using an unsupervised technique? Explain your answer.

6. Explain how a set of If/Then rules could be used to select a food supplier for Majestic. Give an example of five rules that would be pertinent to this problem. Given Majestic's size and culture of the organization, do you think it is likely that it would embrace an expert system? Explain.

7. Explain why a data warehouse is inappropriate for Majestic. Figure 9-7 implies that data marts require the existence of a data warehouse, but this is not always true. Majestic could construct a data mart containing customer, equipment, and food expense without a data warehouse. In this case, the data mart would need to clean and prep its own operational data. Given the nature of Majestic's business, what value might such a data mart provide? List seven decisions that such a data mart might support. Describe the BI system that would support each decision. Explain how such BI systems contribute to Majestic's competitive strategy.

Collaboration Exercise 9 ◉

Before you start this exercise, read Chapter Extensions 1 and 2, which describe collaboration techniques as well as tools for managing collaboration tasks. In particular, consider using Google Docs & Spreadsheets, Google Groups, Microsoft Groove, Microsoft SharePoint, or some other collaboration tool.

1. Reread *MIS in Use 9* on page 221. Discuss with your team why you think Safeway is willing to sacrifice revenue (from discounts) by sponsoring its club-card program. Develop a list of five possible explanations and, as a team, rank them from most important to least important. Justify your ranking.

2. Read CE16, "Database Marketing." Using an example, explain how Safeway could use RFM analysis. There is little evidence, though, that Safeway is using RFM analysis. Explain why this might be so. Write a one-page memo explaining the advantages to Safeway of using RFM.

3. Describe market-basket analysis and explain how Safeway could perform such an analysis using its club-card data. Suppose the lift of high-quality dog food and premium wine is 3.4. Explain what this means. Describe four possible ways that Safeway could use this information. As a team, rank the four possibilities from best to worst and justify your ranking. Explain why Safeway could perform a market-basket analysis without the club-card program.

4. Read CE17, "Reporting Systems and OLAP." Relate the OLAP examples in that chapter extension to Safeway. Describe two possible measures and five possible dimensions of the club-card data. Illustrate with fictitious data two different arrangements of dimensions with one of your measures.

5. Compare your answers to questions 2, 3, and 4. As a team, rank these three applications in terms of the value that you think they generate for Safeway. Justify your ranking. Do you think these applications are worth the cost of this program to Safeway? Explain.

Case Study 9

Building Data for Decision Making at Home Depot

Home Depot is a major retail chain specializing in the sale of construction and home repair and maintenance products. The company has 2,246 retail stores in North America from which it generated $77 billion in sales in 2007. Home Depot carries more than 40,000 products in its stores and employs 331,000 people worldwide.

Suppose you are a buyer for the clothes washer and dryer product line at Home Depot. You work with seven different brands and numerous models within each brand. One of your goals is to turn your inventory as many times a year as you can. In order to do so, you want to identify poorly selling models (and even brands) as quickly as you can. This identification is not as easy as you might think, because competition is intense among washer and dryer manufacturers and a new model can quickly capture a substantial portion of another model's market share. Thus, a big seller this year can be a "dog" (a poor seller) next year.

Another problem is that while some sales trends are national, others pertain to specific regions. A strong seller in the Southeast may not sell as well in the Northwest. Thus, a brand can be a big seller in one region and a dog in another.

In answering the following questions, assume you have total sales data for each brand and model, for each store, for each month. Assume also that you know the store's city and state.

Questions

1. Explain how reporting systems could be helpful to you.

2. Show the structure of one or two reports that you could use to identify poorly selling models. How would you structure the reports to identify different sales trends in different regions?

3. For one of your reports in question 2, write a description of your requirements for an IT professional. Be as complete and thorough as you can in describing your needs.

4. Explain how data-mining systems could be helpful to you.

5. How could cluster analysis help you identify poorly selling brands? How could cluster analysis help you determine differences in sales for different geographic regions? Is the unsupervised nature of cluster analysis an advantage or disadvantage for you?

6. How could regression analysis help you determine poorly selling brands?

7. Do you believe there is an application for a KM system for identifying poorly selling brands? Why or why not?

8. Do you believe there is an application for an expert system for identifying poorly selling brands? Why or why not?

THE
International
Dimension

Global Information Systems

?

Study Questions

Q1 How do global information systems benefit the value chain?

Q2 What are the challenges of international business process management?

Q3 How does Web 2.0 affect international business?

Q4 How do global information systems affect supply chain profitability?

Q5 What is the economic impact of global manufacturing?

The International Dimension

Q1 How Do Global Information Systems Benefit the Value Chain?

Because of information systems, any or all of the value chain activities in Figure 3-5 (page 48) can be performed anywhere in the world. An international company can conduct sales and marketing efforts locally, for every market in which it sells. Emerson Pharmaceuticals, for example, sells in the United States with a U.S. sales force, in France with a French sales force, and in Argentina with an Argentinean sales force. Depending on local laws and customs, those sales offices may be owned by Emerson, or they may be locally owned entities with which Emerson contracts for sales and marketing services. Emerson can coordinate all of the sales efforts of these entities using the same CRM (customer relationship management) system. When Emerson managers need to roll up sales totals for a sales projection, they can do so using an integrated, worldwide system.

Manufacturing of a final product is frequently distributed throughout the world. Components of the Boeing 787 are manufactured in Italy, China, England, and numerous other countries and delivered to Everett, Washington, for final assembly. Each manufacturing facility has its own inbound logistics, manufacturing, and outbound logistics activity, but those activities are linked together via information systems.

For example, Rolls Royce manufactures an engine and delivers that engine to Boeing via its outbound logistics activity. Boeing receives the engine using its inbound logistics activity. All of this activity is coordinated via shared, interorganizational information systems. Rolls Royce's CRM is connected with Boeing's supply processes, using techniques such as CRM and enterprise resource planning (ERP).

Because of the abundance of low-cost, well-educated, English-speaking professionals in India, many organizations have chosen to outsource their service and support functions to India. Some accounting functions are outsourced to India as well.

World time differences enable global virtual companies to operate 24/7. Boeing engineers in Los Angeles can develop a design for an engine support strut and send that design to Rolls Royce in England at the end of their day. The design will be waiting for Rolls Royce engineers at the start of their day. They review the design, make needed adjustments, and send it back to Boeing in Los Angeles, where the reviewed, adjusted design arrives at the start of the workday in Los Angeles. The ability to work around the clock by moving work into other time zones has greatly increased productivity.

Q2 What Are the Challenges of International Business Process Management?

Challenges for international business process management depend on whether the process is functional or cross-functional. As you learned in Chapter 7, functional business processes support particular activities within a single department or business activity. Because the systems operate independently, the organization suffers from islands of automation. Sales and marketing data, for example, are not integrated with operations or manufacturing data.

This lack of integration has *advantages*, however, for international organizations and international systems. Because the order-processing functional system in the United States is separate from and independent of the manufacturing systems in Taiwan, it is unnecessary to accommodate language, business, and cultural differences in a single system. U.S. order-processing systems can operate in English and reflect the practices and culture of the United States. Taiwanese manufacturing information systems can operate in Chinese and reflect the business practices and culture of Taiwan. As long as there is an adequate data interface between the two systems, they can operate independently, sharing data when necessary.

Cross-functional, integrated systems, such as ERP, solve the problems of data isolation by integrating data into databases that provide a comprehensive and organization-wide view. However, because they are integrated, cross-functional systems do not readily accommodate differences in language, business practices, and cultural norms.

For example, consider the ERP system, SAP. SAP software is developed and licensed by SAP, a German software company. Because SAP addresses a global market, SAP software was localized long ago into English and numerous other foreign languages. Suppose that a multinational company with operations in Spain, Italy, Taiwan, Singapore, and Los Angeles uses SAP. Should this company allow the use of different language versions of SAP? As long as the functionality of the versions is the same, no harm occurs by doing so.

But what if employees enter data in different languages? If this is allowed, much of the value of an integrated database is lost. If you speak English, what good are customer contact data recorded in Spanish, Italian, Chinese, and English? Data isolation entered the ERP system via the back door.

Inherent processes are even more problematic. Each software product assumes that the software will be used by people filling particular job functions and performing their actions in a certain way. ERP vendors justify this standardization by saying that their procedures are based on industry-wide best practices and that the organization will benefit by following these standard processes. That statement may be true, but some inherent processes may conflict with cultural norms. If they do, it will be very difficult for management to convince the employees to follow those inherent processes. Or at least it will be difficult in some cultures to do so.

Differences in language, culture, norms, and expectations compound the difficulties of international process management. Just creating an accurate as-is model is difficult and expensive; developing alternative international processes and evaluating them can be incredibly challenging. With cultural differences, it can be difficult just to determine what criteria should be used for evaluating the alternatives, let alone performing the evaluation.

Because of these challenges, in the future it is likely that international business processes will be developed more like interorganizational business processes. A high-level process will be defined to document the service responsibilities of each international unit. Then SOA standards will be used to connect those services into an integrated, cross-functional, international system. Because of encapsulation, the only obligation of an international unit will be to deliver its defined service. One service can be delivered using procedures based on autocratic management policies, and another can be delivered using procedures based on collaborative management policies. The differences will not matter to a SOA-based cross-functional system.

Q3 How Does Web 2.0 Affect International Business?

In truth, we do not know, at least not yet, how Web 2.0 affects international business. We do know that Web 2.0 technologies are used internationally: For example, Google AdWords is available in the Japanese and Indian markets, and social networks are popular in any culture with sufficient connectivity. We do not know, however, how Web 2.0 affects international business. It is possible that Web 2.0 technologies are so culturally biased that they work only in the culture in which they originate. A Facebook social graph of a young college woman in Japan is unlikely to connect in any meaningful way with a similar graph of a male business student in India. Each will have his or her own social network, but they will be domestic, not international.

Similar comments can be made about user-generated content. Teenagers in Chicago are unlikely to be influenced by user-generated tennis shoe designs that are popular in Hanover, Germany. Or are they? Is there a business opportunity for some innovative company to foster user-generated designs in one culture with the express purpose of marketing those designs in another culture? As of August 2008, we do not know.

Opportunities like this will exist for you and your classmates to explore early in your careers. As you use Facebook or MySpace and as you consume or create UGC, think about the international aspects of your activity. Maybe you can be the one to invent the next YouTube!

Meanwhile, we do know that global information systems have and will continue to have an impact on manufacturing, and we consider international manufacturing in the next two questions.

Q4 How Do Global Information Systems Affect Supply Chain Profitability?

In short, global information systems increase supply chain profitability. Supply chain performance is driven by four factors: facilities, inventories, transportation, and information. Every one of these drivers is positively affected by global information systems. Because of global information systems, facilities can be located anywhere in the world. If Amazon.com finds it economically advantageous to warehouse books in Iceland, it can do so. If Rolls Royce can more cheaply manufacture its engine turbine blades in Poland, it can do so.

Furthermore, information systems reduce inventories and hence save costs. They can be used to reduce or eliminate the *bullwhip effect*, a phenomenon in which the variability in the size and timing of orders increases at each stage of the supply chain.

They also support just-in-time (JIT) inventory techniques worldwide. Using information systems, the order of a Dell computer from a user in Bolivia triggers a manufacturing system at Dell, which, in turn, triggers the order of a component from a warehouse in Taiwan—all automatically.

To underscore this point, consider the inventories that exist at this moment in time, worldwide. Every component in one of those inventories represents a waste of the world's resources. Any product or component sitting on a shelf is not being used and is adding no value to the global economy. In the perfect world, a customer would think, "I want a new computer," and that thought would trigger systems all over the world to produce and assemble necessary components, instantly. Given that we live in a world bound by time and space, instantaneous production is forever unreachable. But the goal of worldwide information systems for supply chain inventory management is to come as close to instantaneous as possible.

Consider transportation, the third driver. When you order a book from Amazon.com, you are presented with at least four shipping options. You can choose the speed and attendant price that is appropriate for your needs. Similar systems for businesses allow them to choose the delivery option that optimizes the value they generate. Further, automated systems enable suppliers and customers to track the shipment's location, 24/7, worldwide.

Finally, global information systems produce comprehensive, accurate, and timely information. As you learned in Chapter 9, information systems produce data at prodigious rates, worldwide. That data facilitates operations as just discussed, but it also produces information for planning, organizing, deciding, and other analyses.

Next time you walk into Wal-Mart, think about the impact global information systems had in producing, ordering, and delivering the thousands of items you see.

Q5 What Is the Economic Impact of Global Manufacturing?

Henry Ford pioneered modern manufacturing methods, and in the process he reduced the price of automobiles to the point they were no longer the playthings of the very rich but were affordable to the general population. In 1914, Ford took the unprecedented step of unilaterally increasing his workers' pay from $2.50 per day for 10 hours' work to $5 per day for 8 hours' work. As a consequence, many of his workers could soon afford to purchase an automobile. By paying his workers more, Ford increased demand.

The increase in demand was not due only to purchases by his workers, of course. Because of what economists call the *accelerator effect*, a dollar spent will contribute two or three dollars of activity to the economy. Ford's workers spent their increased pay not just on autos, but also on goods and services in their local community, which benefited via the accelerator effect. That benefit enabled non–Ford workers also to afford an auto. Further, because of the positive publicity he achieved with the pay increase, the community was strongly disposed to purchase a Ford automobile.

Consider those events in light of global manufacturing. For example, if Boeing manufactures airplanes entirely in the United States, the U.S. economy will be the sole beneficiary of that economic activity. If an Italian airline chooses to buy a Boeing plane, the transaction will be a cost to the Italian economy. There will be no accelerator effect, and the transaction will have no consequence on Italians' propensity to fly.

However, if Boeing purchases major components for its airplanes from Italian companies, then that purchase will generate an accelerator effect for the Italian economy. By buying in Italy, Boeing contributes to Italy's economy, and ultimately increases Italians' propensity to fly. That foreign-component purchase will, of course, reduce economic activity in the United States, but if it induces Italians to purchase sufficiently more Boeing airplanes, then it is possible that the loss will be compensated by the increase in airplane sales volume. That purchase will also benefit Boeing's image among Italians and increase the likelihood of sales to the Italian government.

The same phenomenon pertains to Dell computers, Cisco routers, and Microsoft programmers. It also explains why Toyota manufactures cars in the United States.

Active Review

Use this Active Review to verify that you understand the material in the chapter. You can read the entire chapter and then perform the tasks in this review, or you can read the material for just one question and perform the tasks in this review for that question before moving on to the next one.

Q1 How do global information systems benefit the value chain? Using Figure 3-5 (page 48) as a guide, explain how each primary value chain activity can be performed anywhere in the world. Explain how global, virtual companies operate 24/7. Using the answers to this question, explain three ways that Emerson can benefit from a global information system.

Q2 What are the challenges of international business process management? In your own words, explain why the challenges for international process management depend on whether the process is functional or cross-functional. Explain how lack of integration can have advantages. Discuss the particular challenges of inherent processes. Describe how SOA principles facilitate international business process management.

Q3 How does Web 2.0 affect international business? Explain the text's response to this study question. Do you agree or disagree with it? Explain the meaning of the following sentence: "It's possible that Web 2.0 technologies are so culturally biased that they work only in the culture in which they originate." Describe how this situation may create opportunities for you.

Q4 How do global information systems affect supply chain profitability? State the short answer to this question. Name the four drivers of supply chain profitability. Discuss how global information systems affect each driver. Explain how inventories represent waste. Summarize the ways that you think global information systems have in filling the shelves at Wal-Mart.

Q5 What is the economic impact of global manufacturing? Summarize the impact that Henry Ford's act of increasing his workers' pay had on Ford auto sales. Describe how the accelerator effect contributed to the increase in demand. Explain how this same phenomenon pertains to Boeing acquiring major subsystems from manufacturers in Italy or to Toyota building autos in the United States.

Consider Your Net Worth

Examine the questions addressed in Chapters 7 through 9 and consider how those ideas will pertain to you as a future manager and professional businessperson. How can you use the knowledge you've gained to increase your net worth both to your employer and yourself?

1. Summarize the problem that Majestic River Ventures encountered in Chapter 7. Explain how MRV can use business process management to solve that problem and to prevent similar problems in the future. Generalize this situation to your own professional interests. How will business process management be important to you? Describe one way that you envision that you might use BPM in your future. Write one-paragraph defining BPM and explaining its importance. Write that paragraph as if you were going to use those ideas in a job interview.

2. In Chapter 8, Graham is upset that there are no girls, or, more broadly, that there are no people his age on this trip. Explain how MRV can avoid such situations by using social networking in its marketing. Be specific in how MRV can use social networking groups and applications. Generalize this use of social networking to your professional interests. How can you use social networking groups? How can you use social networking applications? Write one paragraph that explains the benefits of social networking to businesses. As in question 1, write that paragraph as if you were going to use it in a job interview.

3. Explain the problem that MRV has in the opening to Chapter 9. How does that problem relate to business intelligence systems? In general, do you think it is unusual for an organization to have valuable information in data that it is unable to access or produce? Why or why not? How does this situation create opportunities for you in the future? Write one paragraph that explains the benefits of business intelligence systems to businesses. As in question 1, write that paragraph as if you were going to use it in a job interview.

Application Exercises

1. Suppose your manager asks you to create a spreadsheet to compute a production schedule. Your schedule should stipulate a production quantity for seven products that is based on sales projections made by three regional managers at your company's three sales regions.

a. Create a separate worksheet for each sales region. Assume that each sheet contains monthly sales projections for each of the past four quarters. Assume that it also contains actual monthly sales for each of those past four quarters.

Finally, assume that each sheet contains a projection for each month in the coming quarter.

b. Fill in sample data for each of the worksheets in part a.

c. On each of the worksheets, use the data from the prior four quarters to compute the discrepancy between the actual sales and the sale projections. This discrepancy can be computed in several ways: You could calculate an overall average, or you could calculate an average per quarter or per month. You could also weigh recent discrepancies more heavily than earlier ones. Choose a method that you think is most appropriate. Explain why you chose the method you did.

d. Modify your worksheets to use the discrepancy factors to compute an adjusted forecast for the coming quarter. Thus, each of your spreadsheets will show the raw forecast and the adjusted forecast for each month in the coming quarter.

e. Create a fourth worksheet that totals sales projections for all of the regions. Show both the unadjusted forecast and the adjusted forecast for each region and for the company overall. Show month and quarter totals.

f. Create a bar graph showing total monthly production. Display the unadjusted and adjusted forecasts using different colored bars.

2. The following figure, which shows a sample bill of materials, was produced using Microsoft Access. Producing such a form is a bit tricky, so this exercise will guide you through the steps required. You can then apply what you learn to produce a similar report. You can also use Access to experiment on extensions of this form.

a. Create a table named PART with columns *PartNumber, Level, Description, QuantityRequired,* and *PartOf.* Description and Level should be text, PartNumber should be AutoNumber, and QuantityRequired and PartOf should be numeric, long integer. Add the PART data shown in the figure below to your table.

b. Create a query that has all columns of PART. Restrict the view to rows having a value of 1 for Level. Name your query *Level1.*

c. Create two more queries that are restricted to rows having values of 2 or 3 for Level. Name your queries *Level2* and *Level3,* respectively.

d. Create a form that contains PartNumber, Level, and Description from Level1. You can use a wizard for this if you want. Name the form *Bill of Materials.*

e. Using the subform tool in the Toolbox, create a subform in your form in part d. Set the data on this form to be all of the columns of Level2. After you have created the subform, ensure that the Link Child Fields property is set to *PartOf* and that the Link Master Fields property is set to *PartNumber.* Close the Bill of Materials form.

f. Open the subform created in part e and create a subform on it. Set the data on this subform to be all of the columns of Level3. After you have created the subform, ensure that the Link Child Fields property is set to *PartOf* and that the Link Master Fields property is set to *PartNumber.* Close the Bill of Materials form.

g. Open the Bill of Materials form. It should appear as shown on the previous page. Open and close the form and add new data. Using this form, add sample bill of materials data for a product of your own choosing.

h. Following the process similar to that just described, create a Bill of Materials Report that lists the data for all of your products.

i. (**Optional, challenging extension**) Each part in our sample bill of materials can be used in at most one assembly (there is space to show just one PartOf value). You can change your design to allow a part to be used in more than one assembly as follows. First, remove *PartOf* from PART. Next, create a second table that has two columns: *AssemblyPartNumber* and *ComponentPartNumber.* The first contains a part number of an assembly and the second a part number of a component. Every component of a part will have a row in this table. Extend the views described earlier to use this second table and to produce a display similar to the one on the previous page.

3. OLAP cubes are very similar to Microsoft Excel pivot tables. If you are unfamiliar with pivot tables, open Excel and search the help system for pivot tables. Select one of the demos to see how pivot tables work. Or you can just follow the instructions that follow. For this exercise, assume that in your organization the purchasing agents rate vendors. You can use a pivot table to display the data in flexible and informative ways.

a. Open Excel and add the following column headings to your spreadsheet: *VendorName, EmployeeName, Date, Year,* and *Rating.* Enter sample data under these headings. Add ratings for at least three vendors and at least three rows for each vendor. Add sufficient data so that each vendor will have at least five ratings, and each employee will have entered at least five ratings. Also, add data for at least two different months and two different years.

b. Under the *Data* tab in Excel, select *Pivot Table* and *Pivot Chart.* (From here on, the exact menu names may vary depending on the version of Excel you have. Look for names that are close to those used here.) A wizard will open. Select *Excel* and *Pivot table* in the first screen. Click *Next.*

c. When asked to provide a data range, drag your mouse over the data you entered so as to select all of the data. Be sure to include the column headings. Excel will fill in the range values in the open dialog box. Click *Next,* select *New worksheet,* and then *Finish.*

d. Excel will create a field list on the right-hand side of your spreadsheet. Drag and drop the field named *VendorName,* on the words "Drop Row Fields Here." Drag and drop *EmployeeName,* on the words "Drop Column Fields Here." Now drag and drop the field named *Rating* on the words "Drop Data Items Here." Voilà! You have a pivot table.

e. To see how the table works, drag and drop more fields on the various sections of your pivot table. For example, drop *Year* on top of *Employee.* Then move *Year* below *Employee.* Now move *Year* below *Vendor.* All of this action is just like an OLAP cube—and, in fact, OLAP cubes are readily displayed in Excel pivot tables. The major difference is that OLAP cubes are usually based on thousands or more rows of data.

4. It is surprisingly easy to create a market-basket report using table data in Access. To do so, however, you will need to enter SQL expressions into the Access query builder. Here, you can just copy SQL statements to type them in. If you take a database class, you will learn how to code SQL statements like those you will use here.

a. Create an Access database with a table named ORDERS having columns *OrderNumber*, *ItemName*, and *Quantity*, with data types Number (*LongInteger*), Text (*50*), and Number (*LongInteger*), respectively. The key of this table is (*OrderNumber*, *ItemName*), but you will not need to define it for this exercise. (If you want to know how to define it, after you have entered the data type definitions of those two columns, drag your mouse to highlight both of them in the design window and then click the key icon.)

b. Now enter sample data. Make sure that there are several items on each order and that some orders have items in common. For example, you might enter [100, 'Cup', 4], [100, 'Saucer', 4], [200, 'Fork', 2], [200, 'Spoon', 2], [200, 'Knife', 2], and [200, 'Cup', 3]. Enter data for at least five orders.

c. Now, to perform the market basket analysis, you will need to enter several SQL statements into Access. To do so, click the *Queries* tab and select *Create query* in Design view. Click *Close* when the Show Table dialog box appears. Right-click in the gray section above the grid in the Select Query window. Select *SQL View*. Now enter the following expression exactly as it appears here:

```
SELECT T1.ItemName as FirstItem, T2.ItemName
  as SecondItem
FROM ORDERS T1, ORDERS T2
WHERE T1.OrderNumber = T2.OrderNumber
AND T1.ItemName <> T2.ItemName;
```

Click the red exclamation point in the toolbar to run the query. Correct any typing mistakes and, once it works, save the query using the name **TwoItemBasket**.

d. Now enter a second SQL statement. Again, click the *Queries* tab and select *Create query* in Design view. Click *Close* when the Show Table dialog box appears. Right-click in the gray section above the grid in the Select Query window. Select *SQL View*. Now enter the following expression exactly as it appears here:

```
SELECT TwoItemBasket.FirstItem,
TwoItemBasket.SecondItem, Count(*)
  AS SupportCount
FROM TwoItemBasket
GROUP BY TwoItemBasket.FirstItem,
TwoItemBasket.SecondItem;
```

Correct any typing mistakes and, once it works, save the query using the name **SupportCount**.

e. Examine the results of the second query and verify that the two query statements have correctly calculated the number of times that two items have appeared together. Explain further calculations you need to make to compute support.

f. Explain the calculations you need to make to compute lift. Although you can make those calculations using SQL, you need more SQL knowledge to do it, and we will skip that here.

g. Explain, in your own words, what the query in part c seems to be doing. What does the query in part d seem to be doing? Again, you will need to take a database class to learn how to code such expressions, but this exercise should give you a sense of the kinds of calculations that are possible with SQL.

Dun and Bradstreet Data via Web Services

Dun and Bradstreet (D&B) collects data on more than 80 million businesses and sells it to customers who use the data for analyzing customer credit, selecting customer prospects, and identifying potential suppliers.

Some customers are willing to buy company reports using a standard commerce server. For others, this process is too slow and cumbersome. For example, consider the customers that use D&B data to assess creditworthiness. Because of competitive pressure, some companies must make credit assessments immediately, in real time, while interacting with their customers. For such applications, buying a prewritten report over the D&B commerce server will not suffice.

Instead, these customers want to use automated processes to access the D&B databases. They want to write credit-analysis programs that obtain needed data from D&B in real time. Consider, for example, the needs of a computer distributor or retailer. The distributor's customers can place large orders using the distributor's Web storefront. The equipment price for a medium-sized network could total $40,000 or $50,000; before accepting the order, the distributor needs to assess the creditworthiness of the customer. In situations like this, the distributor wants its commerce server programs to access D&B data and to use it to evaluate credit programmatically.

To meet this need, D&B developed a version of SOA services that its customers' programs can access. Although the D&B version uses XML documents for data exchange, it does not use all of the SOA standards. In particular, it does not provide a standard service description nor use standard services protocols. Instead, the D&B service provides a proprietary interface for customers. The D&B Web service could not use the current, modern standards, because those standards were not finalized when D&B developed its Web services system.

Still, D&B's Web services do use XML. Consequently, its users can realize the advantages of schema validation, and both D&B and its customers can use XML standards to reformat documents automatically.

In order to use the D&B Web services, customers must enter into an agreement with D&B that specifies which data will be accessed and what and how they will pay for that data access. Then, the customers must learn the D&B interface and develop programs accordingly. D&B provides some technical assistance to customer program developers.

By using Web services to obtain data, customers obtain the latest, up-to-the-minute data. This advantage is important because D&B makes over a million updates to its database every day. Furthermore, D&B Web services provide a single, consistent interface for customers to use. Customers save costs because they need to develop D&B access programs only once; all applications can use those programs to obtain D&B data. Finally, D&B customers can use the Web services interface to request alerts when particular data are updated. Alerts enable customers to update their own databases with the most current data.

Sources: Sean Rhody, "Dun and Bradstreet," *Web Services Journal*, Vol. 1, Issue 1, *http://sys-con.com/webservices* (accessed December 2004); Dun and Bradstreet, "Data Integration Toolkit," PowerPoint Presentation, *http://globalaccess. dnb.com* (accessed December 2004).

Questions

1. Summarize the difference between obtaining D&B data by purchasing reports from the D&B Web commerce server and by obtaining D&B data via SOA services.

2. Explain how schema validation improves the quality of the data exchange. How can D&B and its Web services customers use schema validation to their advantage?

3. As stated, D&B did not describe their Web services in the standard way. What are the consequences to D&B? What are the consequences to D&B's customers? D&B could upgrade its Web services to use these standards. If you worked at D&B, how would you decide whether to make that upgrade? Consider the consequences of the upgrade on both new and existing D&B Web services customers.

4. Besides credit reporting, D&B customers use D&B data to find and assess customer prospects and to determine potential sources of suppliers. Explain how SOA services could be used for these applications as well as for credit analysis.

5. D&B is an international organization that provides data to customers worldwide. What advantages does the use of SOA services provide for non–U.S. customers?

6. How does the D&B Web services interface give D&B a competitive advantage over other data providers?

INFORMATION
SYSTEMS
MANAGEMENT

Emerson Pharmaceuticals and Majestic River Ventures are very different companies. Emerson is a multinational organization with a billion dollars in sales and with facilities, offices, and personnel throughout the world. Emerson U.S. (its U.S. division) has 450 salespeople, plus thousands of other employees in labs, production facilities, and headquarters. Majestic has two small facilities and less than $1 million in sales. The total number of employees and contractors at MRV is 10 percent of the number of salespeople at Emerson.

Both Emerson and MRV use information systems, but they manage them very differently. Emerson U.S. has more than 200 employees in its IT department, and it also outsources several important functions to other vendors. MRV has no IT department; its computer systems, to the extent they are managed at all, are managed by employees and by Eddie, the office manager.

In Part 4, we will consider how both of these companies—one very large and one quite small—develop information systems, how they manage their IT and IS resources, and how they protect their systems with security. Not surprisingly, the two companies take very different approaches to all three of these topics.

This could happen to you

Emerson will have formalized processes for developing systems. The company will have policies and procedures for starting new projects, for managing IS development, and for maintaining systems once they are developed. IT management will be centralized, and the IT department will set standards for computer and network equipment and usage. Emerson will be most concerned about security and will have a staff of professionals devoted exclusively to protecting the company's IT infrastructure. All of these standards, policies, and procedures enhance the quality and reliability of Emerson's systems but can become burdensome and restrict innovative use of IS.

Majestic River Ventures, conversely, is a tiny company with no IS policies or procedures whatsoever. The company has no idea about how to develop information systems, and it knows next to nothing about managing IS resources. Although the company is vaguely aware of the need for security, it has no idea what to do to improve it. As you will see, MRV will pay a considerable price for its ignorance of IS management.

10 Information Systems Development

"Look, Eddie, I think we've outgrown them. They were fine when all we needed was a simple Web site. Maybe not Picassos with graphics, but they made it work."

"But, Sue, what are we gonna do? Put an ad in our local paper under *P* for programmer? We know nothing about this—at least they knew how to build our Web site."

"Yeah, they did, but every time I tried to talk with them about what I want next, they looked like deer in headlights."

This could happen to you

"OK, try it on me. What is it you want?"

"I want to bring our customers closer to us. I want an ongoing relationship with them. We know we're great, but I want them to tell *each other* that we're great.

I want two kinds of Web sites, or something like that. One site for the general public—like we have now, but more of our customers' photos, and more customer comments. Then I want a second site. Maybe it has a password or something. This site is just for people who've gone on trips with us. It has lots of photos, maybe my blog, or Rueben's blog, a survey about future trips. Anything else to keep our customers excited about rafting."

Do I NEED two kinds of web sites?

"Reuben???? He can't tell a standing wave from a tree."

"He's smart, Eddie, and articulate. Plus he's still got his newbie enthusiasm, and I want to harness that for our customers."

"You want me to run the ad? How about 'Wanted: Computer programmer. Free food left over from raft trips.' I can put it on Craig's List."

"Eddie, I want someone who can talk with me about what I want, tell me if it makes sense from a technical standpoint, give me some idea about costs and how long it will take. Then, maybe that person hires the programmer."

"Sounds expensive."

"Maybe. What I do know is that I have an office and a warehouse with five old computers, a slew of spreadsheets, a couple of funky databases, and a graphic artist as a Web developer. I also have a vision of what we could be doing, but I don't know how to make it happen, or even how to start!"

Sue's lament is more common than you might think. She knows what she wants for her business, but she does not know how to proceed. In fact, she needs the knowledge of this chapter. She's not the only one, either. Her graphic artist gets by only because he does simple Web sites. He also needs the knowledge of this chapter. And, finally, you, too, need this knowledge . . . because this could happen to you!

Study Questions

Q1 What is systems development?

Q2 Why is systems development difficult and risky?

Q3 What are the five phases of the SDLC?

Q4 How is system definition accomplished?

Q5 What is the users' role in the requirements phase?

Q6 How are the five components designed?

Q7 How is an information system implemented?

Q8 What are the tasks for system maintenance?

Q9 What are some of the problems with the SDLC?

How does the knowledge in this chapter help MRV and you?

Q1 What Is Systems Development?

Systems development, or **systems analysis and design**, as it is sometimes called, is the process of creating and maintaining information systems. Notice that this process concerns *information systems*, not just computer programs. Developing an *information system* involves all five components: hardware, software, data, procedures, and people. Developing a *computer program* involves software programs, possibly with some focus on data and databases. Figure 10-1 shows that systems development has a broader scope than computer program development.

Because systems development addresses all five components, it requires more than just programming or technical expertise. Establishing the system's goals, setting up the project, and determining requirements require business knowledge and management skill. Tasks like building computer networks and writing computer programs require technical skills; developing the other components requires nontechnical, human relations skills. Creating data models requires the ability to interview users and understand their view of the business activities. Designing procedures, especially those involving group action, requires business knowledge and an understanding of group dynamics. Developing job descriptions, staffing, and training all require human resource and related expertise.

Thus, do not suppose that systems development is exclusively a technical task undertaken by programmers and hardware specialists. Rather, it requires coordinated teamwork of both specialists and nonspecialists with business knowledge.

In Chapter 4, you learned that there are three sources for software: off-the-shelf, off-the-shelf with adaptation, and tailor-made. Although all three sources pertain to software, only two of them pertain to information systems. Unlike software, *information systems are never off-the-shelf.* Because information systems involve your

FIGURE 10-1
Systems Development
Versus Program Development

Computer programming concerned
with programs, some data

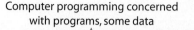
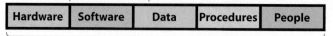

Scope of Systems Development

company's people and procedures, you must construct or adapt procedures to fit your business and people, regardless of how you obtain the computer programs.

As a future business manager, you will have a key role in information systems development. In order to accomplish the goals of your department, you need to ensure that effective procedures exist for using the information system. You need to ensure that personnel are properly trained and are able to use the IS effectively. If your department does not have appropriate procedures and trained personnel, you must take corrective action. Although you might pass off hardware, program, or data problems to the IT department, you cannot pass off procedural or personnel problems to that department. Such problems are your problems. The single most important criterion for information systems success is for users to take ownership of their systems.

Q2 Why Is Systems Development Difficult and Risky?

Systems development is difficult and risky. Many projects are never finished. Of those that are finished, some are 200 or 300 percent over budget. Still other projects finish within budget and schedule, but never satisfactorily accomplish their goals.

You may be amazed to learn that systems development failures can be so dramatic. You might suppose that with all the computers and all the systems developed over the years that by now there must be some methodology for successful systems development. In fact, there *are* systems development methodologies that can result in success, and we will discuss the primary one in this chapter. But, even when competent people follow this or some other accepted methodology, the risk of failure is still high.

In the following sections, we will discuss the five major challenges to systems development displayed in Figure 10-2.

The Difficulty of Requirements Determination

First, requirements are difficult to determine. Consider the system that Sue wants at MRV. What particular features does she want on her two different Web sites? Does MRV actually need different Web sites, or would one site work, with password access required for some features? Sue wants some form of user-generated content for customers to rate MRV, but what? Does she want control over those reviews? What other features does she need?

The proposed MRV system is simple. Consider, instead, the development of a new interorganizational system for supply chain management. What features and functions should it have? What is to be done if different companies have different ideas about the features required? Companies may disagree about the data they are willing to share. How are those differences to be resolved? Hundreds of hours of labor will be required to determine the requirements.

The questions could go on and on. One of the major purposes of the systems development process is to create an environment in which such questions are both asked and answered.

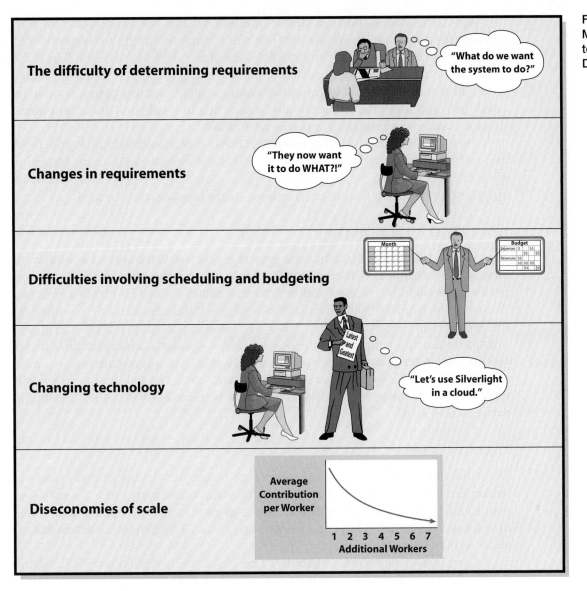

FIGURE 10-2
Major Challenges
to Systems
Development

Changes in Requirements

Even more difficult, systems development aims at a moving target. Requirements change as the system is developed, and the bigger the system and the longer the project, the more the requirements change.

When requirements do change, what should the development team do? Stop work and rebuild the system in accordance with the new requirements? If they do that, the system will develop in fits and starts and may never be completed. Or, should the team finish the system, knowing that it will be unsatisfactory the day it is implemented and will, therefore, need immediate maintenance?

Scheduling and Budgeting Difficulties

Other challenges involve scheduling and budgeting. How long will it take to build a system? That question is not easy to answer. Suppose you are developing a new customer database at MRV. How long will it take to create the data model? Even if you know how long it takes to create the data model, Sue and Eddie and others may disagree with you and with each other. How many times will you need to rebuild the data model until everyone agrees?

Again, the MRV system is a simple problem. What if you are building the new database for the supply chain system? How many hours will it take to create the data model, review, and approve it? Consider database applications. How long will it take to build the forms, reports, queries, and application programs? How long will it take to test all of them? What about procedures and people? What procedures need to be developed, and how much time should be set aside to create and document them, develop training programs, and train the personnel?

Further, how much will all of this cost? Labor costs are a direct function of labor hours; if you cannot estimate labor hours, you cannot estimate labor costs. Moreover, if you cannot estimate how much a system costs, then how do you perform a financial analysis to determine if the system generates an appropriate rate of return?

Changing Technology

Yet another challenge is that while the project is underway, technology continues to change. For example, say that while you are developing the MRV system Microsoft releases Silverlight, a new application product and technology for creating dynamic Web sites. You learn that with Silverlight you can give customers a much more interesting and exciting experience, just what Sue wants. Microsoft claims that it will drastically shorten your development time, halve the costs, and result in a better system. That is, it will do those things if it actually works the way Microsoft says it will.

Even if you believe Silverlight is a viable answer, do you want to stop your development to switch to the new technology? Would it be better to finish developing according to the existing plan?

Diseconomies of Scale

Unfortunately, as development teams become larger, the average contribution per worker decreases. This is true because as staff size increases, more meetings and other coordinating activities are required to keep everyone in sync. There are economies of scale up to a point, but beyond a workgroup of, say, 20 employees, diseconomies of scale begin to take over.

A famous adage known as **Brooks's Law** points out a related problem: *Adding more people to a late project makes the project later.*[1] Brooks's Law is true not only because a larger staff requires increased coordination, but also because new people need training. The only people who can train the new employees are the existing team members, who are, thus, taken off productive tasks. The costs of training new people can overwhelm the benefit of their contribution.

In short, managers of software development projects face a dilemma: They can increase work per employee by keeping the team small, but in doing so they extend the project's timeline. Or, they can reduce the project's timeline by adding staff, but because of diseconomies of scale they will have to add 150 or 200 hours of labor to gain 100 hours of work. And, due to Brooks's Law, once the project is late, both choices are bad.

Furthermore, schedules can be compressed only so far. According to one other popular adage, "Nine women cannot make a baby in one month."

Is It Really So Bleak?

Is systems development really as bleak as the list of challenges makes it sound? Yes and no. All of the challenges just described do exist, and they are all significant hurdles that every development project must overcome. As noted previously, once the project

---

[1]Fred Brooks was a successful senior manager at IBM in the 1960s. After retiring from IBM, he wrote a classic book on IT project management called *The Mythical Man-Month.* Published by Addison-Wesley in 1975, the book is pertinent today and should be read by every IT or IS project manager. It's an enjoyable book, too.

is late and over budget, no good choice exists. "I have to pick my regrets," said one beleaguered manager of a late project.

The IT industry has over 50 years of experience developing information systems, and over those years, methodologies have emerged that successfully deal with these problems. In the next study question, we will consider the systems development life cycle (SDLC), the most common process for systems development.

Q3 What Are the Five Phases of the SDLC?

The **systems development life cycle (SDLC)** is the classical process used to develop information systems. The IT industry developed the SDLC in the "school of hard knocks." Many early projects met with disaster, and companies and systems developers sifted through the ashes of those disasters to determine what went wrong. By the 1970s, most seasoned project managers agreed on the basic tasks that need to be performed to successfully build and maintain information systems. These basic tasks are combined into phases of systems development.

Different authors and organizations package the tasks into different numbers of phases. Some organizations use an eight-phase process, others use a seven-phase process, and still others use a five-phase process. In this book, we will use the following five-phase process:

1. **System definition**
2. **Requirements analysis**
3. **Component design**
4. **Implementation**
5. **System maintenance**

Figure 10-3 shows how these phases are related. Development begins when a business-planning process identifies a need for a new system. We address IS planning processes in Chapter 11. For now, suppose that management has determined, in some

FIGURE 10-3
Phases in the SDLC

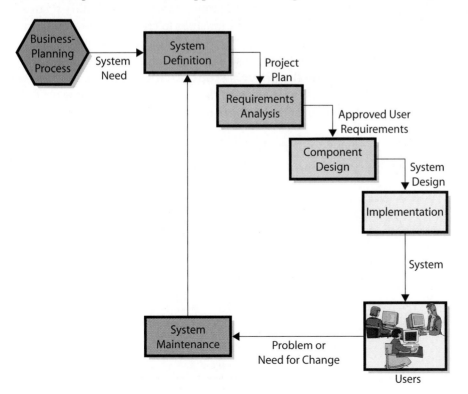

way, that the organization can best accomplish its goals and objectives by constructing a new information system.

Developers in the first SDLC phase—system definition—use management's statement of the system needs in order to begin to define the new system. The resulting project plan is the input to the second phase—requirements analysis. Here, developers identify the particular features and functions of the new system. The output of that phase is a set of approved user requirements, which become the primary input used to design system components. In phase 4, developers implement, test, and install the new system.

Over time, users will find errors, mistakes, and problems. They will also develop new requirements. The description of fixes and new requirements is input into a system maintenance phase. The maintenance phase starts the process all over again, which is why the process is considered a cycle.

In the following sections, we will consider each phase of the SDLC in more detail.

Q4 How Is System Definition Accomplished?

In response to the need for the new system, the organization will assign a few employees, possibly on a part-time basis, to define the new system, to assess its feasibility, and to plan the project. Typically, someone from the IS department leads the initial team, but the members of that initial team are both users and IS professionals. In the case of a small company like MRV, Sue likely will hire an independent contractor who will work with Sue, Eddie, and other key employees to define the system.

Define System Goals and Scope

As Figure 10-4 shows, the first step is to define the goals and scope of the new information system. Information systems exist to facilitate an organization's competitive strategy by supporting business processes or by improving decision making. At this step, the development team defines the goal and purpose of the new system in terms of these purposes.

Consider the new system of Web sites and applications at MRV. What is the purpose of that system? MRV's competitive strategy is to create quality relationships with quality customers and to use those relationships to create new revenue. How does this new system contribute to that strategy? How will it improve the quality of customer relationships? How will it enable MRV to use those relationships to generate revenue?

Another task is to define the project's scope. At MRV, does the new system just foster customer relationships, or does it sell something? Does MRV want to have a commerce server for selling hats and T-shirts or even life jackets and other river gear and equipment?

In other systems, the scope might be defined by specifying the users who will be involved, or the business processes that will be involved, or the plants, offices, and

FIGURE 10-4
SDLC: System Definition Phase

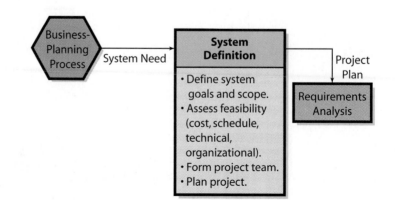

10 Systems Development for Social Networking Development

Many students do not appreciate the need for systems development processes. To help you relate to this need, suppose you work at MRV and Sue gives you the task of defining a project to create a social networking application. In particular, Sue has asked you to investigate the possibility of creating a Facebook application called "Let's Go Rafting."

She wants the application to have some compelling feature that will cause users to recommend it to each other and hence achieve viral distribution. She does not know what that feature is; she expects you to think of it and then create a plan that she can take to a Facebook application developer like Infinistorm (*www.infinistorm.com*). Sue does not know to say this, but she wants you to accomplish the tasks in the *systems definition* and *systems requirements* phases, as summarized in Figures 10-4 and 10-5.

Of course, to have any value, the application must not only have a strong viral hook, but it must also foster MRV's competitive strategy. It needs to further develop quality relationships with quality people and enable MRV to earn revenue from those relationships.

Thus, your task has two major components. First, create features for Let's Go Rafting that will make it viral and accomplish MRV's competitive strategy. Second, create a plan that Sue can take to a developer that accomplishes as many of the steps as possible in the systems definition and requirements stage.

You and a team of your classmates will have an opportunity to accomplish this work in Collaboration Exercise 10 on page 266.

factories that will be involved. At Emerson, for example, Dee might have defined the scope of her blog so as to include only U.S. salespeople, or only U.S. salespeople that sell certain products.

A clear definition of project scope greatly simplifies requirements determination and other subsequent development work. To learn a practical application of systems definition, read in *MIS in Use 10* about the need for a social networking application at MRV.

Assess Feasibility

Once we have defined the project's goals and scope, the next step is to assess feasibility. This step answers the question, "Does this project make sense?" The aim here is to eliminate obviously nonsensible projects before forming a project development team and investing significant labor.

Feasibility has four dimensions: **cost**, **schedule**, **technical**, and **organizational**. Because IS development projects are difficult to budget and schedule, cost and schedule feasibility can be only an approximate, back-of-the-envelope analysis. The purpose is to eliminate any obviously infeasible ideas as soon as possible.

For example, for MRV's Web site, you might investigate how much similar projects have cost in the past. Think about not only development costs, but also the operational costs of hosting the Web site(s) and the cost of employee labor for maintaining the site. It is likely that Sue has some ideas that cost more than the potential benefits they deliver. Or even if those ideas deliver sufficient benefit, the cost may be more than she is willing to spend. In this case, for the project to be cost-feasible, she may need to reduce the project's scope.

For a discussion of ethical issues relating to estimation, see the *Ethics Guide* on pages 252–253.

Like cost feasibility, *schedule feasibility* is difficult to determine because it is difficult to estimate the time it will take to build the system. However, if you determine that it will take, say, no less than 6 months to develop the system and put it into operation, MRV can then decide if it can accept that minimum schedule. At this stage of the project, the company should not rely on either cost or schedule estimates; the purpose of these estimates is simply to rule out any obviously unacceptable projects.

Estimation Ethics

A *buy-in* occurs when a company agrees to produce a system or product for less than it knows the project will require. An example for MRV would be if a consultant agreed to build the system for $15,000 when good estimating techniques indicate it will take $35,000. If the contract for the system or product is written for "time and materials," the customer will ultimately pay the $35,000 for the finished system. Or the customer will cancel the project once the true cost is known. If the contract for the system or product is written for a fixed cost, then the developer will absorb the extra costs. The latter strategy is used if the contract opens up other business opportunities that are worth the $20,000 loss.

Buy-ins always involve deceit. Most would agree that buying in on a time-and-materials project, planning to stick the customer with the full cost later, is unethical and wrong. Opinions vary on buying in on a fixed-priced contract. Some would say buying in is always deceitful and should be avoided. Others say that it is just one of many different business strategies.

What about in-house projects? Do the ethics change if an in-house development team is building a system for use in-house? If team members know there is only $50,000 in the budget for some new system, should they start the project if they believe its true cost is $75,000? If they do start, at some

point senior management will either have to admit a mistake and cancel the project or find the additional $25,000. Project sponsors can make all sorts of excuses for such a buy-in. For example, "I know the company needs this system. If management doesn't realize it and fund it appropriately, then we'll just force their hand."

These issues become even stickier if team members disagree about how much the project will cost. Suppose one faction of the team believes the new system will cost $35,000, another faction estimates $50,000, and a third thinks $65,000. Can the project sponsors justify taking the average? Or, should they describe the range of estimates?

Other buy-ins are more subtle. Suppose you are a project manager of an exciting new project that is possibly a career-maker for you. You are incredibly busy, working 6 days a week and long hours each day. Your team has developed an estimate for $50,000 for your project. A little voice in the back of your mind says that maybe not all costs for every aspect of the project are included in that estimate. You mean to follow up on that thought, but more pressing matters in your schedule take precedence. Soon you find yourself in front of management, presenting the $50,000 estimate. You probably should have found the time to investigate the estimate, but you didn't. Is your behavior unethical?

Or suppose you approach a more senior manager with your dilemma. "I think there may be other costs, but I know that $50,000 is all we've got. What should I do?" Suppose the senior manager says something like, "Well, let's go forward. You don't know of anything else, and we can always find more budget elsewhere if we have to." How do you respond?

You can buy in on schedule as well as cost. If the marketing department says, "We have to have the new product for the trade show," do you agree, even if you know it's highly unlikely? What if marketing says, "If we don't have it by then, we should just cancel the project." Suppose it's not impossible to make that schedule, it's just highly unlikely. How do you respond?

DISCUSSION QUESTIONS

1. Do you agree that buying in on a time-and-materials project is always unethical? Explain your reasoning. Are there circumstances in which it could be illegal?

2. Suppose you learn through the grapevine that your opponents in a competitive bid are buying in on a time-and-materials contract. Does this change your answer to question 1?

3. Suppose you are a project manager who is preparing a request for proposal on a time-and-materials systems development project. What can you do to prevent buy-ins?

4. Under what circumstances do you think buying in on a fixed-price contract is ethical? What are the dangers of this strategy?

5. Explain why in-house development projects are always time-and-materials projects.

6. Given your answer to question 5, is buying in on an in-house project always unethical? Under what circumstances do you think it is ethical? Under what circumstances do you think it is justifiable, even if it is unethical?

7. Suppose you ask a senior manager for advice, as described in the guide. Does the manager's response absolve you of guilt? Suppose you ask the manager and then do not follow her guidance. What problems result?

8. Explain how you can buy in on schedule as well as costs.

9. For an in-house project, how do you respond to the marketing manager who says that the project should be cancelled if it will not be ready for the trade show? In your answer, suppose that you disagree with this opinion—suppose you know the system has value regardless of whether it is done by the trade show.

Technical feasibility refers to whether existing information technology is likely to be able to meet the needs of the new system. At MRV, the new system is most likely well within the capabilities of existing technology. For more advanced systems, this is not always the case. The IRS disaster discussed in Chapter 1 failed, in part, because a rule-based system for examining tax returns was technically infeasible.

Finally, *organizational feasibility* concerns whether the new system fits within the organization's customs, culture, charter, or legal requirements. For example, will MRV incur any legal liability if customers post photos for which they do not have publication rights? If so, the system might be judged to be organizationally infeasible. (In this case, however, MRV can avoid such liability by requiring customers to assert they do have such rights before posting photos—just as Facebook does.) Does MRV have a management policy that prohibits releasing customer data? If so, it may be impossible for them to allow customers to interact with each other on the MRV sites.

Form a Project Team

If the defined project is determined to be feasible, the next step is to form the project team. Normally the team consists of both IT personnel and user representatives. The project manager and IT personnel can be in-house personnel or outside contractors. In Chapter 11, we will describe various means of obtaining IT personnel using outside sources and the benefits and risks of outsourcing.

Typical personnel on a development team are a manager (or managers for larger projects), system analysts, programmers, software testers, and users. **Systems analysts** are IT professionals who understand both business and technology. They are active throughout the systems development process and play a key role in moving the project through the systems development process. Systems analysts integrate the work of the programmers, testers, and users. Depending on the nature of the project, the team may also include hardware and communications specialists, database designers and administrators, and other IT specialists.

The team composition changes over time. During requirements definition, the team will be heavy with systems analysts. During design and implementation, it will be heavy with programmers, testers, and database designers. During integrated testing and conversion, the team will be augmented with testers and business users.

User involvement is critical throughout the system development process. Depending on the size and nature of the project, users are assigned to the project either full or part time. Sometimes users are assigned to review and oversight committees that meet periodically, especially at the completion of project phases and other milestones. Users are involved in many different ways. *The important point is for users to have active involvement and to take ownership of the project throughout the entire development process.*

MRV has no IT department, so the development team will consist, at least initially, of Sue and Eddie. As the project progresses, MRV will need to outsource for professional systems developers and programmers (or hire additional IT personnel).

The first major task for the assembled project team is to plan the project. Members of the project team specify tasks to be accomplished, assign personnel, determine task dependencies, and set schedules.

Q5 What Is the Users' Role in the Requirements Phase?

The primary purpose of the requirements analysis phase is to determine and document the specific features and functions of the new system. For most development projects, this phase requires interviewing dozens of users and documenting potentially hundreds of requirements. Requirements definition is, thus, expensive. It is also difficult, as you will see.

Determine Requirements

Determining the system's requirements is the most important phase in the systems development process. If the requirements are wrong, the system will be wrong. If the requirements are determined completely and correctly, then design and implementation will be easier and more likely to result in success.

Examples of requirements are the contents and the format of Web pages and the functions of buttons on those pages, or the structure and content of a report, or the fields and menu choices in a data entry form. Requirements include not only what is to be produced, but also how frequently and how fast it is to be produced. Some requirements specify the volume of data to be stored and processed.

If you take a course in systems analysis and design, you will spend weeks on techniques for determining requirements. Here, we will just summarize that process. Typically, systems analysts interview users and record the results in some consistent manner. Good interviewing skills are crucial; users are notorious for being unable to describe what they want and need. Users also tend to focus on the tasks they are performing at the time of the interview. Tasks performed at the end of the quarter or end of the year are forgotten if the interview takes place mid-quarter. Seasoned and experienced systems analysts know how to conduct interviews to bring such requirements to light.

As listed in Figure 10-5, sources of requirements include existing systems as well as the Web pages, forms, reports, queries, and application features and functions desired in the new system. Security is another important category of requirements.

If the new system involves a new database or substantial changes to an existing database, then the development team will create a data model. As you learned in Chapter 5, that model must reflect the users' perspective on their business and business activities. Thus, the data model is constructed on the basis of user interviews and must be validated by those users.

Sometimes, the requirements determination is so focused on the software and data components that other components are forgotten. Experienced project managers ensure consideration of requirements for all five IS components, not just for software and data. Regarding hardware, the team might ask: Are there special needs or restrictions on hardware? Is there an organizational standard governing what kinds of hardware may or may not be used? Must the new system use existing hardware? What requirements are there for communications and network hardware?

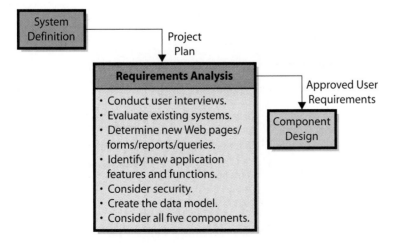

FIGURE 10-5
SDLC: Requirements Analysis Phase

Similarly, the team should consider requirements for procedures and personnel: Do accounting controls require procedures that separate duties and authorities? Are there restrictions that some actions can be taken only by certain departments or specific personnel? Are there policy requirements or union rules that restrict activities to certain categories of employees? Will the system need to interface with information systems from other companies and organizations? In short, requirements need to be considered for all of the components of the new information system.

These questions are examples of the kinds of questions that must be asked and answered during requirements analysis.

Approve Requirements

Once the requirements have been specified, the users must review and approve them before the project continues. The easiest and cheapest time to alter the information system is in the requirements phase. Changing a requirement at this stage is simply a matter of changing a description. Changing a requirement in the implementation phase may require weeks of reworking applications components and the database.

Q6 How Are the Five Components Designed?

Each of the five components is designed in this stage. Typically, the team designs each component by developing alternatives, evaluating each of those alternatives against the requirements, and then selecting among those alternatives. Accurate requirements are critical here; if they are incomplete or wrong, then they will be poor guides for evaluation. Figure 10-6 shows that design tasks pertain to each of the five IS components.

Hardware Design

For hardware, the team determines specifications for the hardware they need and the source of that hardware. For source, they can purchase the hardware, lease it, or lease time from a hosting service in the cloud. (The team is not designing hardware in the sense of building a CPU or a disk drive.)

For MRV, neither Sue nor Eddie has any idea of the hardware requirements for hosting the new system. They will need to rely on their development contractor. Most likely, MRV will lease time from a Web hosting service. Majestic River Ventures is too small and inexperienced to attempt to acquire and operate hardware itself.

FIGURE 10-6
SDLC: Component Design Phase

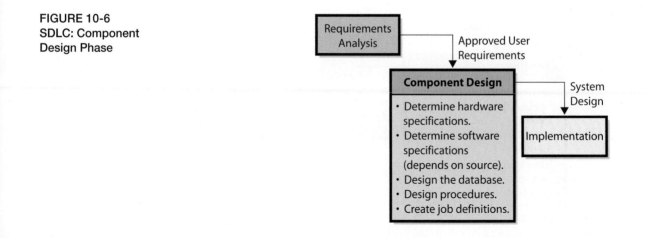

Software Design

Software design depends on the source of the programs. For off-the-shelf software, the team must determine candidate products and evaluate them against the requirements. For off-the-shelf-with-alteration software, the team identifies products to be acquired off-the-shelf and then determines the alterations required. For custom-developed programs, the team produces design documentation for writing program code.

Database Design

If developers are constructing a database, then during this phase they convert the data model to a database design using techniques such as those described in Chapter 5. If developers are using off-the-shelf programs, then little database design needs to be done; the programs will handle their own database processing.

Procedure Design

For a business information system, the system developers and the organization must also design procedures for both users and operations personnel. Procedures need to be developed for normal, backup, and failure recovery operations, as summarized in Figure 10-7. Usually, teams of systems analysts and key users design the procedures.

Design of Job Descriptions

With regard to people, design involves developing job descriptions for both users and operations personnel. Sometimes new information systems require new jobs. If so, the duties and responsibilities for the new jobs need to be defined in accordance with the organization's human resources policies. More often, organizations add new duties and responsibilities to existing jobs. In this case, developers define these new tasks and responsibilities in this phase. Sometimes, the personnel design task is as simple as statements like, "Jason will be in charge of making backups." As with procedures, teams of systems analysts and users determine job descriptions and functions.

	Users	**Operations Personnel**
Normal processing	• Procedures for using the system to accomplish business tasks	• Procedures for starting, stopping, and operating the system
Backup	• User procedures for backing up data and other resources	• Operations procedures for backing up data and other resources
Failure recovery	• Procedures to continue operations when the system fails • Procedures to convert back to the system after recovery	• Procedures to identify the source of failure and get it fixed • Procedures to recover and restart the system

FIGURE 10-7
Procedures to Be Designed

Q7 How Is an Information System Implemented?

Once the design is complete, the next phase in the SDLC is implementation. Tasks in this phase are to build, test, and convert the users to the new system (see Figure 10-8). Developers construct each of the components independently. They obtain, install, and test hardware. They license and install off-the-shelf programs; they write adaptations and custom programs, as necessary. They construct a database and fill it with data. They document, review, and test procedures, and they create training programs. Finally, the organization hires and trains needed personnel.

System Testing

Once developers have constructed and tested all of the components, they integrate the individual components and test the system. So far, we have glossed over testing as if there is nothing to it. In fact, software and system testing are difficult, time-consuming, and complex tasks. Developers need to design and develop test plans and record the results of tests. They need to devise a system to assign fixes to people and to verify that fixes are correct and complete.

A **test plan** consists of sequences of actions that users will take when using the new system. Test plans include not only the normal actions that users will take, but also incorrect actions. A comprehensive test plan should cause every line of program code to be executed. The test plan should cause every error message to be displayed. Testing, retesting, and re-retesting consume huge amounts of labor. Often, developers can reduce the labor cost of testing by writing programs that invoke system features automatically.

Today, many IT professionals work as testing specialists. Testing, or **product quality assurance (PQA)**, as it is often called, is an important career. PQA personnel usually construct the test plan with the advice and assistance of users. PQA test engineers perform testing, and they also supervise user test activity. Many PQA professionals are programmers who write automated test programs.

In addition to IT professionals, users should be involved in system testing. Users participate in the development of test plans and test cases. They also can be part of the test team, usually working under the direction of PQA personnel. Users have the final say on whether the system is ready for use. If you are invited to participate as a user tester, take that responsibly seriously. It will become much more difficult to fix problems after you have begun to use the system in production.

Beta testing is the process of allowing future system users to try out the new system on their own. Software vendors like Microsoft often release beta versions of their products for users to try and to test. Such users report problems back to the

FIGURE 10-8
SDLC: Implementation Phase

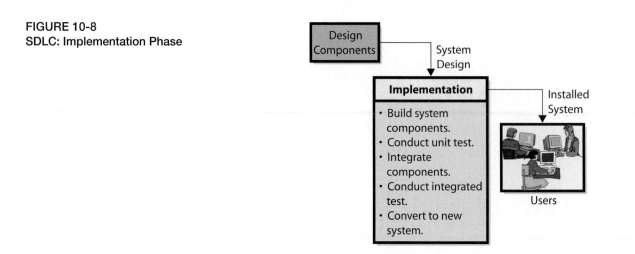

vendor. Beta testing is the last stage of testing. Normally products in the beta test phase are complete and fully functioning; they typically have few serious errors. Organizations that are developing large new information systems sometimes use a beta-testing process just as software vendors do.

System Conversion

Once the system has passed integrated testing, the organization installs the new system. The term **system conversion** is often used for this activity because it implies the process of *converting* business activity from the old system to the new.

Organizations can implement a system conversion in one of four ways:

- Pilot
- Phased
- Parallel
- Plunge

IS professionals recommend any of the first three, depending on the circumstances. In most cases, companies should avoid "taking the plunge!"

With **pilot installation**, the organization implements the entire system on a limited portion of the business. An example would be for MRV to use the new system for a selected portion of its customers. The advantage of pilot implementation is that if the system fails, the failure is contained within a limited boundary. This reduces exposure of the business and also protects the new system from developing a negative reputation throughout the organization(s).

As the name implies, with **phased installation** the new system is installed in phases across the organization(s). Once a given piece works, then the organization installs and tests another piece of the system, until the entire system has been installed. Some systems are so tightly integrated that they cannot be installed in phased pieces. Such systems must be installed using one of the other techniques.

With **parallel installation**, the new system runs in parallel with the old one until the new system is tested and fully operational. Parallel installation is expensive, because the organization incurs the costs of running both systems. Users must work double time, if you will, to run both systems. Then, considerable work is needed to determine if the results of the new system are consistent with those of the old system.

However, some organizations consider the costs of parallel installation to be a form of insurance. It is the slowest and most expensive style of installation, but it does provide an easy fallback position if the new system fails.

The final style of conversion is **plunge installation** (sometimes called *direct installation*). With it, the organization shuts off the old system and starts the new system. If the new system fails, the organization is in trouble: Nothing can be done until either the new system is fixed or the old system is reinstalled. Because of the risk, organizations should avoid this conversion style if possible. The one exception is if the new system is providing a new capability that is not vital to the operation of the organization.

Figure 10-9 summarizes the tasks for each of the five components during the design and implementation phases. Use this figure to test your knowledge of the tasks in each phase.

Q8 What Are the Tasks for System Maintenance?

The last phase of the SDLC is maintenance. Maintenance is a misnomer; the work done during this phase is either to *fix* the system so that it works correctly or to *adapt* it to changes in requirements.

FIGURE 10-9
Design and
Implementation
for the Five
Components

	Hardware	Software	Data	Procedures	People
Design	Determine hardware specifications.	Select off-the-shelf programs. Design alterations and custom programs as necessary.	Design database and related structures.	Design user and operations procedures.	Develop user and operations job descriptions.
Implementation	Obtain, install, and test hardware.	License and install off-the-shelf programs. Write alterations and custom programs. Test programs.	Create database. Fill with data. Test data.	Document procedures. Create training programs. Review and test procedures.	Hire and train personnel.

Unit test each component

Integrated Test and Conversion

Figure 10-10 shows tasks during the maintenance phase. First, there needs to be a means for tracking both failures[2] and requests for enhancements to meet new requirements. For small systems, organizations can track failures and enhancements using word-processing documents. As systems become larger, however, and as the number of failure and enhancement requests increases, many organizations find it necessary to develop a failure-tracking database. Such a database contains a description of each failure or enhancement. It also records who reported the problem, who will make the fix or enhancement, what the status of that work is, and whether the fix or enhancement has been tested and verified by the originator.

Typically, IS personnel prioritize system problems according to their severity. They fix high-priority items as soon as possible, and they fix low-priority items as time and resources become available.

With regard to the software component, software developers group fixes for high-priority failures into a **patch** that can be applied to all copies of a given product. As described in Chapter 4, software vendors supply patches to fix security and other critical problems. They usually bundle fixes of low-priority problems into larger groups called **service packs**. Users apply service packs in much the same way that they apply patches, except that service packs typically involve fixes to hundreds or thousands of problems.

By the way, you may be surprised to learn this, but all commercial software products are shipped with known failures. Usually vendors test their products and remove the most serious problems, but they seldom, if ever, remove all of the defects they know about. Shipping with defects is an industry practice; Microsoft, Adobe, Oracle, IBM, and many others ship products with known problems.

Because an enhancement is an adaptation to new requirements, developers usually prioritize enhancement requests separate from failures. The decision to make an enhancement includes a business decision that the enhancement will generate an acceptable rate of return. Although minor enhancements are made using service packs, major enhancement requests usually result in a new release of a product.

As you read this, keep in mind that although we usually think of failures and enhancements as applying to software, they can apply to the other components as well. There can be hardware or database failures or enhancements. There can also be failures and enhancements in procedures and people, though the latter is usually

---

[2]A *failure* is a difference between what the system does and what it is supposed to do. Sometimes, you will hear the term *bug* used instead of *failure*. As a future user, call failures *failures*, because that's what they are. Don't have a *bugs list*, have a *failures list*. Don't have an *unresolved bug*, have an *unresolved failure*. A few months of managing an organization that is coping with a serious failure will show you the importance of this difference in terms.

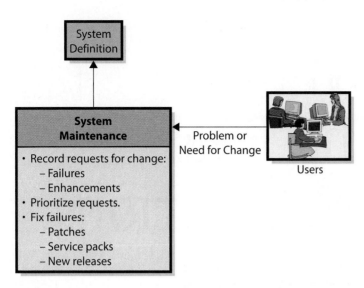

FIGURE 10-10
SDLC: System Maintenance
Phase

expressed in more humane terms than *failure* or *enhancement*. The underlying idea is the same, however.

As stated earlier, note that the maintenance phase starts another cycle of the SDLC process. The decision to enhance a system is a decision to restart the systems development process. Even a simple failure fix goes through all of the phases of the SDLC; if it is a small fix, a single person may work through those phases in an abbreviated form. But each of those phases is repeated, nonetheless.

Q9 What Are Some of the Problems with the SDLC?

Although the industry has experienced notable successes with the SDLC process, there have also been many problems with it, as discussed in this section.

The SDLC Waterfall

One of the reasons for SDLC problems is due to the **waterfall** nature of the SDLC. Like a series of waterfalls, the process is supposed to operate in a sequence of non-repetitive phases. For example, the team completes the requirements phase and goes over the waterfall into the design phase, and on through the process (look back to Figure 10-3, page 249).

Unfortunately, systems development seldom works so smoothly. Often, there is a need to crawl back up the waterfall, if you will, and repeat work in a prior phase. Most commonly, when design work begins and the team evaluates alternatives, they learn that some requirements statements are incomplete or missing. At that point, the team needs to do more requirements work, yet that phase is supposedly finished. On some projects, the team goes back and forth between requirements and design so many times that the project seems to be out of control.

Requirements Documentation Difficulty

Another problem, especially on complicated systems, is the difficulty of documenting requirements in a usable way. I once managed the database portion of a software project at Boeing in which we invested more than 70 labor-years into a requirements statement. When printed, the requirements document was 20-some volumes that stood 7 feet tall when stacked on top of one another.

When we entered the design phase, no one really knew all the requirements that concerned a particular feature. We would begin to design a feature only to find that we

The *Guide* on pages 262–263 states the difficulties with project estimation.

The Real Estimation Process

"I'm a software developer. I write programs in an object-oriented language called C# (pronounced 'C-sharp'). I'm a skilled object-oriented designer, too. I should be—I've been at it 12 years and worked on major projects for several software companies. For the last 4 years, I've been a team leader. I lived through the heyday of the dot-com era and now work in the IT department of a giant pharmaceutical company.

"All of this estimating theory is just that—theory. It's not really the way things work. Sure, I've been on projects in which we tried different estimation techniques. But here's what really happens: You develop an estimate using whatever technique you want. Your estimate goes in with the estimates of all the other team leaders. The project manager sums all those estimates together and produces an overall estimate for the project.

"By the way, in my projects, time has been a much bigger factor than money. At one software company I worked for, you could be 300 percent over your dollar budget and get no more than a slap on the wrist. Be 2 weeks late, however, and you were finished.

"Anyway, the project managers take the project schedule to senior management for approval, and what happens? Senior management thinks they are negotiating. 'Oh, no,' they say, 'that's way too long. You can surely take a month off that schedule. We'll approve the project, but we want it done by February 1 instead of March 1.'

"Now, what's their justification? They think that tight schedules make for efficient work. You know that everyone will work extra hard to meet the tighter timeframe. They know Parkinson's Law—'the time required to perform a task expands to the time available to do it.' So, fearing the possibility of wasting time because of too-lenient schedules, they lop a month off our estimate.

"Estimates are what they are; you can't knock off a month or two without some problem, somewhere. What does happen is that projects get behind, and then management expects us to work longer and longer hours. Like they said in the early years at Microsoft, 'We have flexible working hours. You can work any 65 hours per week you want.'

"Not that our estimation techniques are all that great, either. Most software developers are optimists. They schedule things as if everything will go as planned, and things seldom do. Also, schedulers usually don't allow for vacations, sick days, trips to the dentist, training on new technology, peer reviews, and all the other things we do in addition to writing software.

"So we start with optimistic schedules on our end, then management negotiates a month or two off, and voilà, we have a late project. After a while, management has been burned by late projects so much that they mentally add the month or even more back onto the official schedule. Then both sides work in a fantasy world, where no one believes the schedule, but everyone pretends they do.

"I like my job. I like software development. Management here is no better or worse than in other places. As long as I have interesting work to do, I'll stay here. But I'm not working myself silly to meet these fantasy deadlines."

DISCUSSION QUESTIONS

1. What do you think of this developer's attitude? Do you think he's unduly pessimistic or do you think there's merit to what he says?

2. What do you think of his idea that management thinks they're negotiating? Should management negotiate schedules? Why or why not?

3. Suppose a project actually requires 12 months to complete. Which do you think is likely to cost more: (a) having an official schedule of 11 months with at least a 1-month overrun or (b) having an official schedule of 13 months and following Parkinson's Law, having the project take 13 months?

4. Suppose you are a business manager and an information system is being developed for your use. You review the scheduling documents and see that little time has been allowed for vacations, sick leave, miscellaneous other work, and so forth. What do you do?

5. Describe the intangible costs of having an organizational belief that schedules are always unreasonable.

6. If this developer worked for you, how would you deal with his attitude about scheduling?

7. Do you think there is something different when scheduling information systems development projects than when scheduling other types of projects? What characteristics might make such projects unique? In what ways are they the same as other projects?

8. What do you think managers should do in light of your answer to question 7?

had not considered a requirement buried somewhere in the documentation. In short, the requirements were so unwieldy as to be nearly useless. Additionally, during the requirements analysis interval, the airplane business moved on. By the time we entered the design phase, many requirements were incomplete and some were obsolete. Projects that spend so much time documenting requirements are sometimes said to be in **analysis paralysis**.

Scheduling and Budgeting Difficulties

For a new, large-scale system, schedule and budgeting estimates are so approximate as to become nearly laughable. Management attempts to put a serious face on the need for a schedule and a budget, but when you are developing a large multiyear, multimillion-dollar project, estimates of labor hours and completion dates are approximate and fuzzy. The employees on the project, who are the source for the estimates, know little about how long something will take and about how much they had actually guessed. They know that the total budget and timeline is a summation of everyone's similar guesses. Many large projects live in a fantasy world of budgets and timelines.

In truth, the software community has done much work to improve software development forecasting. But for large projects with large SDLC phases, just too much is unknown for any technique to work well. So, development methodologies other than the SDLC have emerged for developing systems through a series of small, manageable chunks. Rapid application development, object-oriented development, and extreme programming are three such methodologies.

How does **the knowledge** in this chapter help **MRV** and **you**? As stated at the start of this chapter, Sue needs the knowledge in this chapter. In particular, knowledge of the systems development process and the phases of the SDLC will help her organize her thoughts and activities and give her a professional basis on which to approach a development vendor. She also needs to know about the systems definition and requirements phases so that she can both manage them and take an active role in doing the work. Knowledge of the other phases will help her work with her developer as well as assess how well that vendor is performing.

Do I NEED two kinds of web sites?

You, too, need the knowledge in this chapter, and for precisely the same reasons. When considering new information systems, you can use the SDLC to organize your thoughts and work with IS development professionals. You know your role in the definition and requirements phases. You also know how IS professionals should proceed with the design, implementation, and maintenance phases.

Active Review

Use this Active Review to verify that you understand the material in the chapter. You can read the entire chapter and then perform the tasks in this review, or you can read the material for just one question and perform the tasks in this review for that question before moving on to the next one.

Q1 **What is systems development?** Define *systems development*. Explain how systems development differs from program development. Describe the types of expertise needed for systems development projects. Explain why Sue needs the knowledge in this chapter.

Q2 **Why is systems development difficult and risky?** Describe the risk in systems development. Summarize the difficulties posed by the following: requirements definition, requirements changes, scheduling and budgeting, changing technology, and diseconomies of scale.

Q3 **What are the five phases of the SDLC?** Name the five phases in the systems development life cycle, and briefly describe each.

Q4 **How is system definition accomplished?** Using Figure 10-4 as a guide, explain how you would describe to Sue the systems definition task for her new system. Name and describe four elements of feasibility. (*Hint:* The four types of feasibility can be arranged as Cost, Operational, Schedule, Technical; arranged this way, the first letter of each makes the acronym *COST.*)

Q5 **What is the users' role in the requirements phase?** Summarize the tasks in the requirements phase. Describe the role for users in this phase. Discuss what you believe will happen if users are not involved or if users do not take this work seriously. Describe the role users play in requirements approval.

Q6 **How are the five components designed?** Summarize design activities for each of the five components of an information system. Explain six categories of procedure that need to be designed.

Q7 **How is an information system implemented?** Name the two major tasks in systems implementation. Summarize the system testing process. Describe the difference between system and software testing. Explain testing tasks for each of the five components. Name four types of system conversion. Describe each way, and give an example of when each would be effective.

Q8 **What are the tasks for system maintenance?** Explain why the term *maintenance* is a misnomer. Summarize tasks in the maintenance phase.

Q9 **What are some of the problems with the SDLC?** Explain why the SDLC is considered a waterfall process, and describe why this characteristic can be a problem. Describe problems that occur when attempting to develop requirements using the SDLC. Summarize scheduling and budgeting difficulties that the SDLC presents.

Summarize how Sue and Eddie can use the knowledge of the SDLC. Explain how you can use it as well. Use the SDLC and the five components to explain why Sue does not want to run an ad for a programmer.

Key Terms and Concepts

Analysis paralysis 264
Beta testing 258
Brooks's Law 248
Component design phase 249
Cost feasibility 251
Implementation phase 249
Maintenance phase 249
Organizational feasibility 251
Parallel installation 259

Patch 260
Phased installation 259
Pilot installation 259
Plunge installation 259
Product quality assurance (PQA) 258
Requirements analysis phase 249
Schedule feasibility 251
Service pack 260
System conversion 259

System definition phase 249
Systems analysis and design 245
Systems analysts 254
Systems development 245
Systems development life cycle (SDLC) 249
Technical feasibility 251
Test plan 258
Waterfall 261

Using Your Knowledge

1. Assume you work for MRV and you have the conversation with Sue at the start of this chapter. Assume that Sue asks you to take a leadership role in investigating this new system.
   a. Develop a plan for this project using the SDLC.
   b. Specify in detail the tasks to accomplish during the system definition phase.

   c. Write a memo to Sue explaining how you think MRV should proceed.

2. Consider the MRV process problem discussed in Chapter 7, and in particular the design of a new process that uses an equipment database (see Figure 7-11, page 174). Assume that Sue asked you

to investigate the development of this revised system.

  a. Describe the tasks that need to be accomplished for each phase of the SDLC to build such a system.

  b. Specify in detail the tasks to accomplish during the systems definition phase.

Collaboration Exercise 10 ◎

Before you start this exercise, read Chapter Extensions 1 and 2, which describe collaboration techniques as well as tools for managing collaboration tasks. In particular, consider using Google Docs & Spreadsheets, Google Groups, Microsoft Groove, Microsoft SharePoint, or some other collaboration tool.

1. Assume you have been given the tasks described in *MIS in Use 10*, page 251. Ensure that everyone on your team understands the terms *viral marketing* and *viral hook*. Also ensure that everyone understands the purpose and functions of a social networking application. Using a wiki, document these terms on your team site.

2. Visit Facebook or MySpace and find an application that is similar to the one that MRV wants to develop. Do not restrict your search to river-rafting applications (there aren't many). Instead, look for applications that have a similar feel and that probably provide their sponsors a similar value. Create a list of three such applications. Compare and contrast them with the goals you envision for Let's Go Rafting.

3. Brainstorm with your team possible viral hooks for Let's Go Rafting. Create a list of five alternatives. Establish criteria for evaluating those alternatives, and then as a team rank those alternatives. Justify your ranking.

4. Describe how the SDLC pertains to the development of this application. Describe the tasks that need to be accomplished in each phase. Indicate who should perform the tasks: MRV, an outsource development vendor, or both.

5. Develop a list of the top five to seven features of your application. Explain how those features pertain to your viral hook. Explain how those features pertain to MRV's competitive strategy. Evaluate the four dimensions of feasibility for each of your features. Make assumptions as necessary and justify your assumptions.

6. Visit the sites of three social networking application vendors (for example, *www.inifistorm.com*). Explain how you would use your answer to question 4 when you contact that vendor. Judging from the vendors' Web sites, which one do you think would be most amenable to working with you, given that you have some knowledge of the SDLC? Explain how you think your knowledge of the SDLC will improve your interaction and/or results.

7. Define criteria for success for your application. Assess how likely your application is to achieve success. Compare the potential benefit of your social networking application to Sue's idea for new Web sites at the start of this chapter. If you owned MRV, which application would you fund? Justify your answer.

Case Study 10

Slow Learners, or What?

In 1974, when I was teaching at Colorado State University, we conducted a study of the causes of information systems failures. We interviewed personnel on several dozen projects and collected survey data on another 50 projects. Our analysis of the data revealed that the single most important factor in IS failure was a lack of user involvement. The second major factor was unclear, incomplete, and inconsistent requirements.

At the time, I was a devoted computer programmer and IT techie, and frankly, I was surprised. I thought that the significant problems would have been technical issues.

I recall one interview in particular. A large sugar producer had attempted to implement a new system for paying sugar-beet farmers. The new system was to be implemented at some 20 different sugar-beet collection sites, which were located in small farming communities, adjacent to rail yards. One of the benefits of the new system was significant cost savings, and a major share of those savings occurred because the new system eliminated the need for local comptrollers. The new system was expected to eliminate the jobs of 20 or so senior people.

The comptrollers, however, had been paying local farmers for decades; they were popular leaders not just within the company, but in their communities as well. They were well liked, highly respected, important people. A system that caused the elimination of their jobs was, using a term from this chapter, *organizationally infeasible*, to say the least.

Nonetheless, the system was constructed, but an IS professional who was involved told me, "Somehow, that new system just never seemed to work. The data were not entered on a timely basis, or they were in error, or incomplete; sometimes the data were not entered at all. Our operations were falling apart during the key harvesting season, and we finally backed off and returned to the old system." Active involvement of system users would have identified this organizational infeasibility long before the system was implemented.

That's ancient history, you say. Maybe, but in 1994 the Standish Group published a now famous study on IS failures. Entitled "The CHAOS Report," the study indicated the leading causes of IS failure are, in descending order: (1) lack of user input, (2) incomplete requirements and specifications, and (3) changing requirements and specifications (*www.standishgroup.com*). That study was completed some 20 years after our study.

In 2004, Professor Joseph Kasser and his students at the University of Maryland analyzed 19 system failures to determine their cause. They then correlated their analysis of the cause with the opinions of the professionals involved in the failures. The correlated results indicate the first-priority cause of system failure was "Poor requirements"; the second-priority cause was "Failure to communicate with the customer" (*www.softwaretechnews.com/technews2-2/trouble.html*).

In 2003, the IRS Oversight Board concluded the first cause of the IRS BSM failure (see Case Study 1) was "inadequate business unit ownership and sponsorship of projects. This resulted in unrealistic business cases and continuous project scope 'creep.'"

For over 30 years, studies have consistently shown that leading causes of system failures are a lack of user involvement and incomplete and changing requirements. Yet failures from these very failures continue to mount.

Sources: www.standishgroup.com; www.softwaretechnews.com/technews2-2/trouble.html.

Questions

1. Using the knowledge you have gained from this chapter, summarize the roles that you think users should take during an information systems development project. What responsibilities do users have? How closely should they work with the IS team? Who is responsible for stating requirements and constraints? Who is responsible for managing requirements?

2. If you ask users why they did not participate in requirements specification, some of the common responses are the following:
   a. "I wasn't asked."
   b. "I didn't have time."
   c. "They were talking about a system that would be here in 18 months, and I'm just worried about getting the order out the door today."
   d. "I didn't know what they wanted."
   e. "I didn't know what they were talking about."
   f. "I didn't work here when they started the project."
   g. "The whole situation has changed since they were here; that was 18 months ago!"

   Comment on each of these statements. What strategies do they suggest to you as a future user and as a future manager of users?

3. If you ask IS professionals why they did not obtain a complete and accurate list of requirements, common responses are:
   a. "It was nearly impossible to get on the users' calendars. They were always too busy."
   b. "The users wouldn't regularly attend our meetings. As a result, one meeting would be dominated by the needs of one group, and another meeting would be dominated by the needs of another group."
   c. "Users didn't take the requirement process seriously. They wouldn't thoroughly review the requirements statements before review meetings."
   d. "Users kept changing. We'd meet with one person one time and another person a second time, and they'd want different things."
   e. "We didn't have enough time."
   f. "The requirements kept changing."

   Comment on each of these statements. What strategies do they suggest to you as a future user and a future manager of users?

4. If it is widely understood that one of the principal causes of IS failures is a lack of user involvement, and if this factor continues to be a problem after 30+ years of experience, does this mean that the problem cannot be solved? For example, everyone knows that you can maximize your gains by buying stocks at their annual low price and selling them at their annual high price, but doing so is very difficult. Is it equally true that although everyone knows that users should be involved in requirements specification, and that requirements should be complete, it just cannot be done? Why or why not?

11 Information Systems Management

Dee Clark created a blog for communicating to her sales force, and she wanted to restrict access to that blog to authorized Emerson personnel. The easiest way to protect her blog from outside eyes was to put it inside the corporate network where the salespeople could access it using Emerson's VPN.

Of course, to place the blog software on an Emerson server, Dee needed the permission and help of the IT department. Dee didn't understand the IT department's mission and was surprised when she met substantial resistance. Her response was to use her manager's manager to bludgeon the IT department into submission. In the process, her management chain exposed Emerson to an enormous security risk. Once Dee's consultant, Don Gray, was inside the system, given his knowledge and experience, he could have played havoc with their internal information systems. Dee should have known about that risk. Even if she didn't know, her boss's boss ought to have known about it.

Dee's problems were compounded because she did not understand the IT department's responsibilities, nor did she know their problems and concerns. Consequently, she didn't know how to talk with them. Dee's strength was not empathy, and with no knowledge of the responsibilities of the IT department, she was unable to practice empathetic thinking (see page 36) when she made her request. Had she approached the IT department with knowledge of its concerns, she would have had a more supportive response and could have avoided exposing Emerson to such risk.

Our computer systems are a MESS.

MRV, however, does not have an IT department. It needs someone to perform the services of an IT department, but on a much smaller scale. In MRV's case, those services will be provided by employees on a part-time basis or by outside contractors.

This chapter will explain the organization and operation of typical IT departments. If you find yourself in the position Dee was or in the position that MRV is, you will have the knowledge to interact with IT personnel in a more professional and effective way.

This could happen to you

Study Questions

Q1 Why do you need to know about the IT department?

Q2 What are the responsibilities of the IT department?

Q3 How is the IT department organized?

Q4 What IS-related job positions exist?

Q5 How do organizations decide how much to spend on IT?

Q6 What are your IS rights and responsibilities?

How does the knowledge in this chapter help Dee, MRV, and you?

Q1 Why Do You Need to Know About the IT Department?

You need to know about the IT department for three principal reasons. First, like Dee, you need to understand the responsibilities and duties of the IT department so you can be an effective consumer of the IT department's resources. If you understand what the IT department does and how it is organized, you'll know how better to obtain the equipment, services, or systems you (and organizations you manage) need.

Second, you need to know about the functions of the IT department to be a better informed and effective manager or executive. For example, more than one merger or acquisition has been negotiated, signed, and planned, without anyone thinking of the IT departments. As you can now understand, marrying the infrastructure and systems of two organizations requires extensive planning.

Or suppose you sponsor a new business initiative or work on a team that is sponsoring a new initiative. You need to know to think about the needs of the IT department in supporting that new initiative. Dee's blog is an example of a very small initiative. Suppose, instead, you're working on a team to set up selling in teams with, say, the supplier of a companion product. Perhaps your company sells DSL (digital subscriber line) modems, and you're thinking of partnering sales efforts with a phone company that leases DSL lines to business customers. Many questions arise, one of which is, "Which company will provide customer support?" With knowledge of the IT department's functions, you'll know to ask how this new initiative will impact your existing customer support systems.

Finally, if you are a manager in a small company, like MRV, you need to ensure that the functions of the IT department are performed. Your responsibility will actually be greater in a small company, because there will be no IS professionals to raise management's attention to serious IT matters such as backup and recovery and security. Read *MIS in Use 11* for more discussion of MRV's IT needs.

11 Managing IT at Majestic River Ventures

MRV does not have an IT department, but it does have information systems. In particular, it has its current Web site that it uses to attract prospects and that is hosted by an independent hosting vendor. MRV is considering developing both an expanded Web site (as indicated in the Chapter 10 opening on page 244) and a social networking application. Those sites will also be hosted by independent vendors. MRV keeps track of its customers using an Access database in the company office in Boise, Idaho. Additionally, it tracks equipment using Access in its warehouse in Baker, Oregon. Food and equipment needs are computed using Excel spreadsheets on laptop computers used by trip leaders in both facilities as well as on the road during trips. MRV uses QuickBooks for accounting. MRV maintains wireless networks in both its Boise and Baker facilities.

Even though MRV has this array of information systems, it has no in-house IT department, nor can it afford one. The lack of that department does not mean, however, that the responsibilities of such a department can go unaddressed.

You and your team of classmates will have an opportunity to formulate an IT plan for MRV in Collaboration Exercise 11 on page 283.

Q2 What Are the Responsibilities of the IT Department?

The IT department[1] has four primary responsibilities, as shown in Figure 11-1. We'll consider each.

Plan for Information Systems and IT Infrastructure

Information systems exist to further the organization's competitive strategy. They exist to facilitate business processes and to help improve decision making. Thus, there are no "IS projects"; instead, all projects involving IS are a part of some other business system or facilitate some business goal.

The IT department has the responsibility of aligning all of its activities with the organization's primary goals and objectives. As new technology emerges, the IT department is responsible for assessing that technology and determining if it can be used to advance the organization's goals. Furthermore, as the business changes, the IT department is responsible for adapting infrastructure and systems to the new business goals.

Several years ago, Microsoft began to use the term **agile enterprise** in its advertising. Today, many executives use the term to refer to an organization that

FIGURE 11-1
Primary Responsibilities
of the IT Department

> 1. Plan for information systems and IT infrastructure.
>
> 3. Develop and adapt information systems and IT infrastructure.
>
> 5. Maintain information systems and operate and manage infrastructure.
>
> 4. Protect infrastructure and data.

[1]Notice that the IT department has responsibility for the information system and not just information technology. Therefore, the term *IS department* would be more appropriate. However, for some reason, that term is less often used in real-world settings. So, when you read or hear "IT department," think "IS department" instead.

can quickly adapt to changes in the market, industry, product, law, or other significant external factors. Microsoft used this term because IT infrastructure and systems are known to be particularly difficult to adapt to change, and it claimed its products would change this characteristic. This might be the case, but the one certain effect of its campaign was to alert IT managers and business executives to the need to be agile.

Develop and Adapt Information Systems and IT Infrastructure

Given a plan, the next task for the IT department is to create, develop, and adapt both information systems and IT infrastructure. We discussed systems development in Chapter 10; we need not say any more about that topic here.

In addition to systems development, the IT department is responsible for creating and adapting infrastructure, such as computer networks, servers, data centers, data warehouses, data marts, and other IT resources. The IT department is also charged with creating systems infrastructures, such as email systems, VPNs, instant messaging, blogs, online meetings, and any other IT-based infrastructure the company needs.

In most organizations, user departments pay for computers and related equipment out of their own budgets. However, because the IT department is responsible for maintaining that equipment and for connecting it to the organizational networks, the IT department will specify standard computer systems and configurations that it will support. The IT department is responsible for defining those specifications.

Maintain Information Systems and Operate and Manage Infrastructure

We discussed information systems maintenance in Chapter 10 and will not repeat that discussion here. Regarding the operation and management of infrastructure, realize that IT infrastructure is not like the building's plumbing or wiring. You cannot install a network or a server and then forget it. IT infrastructure must be operated and managed. Networks and servers need to be powered on, and they need to be monitored. From time to time, they need to be adjusted, or **tuned**, to changes in the workload. Components fail, and when they do, the IT department is called upon to repair the problem.

To understand the importance of this function, consider what happens when a network fails. Users cannot connect to their local servers; they cannot run the information systems they need to perform their jobs. Users cannot connect with the Internet or send or receive email. Users may not even be able to reach their contact lists to find phone numbers to make telephone calls to explain why they are not responding. Truly, the business stops. And if, like Emerson, information systems have been distributed to customers or suppliers, personnel in other businesses are impacted as well.

Because of the high cost and serious disruption of system outages, information systems personnel are particularly sensitive to possible threats to that infrastructure. The Emerson IT personnel had every right to object to Dee's allowing a consultant to access their network. Had a problem occurred, had the consultant done something to disrupt the network, the IT department would be accountable. Most of the company would judge the problem to have been an IT failure, even though Dee and her bosses were the true source of the problem. No one—including the CEO or even the sales vice president who applied the pressure—would care. This point leads to the last IT department responsibility.

Protect Infrastructure and Data from Threats

The IT department is responsible to protect infrastructure and data from threats. We will discuss threats and safeguards against them in Chapter 12. For now, just understand that threats to infrastructure and data arise from three sources: human error and mistakes, malicious human activity, and natural events and disasters.

The IT department helps the organization manage risk. The department needs to identify potential threats, estimate both financial and other risks, and specify appropriate safeguards. Nothing is free, including safeguards, and, indeed, some safeguards are very expensive. The IT department works with the CFO and others in the organization to determine what safeguards to implement, or stated differently, what level of risk to assume. See Chapter 12 for more information.

Q3 How Is the IT Department Organized?

Figure 11-2 shows typical top-level reporting relationships. As you will learn in your management classes, organizational structure varies depending on the organization's size, culture, competitive environment, industry, and other factors. Larger organizations with independent divisions will have a group of senior executives like those shown here for each division. Smaller companies may combine some of these departments. Consider the structure in Figure 11-2 as a typical example.

The title of the principal manager of the IT department varies from organization to organization. A common title is **chief information officer (CIO)**. Other common titles are *vice president of information services, director of information services*, and, less commonly, *director of computer services.*

In Figure 11-2, the CIO, like other senior executives, reports to the chief executive officer (CEO), although sometimes these executives report to the chief operating officer (COO), who in turn reports to the CEO. In some companies, the CIO reports to the chief financial officer (CFO). That reporting arrangement may make sense if the primary information systems support accounting and finance activities. In organizations that operate significant nonaccounting information systems, such

FIGURE 11-2
Typical Senior-Level
Reporting Relationships

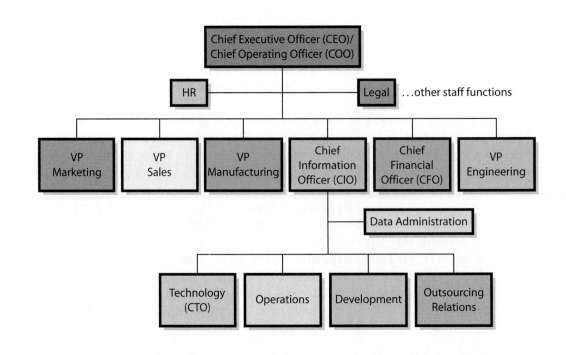

as manufacturers, the arrangement shown in Figure 11-2 is more common and effective.

The structure of the IT department also varies among organizations. Figure 11-2 shows a typical IT department with four groups and a data-administration staff function.

Most IT departments include a *technology* office that investigates new information systems technologies and determines how the organization can benefit from them. For example, today many organizations are investigating SOA, social networking, and UGC and planning on how they can best use those technologies to accomplish their goals and objectives. An individual called the **chief technology officer (CTO)** often heads the technology group. The CTO sorts through new ideas and products to identify those that are most relevant to the organization. The CTO's job requires deep knowledge of information technology and the ability to envision how new IT will affect the organization over time.

The next group in Figure 11-2, *operations*, manages the computing infrastructure, including individual computers, computer centers, networks, and communications media. This group includes system and network administrators. As you will learn, an important function for this group is to monitor user experience and respond to user problems.

The third group in the IT department in Figure 11-2 is *development*. This group manages the process of creating new information systems as well as maintaining existing information systems. (Recall from Chapter 10 that in the context of information systems, *maintenance* means either removing problems or adapting existing information systems to support new features and functions.)

The size and structure of the development group depends on whether programs are developed in-house. If not, this department will be staffed primarily by systems analysts who work with users, operations, and vendors to acquire and install licensed software and to set up the system components around that software. If the organization develops programs in-house, then this department will include programmers, test engineers, technical writers, and other development personnel.

The last IT department group in Figure 11-2 is *outsourcing relations*. This group exists in organizations that have negotiated outsourcing agreements with other companies to provide equipment, applications, or other services.

Figure 11-2 also includes a *data administration* staff function. The purpose of this group is to protect data and information assets by establishing data standards and data management practices and policies.

There are many variations on the structure of the IT department shown in Figure 11-2. In larger organizations, the operations group may itself consist of several different departments. Sometimes, there is a separate group for data warehousing and data marts.

As you examine Figure 11-2, keep in mind the distinction between IS and IT. Information systems (IS) exist to help the organization achieve its goals and objectives. Information systems have the five components we have discussed throughout this text. Information technology (IT) is just technology. It concerns the products, techniques, procedures, and designs of computer-based technology. IT must be placed into the structure of an IS before an organization can use it.

Q4 What IS-Related Job Positions Exist?

The IS industry has a wide range of interesting and well-paying jobs. Many students enter the MIS class thinking that the IS industry consists only of programmers and computer technicians. If you reflect on the five components of an information

FIGURE 11-3
Job Positions
in the
Information
Systems
Industry

Title	Responsibilities	Knowledge, Skill, and Characteristics Requirements	2008 U.S. Salary Range (USD)
System analyst	Work with users to determine system requirements, design and develop job descriptions and procedures, help determine system test plans.	Strong interpersonal and communications skills. Knowledge of both business and technology. Adaptable.	$65,000–$150,000
Programmer	Design and write computer programs.	Logical thinking and design skills, knowledge of one or more programming languages.	$50,000–$150,000
PQA test engineer	Develop test plans, design and write automated test scripts, perform testing.	Logical thinking, basic programming, superb organizational skills, eye for detail.	$40,000–$95,000
Technical writer	Write program documentation, help-text, procedures, job descriptions, training materials.	Quick learner, clear writing skills, high verbal communications skills.	$40,000–$95,000
User support representative	Help users solve problems, provide training.	Communications and people skills. Product knowledge. Patience.	$40,000–$65,000
Computer technician	Install software, repair computer equipment and networks.	Associate degree, diagnostic skills.	$30,000–$65,000
Network administrator	Monitor, maintain, fix, and tune computer networks.	Diagnostic skills, in-depth knowledge of communications technologies and products.	$75,000–$200,000+
Consultant	Wide range of activities: programming, testing, database design, communications and networks, project management, security and risk management, strategic planning.	Quick learner, entrepreneurial attitude, communications and people skills. Respond well to pressure. Particular knowledge depends on work.	From $35 per hour for a contract tester to more than $500 per hour for strategic consulting to executive group.
Salesperson	Sell software, network, communications, and consulting services.	Quick learner, knowledge of product, superb professional sales skills.	$65,000–$200,000+
Small-scale project manager	Initiate, plan, manage, monitor, and close down projects.	Management and people skills, technology knowledge. Highly organized.	$75,000–$150,000
Large-scale project manager	Initiate, plan, monitor, and close down complex projects.	Executive and management skills. Deep project management knowledge.	$150,000–$250,000+
Database administrator	Manage and protect database (see Chapter 12).	Diplomatic skills, database technology knowledge.	$75,000–$250,000
Chief technology officer (CTO)	Advise CIO, executive group, and project managers on emerging technologies.	Quick learner, good communication skills, deep knowledge of IT.	$125,000–$300,000+
Chief information officer (CIO)	Manage IT department, communicate with executive staff on IT- and IS-related matters. Member of the executive group.	Superb management skills, deep knowledge of business, and good business judgment. Good communicator. Balanced and unflappable.	$150,000–$500,000, plus executive benefits and privileges.

system, you can understand why this cannot be true. The data, procedure, and people components of an information system require professionals with highly developed interpersonal communications skills.

Figure 11-3 summarizes the major job positions in the IS industry. With the exception of computer technician and possibly of PQA test engineer, all of these positions require a 4-year degree. Furthermore, with the exception of programmer and PQA test engineer, all of these positions require business knowledge. In most cases, successful professionals have a degree in business. Note, too, that most positions require good verbal and written communications skills. Business, including information systems, is a social activity.

Many of the positions in Figure 11-3 have a wide salary range. Lower salaries are for professionals with limited experience or for those who work in smaller companies or work on small projects. The larger salaries are for those with deep knowledge and experience who work for large companies on large projects. Do not expect to begin your career at the high end of these ranges. As noted, all salaries are for positions in the United States and are shown in U.S. dollars.

In the nearly 40 years of my career, I have worked as a systems analyst, programmer, small- and large-scale project manager, consultant, and chief technology officer (CTO). It's been great fun, and the industry becomes more and more interesting each year. Give these careers some thought.

By the way, for all but the most technical positions, knowledge of a business specialty can add to your marketability. If you have the time, a dual major can be an excellent choice. Popular and successful dual majors are: accounting and information systems, marketing and information systems, and management and information systems.

Keep in mind that the changing nature of technology—and of business generally—will demand that you remain agile, as discussed in the *Guide* on pages 276–277.

Q5 How Do Organizations Decide How Much to Spend on IT?

Information systems and information technology are expensive. Consequently, organizations need to address the investment in IS and IT in the same way that they address investments in plant, inventories, or any other substantial project. Typically, decisions to invest in any business project involve an analysis of the costs and benefits.

All such analysis requires estimates of the costs and benefits of the project. However, to compare costs to benefits, both the costs and benefits need to be expressed in dollars or some other currency. Estimating dollar costs of IS or IT projects is not more difficult than estimating them for other projects. The difficulty arises when attempting to place a dollar value on benefits. For example, what is the dollar value of an email system? Employees require access to email in order to do any work. Asking the dollar value of the email system is like asking the dollar value of the restroom. How can you compute it?

Other value computations are difficult, but possible. For example, if a customer support information system reduces the likelihood of losing a customer, then the value of that system can be computed by multiplying the probability of loss times the lifetime value of that customer. Or, if an information system enables customer support representatives to service customers 10 percent faster, then the dollar value of that system is 10 percent of the anticipated customer support costs.

Most IS and IT investment analyses divide benefits into two categories: tangible and intangible. **Tangible benefits** are those for which a dollar value can be computed. Reducing customer support costs by 10 percent is a tangible benefit. **Intangible benefits**

Jumping Aboard the Bulldozer

A recent popular theme in the media is how overseas outsourcing is destroying the U.S. labor market. The "jobless recovery" is how it's headlined. However, a closer look reveals that overseas outsourcing is not the culprit. Brainard and Litan cite research that indicates that organizations will move approximately 250,000 jobs per year overseas between now and 2015.[1] Although that may sound like a lot, in the context of the 137 million U.S. workers, and in the context of the 15 million Americans who lose their jobs due to other factors, 250,000 jobs overseas is not much.

The culprit—if *culprit* is the right word—is not overseas outsourcing; it is productivity. Because of information technology, Moore's Law, and all the information systems that you have learned about in this book, worker productivity continues to increase, and it is possible to have an economic recovery without a binge of new hiring.

The Austrian economist Joseph Schumpeter called such processes "creative destruction" and said that they are the cleansers of the free market.[2] Economic processes operate to remove unneeded jobs, companies, and even industries, thereby keeping the economy growing and prospering. In fact, the lack of

such processes hindered the growth of Japan and some European nations in the 1990s.

(By the way, there's a historical irony here, because creative destruction gave rise to one of the first information systems. This system consisted of a group of human "calculators" who were employed by the French in the 1790s to compute scientific tables for the then-new metric system. According to Ken Alder, the human calculators were wigmakers, who became unemployed due to the French Revolution.[3] The guillotine not only reduced the size of the market for wigs, but also made aristocratic hairstyles less popular, and so wigmakers became human calculators.)

This idea of creative destruction is all well and good for an economic theory, but what do you, as a student in the first decade of the twenty-first century, do? How do you respond to the dynamics of shifting work and job movements? You can take a lesson from the railroads in the 1930s. They were blindsided by air transportation. In a now-classic marketing blunder, the railroads perceived themselves as purveyors of railroad transportation instead of purveyors of transportation more generally. The railroads were well positioned to take advantage of air transportation, but they did nothing and were overtaken by the new airline companies.

How does this apply to you? As you have learned, MIS is the development and use of information systems that enable organizations to achieve their goals and objectives. When you work with information systems, you are not a professional

[1] Lial Brainard and Robert Litan, "Services Offshoring Bane or Bone and What to Do?" *CESifo Forum*, Summer 2004, Vol. 5, Issue 2, p. 307.
[2] Joseph Schumpeter, *Capitalism, Socialism, and Democracy* (New York: Harper, 1975), pp. 82–85.

[3] Ken Alder, *The Measure of All Things* (New York: The Free Press, 2002), p. 142.

of a particular system or technology; rather, you are a developer or user of a system that helps your organization achieve its goals and objectives.

Suppose, for example, you work with an email-based purchasing system. If you view yourself as an expert in email-based purchasing, then you are doomed, because it will be supplanted by SOA systems. Are you better off to define yourself as an expert in some aspect of SOA, say XML coding? No, because SOA will someday be replaced with something else, and writing XML schemas is work that can easily be moved offshore. Instead, define yourself more generally as someone who specializes in the application of emerging technology to help your business achieve its goals and objectives.

From this perspective, the technology you learned in this class can help you start your career. If IS-based productivity is the bulldozer that is mowing down traditional jobs, then use what you have learned here to jump aboard that bulldozer. Not as a technologist, but as a business professional who can determine how best to use that bulldozer to enhance your career.

In the case of purchasing, learn something about SOA and XML and apply that knowledge to gain employment in a company that uses them to accomplish its goals and objectives. But realize that SOA/XML only helps you get that job; it just gets you started. Your long-term success depends not on your knowledge of those particular technologies, but rather on your ability to think, to solve problems, to collaborate, and to use technology and information systems to help your organization achieve its goals and objectives.

Discussion Questions

1. Describe several ways that the overseas outsourcing problem is overstated.

2. Summarize the argument that the "culprit" is not overseas outsourcing, but rather productivity.

3. Why is it incorrect to consider productivity as a culprit?

4. Explain the phenomenon of creative destruction.

5. Why are your career prospects limited if you define yourself as an expert in SOA and XML?

6. Apply the line of reasoning you used in your answer to question 5 to some other technology or system, such as CRM, ERP, OLAP, RFM, or some other technology.

7. Explain how you can use one of the technologies in question 6 to help you start your career. To be successful, what perspective must you then maintain?

are those for which it is impossible to compute a dollar value. The benefits of the email system are intangible.

One common method for justifying IS and IT projects is to compute the costs and tangible benefits of the system and to perform a financial analysis. If the project can be justified on tangible benefits alone, then the favorable decision is made. If it cannot be justified on the basis of tangible benefits, then the intangible benefits are considered, and a subjective decision is made as to whether the intangibles are sufficiently valuable to overcome the missing tangible benefits that would be required.

Q6 What Are Your IS Rights and Responsibilities?

We conclude this chapter with a summary of your rights and responsibilities with regard to the IT department. Figure 11-4 lists what you are entitled to receive and indicates what you are expected to contribute.

Your Rights

You have a right to have the computing resources you need to perform your work as proficiently as you want. You have a right to the computer hardware and programs that you need. If you process huge files for data-mining applications, you have a right to the huge disks and the fast processor that you need. However, if you merely receive email and consult the corporate Web portal, then your right is for more modest requirements (leaving the more powerful resources for those in the organization who need them).

You have a right to reliable network and Internet services. Reliable means that you can process without problems almost all of the time. It means that you never go to work wondering, "Will the network be available today?" Network problems should be a rare occurrence.

You also have a right to a secure computing environment. The organization should protect your computer and its files, and you should not normally even need to

FIGURE 11-4
User's IS Rights and Responsibilities

You have a right to:	You have a responsibility to:
– Computer hardware and programs that allow you to perform your job proficiently	– Learn basic computer skills
– Reliable network and Internet connections	– Learn standard techniques and procedures for the applications you use
– A secure computing environment	– Follow security and backup procedures
– Protection from viruses, worms, and other threats	– Protect your password(s)
– Contribute to requirements for new system features and functions	– Use computer resources according to your employer's computer-use policy
– Reliable systems development and maintenance	– Make no unauthorized hardware modifications
– Prompt attention to problems, concerns, and complaints	– Install only authorized programs
– Properly prioritized problem fixes and resolutions	– Apply software patches and fixes when directed to do so
– Effective training	– When asked, devote the time required to respond carefully and completely to requests for requirements for new system features and functions
	– Avoid reporting trivial problems

think about security. From time to time, the organization may ask you to take particular actions to protect your computer and files, and you should take those actions. But such requests should be rare and related to specific outside threats.

You have a right to participate in requirements meetings for new applications that you will use and for major changes to applications that you currently use. You may choose to delegate this right to others, or your department may delegate that right for you, but if so, you have a right to contribute your thoughts through that delegate.

You have a right to reliable systems development and maintenance. Although schedule slippages of a month or two are common in many development projects, you should not have to endure schedule slippages of 6 months or more. Such slippages are evidence of incompetent systems development.

Additionally, you have a right to receive prompt attention to your problems, concerns, and complaints about information services. You have a right to have a means to report problems, and you have a right to know that your problem has been received and at least registered with the IT department. You have a right to have your problem resolved, consistent with established priorities. This means that an annoying problem that allows you to conduct your work will be prioritized below another's problem that interferes with his or her ability to do the job.

Finally, you have a right to effective training. It should be training that you can understand and that enables you to use systems to perform your particular job. The organization should provide training in a format and on a schedule that is convenient to you.

Your Responsibilities

You also have responsibilities toward the IT department and your organization. Specifically, you have a responsibility to learn basic computer skills and to learn the basic techniques and procedures for the applications you use. You should not expect hand-holding for basic operations. Nor should you expect to receive repetitive training and support for the same issue.

You have a responsibility to follow security and backup procedures. This is especially important because actions that you fail to take may cause problems for your fellow employees and your organization as well as for you. In particular, you are responsible for protecting your password(s). In the next chapter, you will learn that this is important not only to protect your computer, but, because of intersystem authentication, it is important to protect your organization's networks and databases as well.

You have a responsibility for using your computer resources in a manner that is consistent with your employer's policy. Many employers allow limited email for critical family matters while at work, but discourage frequent and long casual email. You have a responsibility to know your employer's policy and to follow it.

See the *Ethics Guide* on pages 280–281 for additional discussions on computer-use policy.

You also have a responsibility to make no unauthorized hardware modifications to your computer and to install only authorized programs. One reason for this policy is that your IT department constructs automated maintenance programs for upgrading your computer. Unauthorized hardware and programs may interfere with these programs. Additionally, the installation of unauthorized hardware or programs can cause you problems that the IT department will have to fix.

You have a responsibility to install computer patches and fixes when asked to do so. This is particularly important for patches that concern security and backup and recovery. When asked for input to requirements for new and adapted systems, you have a responsibility to take the time necessary to provide thoughtful and complete responses. If you do not have that time, you should delegate your input to someone else.

6. As a group, reflect on the lists that you have made in your answers to questions 2 through 5. Because of its limited budget, MRV will need to prioritize among these tasks. List the top-10 priority tasks and explain how each task is a top priority. If you think more than 10 tasks should be top priority, explain why.

7. If you managed MRV, how would you accomplish the tasks you identified in your answer to question 6? Would you consciously choose not to perform some of these tasks? What would be the consequences of such a choice? If you know that a task needs to be done but choose for cost reasons not to do it, are you better off than if you do not know that the task needs to be done? Why or why not?

8. To what extent do you believe that MRV's experience is shared by other small businesses? What conclusions do you draw from this exercise about the need for MIS knowledge among small business owners?

Case Study 11

Marriott International, Inc.

Marriott International, Inc., operates and franchises hotels and lodging facilities throughout the world. Its 2007 revenue was just over $12.9 billion. Marriott groups its business into segments according to lodging facility. Major business segments are full-service lodging, select-service lodging, extended-stay lodging, and timeshare properties. Marriott states that its three top corporate priorities are profitability, preference, and growth.

In the mid-1980s, the airlines developed the concept of *revenue management*, which adjusts prices in accordance with demand. The idea gained prominence in the airline industry, because an unoccupied seat represents revenue that is forever lost. Unlike a part in inventory, an unoccupied seat on today's flight cannot be sold tomorrow. Similarly, in the lodging industry today's unoccupied hotel room cannot be sold tomorrow. So, for hotels revenue management translates to raising prices on Monday when a convention is in town and lowering them on Saturday in the dead of winter when few travelers are in sight.

Marriott had developed two different revenue-management systems, one for its premium hotels and a second one for its lower-priced properties. It developed both of these systems using pre-Internet technology; systems upgrades required installing updates locally. The local updates were expensive and problematic. Also, the two systems required two separate interfaces for entering prices into the centralized reservation system.

In the late-1990s, Marriott embarked on a project to create a single revenue-management system that could be used by all of its properties. The new system, called OneSystem, was developed in-house, using a process similar to those you learned about in Chapter 10.

The IT professionals understood the importance of user involvement, and they formed a joint IT–business user team that developed the business case for the new system and jointly managed its development. The team was careful to provide constant communication to the system's future users, and it used prototypes to identify problem areas early. Training is a continuing activity for all Marriott employees, and the company integrated training facilities into the new system.

OneSystem recommends prices for each room, given the day, date, current reservation levels, and history. Each hotel property has a revenue manager who can override these recommendations. Either way, the prices are communicated directly to the centralized reservation system. OneSystem uses Internet technology so that when the company makes upgrades to the system, it makes them only at the Web servers, not at the individual hotels. This strategy saves considerable maintenance cost, activity, and frustration.

OneSystem computes the theoretical maximum revenue for each property and compares actual results to that maximum. Using OneSystem, the company has increased the ratio of actual to theoretical revenue from 83 percent to 91 percent. That increase of 8 percentage points has translated into a substantial increase in revenues.

Source: Case based on *www.cio.com/article/119209/The_Price_Is_Always_Right* (accessed October 2008).

Questions

1. How does OneSystem contribute to Marriott's objectives?

2. What are the advantages of having one revenue-management system instead of two? Consider both users and the IT department in your answer.

3. At the same time it was developing OneSystem in-house, Marriott chose to outsource its human relations information system. Why would it choose to develop one system in-house but outsource the other? Consider the following factors in your answer:

   - Marriott's objectives
   - The nature of the systems
   - The uniqueness of each system to Marriott
   - Marriott's in-house expertise

4. How did outsourcing HR contribute to the success of OneSystem?

"Sue, I told you Trevor would leave us."

"Yeah, Eddie, you did."

"He didn't like his tiny bonus—part of *your* new incentive computation—and I heard he's now working for Granite River Rafting."

"He was working for them."

"What do you mean?"

"Jason Taylor over at Granite just called me. He fired him."

"What, so soon? What did he do?"

"Stole our data."

"What are you saying?"

"Apparently, the day Trevor quit us, he was in this office by himself. He knew where all our customer data is stored, and he made a copy on a CD. Took it with him."

"You're kidding."

"I am not. He told Jason what he'd done, offered to give Jason all that data, and Jason let him go."

"I called Trevor and told him to give the data back. He says he'll mail it to me."

"How do we know he doesn't make a copy?"

"We don't."

"Jason's a straight-up guy. He'd tell us. But there are people on these rivers who aren't nearly so honest. What do we do about them?"

"Nothing we can do. I'm wondering if we should tell our customers. Thank heavens we don't store credit card data.

I'm sorry. One of our employees stole your e-mail address.

He did get all their email addresses, though. I guess I'd better call our lawyer. Not how I wanted to start the day. . . . Let's thank Jason with one of those big Copper River salmon we caught last month. . . . I'll write a note to go with it."

As stated at the end of Chapter 11, one of the responsibilities of the IT department is to protect information systems, data, and infrastructure. In this chapter, we will survey various threats and safeguards for countering those threats. As you will learn, safeguards fall into three categories: technical safeguards, which include hardware and software; data safeguards, which are concerned with protecting data and enforcing data policies; and human safeguards, which focus on people and the procedures they operate by. In particular, the company has to know what actions to take when personnel leave the organization. Of course, MRV has no IT department, and no one there had thought about such safeguards. As it turns out, MRV could have prevented its problems with a few simple human safeguards. You can use the knowledge of this chapter to protect your organization. Read carefully, because this could happen to you!

Study Questions

Q1 What are the sources and types of security threats?

Q2 What are the elements of a security program?

Q3 How can technical safeguards protect against security threats?

Q4 How can data safeguards protect against security threats?

Q5 How can human safeguards protect against security threats?

Q6 What is necessary for disaster preparedness?

Q7 How should organizations respond to security incidents?

How does the knowledge in this chapter help MRV and you?

Q1 What Are the Sources and Types of Security Threats?

We begin by describing security threats. We will first summarize the sources of threats and then describe specific problems that arise from each source. Three sources of **security threats** are human error and mistakes, malicious human activity, and natural events and disasters.

Human errors and mistakes include accidental problems caused by both employees and nonemployees. An example is an employee who misunderstands operating procedures and accidentally deletes customer records. Another example is an employee who, in the course of backing up a database, inadvertently installs an old database on top of the current one. This category also includes poorly written application programs and poorly designed procedures. Finally, human errors and mistakes include physical accidents like driving a forklift through the wall of a computer room.

The second source of security problems is *malicious human activity.* This category includes employees and former employees who intentionally destroy data or other system components. It also includes both hackers who break into a system as well as virus and worm writers who infect computer systems. Malicious human activity also includes outside criminals who break into a system to steal for financial gain; it also includes terrorism.

Natural events and disasters are the third source of security problems. This category includes fires, floods, hurricanes, earthquakes, tsunamis, avalanches, and other acts of nature. Problems in this category include not only the initial loss of capability and service, but also losses stemming from actions to recover from the initial problem.

Figure 12-1 summarizes threats by type of problem and source. Five types of security problems are listed: unauthorized data disclosure, incorrect data modification, faulty service, denial of service, and loss of infrastructure. We will consider each type.

FIGURE 12-1
Security Threats

		Source		
		Human Error	**Malicious Activity**	**Natural Disasters**
Problem	**Unauthorized data disclosure**	Procedural mistakes	Pretexting Phishing Spoofing Sniffing Computer crime	Disclosure during recovery
	Incorrect data modification	Procedural mistakes Incorrect procedures Ineffective accounting controls System errors	Hacking Computer crime	Incorrect data recovery
	Faulty service	Procedural mistakes Development and installation errors	Computer crime Usurpation	Service improperly restored
	Denial of service	Accidents	DOS attacks	Service interruption
	Loss of infrastructure	Accidents	Theft Terrorist activity	Property loss

Unauthorized Data Disclosure

Unauthorized data disclosure can occur by human error when someone inadvertently releases data in violation of policy. An example at a university would be a new department administrator who posts student names, numbers, and grades in a public place, when the releasing of names and grades violates state law. Another example is employees who unknowingly or carelessly release proprietary data to competitors or to the media.

The popularity and efficacy of search engines has created another source of inadvertent disclosure. Employees who place restricted data on Web sites that can be reached by search engines may mistakenly publish proprietary or restricted data over the Web.

Of course, proprietary and personal data can also be released maliciously. **Pretexting** occurs when someone deceives by pretending to be someone else. A common scam involves a telephone caller who pretends to be from a credit card company and claims to be checking the validity of credit card numbers: "I'm checking your MasterCard number; it begins 5491. Can you verify the rest of the number?" MasterCard numbers commonly start with 5491; the caller is attempting to steal a valid number.

Phishing is a similar technique for obtaining unauthorized data that uses pretexting via email. The *phisher* pretends to be a legitimate company and sends an email requesting confidential data, such as account numbers, Social Security numbers, account passwords, and so forth. Phishing compromises legitimate brands and trademarks. *MIS in Use 12* (pages 290–291) looks in more detail at examples of phishing.

Spoofing is another term for someone pretending to be someone else. If you pretend to be your professor, you are spoofing your professor. **IP spoofing** occurs when an intruder uses another site's IP address as if it were that other site. **Email spoofing** is a synonym for phishing.

Sniffing is a technique for intercepting computer communications. With wired networks, sniffing requires a physical connection to the network. With wireless networks, no such connection is required: **Drive-by sniffers** simply take computers with wireless connections through an area and search for unprotected wireless networks. They can monitor and intercept wireless traffic at will. Even protected wireless networks are vulnerable, as you will learn. Spyware and adware are two other sniffing techniques discussed later in this chapter.

Other forms of computer crime include breaking into networks to steal data such as customer lists, product inventory data, employee data, and other proprietary and confidential data.

Finally, people may inadvertently disclose data during recovery from a natural disaster. Usually, during a recovery, everyone is so focused on restoring system capability that they ignore normal security safeguards. A request like "I need a copy of the customer database backup" will receive far less scrutiny during disaster recovery than at other times.

Incorrect Data Modification

The second problem category in Figure 12-1 is *incorrect data modification*. Examples include incorrectly increasing a customer's discount or incorrectly modifying an employee's salary, earned days of vacation, or annual bonus. Other examples include placing incorrect information, such as incorrect price changes, on the company's Web site or company portal.

Incorrect data modification can occur through human error when employees follow procedures incorrectly or when procedures have been incorrectly designed. For proper internal control on systems that process financial data or that control inventories of assets, like products and equipment, companies should ensure separation of duties and authorities and have multiple checks and balances in place.

A final type of incorrect data modification caused by human error includes *system errors*. An example is the lost-update problem discussed in Chapter 5 (page 111).

Hacking occurs when a person gains unauthorized access to a computer system. Although some people hack for the sheer joy of doing it, other hackers invade systems for the malicious purpose of stealing or modifying data. Computer criminals invade computer networks to obtain critical data or to manipulate the system for financial gain. Examples are reducing account balances or causing the shipment of goods to unauthorized locations and customers.

Finally, faulty recovery actions after a disaster can result in incorrect data changes. The faulty actions can be unintentional or malicious.

Faulty Service

The third problem category, *faulty service*, includes problems that result because of incorrect system operation. Faulty service could include incorrect data modification, as just described. It also could include systems that work incorrectly by sending the wrong goods to the customer or the ordered goods to the wrong customer, incorrectly billing customers, or sending the wrong information to employees. Humans can inadvertently cause faulty service by making procedural mistakes. System developers can write programs incorrectly or make errors during the installation of hardware, software programs, and data.

Usurpation occurs when unauthorized programs invade a computer system and replace legitimate programs. Such unauthorized programs typically shut down the legitimate system and substitute their own processing. Faulty service can also result from mistakes made during the recovery from natural disasters.

Denial of Service

Human error in following procedures or a lack of procedures can result in **denial of service (DOS)**. For example, humans can inadvertently shut down a Web server or corporate gateway router by starting a computationally intensive application. An OLAP application that uses the operational DBMS can consume so many DBMS resources that order-entry transactions cannot get through.

12 Phishing for Credit Card Accounts

Before you read further, realize that the graphics in this case are fake. They were not produced by a legitimate business, but were generated by a phisher. A *phisher* is an operation that spoofs legitimate companies in an attempt to illegally capture credit card numbers, email accounts, driver's license numbers, and other data. Some phishers even install malicious program code on users' computers.

Phishing is usually initiated via an email. Go to *www.fraudwatchinternational.com/phishing* and examine several of the phishing attacks. As of September 2008, you can see phishing attacks on PayPal, Google, Bank of America, and dozens of other companies. The most common phishing attack is initiated with a bogus email. For example, you might receive the email shown in Figure 1.

This bogus email is designed to cause you to click on the "See more details here" link. When you do so, you will be connected to a site that will ask you for personal data, such as credit card numbers, card expiration dates, driver's license number, Social Security number, or other data. In this particular case, you will be taken to a screen that asks for your credit card number (see Figure 2).

This Web page is produced by a nonexistent company and is entirely fake, including the link "Inform us about fraud." The only purpose of this site is to illegally capture your card number. It might also install spyware, adware, or other malware (see page 294) on your computer.

If you were to get this far, you should immediately close your browser and restart your computer. You should also run anti-malware scans on your computer to determine if the phisher has installed program code on your computer. If so, use the anti-malware software to remove that code.

How can you defend yourself from such attacks? First, you know that you did not purchase two first class tickets to

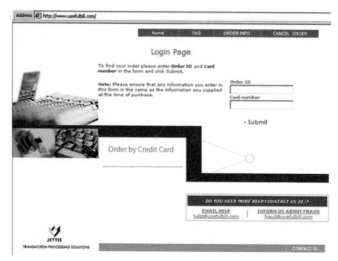

FIGURE 2
Fake Phishing Screen

Your Order ID: "17152492"
Order Date: "09/07/07"
Product Purchased: "Two First Class Tickets to Cozumel"
Your card type: "CREDIT"
Total Price: "$349.00"

Hello, when you purchased your tickets you provided an incorrect mailing address.
See more details here
Please follow the link and modify your mailing address or cancel your order. If you have questions, feel free to contact with us account@usefulbill.com

FIGURE 1
Fake Phishing Email

Cozumel. (Had you by odd circumstance just purchased airline tickets to Cozumel, you should contact the legitimate vendor's site *directly* to determine if there had been some mix up.) Because you have not purchased such tickets, suspect a phisher.

Second, notice the implausibility of the email. It is exceedingly unlikely that you can buy two first-class tickets to any foreign country for $349. Additionally, note the misspelled word and the poor grammar ("cortact with us"). All of these facts should alert you to the bogus nature of this email.

Third, do not be misled by legitimate-looking graphics. Phishers are criminals; they do not bother to respect international agreements on legitimate use of trademarks. The phisher might use names of legitimate companies like Visa, MasterCard, Discover, and American Express on the Web page, and the presence of those names might lull you into thinking this is legitimate. The phisher is illegally using those names. In other instances, the phisher will copy the entire look and feel of a legitimate company's Web site.

Phishing is a serious problem. To protect yourself, be wary of unsolicited email, even if the email appears to be from a legitimate business. If you have questions about an email, contact the company directly (*not* using the addresses provided by the phisher!) and ask about the email. Above all, never give confidential data such as account numbers, Social Security numbers, driver's license numbers, or credit card numbers in response to any *unsolicited* email.

Several characteristics of phishing make it difficult to eliminate. First, attacks often are indirect. Organizations do not know that their name, brand, and graphics are being used to deceive their own customers until someone reports the attack. Second, it is difficult to gauge the size of the attack, and thus it is difficult to calibrate a response. Notifying every customer will alarm the customer base and create a negative brand impression. If the attack is limited, such a warning may not be justified, but who knows if the worst of the attack is yet to come?

Third, according to the Financial Services Technology Consortium, phishing is seldom perpetrated by a single individual, but is perpetrated by organized criminal enterprises. These crime organizations hire technical specialist contractors to phish, but these contractors give the results to the organization, which quickly disseminates them to criminals throughout the world.

Phishing is an attack on an organization's brand, which can be worth millions, even billions, of dollars. The phishing attack is clothed in the brand image, using the brand's familiar graphics. After the attack, in the mind of the customer the brand may be paired with deception, problems, and financial loss. These are not the emotions that any marketer wants paired with its brand.

Additionally, the financial consequence of each incident may be small to the spoofed organization, and so the organization may not be moved to respond. It is only in the aggregate that the tangible and intangible costs mount. Consequently, the cost/benefit ratio of helping a single customer is high. Yet, there does not seem to be any way to resolve the problem except one by one.

Finally, enforcement and punishment of phishers is exceedingly difficult. It is easy for phishers to operate in countries where such activity is tolerated. Also, the victims of a given attack potentially are spread worldwide. Who is available to punish the phishers?

You and a team of your classmates will have a chance to investigate phishing further in Collaboration Exercise 12 on page 310. ◉

Denial-of-service attacks can be launched maliciously. A malicious hacker can flood a Web server, for example, with millions of bogus service requests that so occupy the server that it cannot service legitimate requests. As you learned in Chapter 4 (page 92), computer worms can infiltrate a network with so much artificial traffic that legitimate traffic cannot get through. Finally, natural disasters may cause systems to fail, resulting in denial of service.

Loss of Infrastructure

Human accidents can cause *loss of infrastructure.* Examples are a bulldozer cutting a conduit of fiber-optic cables and the floor buffer crashing into a rack of Web servers.

Theft and terrorist events also cause loss of infrastructure. A disgruntled, terminated employee can walk off with corporate data servers, routers, or other crucial equipment. Terrorist events can also cause the loss of physical plants and equipment.

Natural disasters present the largest risk for infrastructure loss. A fire, flood, earthquake, or similar event can destroy data centers and all they contain. The devastation of the Indian Ocean tsunami in December 2004 and of hurricanes Katrina and Rita in the fall of 2005 are potent examples of the risks to infrastructure from natural causes.

You may be wondering why Figure 12-1 does not include viruses, worms, and Trojan horses. The answer is that viruses, worms, and Trojan horses are *techniques* for causing some of the problems in the figure. They can cause a denial-of-service attack, or they can be used to cause malicious, unauthorized data access, or data loss.

Q2 What Are the Elements of a Security Program?

All of the problems listed in Figure 12-1 are real and as serious as they sound. Accordingly, organizations must address security in a systematic way. A security program[1] has three components: senior management involvement, safeguards of various kinds, and incident response.

---

[1]Note the word *program* is used here in the sense of a management program that includes objectives, policies, procedures, directives, and so forth. Do not confuse this term with a *computer program.*

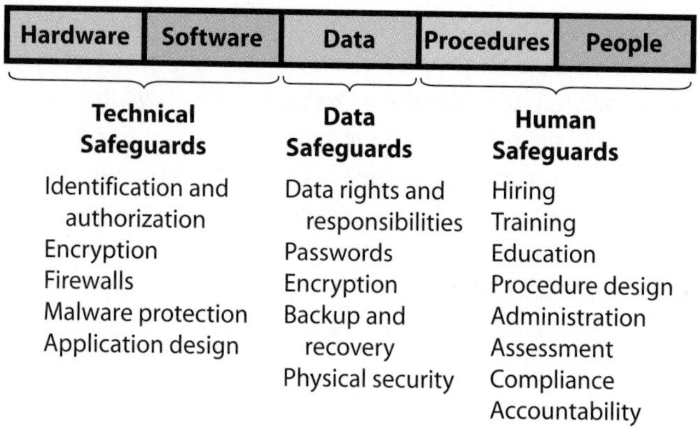

FIGURE 12-2
Security Safeguards as
They Relate to the Five
Components

Hardware	Software	Data	Procedures	People

Technical Safeguards	Data Safeguards	Human Safeguards
Identification and authorization	Data rights and responsibilities	Hiring
Encryption	Passwords	Training
Firewalls	Encryption	Education
Malware protection	Backup and recovery	Procedure design
Application design	Physical security	Administration
		Assessment
		Compliance
		Accountability

FIGURE 12-2
Security Safeguards as
They Relate to the Five
Components

Effective security requires balanced attention to all five components! Senior management has two critical security functions: First, senior management must establish the security policy. This policy sets the stage for the organization's response to security threats. However, because no security program is perfect, there is always risk. Management's second function, therefore, is to manage risk by balancing the costs and benefits of the security program.

Safeguards are protections against security threats. A good way to view safeguards is in terms of the five components of an information system, as shown in Figure 12-2. Some of the safeguards involve computer hardware and software. Some involve data; others involve procedures and people. In addition to these safeguards, organizations must also consider disaster recovery safeguards. An effective security program consists of a balance of safeguards of all these types.

The final component of a security program consists of the organization's planned response to security incidents. Clearly, the time to think about what to do is not when the computers are crashing all around the organization. We will discuss incident response in the last section of this chapter.

Q3 How Can Technical Safeguards Protect Against Security Threats?

Technical safeguards involve the hardware and software components of an information system. Figure 12-3 lists primary technical safeguards. We have discussed all of these in prior chapters. Here we will just supplement those prior discussions.

Identification and Authentication

Every information system today should require users to sign on with a user name and password. The user name *identifies* the user (the process of **identification**), and the password *authenticates* that user (the process of **authentication**). Review the material

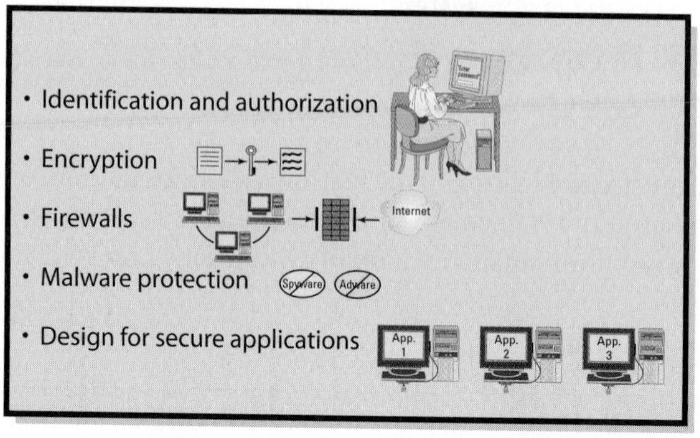

FIGURE 12-3
Technical Safeguards

- Identification and authorization
- Encryption
- Firewalls
- Malware protection
- Design for secure applications

on strong passwords and password etiquette in Chapter 1 (pages 14–15) if you have forgotten that discussion.

Passwords have important weaknesses. For one, users tend to be careless in their use. Despite repeated warnings to the contrary, yellow sticky notes holding written passwords adorn many computers. In addition, users tend to be free in sharing their passwords with others. Finally, many users choose ineffective, simple passwords. With such passwords, intrusion systems can very effectively guess passwords.

These deficiencies can be reduced or eliminated using smart cards and biometric authentication.

Smart Cards

A **smart card** is a plastic card similar to a credit card. Unlike credit, debit, and ATM cards, which have a magnetic strip, smart cards have a microchip. The microchip, which holds far more data than a magnetic strip, is loaded with identifying data. Users of smart cards are required to enter a **personal identification number (PIN)** to be authenticated.

Biometric Authentication

Biometric authentication uses personal physical characteristics such as fingerprints, facial features, and retinal scans to authenticate users. Biometric authentication provides strong authentication, but the required equipment is expensive. Often, too, users resist biometric identification because they feel it is invasive.

Biometric authentication is in the early stages of adoption. Because of its strength, it likely will see increased usage in the future. It is also likely that legislators will pass laws governing the use, storage, and protection requirements for biometric data. For more on biometrics, see *http://searchsecurity.techtarget.com*.

Note that authentication methods fall into three categories: what you know (password or PIN), what you have (smart card), and what you are (biometric).

Single Sign-on for Multiple Systems

Information systems often require multiple sources of authentication. For example, when you sign on to your personal computer, you need to be authenticated. When you access the LAN in your department, you need to be authenticated again. When you traverse your organization's WAN, you will need to be authenticated to even more networks. Also, if your request requires database data, the DBMS server that manages that database will authenticate you yet again.

It would be annoying to enter a name and password for every one of these resources. You might have to use and remember five or six different passwords just to access the data you need to perform your job. It would be equally undesirable to send your password across all of these networks. The further your password travels, the greater the risk it can be compromised.

Instead, today's operating systems have the capability to authenticate you to networks and other servers. You sign on to your local computer and provide authentication data; from that point on, your operating system authenticates you to another network or server, which can authenticate you to yet another network and server, and so forth.

Encryption and Firewalls

The next two categories of technical safeguards in Figure 12-3 are encryption and firewalls. They were described in Chapter 6, on pages 134–136. We will not repeat that discussion here. Just realize that they are very important technical safeguards. (Review the material in Chapter 6 if you need to refresh that knowledge.)

Malware Protection

The next technical safeguard in our list in Figure 12-3 is malware. The term **malware** has several definitions. Here we will use the broadest one: *malware* is viruses, worms, Trojan horses, spyware, and adware. We discussed viruses, worms, and Trojan horses in Chapter 4 (pages 92–93); you should review that material now if you have forgotten their definitions.

Spyware and Adware

Spyware programs are installed on the user's computer without the user's knowledge or permission. Spyware resides in the background and, unknown to the user, observes the user's actions and keystrokes, monitors computer activity, and reports the user's activities to sponsoring organizations. Some malicious spyware captures keystrokes to obtain user names, passwords, account numbers, and other sensitive information. Other spyware supports marketing analyses, observing what users do, Web sites visited, products examined and purchased, and so forth.

Adware is similar to spyware in that it is installed without the user's permission and it also resides in the background and observes user behavior. Most adware is benign in that it does not perform malicious acts or steal data. It does, however, watch user activity and produce pop-up ads. Adware can also change the user's default window or modify search results and switch the user's search engine. For the most part, it is just annoying, but users should be concerned any time they have unknown programs on their computers that perform unrequested functions.

Figure 12-4 lists some of the symptoms of adware and spyware. Sometimes these symptoms develop slowly over time as more malware components are installed. Should these symptoms occur on your computer, remove the spyware or adware using anti-malware programs.

Malware Safeguards

Fortunately, it is possible to avoid most malware using the following malware safeguards:

1. *Install antivirus and antispyware programs on your computer.* Your IT department will have a list of recommended (perhaps required) programs for this purpose. If you choose a program for yourself, choose one from a reputable vendor. Check reviews of anti-malware software on the Web before purchasing.

2. *Set up your anti-malware programs to scan your computer frequently.* You should scan your computer at least once a week and possibly more often. When you detect malware code, use the anti-malware software to remove it. If the code cannot be removed, contact your IT department or anti-malware vendor.

3. *Update malware definitions.* **Malware definitions**—patterns that exist in malware code—should be downloaded frequently. Anti-malware vendors update these definitions continuously, and you should install these updates as they become available.

4. *Open email attachments only from known sources.* Also, even when opening attachments from known sources, do so with great care. According to professor and security expert Ray Panko, about 90 percent of all viruses are spread by

FIGURE 12-4
Spyware and Adware
Symptoms

- Slow system start up
- Sluggish system performance
- Many pop-up advertisements
- Suspicious browser homepage changes
- Suspicious changes to the taskbar and other system interfaces
- Unusual hard-disk activity

email attachments.[2] This statistic is not surprising, because most organizations are protected by firewalls. With a properly configured firewall, email is the only outside-initiated traffic that can reach user computers.

Most anti-malware programs check email attachments for malware code. However, all users should form the habit of *never* opening an email attachment from an unknown source. Also, if you receive an unexpected email from a known source or an email from a known source that has a suspicious subject, odd spelling, or poor grammar, do not open the attachment without first verifying with the known source that the attachment is legitimate.

5. *Promptly install software updates from legitimate sources.* Unfortunately, all programs are chock full of security holes; vendors are fixing them as rapidly as they are discovered, but the practice is inexact. Install patches to the operating system and application programs promptly.

6. *Browse only in reputable Internet neighborhoods.* It is possible for some malware to install itself when you do nothing more than open a Web page. Don't go there!

Malware Is a Serious Problem

America Online (AOL) and the National Cyber Security Alliance conducted a malware study using Internet users in 2004. They asked the users a series of questions and then, with the users' permission, scanned the users' computers to determine how accurately the users understood malware problems on their own computers. This fascinating study can be found online at *www.staysafeonline.info/news/2004press.html.*

Figure 12-5 shows a few important results from this study. Among the users, 6 percent thought they had a virus, but 19 percent actually did. Further, half of those surveyed did not know if they had a virus. Of those computers having viruses, an average of 2.4 viruses were found, and the maximum number of viruses found on a single computer was 213!

Question	User Response	Scan Results
Do you have a virus on your computer?	Yes: 6%	Yes: 19%
	No: 44%	No: 81%
	Don't know: 50%	
Average (maximum) number of viruses on infected computer		2.4 (213)
How often do you update your antivirus software?	Last week: 71%	Last week: 33%
	Last month: 12%	Last month: 34%
	Last 6 months: 5%	Last 6 months: 6%
	Longer than 6 months: 12%	Longer than 6 months: 12%
Do you think you have spyware or adware on your computer?	Yes: 53%	Yes: 80%
	No: 47%	No: 20%
Average (maximum) number of spyware/adware components on computer		93 (1,059)
Did you give permission to someone to install these components on your computer?	Yes: 5% No: 95%	

FIGURE 12-5
Malware Survey Results

Source: AOL/NCSA Online Safety Study, October 2004, *www.staysafeonline.info/news/safety_study_v04.pdf* (accessed March 2005).

---

[2]Ray Panko, *Corporate Computer and Network Security* (Upper Saddle River, NJ: Prentice Hall, 2004), p. 165.

When asked how often they update their antivirus definitions, 71 percent of the users reported that they had done so within the last week. Actually, only one-third of the users had updated their definitions that recently.

Figure 12-5 shows similar results for spyware. The average user computer had 93 spyware components. The maximum number found on a computer was 1,059. Note that only 5 percent of the users had given permission for the spyware to be installed.

Although the problem of malware will never be eradicated, you can reduce its size by following the six safeguards listed in the previous subsection. You should take these actions as a habit, and you should ensure that employees you manage take them as well.

Design for Secure Applications

The final technical safeguard in Figure 12-3 concerns the design of applications. As a future IS user, you will not design programs yourself. However, you should ensure that any information system developed for you and your department includes security as one of the application requirements.

Q4 How Can Data Safeguards Protect Against Security Threats?

Data safeguards protect databases and other organizational data. Two organizational units are responsible for data safeguards. **Data administration** refers to an organization-wide function that is in charge of developing data policies and enforcing data standards. Data administration is a staff function to the CIO, as discussed in Chapter 11.

Database administration refers to a function that pertains to a particular database. The ERP, CRM, and MRP databases each have a database administration function. Database administration ensures that procedures exist to ensure orderly multiuser processing of the database, to control changes to the database structure, and to protect the database.

Both data and database administration are involved in establishing the data safeguards in Figure 12-6. First, data administration should define data policies such as "We will not share identifying customer data with any other organization" and the like. Then, data administration and database administration(s) work together to specify user data rights and responsibilities. Third, those rights should be enforced by user accounts that are authenticated at least by passwords.

The organization should protect sensitive data by storing it in encrypted form. Such encryption uses one or more keys in ways similar to that described for data communication encryption. One potential problem with stored data, however, is that the key might be lost or that disgruntled or terminated employees might destroy it. Because of this possibility, when data are encrypted, a trusted party should have a copy of the encryption key. This safety procedure is sometimes called **key escrow**.

Another data safeguard is to periodically create backup copies of database contents. The organization should store at least some of these backups off premises, possibly in a remote location. Additionally, IT personnel should periodically practice

FIGURE 12-6
Data Safeguards

- Define data policies
- Data rights and responsibilities
- Rights enforced by user accounts authenticated by passwords
- Data encryption
- Backup and recovery procedures
- Physical security

recovery to ensure that the backups are valid and that effective recovery procedures exist. Do not assume that just because a backup is made, the database is protected.

Physical security is another data safeguard. The computers that run the DBMS and all devices that store database data should reside in locked, controlled-access facilities. If not, they are subject not only to theft, but also to damage. For better security, the organization should keep a log showing who entered the facility, when, and for what purpose.

In some cases, organizations contract with other companies to manage their databases. If so, all of the safeguards in Figure 12-6 should be part of the service contract. Also, the contract should give the owners of the data permission to inspect the premises of the database operator and to interview its personnel on a reasonable schedule.

Q5 How Can Human Safeguards Protect Against Security Threats?

Human safeguards involve the people and procedure components of information systems. In general, human safeguards result when authorized users follow appropriate procedures for system use and recovery. Restricting access to authorized users requires effective authentication methods and careful user account management. In addition, appropriate security procedures must be designed as part of every information system, and users should be trained on the importance and use of those procedures. In this section, we will consider the development of human safeguards first for employees and then for nonemployee personnel.

Human Safeguards for Employees

Figure 12-7 lists security considerations for employees. The first is position definitions.

Position Definitions

Effective human safeguards begin with definitions of job tasks and responsibilities. In general, job descriptions should provide a separation of duties and authorities. For example, no single individual should be allowed both to approve expenses and write checks. Instead, one person should approve expenses, another pay them, and a third should account for the payment. Similarly, in inventory, no single person should be allowed to authorize an inventory withdrawal and also to remove the items from inventory.

Given appropriate job descriptions, user accounts should be defined to give users the *least possible privilege* needed to perform their jobs. For example, users whose job description does not include modifying data should be given accounts with read-only privilege. Similarly, user accounts should prohibit users from accessing data their job description does not require. Because of the problem of semantic security, even access to seemingly innocuous data may need to be limited.

Finally, the security sensitivity should be documented for each position. Some jobs involve highly sensitive data (e.g., employee compensation, salesperson quotas, and proprietary marketing or technical data). Other positions involve no sensitive data. Documenting *position sensitivity* enables security personnel to prioritize their activities in accordance with the possible risk and loss.

Hiring and Screening

Security considerations should be part of the hiring process. Of course, if the position involves no sensitive data and no access to information systems, then screening for information systems security purposes will be minimal. When hiring for high-sensitivity positions, however, extensive interviews, references, and background investigations are

Account Administration

The third human safeguard is account administration. The administration of user accounts, passwords, and help-desk policies and procedures are important components of the security system.

Account Management

Account management concerns the creation of new user accounts, the modification of existing account permissions, and the removal of unneeded accounts. Information system administrators perform all of these tasks, but account users have the responsibility to notify the administrators of the need for these actions. The IT department should create standard procedures for this purpose. As a future user, you can improve your relationship with IS personnel by providing early and timely notification of the need for account changes.

The existence of accounts that are no longer necessary is a serious security threat. IS administrators cannot know when an account should be removed; it is up to users and managers to give such notification.

Password Management

Passwords are the primary means of authentication. They are important not just for access to the user's computer, but also for authentication to other networks and servers to which the user may have access. Because of the importance of passwords, the National Institute of Standards and Technology (NIST) recommends that employees be required to sign statements similar to that shown in Figure 12-8.

When an account is created, users should immediately change the password they are given to a password of their own. In fact, well-constructed systems require the user to change the password on first use.

Additionally, users should change passwords frequently thereafter. Some systems will require a password change every 3 months or perhaps more frequently. Users grumble at the nuisance of making such changes, but frequent password changes reduce not only the risk of password loss, but also the extent of damage if an existing password is compromised.

Some users create two passwords and switch back and forth between those two. This strategy results in poor security, and some password systems do not allow the user to reuse recently used passwords. Again, users may view this policy as a nuisance, but it is important.

Help-Desk Policies

In the past, help desks have been a serious security risk. A user who had forgotten his password would call the help desk and plead for the help-desk representative to tell him his password or to reset the password to something else. "I can't get this report out without it!" was (and is) a common lament.

FIGURE 12-8
Sample Account
Acknowledgment Form

Source: National Institute of Standards and Technology, *Introduction to Computer Security: The NIST Handbook*, Publication 800–812, p. 114.

> I hereby acknowledge personal receipt of the system password(s) associated with the user IDs listed below. I understand that I am responsible for protecting the password(s), will comply with all applicable system security standards, and will not divulge my password(s) to any person. I further understand that I must report to the Information Systems Security Officer any problem I encounter in the use of the password(s) or when I have reason to believe that the private nature of my password(s) has been compromised.

The problem for help-desk representatives is, of course, that they have no way of determining that they are talking with the true user and not someone spoofing a true user. But, they are in a bind: If they do not help in some way, the help desk is perceived to be the "unhelpful desk."

To resolve such problems, many systems give the help-desk representative a means of authenticating the user. Typically, the help-desk information system has answers to questions that only the true user would know, such as the user's birthplace, mother's maiden name, or last four digits of an important account number. Usually, when a password is changed, notification of that change is sent to the user in an email. Email, as you learned, is sent as plaintext, however, so the new password itself ought not to be emailed. If you ever receive notification that your password was reset when you did not request such a reset, immediately contact IT security. Someone has compromised your account.

All such help-desk measures reduce the strength of the security system, and, if the employee's position is sufficiently sensitive, they may create too large a vulnerability. In such a case, the user may just be out of luck. The account will be deleted, and the user must repeat the account-application process.

Systems Procedures

Figure 12-9 shows a grid of procedure types—normal operation, backup, and recovery. Procedures of each type should exist for each information system. For example, the order-entry system will have procedures of each of these types, as will the Web storefront, the inventory system, and so forth. The definition and use of standardized procedures reduces the likelihood of computer crime and other malicious activity by insiders. It also ensures that the system's security policy is enforced.

Procedures exist for both users and operations personnel. For each type of user, the company should develop procedures for normal, backup, and recovery operations. As a future user, you will be primarily concerned with user procedures. Normal-use procedures should provide safeguards appropriate to the sensitivity of the information system.

Backup procedures concern the creation of backup data to be used in the event of failure. Whereas operations personnel have the responsibility for backing up system databases and other systems data, departmental personnel have the need to back up data on their own computers. Good questions to ponder are, "What would happen if I lost my computer (or PDA) tomorrow?" "What would happen if someone dropped my computer during an airport security inspection?" "What would happen if my computer were stolen?" Employees should ensure that they back up critical business data on their computers. The IT department may help in this effort by designing backup procedures and making backup facilities available.

	System Users	Operations Personnel
Normal operation	Use the system to perform job tasks, with security appropriate to sensitivity.	Operate data center equipment, manage networks, run Web servers, and do related operational tasks.
Backup	Prepare for loss of system functionality.	Back up Web site resources, databases, administrative data, account and password data, and other data.
Recovery	Accomplish job tasks during failure. Know tasks to do during system recovery.	Recover systems from backed up data. Perform role of help desk during recovery.

FIGURE 12-9
System Procedures

Finally, systems analysts should develop procedures for system recovery. First, how will the department manage its affairs when a critical system is unavailable? Customers will want to order, and manufacturing will want to remove items from inventory even though a critical information system is unavailable. How will the department respond? Once the system is returned to service, how will records of business activities during the outage be entered into the system? How will service be resumed? The system developers should ask and answer these questions and others like them and develop procedures accordingly.

Security Monitoring

Security monitoring is the last of the human safeguards we will consider. Important monitoring functions are activity log analyses, security testing, and investigating and learning from security incidents.

Many information system programs produce *activity logs*. Firewalls produce logs of their activities, including lists of all dropped packets, infiltration attempts, and unauthorized access attempts from within the firewall. DBMS products produce logs of successful and failed log-ins. Web servers produce voluminous logs of Web activities. The operating systems in personal computers can produce logs of log-ins and firewall activities.

None of these logs adds any value to an organization unless someone looks at them. Accordingly, an important security function is to analyze these logs for threat patterns, successful and unsuccessful attacks, and evidence of security vulnerabilities.

Additionally, companies should test their security programs. Both in-house personnel and outside security consultants should conduct such testing.

Another important monitoring function is to investigate security incidents. How did the problem occur? Have safeguards been created to prevent a recurrence of such problems? Does the incident indicate vulnerabilities in other portions of the security system? What else can be learned from the incident?

Security systems reside in a dynamic environment. Organization structures change. Companies are acquired or sold; mergers occur. New systems require new security measures. New technology changes the security landscape, and new threats arise. Security personnel must constantly monitor the situation and determine if the existing security policy and safeguards are adequate. If changes are needed, security personnel need to take appropriate action.

Security, like quality, is an ongoing process. There is no final state that represents a secure system or company. Instead, companies must monitor security on a continuing basis.

Q6 What Is Necessary for Disaster Preparedness?

A disaster is a substantial loss of computing infrastructure caused by acts of nature, crime, or terrorist activity. As stated several times, the best way to solve a problem is not to have it. The best safeguard against a disaster is appropriate location. If possible, place computing centers, Web farms, and other computer facilities in locations not prone to floods, earthquakes, hurricanes, tornados, or avalanches. Even in those locations, place infrastructure in unobtrusive buildings, basements, backrooms, and similar locations well within the physical perimeter of the organization. Also, locate computing infrastructure in fire-resistant buildings designed to house expensive and critical equipment.

However, sometimes business requirements necessitate locating the computing infrastructure in undesirable locations. Also, even at a good location, disasters do occur. Therefore, some businesses prepare backup processing centers in locations geographically removed from the primary processing site.

> • Locate infrastructure in safe location.
> • Identify mission-critical systems.
> • Identify resources needed to run those systems.
> • Prepare remote backup facilities.
> • Train and rehearse.

FIGURE 12-10
Disaster Preparedness
Guidelines

Figure 12-10 lists major disaster preparedness tasks. After choosing a safe location for the computing infrastructure, the organization should identify all mission-critical applications. These are applications without which the organization cannot carry on and which, if lost for any period of time, could cause the organization's failure. The next step is to identify all resources necessary to run those systems. Such resources include computers, operating systems, application programs, databases, administrative data, procedure documentation, and trained personnel.

Next, the organization creates backups for the critical resources at the remote processing center. So-called **hot sites** are remote processing centers run by commercial disaster-recovery services. For a monthly fee, they provide all the equipment needed to continue operations following a disaster. See *www.ragingwire.com/managed_services?p=recovery* for information about services provided by a typical vendor. **Cold sites**, in contrast, provide office space, but customers themselves provide and install the equipment needed to continue operations.

Once the organization has backups in place, it must train and rehearse cutover of operations from the primary center to the backup. Periodic refresher rehearsals are mandatory.

Preparing a backup facility is very expensive; however, the costs of establishing and maintaining that facility are a form of insurance. Senior management must make the decision to prepare such a facility, by balancing the risks, benefits, and costs.

Q7 How Should Organizations Respond to Security Incidents?

The last component of a security plan that we will consider is incident response. Figure 12-11 lists the major factors. First, every organization should have an incident-response plan as part of the security program. No organization should wait until some asset has been lost or compromised before deciding what to do. The plan should include how employees are to respond to security problems, whom they should contact, the reports they should make, and steps they can take to reduce further loss.

Consider, for example, a virus. An incident-response plan will stipulate what an employee should do when he notices the virus. It should specify whom to contact and what to do. It may stipulate that the employee should turn off his computer and physically disconnect from the network. The plan should also indicate what users with wireless computers should do.

The plan should provide centralized reporting of all security incidents. Such reporting will enable an organization to determine if it is under systematic attack or whether an incident is isolated. Centralized reporting also allows the organization to learn about security threats, take consistent actions in response, and apply specialized expertise to all security problems.

When an incident does occur, speed is of the essence. Viruses and worms can spread very quickly across an organization's networks, and a fast response will help to mitigate the consequences. Because of the need for speed, preparation pays. The incident-response plan should identify critical personnel and their off-hours contact information. These personnel should be trained on where to go and what to do when

That's it! You've reached the end of the book. Take a moment to reflect on how you will use what you will learn, as described in the *Guide* on pages 306–307.

FIGURE 12-11
Factors in Incident Response

> • Have plan in place
> • Centralized reporting
> • Specific responses
>   – Speed
>   – Preparation pays
>   – Don't make problem worse
> • Practice!

The Final, Final Word

Congratulations! You've made it through the entire book. With this knowledge you are well prepared to be an effective user of information systems. And with work and imagination, you can be much more than that. Many interesting opportunities are available to those who can apply information in innovative ways. Your professor has done what she can do, and the rest, as they say, is up to you.

As stated several times, today computer communications and data storage are free—or so close to free that the cost is not worth mentioning. What are the consequences? Amazon.com, YouTube, Facebook, UGC, and on and on. Are the best opportunities gone? I very much doubt it.

Although the rate of new technology development may slow in the next 5 years, the introduction of innovative applications of technology will continue to explode. According to Harry Dent, technology waves always occur in pairs.[3] The first phase is wild exuberance, in which new technology is invented, its capabilities flushed out, and its characteristics understood. That first phase always results in overbuilding. But it sets the stage for the second phase, in which surviving companies and entrepreneurs purchase the overbuilt infrastructure for pennies on the dollar and use it for new business purposes.

The automotive industry, for example, proceeded in two stages. The irrational exuberance phase culminated in a technology crash; General Motors' stock fell 75 percent from 1919 to 1921. However, that exuberance led to the development of the highway system, the development of the petroleum industry, and a complete change in the conduct of commerce in the United States. Every one of those consequences created opportunities for businesspeople alert to the changing business environment.

I believe we are seeing today a similar second stage in the adoption of information technology. Businesses are innovating to take advantage of the new opportunities. Many businesses have already developed innovations for Web 2.0, social networking, and UGC, and more are being developed even as you read this Guide.

Fiber-optic cable will come to my home (and yours) when telecom companies buy today's dark fiber for pennies on the dollar and light it up. With fiber-optic cable to my house, goodbye video store! Hello DK Enterprises—Internet broadcaster of my music library and sailing photos. Or, maybe it won't be fiber; it might be very high-speed wireless that comes to our homes. Either way, the opportunity for innovation will be great.

So as you finish your business degree, stay alert for new technology-based opportunities. Watch for the second wave and catch it. If you found this course interesting, take more IS classes. Enroll in a database class or a systems development class, even if you don't want to be an IS major. If you're

[3]Harry Dent, *The Next Great Bubble Boom* (New York: The Free Press, 2004).

technically oriented, take a data communications class or a security class. If you enjoy this material, become an IS major. If you want to program a computer, great, but if you do not, then don't. There are tremendous opportunities for nonprogrammers in the IS industry. Look for novel applications of IS technology to the emerging business environment. Hundreds of them abound! Find them and have fun!

Discussion Question

How will you further your career with what you've learned in this class? Give that question serious thought, and write a memo to yourself to read from time to time as your career progresses.

they get there. Without adequate preparation, there is substantial risk that the actions of well-meaning people will make the problem worse. Also, the rumor mill will be alive with all sorts of nutty ideas about what to do. A cadre of well-informed, trained personnel will serve to dampen such rumors.

Finally, organizations should periodically practice incident response. Without such practice, personnel will be poorly informed on the response plan, and the plan itself may have flaws that only become apparent during a drill.

How does the knowledge in this chapter help MRV and you?

MRV desperately needs the knowledge in this chapter. Sue and Eddie can use it to understand the threats to which MRV is exposed and to learn about security safeguards it can be using. MRV needs to query its hosting vendor(s) about their safeguards, and it needs to go through the safeguards described in this chapter to determine which are appropriate, given the company's exposure. Certainly, given the recent theft of data, MRV needs to review the safeguards on all of the customer data. In particular, the company needs to ensure that employees are given access only to data they need, and it should develop procedures for dealing with terminated or recently resigned employees.

I'm sorry. One of our employees stole your e-mail address.

You can use this knowledge in your own career. You know what threats you and your company are exposed to, and you understand the need for security safeguards. If you manage your own department, you can use the guidelines in Figure 12-7 to establish and maintain appropriate human safeguards in your department. Security issues are important. To you, as a future manager, Figure 12-7 is one of the most important figures in this textbook.

Active Review

Use this Active Review to verify that you understand the material in the chapter. You can read the entire chapter and then perform the tasks in this review, or you can read the material for just one question and perform the tasks in this review for that question before moving on to the next one.

Q1 **What are the sources and types of security threats?** Explain the difference among security threats, threat sources, and threat types. Give one example of a security threat for each cell in the grid in Figure 12-1. Describe a phishing attack. Explain the threat of phishing to individuals. Explain the threat of phishing to company and product brands.

Q2 **What are the elements of a security program?** Define *technical, data,* and *human safeguards.* Show how these safeguards relate to the five components of an information system.

Q3 **How can technical safeguards protect against security threats?** List five technical safeguards. Define *identification* and *authentication.* Describe three types of authentication. Define *malware,* and name five types of malware. Describe six ways to protect against malware. Summarize why malware is a serious problem.

Q4 **How can data safeguards protect against security threats?** Define *data administration* and *database administration,* and explain their difference. List data safeguards.

Q5 **How can human safeguards protect against security threats?** Summarize human safeguards for each activity in Figure 12.7. Summarize safeguards that pertain to nonemployee personnel. Describe three dimensions of safeguards for account administration. Explain how system procedures can serve as human safeguards. Describe security monitoring techniques.

Q6 What is necessary for disaster preparedness? Define *disaster.* List major considerations for disaster preparedness. Explain the difference between a hot site and a cold site.

Q7 How should organizations respond to security incidents? Summarize the actions that an organization should take when dealing with a security incident.

How does **the knowledge** in this chapter **help MRV** and **you?**

Describe the ways MRV can use the knowledge from this chapter. Explain how you can use the knowledge of this chapter to become a better business professional.

Key Terms and Concepts

Adware 294
Authentication 292
Biometric authentication 293
Cold site 305
Data administration 296
Database administration 296
Data safeguards 296
Denial of service (DOS) 289
Drive-by sniffer 288
Email spoofing 288
Hacking 289

Hardening 299
Hot site 305
Human safeguards 297
Identification 292
IP spoofing 288
Key escrow 296
Malware 294
Malware definitions 294
Personal identification number (PIN) 293

Phishing 288
Pretexting 288
Security threat 287
Smart cards 293
Sniffing 288
Spoofing 288
Spyware 294
Technical safeguards 292
Unauthorized data disclosure 288
Usurpation 289

Using Your Knowledge

1. Credit reporting agencies are required to provide you with a free credit report each year. Most such reports do not include your credit score, but they do provide the details on which your credit score is based. Use one of the following companies to obtain your free report. *www.equifax.com, www.experion. com,* and *www.transunion.com.*
   a. You should review your credit report for obvious errors. However, other checks are appropriate. Search the Web for guidance on how best to review your credit records. Summarize what you learn.
   b. What actions can you take if you find errors in your credit report?
   c. Define *identity theft.* Search the Web and determine the best course of action if someone thinks he has been the victim of identity theft.

2. Suppose you lose your company laptop at an airport. What should you do? Does it matter what data is stored on your disk drive? If the computer contained sensitive or proprietary data, are you necessarily in trouble? Under what circumstances should you now focus on updating your resume?

3. Suppose you alert your boss to the security threats in Figure 12-1 and to the safeguards in Figure 12-2. Suppose he says, "Very interesting. Tell me more." In preparing for the meeting, you decide to create a list of talking points.
   a. Write a brief explanation of each threat in Figure 12-1.
   b. Explain how the five components relate to safeguards.
   c. Describe two to three technical, two to three data, and two to three human safeguards.
   d. Write a brief description on the safeguards in Figure 12-7.
   e. List security procedures that pertain to you, a temporary employee.
   f. List procedures that your department should have with regard to disaster planning.

4. Dee's consultant was given permission to install software on a server inside Emerson's network. Suppose he had been a computer criminal.
   a. Using Figure 12-1 as a guide, what might he have done?
   b. Suppose he maliciously deleted critical CRM data. What could Emerson do?
   c. Explain how Figure 12-11 pertains to this situation.

d. In this circumstance, what is likely to happen to Dee? To the manager of the IT department? To the employee who authorized access to the consultant?

5. Suppose you need to terminate an employee who works in your department. Summarize security protections you must take. How would you behave differently if this termination were a friendly one?

Collaboration Exercise 12 ◎

Before you start this exercise, read Chapter Extensions 1 and 2, which describe collaboration techniques as well as tools for managing collaboration tasks. In particular, consider using Google Docs & Spreadsheets, Google Groups, Microsoft Groove, Microsoft SharePoint, or some other collaboration tool.

Read about phishing in *MIS in Use 12* page 290, if you have not done so already.

1. Visit *www.fraudwatchinternational.com/phishing*. Select five of what you consider to be the most outrageous phishing examples. In each case, identify the following:
   a. The data the attack was designed to obtain
   b. How the target person could have detected the attack
   c. The damage that occurred to the company that was spoofed

2. Suppose that you work for Barclays, PayPal, Visa, or any other major organization that is vulnerable to phishing. (It will be easier to answer this question if you choose an organization for which you are a customer.)
   a. Using the information in this chapter, write a single-page memo that describes the phishing threat to your company and explains why the threat is difficult for the company to address.

   b. List possible actions, if any, that your company can take to eliminate the phishing threat.
   c. List possible actions that your company can take to lessen the consequences of the phishing threat.
   d. Write a specific policy that you think your organization should take concerning phishing.
   e. Suppose you manage your company's customer help desk. Describe a procedure for the help-desk employees to take when a customer reports a phishing attack.
   f. Describe the elements of a phishing incident-reporting system for your company.

3. Phishing is an industry-wide problem. Organizations may better be able to solve phishing problems or mitigate their consequences by working together.
   a. Name and describe three specific industry initiatives that could be created to address phishing problems.
   b. Search the Internet for evidence that any of the initiatives you described in part a already exists. If you find such evidence, explain how your initiative has been implemented. If you do not find such evidence, describe why you think your idea may not have been implemented.

4. Summarize the damage that a phishing attack causes an organization's brand. What can organizations do to minimize this damage?

Case Study 12

The ChoicePoint Attack

ChoicePoint, a Georgia-based corporation, provides risk-management and fraud-prevention data. Traditionally, ChoicePoint provided motor vehicle reports, claims histories, and similar data to the automobile insurance industry; in recent years, it broadened its customer base to include general business and government agencies. Today, it also offers data for volunteer and job-applicant screening and data to assist in the location of missing

children. ChoicePoint has over 4,000 employees, and its 2007 revenue was $982 million.

In the fall of 2004, ChoicePoint was the victim of a fraudulent spoofing attack in which unauthorized individuals posed as legitimate customers and obtained personal data on more than 145,000 individuals. According to the company's Web site:

These criminals were able to pass our customer authentication due-diligence processes by using stolen identities to create and produce the documents needed to appear legitimate. As small business customers of ChoicePoint, these fraudsters accessed products that contained basic telephone directory-type data (name and address information) as well as a combination of Social Security numbers and/or driver's license numbers and, at times, abbreviated credit reports. They were also able to obtain other public record information including, but not limited to bankruptcies, liens, and judgments; professional licenses; and real property data.

ChoicePoint became aware of the problem in November 2004, when it noticed unusual processing activity on some accounts in Los Angeles. Accordingly, the company contacted the Los Angeles Police Department, which requested that ChoicePoint not reveal the activity until the department could conduct an investigation. In January, the LAPD notified ChoicePoint that it could contact the customers whose data had been compromised.

This crime is an example of a failure of authentication, not a network break-in. ChoicePoint's firewalls and other safeguards were not overcome. Instead, the criminals spoofed legitimate businesses. The infiltrators obtained valid California business licenses, and until their unusual processing activity was detected they appeared to be legitimate users.

In response to this problem, ChoicePoint established a hotline for customers whose data had been compromised. It also purchased a credit report for each victim and paid for a credit-report-monitoring service for one year. In February 2005, attorneys initiated a class-action lawsuit for all 145,000 customers, with an initial loss claim of $75,000 each. At the same time, the U.S. Senate announced that it would conduct an investigation.

Ironically, ChoicePoint exposed itself to a public relations nightmare, considerable expense, a class-action lawsuit, a Senate investigation, and a 20-percent drop in its share price because it contacted the police and cooperated in the attempt to apprehend the criminals. When ChoicePoint noticed the unusual account activity, had it simply shut down data access for the illegitimate businesses, no one would have known. Of course, the 145,000 customers whose identities had been compromised would have unknowingly been subject to identity theft, but it is unlikely that such thefts could have been tracked back to ChoicePoint.

As a data utility, ChoicePoint maintains relationships with many different entities. It obtains its data from both public and private sources. It then sells access to this data to its customers. Much of the data, by the way, can be obtained directly from the data vendor. ChoicePoint adds value by providing a centralized access point for many data needs. In addition to data sources and customers, ChoicePoint maintains relationships with partners such as the vital records departments in major cities. Finally, ChoicePoint also has relationships with the people and organizations on which it maintains data.

Questions

1. ChoicePoint exposed itself to considerable expense, many problems, and a possible loss of brand confidence because it notified the Los Angeles Police Department, cooperated in the investigation, and notified the individuals whose records had been compromised. It could have buried the theft and possibly avoided any responsibility. Comment on the ethical issues and ChoicePoint's response. Did ChoicePoint choose wisely? Consider that question from the viewpoint of customers, law enforcement personnel, investors, and management.

2. Given ChoicePoint's experience, what is the likely action of similar companies whose records are compromised in this way? Given your answer, do you think federal regulation and additional laws are required? What other steps could be taken to ensure that data vendors notify people harmed by data theft?

3. Visit *www.choicepoint.com*. Summarize the products that ChoicePoint provides. What seems to be the central theme of this business?

4. Suppose that ChoicePoint decides to establish a formal security policy on the issue of inappropriate release of personal data. Summarize the issues that ChoicePoint should address in this policy.

THE International Dimension

International IT Development and Management

Study Questions

- **Q1** What characteristics make international IT management challenging?
- **Q2** Why is international information systems development difficult?
- **Q3** What are the challenges of international project management?
- **Q4** What are the challenges of international IT management?
- **Q5** How does the international dimension affect computer security risk management?

The International Dimension

Q1 What Characteristics Make International IT Management Challenging?

Size and complexity make international IT management challenging. International information systems are larger and more complex. Projects to develop them are larger and more complicated to manage. International IT departments are bigger and composed of people from many cultures with many different native languages. International organizations have more IS and IT assets, and those assets are exposed to more risk and greater uncertainty. Security incidents are more complicated to investigate.

We will consider each of these impacts in more detail in the following questions. The bottom line, however, is size and complication.

Q2 Why Is International Information Systems Development Difficult?

Before considering this question, realize that the factors that affect international information systems development are more challenging than those that affect international software development. If the *system* is truly international, if many people from many different countries will be using the system, then the development project is exceedingly complicated. For example, consider the effort required for a multinational company like 3M to create an integrated, worldwide CRM. Such a project is massive!

In contrast, creating localized software (one or more programs available in different human-language versions) is challenging, but not nearly as daunting. As stated in the International Dimension for Part 2, localizing a program is a matter of designing it to accept program menus, messages, and help text from external files and of translating those files. Of course, different character sets, different sorting orders, different currency symbols, and other complications must be accounted for, but these challenges are surmountable with good software design and development.

Think about the five components of an information system. Running hardware in different countries is not a problem, and localizing software is manageable. Databases pose some problems, namely determining the language, currency, and units of measure used to record data, but these problems are surmountable. A substantial problem arises, however, when we consider procedures.

An international system is used by people who live and work in cultures that are vastly different from one

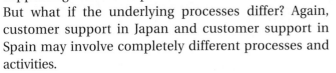

another. The way that customers are treated in Japan differs substantially from the way that customers are treated in Spain, which differs substantially from the way that customers are treated in the United States. The procedures for using a CRM will be correspondingly different.

Consider the phases of the SDLC. During systems definition, we are supposed to determine the purpose and scope of the system. As you know by now, information systems should facilitate the organization's competitive strategy by supporting business processes. But what if the underlying processes differ? Again, customer support in Japan and customer support in Spain may involve completely different processes and activities.

Even if the purpose and scope can be defined in some unified way, how are requirements to be determined? Again, if the underlying business processes differ, then the specific requirements for the information system will differ. Managing requirements for a system in one culture is difficult, but managing requirements for international systems can be many times more difficult.

There are two responses to such challenges: (1) either define a set of standard business processes or (2) develop alternative versions of the system that support different processes in different countries. Both responses are problematic. The first response requires conversion of the organization to different work processes, and, as you learned in Chapter 7, such conversion can be exceedingly difficult. People resist change, and they will do so with vehemence if the change violates cultural norms.

The second response is easier to implement, but it creates system design challenges. It also means that, in truth, there is not one system, but many.

In spite of the problems, both responses are used. For example, SAP, Oracle, and other ERP vendors define standard business processes via the inherent procedures in their software products. Many organizations attempt to enforce those standard procedures. When it becomes organizationally infeasible to do so, organizations develop exceptions to those inherent procedures and develop programs to handle the exceptions. This choice means high maintenance expense.

Q3 What Are the Challenges of International Project Management?

Managing a global information systems development project is difficult because of project size and complexity. Requirements are complex, many resources are required, and numerous people are involved. Team members speak different languages, live in different cultures, work in different time zones, and seldom meet face-to-face.

One way to understand how these factors impact global project management is to consider each of the project management knowledge areas as set out by the international Project Management Institute's document, the *PMBOK®* Guide (*www.pmi.org/Marketplace/Pages/ProductDetail.aspx?GMProduct=00100035801*). Figure 1 summarizes challenges for each knowledge area. Project integration is more difficult because international development projects require the complex integration of results from distributed work groups. Also, task dependencies can span teams working in different countries, increasing the difficulty of task management.

The scope and requirements definition for international IS is more difficult for the reasons discussed in Q2. Time management is more difficult because teams in different cultures and countries work at different rates. Some cultures have a 35-hour workweek, and some have a 60-hour workweek. Some cultures expect 6-week vacations, and some expect 2 weeks. Some cultures thrive on efficiency of labor, and others thrive on considerate working relationships. There is no standard rate of development for an international project.

FIGURE 1
Challenges for International IS
Project Management

Knowledge Areas	Challenge
Project integration	Complex integration of results from distributed work groups. Management of dependencies of tasks from physically and culturally different work groups.
Scope (requirements)	Need to support multiple versions of underlying business processes. Possibly substantial differences in requirements and procedures.
Time	Development rates vary among cultures and countries.
Cost	Cost of development varies widely among countries. Two members performing the same work in different countries may be paid substantially different rates. Moving work among teams may dramatically change costs.
Quality	Quality standards vary among cultures. Different expectations of quality may result in an inconsistent system.
Human resources	Worker expectations differ. Compensation, rewards, work conditions vary widely.
Communications	Geographic, language, and cultural distance among team members impedes effective communication.
Risk	Development risk is higher. Easy to lose control.
Procurement	Complications of international trade.

In terms of cost, different countries and cultures pay vastly different labor rates. Using critical path analysis, managers may choose to move a task from one team to another. Doing so, however, may substantially increase costs. Thus, management may choose to accept a delay rather than move work to an available (but more expensive) team. The complex trade-offs that exist between time and cost become even more complex for international projects.

Quality and human resources are also more complicated for international projects. Quality standards vary among countries. The IT industry in some nations, like India, has invested heavily in development techniques that increase program quality. Other countries, like the United States, have been less willing to invest in quality. In any case, the integration of programs of varying quality results in an inconsistent system.

Worker expectations vary among cultures and nations. Compensation, rewards, and worker conditions vary, and these differences can lead to misunderstandings, poor morale, and project delays.

Because of these factors, effective team communication is exceedingly important for international projects, but because of language and culture differences and geographic separation, such communication is difficult. Effective communication is also more expensive. Consider, for example, just the additional expense of maintaining a team portal in three or four languages.

If you consider all of the factors in Figure 1, it is easy to understand why project risk is high for international IS development projects. So many things can go wrong. Project integration is complex; requirements are difficult to determine; cost, time, and quality are difficult to manage; worker conditions vary widely; and communication is difficult. Finally, project procurement is complicated by the normal challenges of international commerce.

Q4 What Are the Challenges of International IT Management?

Chapter 11 defined the four primary responsibilities of the IT department: plan, operate, develop, and protect information systems and IT infrastructure. Each of these responsibilities becomes more challenging for international IT organizations.

Regarding planning, the principal task is to align IT and IS resources with the organization's competitive strategy. The task does not change character for international companies; it just becomes more complex and difficult. Multinational organizations and operations are complicated, and the business processes that support their competitive strategies tend also to be complicated. Further, changes in global economic factors can mean dramatic changes in processes and necessitate changes in IS and IT support. Technology adoption can also cause remarkable change. The increasing use of cell phones in developing countries, for example, changes the requirements for local information systems. The rising price of oil will also change international business processes. So planning tasks for international IT are larger and more complex.

Three factors create challenges for international IT operations. First, conducting operations in different countries, cultures, and languages adds complexity. Go to the Web site of any multinational corporation, say *www.mmm.com* or *www.dell.com*, and you'll be asked to click on the country in which you reside. When you click, you are likely to be directed to a Web server running in some other country. Those Web servers need to be managed consistently, even though they are operated by people living in different cultures and speaking different languages.

The second operational challenge of international IS is the integration of similar, but different, systems. Consider inventory. A multinational corporation might have dozens of different inventory systems in use throughout the world. To enable the movement of goods, many of these systems need to be coordinated and integrated.

Or consider customer support that operates from three different support centers in three different countries. Each support center may have its own information system, but the data among those systems will need to be exported or otherwise shared. If not, then a customer who contacts one center will be unknown to the others.

The third complication for operations is outsourcing. Many organizations have chosen to outsource customer support, training, logistics, and other backroom activities. International outsourcing is particularly advantageous for customer support and other functions that must be operational 24/7. Amazon.com, for example, operates customer service centers in the United States, India, and Ireland. Many companies outsource logistics to United Parcel Service (UPS), because doing so offers comprehensive, worldwide shipping and logistical support. The organization's information systems usually need to be integrated with outsource vendors' information systems, and this may need to be done for different systems, all over the world. The challenges for the development of international information systems were addressed in questions Q1 and Q2.

International IS/IT outsourcing is not without controversy, however. It is one thing to shift a job making tennis shoes to Singapore, or even to hire customer support representatives in India. But there was consternation and wringing of hands when IBM announced that it was shifting nearly 5,000 computer-programming jobs to India. Some perceive the moving of such high-tech, high-skill jobs overseas as a threat to U.S. technology leadership. Others say it is just economic factors guiding jobs to places where they are most efficiently performed.

The fourth IT department responsibility is protecting IS and IT infrastructure. We consider that function in the next question.

Q5 How Does the International Dimension Affect Computer Security Risk Management?

Computer security risk management is more difficult and complicated for international information systems. First, IT assets are subject to more threats. Infrastructure

will be located in sites all over the world, and those sites differ in the threats to which they are exposed. Some will be subject to political threats, others to the threat of civil unrest, others to terrorists, and still others will be subject to threats of natural disasters of every conceivable type. Place your data center in Kansas, and it's subject to tornados. Place your data center internationally, and it's potentially subject to typhoons/hurricanes, earthquakes, floods, volcanic eruption, or mudslides. And don't forget epidemics that will affect the data center employees.

Second, the likelihood of a threat is more difficult to estimate for international systems. What is the likelihood that the death of Fidel Castro will cause civil unrest and threaten your data center in Havana? How does an organization assess that risk? What is the likelihood that a computer programmer in India will insert a Trojan horse into code that she writes on an outsourcing contract?

In addition to risk, international information systems are subject to far greater uncertainty. Uncertainty reflects the likelihood that something that "we don't know we don't know" will cause an adverse outcome. Because of the multitudinous cultures, religions, nations, beliefs, political views, and crazy people in the world, uncertainty

about risks to IS and IT infrastructure is high. Again, if you place your data center in Kansas, you have some idea of the magnitude of the uncertainty to which you are exposed, even if you don't know exactly what it is. Place a server in a country on every continent of the world, and you have no idea of the potential risks to which they are exposed.

Regarding safeguards, technical and data safeguards do not change for international information systems. Because of greater complexity there may be a need for more safeguards or for more complex ones, but the technical and data safeguards described in Chapter 12 all work for international systems. Human safeguards are another matter. For example, can an organization depend on the control of separation of duties and authorities in a culture for which graft is an accepted norm? Or, what is the utility of a personal reference in a culture in which it is considered exceedingly rude to talk about someone when they are not present? Because of these differences, human safeguards need to be chosen and evaluated on a culture-by-culture basis.

In short, risk management for both international information systems and IT infrastructure is more complicated, more difficult, and subject to greater uncertainty.

Active Review

Use this Active Review to verify that you understand the material in the International Dimension. You can read the entire mini chapter and then perform the tasks in this review, or you can read the material for just one question and perform the tasks in this review for that question before moving on to the next one.

Q1 **What characteristics make international IT management challenging?** State the two characteristics that make international IT management challenging. Explain how those factors pertain to IS development, IT management, and risk management.

Q2 **Why is international information systems development difficult?** Explain the difference between international systems development and international software development. Using the five-component framework, explain why

international systems development is more difficult. Describe difficulties that arise during the systems definition and requirements phases during the development of an international IS. Describe two responses to these difficulties, and explain why both are problematic. Give an example of how each is used.

Q3 **What are the challenges of international project management?** Provide two words that characterize the difficulty of international project management. Explain how each of the knowledge areas in Figure 1 are more complicated for international projects. Give an example of one complication for each knowledge area.

Q4 **What are the challenges of international IT management?** State the four responsibilities for IT departments. Explain how each of these responsibilities is more challenging for international IT organizations. Describe three factors that create challenges for international IT operations.

Q5 How does the international dimension affect computer security risk management? Explain why international IT assets are subject to more threats. Give three examples. Explain why the likelihood of international threats is more difficult to determine. Describe uncertainty, and explain why it is higher for international IT organizations. Explain how technical, data, and human safeguards differ for international IT organizations. Give two examples of problematic international human safeguards.

PART 4

review

Consider Your Net Worth

1. Assume you have graduated and are working in your chosen field of study: sales, marketing, finance, general management, or IT. Suppose that you learn there is a systems development project underway, and suppose you decide to volunteer for the project. You do so because you know that it will give you a chance to relate to your boss in a new way and because you will be able to network with others in your organization. (If you are majoring in IT, answer the questions below assuming you are a junior member of the team.)

   a. If the project is being developed using the SDLC, summarize your possible role(s). What tasks might you be asked to perform? How will your knowledge of the SDLC help you? How can your knowledge of the SDLC give you a competitive advantage?

   b. Suppose that you learn that a new information systems project is being proposed, and suppose you do *not* volunteer to be a user representative to the team. What is the opportunity cost of your decision?

2. Suppose you have just taken over the management of a department that has just begun to use a new information system. Assume that the information system has not been reliable and is difficult to use. It is so difficult, in fact, that the employees in your new department ridicule the new system.

   a. Summarize your management problem.

   b. Suppose you decide to investigate the origin of the problems before you do anything. Describe what you might want to learn.

   c. Suppose you learn that many of the problems your department is experiencing are due to the fact that your predecessor did not take the task of specifying requirements seriously. What do you do with that knowledge?

   d. Describe three alternatives for approaching the IT department with these complaints. Which of these three is the most professional? Which of these three is most likely to improve the situation?

   e. Describe three alternatives for handling the situation with your department. Which do you think is most likely to generate confidence in you among your team? Which is most likely to improve the situation?

3. Assume that you have just taken over the management of a department that depends on a particular information system to do its work. You ask your employees to show you the procedures for departmental operations in case of system failure, and you learn there are none.

a. What do you suppose will happen if the system fails?

b. Suppose you conduct an informal risk management of the situation and conclude no such procedures are necessary. Speculate on the characteristics of the situation that would cause you to form this conclusion.

c. If, on the basis of your informal risk management assessment, you conclude that such procedures are necessary, how would you proceed? Would you involve the IT department? Why or why not?

d. Assume you decide to involve the IT department. Describe whom you would want to meet and what you would communicate when you did meet him or her.

4. Turn to the Contents Overview on pages x–xi, and reflect on what you've learned from this textbook.

a. Which chapter or chapter extension was the most interesting to you?

b. How can you use your answer to part a to guide your career choice or what you do within the career you've already chosen?

c. Which chapter or chapter extension do you believe will be the most helpful to you in your career? Explain.

d. Which chapter or chapter extension do you believe will be the least helpful to you in your career? Explain.

5. Summarize the ways that you believe the knowledge you have gained about MIS will be helpful to you in your career. Give specific examples using at least five chapters or chapter extensions.

6. Suppose that you work for a company in an internship in your chosen field of study. Write a memo to your boss requesting that your employer pay the tuition for this class. In your memo, explain how the knowledge you have learned in this class pertains to your work.

Application Exercises

1. Suppose you are given the task of keeping track of the number of labor hours invested in meetings for systems development projects. Assume your company uses the traditional SDLC and that each phase requires two types of meetings: *Working meetings* involve users, systems analysts, programmers, and PQA test engineers. *Review meetings* involve all of those people, plus level-1 and level-2 managers of both user departments and the IT department.

a. Construct a spreadsheet that computes the total labor hours invested in each phase of a project. When a meeting occurs, assume you enter the project phase, the meeting type, the start time, the end time, and the number of each type of personnel attending. Your spreadsheet should calculate the number of labor hours and should add the meeting's hours to the totals for that phase and for the project overall.

b. Change your spreadsheet to include a budget of the number of labor hours for each type of employee for each phase. In your spreadsheet, show the difference between the number of hours budgeted and the number actually consumed.

c. Change your spreadsheet to include the budgeted cost and actual cost of labor. Assume that you enter, once, the average labor cost for each type of employee.

2. Use Access to develop a failure-tracking database application. For each failure, your application should record the following:

FailureNumber (Use an Access autonumber data type.)

DateReported

FailureDescription

ReportedBy (the name of the PQA engineer reporting the failure)

FixedBy (the name of the programmer who is assigned to fix the failure)

DateFailureFixed

FixDescription

DateFixVerified

VerifiedBy (the name of the PQA engineer verifying the fix)

a. Create a FAILURE table, a PQA ENGINEER table, and a PROGRAMMER table. The last two tables should have *Name* (assume names are unique in each table) and *Email* columns. Add other appropriate columns to each table.

b. Create one or more forms that can be used to report a failure, to report a failure fix, and to report a failure verification. Create the form(s) so that the user can just pull down the name of a PQA engineer or programmer from the appropriate table to fill in the *ReportedBy, FixedBy,* and *VerifiedBy* fields.

c. Construct a report that shows all failures sorted by reporting PQA engineer and then by *DateReported.*

d. Construct a report that shows only fixed and verified failures

e. Construct a report that shows only fixed but unverified failures.

3. Suppose you work for a small manufacturer of industrial-handling equipment, such as conveyor belts, wheeled carts, dollies, and so on. Assume your company employs 80 people in standard functions, such as product design, manufacturing, sales, and marketing. You work in accounting and have been asked to recommend three outsource vendors to manage the employees' 401(k) retirement plans. Use the Web to answer the following questions.

a. Explain what a 401(k) retirement plan is.

b. List three vendors that outsource such plans.

c. Summarize the product offerings from each of the vendors in your answer to part b.

d. Compare the costs of each of the products in your answer to part c.

e. Based on the data you have, summarize the advantages and disadvantages of each of the alternatives in your answer to part d. Make and state assumptions, if necessary.

4. Suppose you manage a department of 20 employees and you wish to build an information system to track their computers, the software that resides on those computers, and the licenses for each software product. Assume that employees can have more than one computer and that each computer has multiple software products. Each product has a single license. The license can be either a *site license* (meaning your organization paid for everyone in the company to be able to use that program) or the license is a purchase order number and date for the order that paid for the license.

a. Design a spreadsheet for keeping track of the employees, computers, and licenses. Insert sample data for three employees and at least five computers with typical software.

b. Design a database for keeping track of the employees, computers, and licenses. Assume your database has an EMPLOYEE table, a COMPUTER table, and a SOFTWARE_LICENSE table. Place appropriate columns in these tables and construct the relationship. Insert sample data for three employees, five computers, and multiple software licenses per computer.

c. Compare the spreadsheet and database solutions to this problem. Which is easier to set up? Which is easier to maintain?

d. Use whichever of your solutions you prefer for producing the following two reports:

- *A list of employees and their computers, sorted by employee*
- A list of software products, the computers on which they reside, and the employees assigned those computers, sorted by software product name

5. Assume you have been given the task of compiling evaluations that your company's purchasing agents make of their vendors. Each month, every purchasing agent evaluates all of the vendors that he or she has worked with in the past month on three factors: price, quality, and responsiveness. Assume the ratings are from 1 to 5, with 5 being the best. Because your company has hundreds of vendors and dozens of purchasing agents, you decide to use Access to compile the results.

a. Create a database with three tables: VENDOR (*VendorNumber, Name, Contact*), PURCHASER (*EmpNumber, Name, Email*), and RATING (*EmpNumber, VendorNumber, Month, Year, PriceRating, QualityRating, ResponsivenessRating*). Assume *VendorNumber* and *EmpNumber* are the keys of VENDOR and PURCHASER, respectively. Decide what you think is the appropriate key for RATING.

b. Create appropriate relationships using Tools/Relationships.

c. Using the table view of each table, enter sample data for vendors, employees, and ratings.

d. Create a query that shows the names of all vendors and their average scores.

e. Create a query that shows the names of all employees and their average scores. (*Hint:* In this and in question f, you will need to use the Group By function in your query.)

f. Create a parameterized query that you can use to obtain the minimum, maximum, and average ratings on each criterion for a particular vendor. Assume you will enter *VendorName* as the parameter.

6. Develop a spreadsheet model of the cost of a virus attack in an organization that has three types of computers: employee workstations, data servers, and Web servers. Assume the number of computers affected by the virus depends on the severity of the virus. For the purposes of your model, assume that there are three levels of virus severity: *Low-severity* incidents affect fewer than 30 percent of the user workstations and none of the data or Web servers. *Medium-severity* incidents affect up to 70 percent of the user workstations, up to half of the Web servers, and none of the data servers. *High-severity* incidents can affect all organizational computers.

Assume 50 percent of the incidents are low severity, 30 percent are medium severity, and 20 percent are high severity.

Assume employees can remove viruses from workstations themselves, but that specially trained technicians are required to repair the servers. The time to eliminate a virus from an infected computer depends on the computer type. Let the time to remove the virus from each type be inputs to your model. Assume that when users eliminate the virus themselves they are unproductive for twice the time required for the removal. Let the average employee hourly labor cost be an input to your model. Let the average cost of a technician also be an input to your model. Finally, let the total number of user computers, data servers, and Web servers be inputs to your model.

Run your simulation 10 times. Use the same inputs for each run, but draw a random number (assume a uniform distribution for all random numbers) to determine the severity type. Then, draw random numbers to determine the percentage of computers of each type affected, using the constraints stated previously. For example, if the attack is of medium severity, draw a random number between 0 and 70 to indicate the percentage of infected user workstations, and a random number between 0 and 50 to indicate the percentage of infected Web servers.

For each run, calculate the total of lost employee hours, the total dollar cost of lost employee labor hours, the total hours of technicians to fix the servers, and the total cost of technician labor. Finally, compute the total overall cost. Show the results of each run. Show the average costs and hours for the 10 runs.

The Need for Technical Feasibility

The U.S. Internal Revenue Service (IRS) Business Systems Modernization (BSM) project has been a multiyear attempt to replace the existing tax-processing information systems with systems based on modern technology. Review page 20 for a discussion of the underlying need, problems, and suggested problem solutions.

The subsystem that has generated the most controversy and been the cause of the most serious delays is the Customer Account Data Engine (CADE). CADE is an expert system that uses a database of business rules. Unlike most databases that contain facts and figures like CustomerName, Email, Balance, and so forth, the CADE database contains expert-system business rules, which are statements about how an organization conducts its business. In the context of the IRS, this database contains rules about tax laws and the processing of tax forms. An example of such a rule is:

```
Rule 10:
IF the amount on line 7 of Form 1040EZ is greater
  than zero,
THEN invoke Rule 15.
```

With a rule-based approach, the IRS need only develop programs that access the database and follow the rules. No other programs need to be developed.

Rule-based systems differ substantially from traditional application programs. Using traditional technology, the developers interview the users, determine what the business rules are, and then write computer code that operates in accordance with the rules. The disadvantage of such traditional programming is that only technically trained programmers can decipher the rules in the program code. Also, only trained programmers can add, change, or delete rules.

The advantage of rule-based systems like CADE is that the business rules are stored in the database and can be read, added, changed, or deleted by personnel with business knowledge but little computer training. Hence, in theory, CADE is more adaptable to changing requirements than a system written with traditional programming languages.

Unfortunately, the technical feasibility of using a rule-based system for a problem as large and complex as IRS tax processing is unknown. It appears that, at least from public records, no one ever tried to estimate that feasibility. The result has been a string of schedule delays and cost overruns. The first CADE release, which processes only the simplest individual tax returns (those using IRS Form 1040EZ), was to be completed by January 2002. It was delayed once until August 2003, and then delayed again to September 2004. At that point, a limited version of this first release was demonstrated.

The database for these simple returns has some 1,200 business rules, but no reliable estimate has yet been developed for the number of rules required for the full system. The lack of an estimate is particularly serious because some experts believe the difficulty and complexity of creating rules increases geometrically with the number of rules. Meanwhile, $33 million was invested in 2003, and another $84 million was spent in 2004.

Given the history of problems, the IRS hired the Software Engineering Institute (SEI) of Carnegie Mellon University to conduct an independent audit of the project. SEI

Chapter Extension 1

Chapter 1 provides the background for this Extension.

Improving Your Collaboration Skills

Q1 Why Learn Collaboration Skills?

You don't need to be told that collaboration is important. You probably have a team project in every one of your business school classes. You may have heard experts like Robert Reich, the former U.S. Secretary of Labor, say that collaboration is a key business skill for workers in the twenty-first century.[1] Or, you might know professionals like Lily Shen, an information systems project manager at Hitachi Systems. Lily works in Houston, Texas; her major client is located in China; and her team is scattered all over the world. She manages a distributed collaborative team. According to the RAND Corporation,[2] jobs like Lily's will become increasingly common, important, and remunerative for workers in the Information Age.

But have you thought, seriously, that collaboration requires skill? Do you realize that collaboration is like tennis or golf—you start with a certain native ability but you can improve that ability with coaching and practice? It is likely that you've been going to team meetings since grade school. Do you just show up, offer your thoughts, do something toward a common goal, and just turn it in? Ever wonder how you could collaborate better? How your team could work better together? Whether you might have created a better product with less work? Have you asked yourself if it is possible to create a team that has conflict yet is still a productive group? One that you looked forward to meeting with? Or, one that produced a product that was better than anything any one of you could have done individually?

Learning effective collaboration skills is a lifelong project. Start now. Think about the ways that you interact with your teammates; think about the structure of your team; think about how you handle conflict. When you become a skilled collaborator, you can help your team to do better work, faster.

This textbook can help you improve your collaboration skills in two ways. In this chapter extension, we consider collaboration *behaviors*; in Chapter Extension 2 we consider information systems *tools* that your team can use to collaborate more efficiently, and maybe even more effectively.

Q2 What Is Collaboration?

Collaboration occurs when two or more people work together to achieve a common goal, result, or work product. When collaboration is effective, the results of the group are greater than could be produced by any of the individuals working alone. Collaboration involves coordination and communication, but it is greater than either of those.

---

[1]Robert B. Reich, *The Work of Nations* (New York: Alfred A. Knopf, 1991), p. 174.
[2]Lynn A. Karoly and Constantijn A. Panis, *The 21st Century at Work* (Santa Monica, CA: RAND Corporation, 2004), p. xiv.

Consider an example of a student team that is assigned a term project. Suppose the team meets and divides the work into sections, and then team members work independently on their individual pieces. An hour before the project is due the team members meet again to assemble their independent pieces into a whole. Such a process is *not* collaboration. Although the members of such a team are *cooperating*, they are not *collaborating*.

The Importance of Feedback and Iteration

Collaboration involves *feedback* and *iteration*. In a collaborative team, group members review each others' work product and revise that product as a result. The effort proceeds in a series of steps, or iterations, in which one person produces something, others comment on what was produced, a revised version is produced, and so forth. Further, in the process of reviewing others' work, team members learn from each other and change the way they work and what they produce. The feedback and iteration enable the group to produce something greater than any single person could accomplish working independently.

It is not possible to collaborate at the last minute. You cannot produce a document at midnight the day before the project is due and expect your teammates to review it in time for you or someone else to revise. In most student teams, collaboration proceeds over a period of weeks, not hours.

Critical Collaboration Drivers

The effectiveness of a collaborative effort is driven by three critical factors:

- Communication
- Content management
- Workflow control

Communication has two key elements. The first is the communication skills and abilities of the group members. The ability to give and receive critical feedback is particularly important, as you will see. The product can improve only when group members can criticize each others' work without creating rancor and resentment and can improve their contributions based on criticism received.

The second key communication element is the availability of effective communication systems. Today, few collaborative meetings are conducted face-to-face. Group members may be geographically distributed, or they may be unable to meet at the same time, or both. In such cases, the availability of email and more sophisticated and effective communications systems is crucial.

Most students today should give up on face-to-face meetings. It is too difficult to get everyone together in one place at one time. Instead, use information systems to meet virtually and maybe not all at the same time. Chapter Extension 2 describes the use of several such systems.

The second driver of effective collaboration is *content management*. When multiple users are contributing and changing documents, schedules, task lists, assignments, and so forth, one user's work might interfere with another's. Users need to manage content so that such conflict does not occur. Also, it is important to know who made what changes, when, and why. Content management systems track and report such data. Finally, in some collaborations members have different rights and privileges. Some team members have full permissions to create, edit, and delete content, others are restricted to editing, and still others are restricted to a read-only status. Information systems play a key role in enforcing such restrictions.

Workflow control is the third key driver of effective collaboration. A *workflow* is a process or procedure by which content is created, edited, used, and disposed. For a team that supports a Web site, for example, a workflow design might specify that certain members create Web pages, others review those pages, and still others post the reviewed and approved pages to the Web site. The workflow specifies particular ordering of tasks and includes processes for handling rejected changes as well as for dealing with exceptions.

The three collaboration drivers are not equally important for all collaborations. For one-time, *ad hoc* workgroups, it is seldom worthwhile to create and formalize workflows. For such groups, communication is the most important driver. However, for a team of engineers designing a new airplane a formally defined workflow is crucial.

In Chapter Extension 2, you can learn about information systems tools that will facilitate collaboration in your team projects at school as well as later as a working professional.

Q3 What Is an Effective Team?

Some teams are more effective than others, and considerable research has been done to determine why. Before we address that question, first consider what we mean by **team**. Katzenbach and Smith[3] define a *team* as:

> A small number of people with complementary skills who are committed to a common purpose, performance goals, and approach for which they hold themselves mutually accountable. (p. 45)

The authors define *small* as fewer than 25, but their book was published in the 1990s, prior to the emergence of information systems collaboration technology. Today, a small team might be fewer than 50, or maybe even 75. Notice the key phrases in this definition:

- "Complementary skills"
- "Committed to a common purpose, goals, and approach"
- "Hold themselves mutually accountable"

As stated earlier, some teams are more effective than others. Richard Hackman, a Harvard professor who has been conducting research on teams for more than 30 years, identifies three characteristics of an **effective team**:[4]

1. The team accomplishes its goals and objectives in a way that satisfies the team's sponsors and clients.
2. Over time, the team increases in capability. Working together becomes easier and more effective.
3. Team members learn and feel fulfilled as a result of working on the team.

Consider each of these elements in turn.

Accomplishing Goals and Objectives

Your situation for teams at school is different than for the industry teams that Hackman studies. In school, your professor is the sponsor of your team, and he or she will determine the official assessment of your team's work. If you are like many students, you prefer projects with clearly defined goals and definite answers. Unfortunately, in the business world goals and objectives are seldom so cut-and-dried.

---

[3]Jon Katzenbach and Douglas Smith, *The Wisdom of Teams* (New York: Harper Business, 1999), p. 45.
[4]Richard Hackman, *Leading Teams* (Boston: Harvard University Press, 2002), p. 213.

For example, in industry a team might be given a goal such as, "Find the best possible use for Microsoft Surface for accomplishing our competitive strategy." The team might not even know what Microsoft Surface is (see Chapter 4, p. 84). How will they ever be able to determine if they have found the *best possible use*?

If your professor gives you fuzzy goals like this one, be grateful, not critical. It isn't that he or she doesn't care or is poorly organized. Rather, your professor knows that in business, the only questions that have definite answers are those that are not worth asking.

However, in such situations it is critical that your team have a common understanding of the goals and objectives of the project. Invest the time to ensure that everyone is working toward the same end. If not, considerable team energy will be wasted.

Improve the Ability for the Team to Work Together

Most students stop right there, after the first element. Their one and only concern is to earn a high grade for the project. But Hackman defines two other measures of team effectiveness. One such measure concerns the team itself: Did the team become more effective as time went on? Did team members learn each others' strengths and how to use them wisely? Did team members learn each others' weaknesses and hot buttons and learn how to work around or otherwise manage them?

As stated, collaboration always involves feedback and iteration. Did team members learn how to give and receive critical feedback to one another? Did team members gain in their proficiency at using that critical feedback?

When teams improve their ability to work together, team members often come to like and enjoy each other more. But, such enjoyment is not essential to teamwork. Sometimes team members are just too different in personal perspective. What is essential, however, is that team members come to respect and trust each other.

Learning and Fulfillment

According to Hackman, teams have much to offer their members in terms of gaining new knowledge and skills from one another and learning from the different world perspectives of members on the team. Teams can provide a sense of belonging and serve to facilitate the development of new friendships.[5]

For a group to be considered successful, the group should enable members to do what they want and need to do, it should foster members' personal learning, and membership on the team should generate positive emotions about having worked with the group.

Q4 What Skills Are Important for Effective Collaboration?

The behavior of people in groups varies tremendously. Some people have a natural ability to collaborate, whereas others find it difficult, frustrating, or inefficient. Most people, though, with coaching and experience, can improve their collaboration skills. Before addressing specific skills, consider the factors that influence team member behaviors.

[5]*Ibid.*, pp. 28, 29.

Factors That Influence Team Member Behavior

Psychologists and social scientists who have devoted considerable research to teamwork generally agree that team members' behavior is influenced by:

- Natural skills and abilities
- Childhood formative environment
- Past team experiences
- Attitude (and skill) of the team leader
- Nature of the work

People are born with different social abilities. Some people are naturally empathetic. Some are born leaders. Some people are shy and do not like to be in the center of activities. Beyond natural ability, the team members' formative environment influences their ability to collaborate. Team members who were born as the middle child in a family with nine children will have learned collaboration skills that someone raised as an only child will not know. Further, team members bring memories of their past experiences, and those memories determine their initial expectations for the team.

Team leaders have a major impact on team members' behavior. A team leader who is actively involved, who encourages participation, and who expects (and welcomes) conflict creates an environment that fosters collaboration. Finally, the nature of the work and its relationship to the interests and abilities of the team influence team behavior. Most people find it hard to collaborate on a project they find unimportant or boring.

Key Skills for Collaborators

Ditkoff, Allen, Moore, and Pollard[6] surveyed 108 business professionals on the qualities, attitudes, and skills that make a good collaborator. Their results found no significant differences in response to the top 10 qualities with regard to the respondents' age, gender, experience, or occupation. All respondents seemed to agree on the top 10.

The table in Figure CE1-1 lists the most and least important characteristics reported in the survey. Three of the top seven characteristics involve disagreement: speaking an unpopular viewpoint (3), willingness to engage in difficult conversations (5), and skill at giving and receiving critical feedback (7). Note, too, that these three fall *after* enthusiasm for the subject (1) and being curious and open-minded (2). The respondents seem to be saying, "You need to care, you need to be open-minded, but you need to be able to deal with conflict, effectively disagree, and receive opinions that are different from your own."

These results are not surprising when we think about collaboration as an iterative process in which team members give and receive feedback. During collaboration, team members learn from each other, and it will be difficult to learn if no one is willing to express unpopular or contentious ideas. The respondents also seem to be saying, "You can, even should, be negative, as long as you care about what we're doing." These collaboration skills do not come naturally to people who have been taught to "play well with others," and that may be why they were ranked so highly in the survey.

The characteristics rated as not relevant also are revealing. Experience as a collaborator or in business does not seem to matter. Being popular also is not important. A big surprise, however, is that being well organized was rated 31st out of 39 characteristics. Perhaps collaboration itself is not a very well-organized process?

---

[6]Mitch Ditkoff, Tim Moore, Carolyn Allen, and Dave Pollard, "What Qualities, Attitudes, and Skills Help Make a Good Collaborator?" *http://blogs.salon.com* (accessed November 2005).

Rankings of Individual Collaboration Characteristics:
Essential:
Enthusiastic (1)
Curious and open-minded (2)
Says what they think, even if an unpopular perspective (3)
Highly Appreciated:
Responds promptly (4)
Can engage in difficult conversations (5)
Good listener (6)
Good with critical feedback (giving & receiving) (7)
Will voice unpopular ideas (8)
Easy to work with (9)
Does what commits to do (10)
Enthusiastic learner (11)
Provides different perspectives (12)
Not Important:
Well organized (31)
Similar personality (32)
Trust based on past experience (33)
Experienced with collaboration (34)
Effective presentation skills (35)
Outgoing and social (36)
Someone I already know (37)
Reputation as experienced collaborator (38)
Seasoned business experience (39)

Q5 What Characterizes Productive Conflict?

All of the research on collaboration indicates that conflict is common and, when properly conducted and managed, is a productive and positive factor for the team's performance. Student teams often fail because of an unwillingness to engage in conflict. Students might not want to be seen as unpopular or as not fitting in with the group, or perhaps students do not yet understand the importance of raising contrary or unpopular opinions. For whatever reason, many students will remain silent and walk away rather than express ideas that run counter to the rest of the group.

(There are some students whose standard behavior is to be negative and contrarian. They do not have problems avoiding conflict; they revel in it. But there are many other students, normally pleasant and anxious to please, who cannot bring themselves to express negative or opposing thoughts. If you are such a student, you will have greater success in business if you learn to behave differently.)

Among rational people, conflict occurs because of differences in perspective. One person understands the task differently from another, one person views a nuance in the situation that others do not see, or perhaps someone has experience that other team members do not have. When conflict occurs, it is important to understand the idea of differences in perspective and to use empathetic thinking to elicit the differences in behavior.

See the "Understanding Perspectives" Guide on page 28 and the "Empathetic Thinking" Guide on page 36 for more information about ways of accommodating different perspectives.

When differences in perspective are identified, the team must decide if those differences are consequential. Will those differences make a difference to the team's effectiveness? Note, too, that if you subscribe to Hackman's definition of team effectiveness, this means asking two additional questions: Will the difference matter to accomplishing team goals? Will the difference hamper the team's ability to grow as a team or inhibit the individual growth of the team members?

If the differences are consequential, then the team needs to keep communicating. Team members should strive to hear, learn, and adapt, when appropriate. The understanding of differences and their resolution can be frustrating. But team members must avoid personal attacks. *All of the literature on team performance indicates that attacks on a team member's personality, appearance, intelligence, or any other personal characteristic does* **irreparable** *harm to the team.* Never engage in such behavior. Instead, focus on the task at hand and on the differences that you have with regard to the team's work.

Sometimes when teams are stuck in seemingly unending conflict, the problem is caused by team members unknowingly using different criteria. As a simple example, one team member might believe that cost is the most important factor for judging an alternative, whereas another team member might believe that the delivery schedule is more important. They may not know that they are using different criteria. In such cases, no progress can be made until the difference is made explicit and the team agrees on a common set of criteria. This sometimes leads to a discussion of what criteria should be used to select the criteria. If so, carry the discussion through until the team has arrived at a common set of "criteria for criteria" and then a common set of criteria.

To repeat, all of the literature on teamwork indicates that conflict is inevitable and, when properly managed, results in better team performance. Do not shy away from productive conflict.

Q6 How Can You Improve Your Collaboration Skills?

As stated, collaboration skills are like any other skills; they can be improved by practice. Important behaviors to practice are listed in Figure CE1-2. The first requirement for improving your collaboration skills is to show up and get involved. You need to play tennis to improve tennis, and you need to collaborate to improve your collaboration skills. You need to believe that you can be better at collaboration and make a conscious and active effort to do so.

Assess yourself. Go through the list of behaviors in Figure CE1-1 and score yourself on the first 10 items in the list. Find the two or three items on which you score yourself the worst and identify ways to improve. There is an old management that says, "If you always do what you've always done, then you'll always get what you've always gotten." As the saying suggests, in order to improve your collaboration skills you must try some new behavior(s), no matter how awkward or uncomfortable you

- Show up...get involved.
- Assess yourself.
- Try new behaviors...and watch what happens.
- Keep Hackman's three goals of an effective team in mind.
- Engage in productive conflict.
- Ask for feedback and listen to it.
- Keep at it.

FIGURE CE1-2
Ways to Improve Your Collaboration Skills

feel. If you have difficulty expressing contrary opinions, make a goal of expressing at least one in a future meeting.

Keep Hackman's three criteria in mind as you practice new skills. An effective team is one that not only accomplishes the given task, but one that also grows as a team and fosters the individual growth of team members. What new behaviors can you engage in to foster the second two?

It is very difficult for any of us to assess our own social skills. We're just too biased an observer. Ask your teammates for feedback. Or, if that is too personal, create a policy in your team for team members to provide feedback for everyone. Do this for your own growth, even if your instructor does not require it.

Finally, keep at it. Acquiring strong collaboration skills is a lifelong process. It may also be the single most important skill in business, because business is a social activity; people do business with people. When you are 60 years old and a vice president of whatever, you will still be collaborating, and you will still be perfecting your collaboration skills. Start now.

Active ? Review

Use this Active Review to verify that you understand the material in the chapter. You can read the entire chapter and then perform the tasks in this review, or you can read the text material for just one question and perform the tasks in this review for that question before moving on to the next one.

Q1 Why learn collaboration skills? In your own words, explain why collaboration is important and how collaboration is like tennis or golf. Identify reasons for improving your collaboration skills. Name your best collaboration skill and your worst collaboration skill. Explain your selection.

Q2 What is collaboration? Define *collaboration*. Explain why collaboration is more than just cooperation. Identify the two critical characteristics of collaboration and explain them. Explain why you cannot collaborate at the last minute. Identify three critical collaboration drivers and summarize each. Explain why the textbook discourages face-to-face meetings.

Q3 What is an effective team? Define *team*. Name and explain the key terms in the definition. List Hackman's three characteristics of an effective team. Explain each characteristic. Besides accomplishing the goal of the project, do you agree with the effectiveness criteria? Why or why not? Do differences between teams in school and teams in business mean that Hackman's effectiveness criteria are inappropriate for school teams? Why or why not?

Q4 What skills are important for effective collaboration? Summarize the factors that influence a team member's collaborative behavior. Describe which, if any, of those factors are within the control of the team. Explain how the team might accommodate factors that are not within its control. Summarize the indispensible and very important behaviors that Ditkoff et al. found for collaboration. Summarize the not-relevant factors. Describe what you believe are the three most surprising behaviors in this survey and explain why you find them surprising.

Q5 What characterizes productive conflict? Explain why it is naïve and incorrect to not expect conflict in collaboration teams. Describe why you think students tend to avoid conflict in team meetings. Explain the role of perspectives in group conflict. Name a situation in which a difference in perspective is consequential and one in which it is not. Describe the role of criteria in assessing how consequential a difference might be. Describe behavior in conflict situations that must be avoided at all costs. Give an example of criteria and of "criteria for criteria."

Q6 How can you improve your collaboration skills? Summarize techniques for improving your collaboration skills. Assess your skills in terms of Figure CE1-1. Describe your three weakest skills. Develop tasks for you to accomplish to address correcting those three weakest skills.

Key Terms and Concepts

Collaboration 327   Effective team 329   Team 329

Using Your Knowledge

1. Explain why collaboration is important in business.

2. What is the relationship between collaboration and teams? Are all teams collaborative? Does every collaborative activity involve a team? Consider a team of five students painting a house. Is that team collaborative? Does it proceed via a sequence of steps using feedback and iteration? Are teams that are cooperative but not collaborative bad?

3. Consider a team of students given the task of recommending ways to improve campus security. Explain why such a team is likely to be collaborative. Identify three issues that such a team might address, and explain why those issues would need feedback and iteration.

4. Consider the following statement: "In business, the only questions that have definite answers are those that are not worth asking." What do you think this means? Do you agree or disagree? Explain.

5. The text states that if your professor gives you an ambiguous problem statement, you should be grateful, not critical. Why do you think the author wrote that sentence? Do you agree or disagree? How common do you think ambiguous problems are in business?

6. The number one characteristic in the Ditkoff et al. survey is enthusiasm for the subject of the collaboration. Suppose you are assigned to a collaborative team that has been given a task that you find tedious and boring. Besides resigning yourself to failing in a horrible experience, describe three creative ways you can respond to this challenge. How might this situation differ at work from that at school?

7. Consider the following statement: "All of the literature on team performance indicates that attacks on a team member's personality, appearance, intelligence, or any other personal characteristic does *irreparable* harm to the team." Define the term *irreparable*. If, in a moment of frustration and anger, you tell someone that he or she is stupid, what can you do to repair the damage? What can your teammates do? Suppose in that moment of anger and frustration you have the thought that the person with whom you are conversing is stupid. What can you do that will increase the effectiveness of your team? Keep Hackman's three criteria in mind as you answer. Explain the statement, "The easiest way to solve a problem is not to have it."

Chapter Extension 2

Chapter 1 provides the background for this Extension.

Using Collaboration Information Systems

Study Questions

Q1 Why use information systems for collaboration?

Q2 How can you use collaboration systems to improve team communication?

Q3 How can you use collaboration systems to manage content?

Q4 How can you use collaboration systems to control workflow?

Q5 What are the differences among Google Docs & Spreadsheets, Microsoft Groove, and Microsoft SharePoint?

Q6 What are recommended uses for particular collaboration tools?

Q1 Why Use Information Systems for Collaboration?

Collaboration is critical in business, and numerous software vendors and open-source developers (see Chapter 4) have created computer programs to facilitate various collaborative tasks. Notice, by the way, that they have created *computer programs*, not information systems. If you choose to use one or more of these tools, it will be up to you to create the *information system*, especially the procedure and training components.

Why should you do that? Why should your team choose to use a collaboration information system? For one, it will make your life easier. Once you and your team learn how to use the tools, once you have developed procedures for using them in your group, teamwork will be easier. You will no longer need to get everyone together face-to-face. You will no longer lose work; you will be able to determine who is contributing and who is not.

By the way, in some cases you will be applying skills you already possess. If you use multiparty text chat (discussed in Q2, next), you are applying texting skills that you already know. Similarly, you may already know how to participate in a discussion group or read or contribute to a wiki; if so, using a collaboration IS will give you a forum to apply those skills to your group work.

Another reason for using a collaboration system is that you will create better results. Such systems facilitate true collaboration, which, as discussed in Chapter Extension 1, means feedback and iteration. Each team member can produce documents, and others can comment and make revisions to them. Your work can evolve into something much better than you'd originally planned.

Additionally, collaboration skills are highly marketable. Take the example of Microsoft SharePoint. SharePoint is the fastest-growing product in Microsoft history. It reached $1 billion in sales faster than any other Microsoft product. Between 2004 and 2007, its compound annual growth rate of sales was greater than 50 percent. This success means that many organizations are beginning to use SharePoint. Note the word *beginning*. Few people in business today know how to use SharePoint, so if you do, you will have a competitive advantage. Based on the experience of many students, job recruiters are impressed with SharePoint knowledge.

In the next three questions, we will illustrate collaboration tools that you can use for each of the collaboration drivers described in Chapter Extension 1—communication, content management, and workflow control.

Q2 How Can You Use Collaboration Systems to Improve Team Communication?

If you truly are going to *collaborate* on your team projects, if you are going to create work products (such as documents), encourage others to criticize those products, and revise those products in accordance with the criticism, then you will need to communicate. Similarly, if you are going to review others' work, make critical comments, and help them improve their product, then you will also need to communicate. So, improving communication capabilities is key to collaboration success.

Figure CE2-1 summarizes technology available to facilitate communication. **Synchronous communication** occurs when all team members meet at the same time, such as with face-to-face meetings or conference calls. **Asynchronous communication** occurs when team members do not meet at the same time. Employees who work different shifts at the same location or team members who work in different time zones around the world must meet asynchronously.

Most student teams attempt to meet face-to-face, at least at first. Arranging such meetings is always difficult, however, because student schedules and responsibilities differ. If you are going to arrange such meetings, consider creating an online group calendar in which team members post their availability, week by week. Also, use the meeting facilities in Microsoft Outlook to issue invitations and gather RSVPs. If you don't have Outlook, use an Internet site such as Evite (*www.evite.com*) for this purpose. For face-to-face meetings, you will need little other technology beyond standard Office applications such as Word and PowerPoint. Given today's communication technology, most students should forgo face-to-face meetings. They are too difficult to arrange and seldom worth the trouble. Instead, learn to use **virtual meetings** in which participants do not meet in the same place and possibly not at the same time.

If your virtual meeting is synchronous (all meet at the same time), you can use **conference calls** or **multiparty text chat**. Some students find it weird to use text chat for school projects, but why not? You can attend meetings wherever you are, silently. In the next section, we will describe Microsoft Groove, a tool you should consider because of its easy-to-use multiparty text chat, along with several other useful features.

If everyone on your team has a camera on his or her computer, you can also do **videoconferencing**, like that shown in Figure CE2-2. Microsoft NetMeeting is one such product, but you can find others on the Internet. Videoconferencing is more intrusive than text chat; you have to comb your hair, but it does have a more personal touch. Sometime during your student career you should use it to see what you think.

In some (most?) classes and situations, synchronous meetings, even virtual ones, are impossible to arrange. You just cannot get everyone together at the same time. In this circumstance, when the team must meet asynchronously, most students try to

FIGURE CE2-1
Information Technology for Communication

	Synchronous		Asynchronous
Shared calendars Invitation and attendance			
Single location	Multiple locations		Single or multiple locations
Office applications such as Word and PowerPoint	Conference calls Multiparty text chat Microsoft Groove Videoconferencing		Email Discussion forums Team surveys

Virtual meetings

FIGURE CE2-2
User Participating in NetMeeting

Source: Courtesy of Zigy Kaluzny, Getty Images/Getty Images, Inc.

communicate via **email**. The problem with email is that there is too much freedom. Not everyone will participate, because it is easy to hide from email. Discussion threads become disorganized and disconnected. After the fact, it is difficult to find particular emails, comments, or attachments.

Discussion forums are an alternative. Here, one group member posts an entry, perhaps an idea, a comment, or a question, and other group members respond. Figure CE2-3 shows an example. Such forums are better than email because it is harder for the discussion to get off track. Still, however, it remains easy for some team members not to participate.

Team surveys are another form of communication technology. With these, one team member creates a list of questions and other team members respond. Surveys are

---

Posted: 5/8/2007 12:18 PM by Adrian Menstell   View Properties   Reply

Well,

I decided Is hould try and be more productive so I wrote up the needs and output text as well. This draft will replace the second draft rather than a new one, or soemthing like that I am still trying to work this all out but it will be both on th shared and the marketing forlders. I would really love some feed back on anything and everything.

Adrian

⊻ **Show Quoted Messages**

Posted: 5/8/2007 2:08 PM by Lori McGovern   View Properties   Reply

Adrian,
Looks great from the accting standpoint.
Lori

⊻ Show Quoted Messages

Posted: 5/8/2007 2:35 PM by Sandra Combs   View Properties   Reply

Adrian
When i added my thoughts to the marketing project it erased the original document. Sorry about that. And as far as the HR dept. I get where you are coming from now in regards to which section it would be under. I think then that we should move that piece to the sales dept. Just because within our group there is no specific HR dept. Thanks.

⊻ Show Quoted Messages

Posted: 5/8/2007 2:39 PM by Adrian Menstell   View Properties   Reply

well the absence of an HR department is a big deal for sure. To be honest I am not sure what all the departmennts, I just lifted them off the other papers.
HR to sales, I am curious why you feel the sales would be the best fit, I am not disagreeing but inorder for me to move it I need to be able to explain why it fits there.
My thought was possible operations (just 'cause the term operations is so vauge we could lump so much into it)

what are your thoughts?
Adrian

FIGURE CE2-3
Example of a Discussion Forum

FIGURE CE2-4
Portion of a Sample Team
Survey

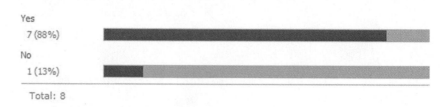

1. Have you read the Project 3 and 4 instructions from the power point slides? (Check box if yes)

Yes
7 (88%)

No
1 (13%)

Total: 8

2. Do you understand the requirements for Project 3?

Yes
6 (75%)

No
2 (25%)

Total: 8

3. Do you understand the requirements for project 4?

Yes
7 (88%)

No
1 (13%)

Total: 8

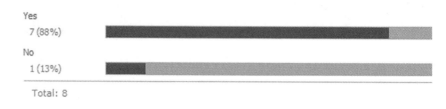

4. What confusions (if any) do you have in regards to Project 3?

Is it to be a research project? Are we supposed to find information on collaboration and post it?
1 (14%)

None.

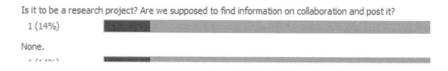

an effective way to obtain team opinions; they are generally easy to complete, so most team members will participate. Also, it is easy to determine who has not yet responded. Figure CE2-4 shows the results of one team survey. Confirmit (*www.confirmit.com*) is one common survey application program. You can find others on the Internet. Microsoft SharePoint (discussed later) has a built-in survey capability.

Q3 How Can You Use Collaboration Systems to Manage Content?

The second driver of collaboration performance is content management. You and your teammates will need to share documents, illustrations, spreadsheets, and other data. The information systems you use for sharing content depend on the degree of control that you want. Figure CE2-5 lists three categories of content-management control: no control, version tracking, and version management. Consider each.

Shared Content with No Control

The most primitive way to share content is via email attachments. It is easy to share content this way, but email attachments have numerous problems. For one, there is always the danger that someone does not receive an email, does not notice it in his or her inbox, or does not bother to save the attachments. Then, too, if three users obtain

Alternatives for Sharing Content		
No Control	Version Management	Version Control
Email with attachments Shared files on a server	Wikis Google Docs & Spreadsheets Microsoft Groove	Microsoft SharePoint

Increasing degree of content control

the same document as an email attachment, each user changes it, and each sends back the changed documents via email, different, incompatible versions of that document will be floating around. So, although email is simple, easy, and readily available, it will not suffice for collaborations in which there are many document versions or for which there is a desire for content control.

Another way to share content is to place it on a shared file server. You will learn more about servers in Part 2, but for now just understand that a server is a computer that provides a service. In this case, the service is content storage. If your team has access to a file server, you can put documents on the server and others can download them, make changes, and upload them back onto the server. Often a technology called **FTP** is used to get and place documents (discussed in Chapter 6).

Storing documents on servers is better than using email attachments because documents have a single storage location. They are not scattered in different team members' email boxes. Team members have a known location for finding documents.

However, without any additional control it is possible for team members to interfere with one another's work. For example, suppose team members A and B download a document and edit it, but without knowing about the other's edits. Person A stores his version back on the server and then person B stores her version back on the server. In this scenario, person A's changes will be lost.

Furthermore, without any version management it will be impossible to know who changed the document and when. Neither person A nor person B will know whose version of the document is on the server. To avoid such problems, some form of version management is recommended.

Shared Content with Version Management

Systems that provide **version management** track changes to documents and provide features and functions to accommodate concurrent work. The means by which this is done depends on the particular system used. In this section, we consider three systems that you should consider for your team's work: wikis, Google Docs & Spreadsheets, and Microsoft Groove.

Wikis

The simplest version-management systems are wikis. A **wiki** (pronounced *we-key*) is a shared knowledge base in which the content is contributed and managed by the wiki's users. The most famous wiki is Wikipedia (*www.wikipedia.org*), a general encyclopedia available to the public (see Figure CE2-6).

Collaborative teams can use wiki technology to create and maintain private wikis that serve as a repository of team knowledge. When a user contributes a wiki entry, the system tracks who created the entry and the date of creation. As others modify the entry, the wiki software tracks the identity of the modifier, the date, and possibly other data. Some users are given permission to delete wiki entries.

FIGURE CE2-6
A Wikipedia Entry

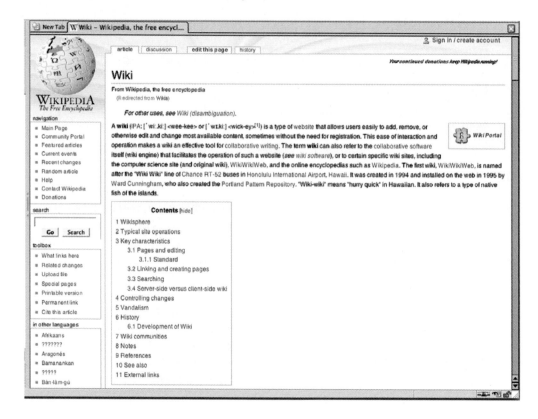

Google Docs & Spreadsheets

Google Docs & Spreadsheets is a system for sharing documents and spreadsheet data. (This application is rapidly evolving; by the time you read this, Google may have added additional file types or changed the system from what is described here. Google the name "Google Docs & Spreadsheets" to obtain the latest information about it.)

With Google Docs & Spreadsheets, anyone who edits a document must have a Google account. (A Google account is not the same as a Gmail account.) You can establish a Google account with a Hotmail, a university, or any other email account. Your Google account will be affiliated with whatever email account you enter.

To create a Google document, go to *http://docs.google.com* (note there is no *www* in this address). Sign into (or create) your Google account. From that point on, you can upload documents and spreadsheets, share them with others, and download them to common file formats.

You can then make the document available to others by entering their email addresses (which need not be Google accounts). Those users are notified that the document exists and are given a link by which they can access it. If they have (or create) a Google account, they can edit the document.

With Google Docs & Spreadsheets, documents are stored on a Google server. Users can access the documents from Google and simultaneously see and edit documents. In the background, Google merges the users' activities into a single document. You are notified that another user is editing a document at the same time as you are, and you can refresh the document to see their latest changes. Google tracks document revisions, with brief summaries of changes made. Figure CE2-7 shows a sample revision for a sample document that has been shared among three users.

Google Docs & Spreadsheets is free, but all documents must be processed by Google programs. A Microsoft Word or Excel document can be uploaded to a Google Docs & Spreadsheets site, but the document must be edited by Google programs. Documents can be saved in Word, Excel, or other common file formats. As of this writing, some common files, such as PowerPoint, cannot be shared. That may change in the future, however.

FIGURE CE2-7
Sample Google Docs &
Spreadsheet Document
Version

Source: Google Docs &
Spreadsheets™. Google is
a trademark of Google Inc.

Microsoft Office Groove

Microsoft Office Groove is a collaboration product that includes version management and other useful tools. Using Groove, a user creates a **workspace**, which is a collection of tools, documents, and users. The creator of the workspace invites others to join by sending them an email. The invitee accepts or declines the invitation. If the invitee accepts, he or she joins the workspace and can view all of the workspace content, including documents, schedules, drawings, announcements of meetings, and so forth.

When a user changes a document, Groove automatically propagates that change to workspaces on other users' computers. If two users attempt to change the same document at the same time, Groove disallows one of them until the other is finished. Groove provides a wide number of tools, including document repositories, discussion forums, to-do lists, meeting agendas, drawing spaces, calendars, and other features. Whenever a team member makes changes to the workspace—say, adding a calendar or a file of drawings or setting up a sequence of meetings—Groove propagates those changes to all team members' computers.

Groove can be used synchronously or asynchronously. For the former, Groove supports multiuser text chat. It also uses **Voice over IP (VoIP)** (discussed in Chapter 6) to enable meeting participants to conduct telephone conversations using the Internet connection. No separate phone line is necessary.

Team members can use Groove asynchronously. Working alone, they can modify documents, leave messages for one another, create new tasks, and so forth. As other team members rejoin the workspace, Groove will show them all work that was done while they were away. Groove can be hosted on any personal computer, and it can also be hosted on a server. If it is hosted on a server, then the workspace is always available. If it is hosted on a personal computer, then the workspace is available only when that computer is connected to the Internet.

Figure CE2-8 shows a sample Groove workspace. Shared files are listed in the middle column. The users in the workspace are listed in the pane in the upper right-hand corner, a chat session appears in the middle pane on the right-hand side, and a list of tasks appears in the lower right-hand corner.

The downside to Groove is that to participate all users must have purchased a license for Groove and have it installed on his or her computer. However, if your university participates in the Microsoft Developer Network Academic Alliance (and this is likely), you can obtain a license-free version of Groove through that program. Ask your instructor for more information.

Both Google Docs & Spreadsheets and Microsoft Groove are easy to set up and learn. Both are incredibly useful products that can make your collaborative work easier and result in higher-quality output. Take a look at them!

FIGURE CE2-8
Sample Groove Workspace

Source: Microsoft Office Groove
Workspace. Reprinted with permission
from Microsoft Corporation.

Shared Content with Version Control

Version-management systems improve the tracking of shared content and potentially eliminate problems caused by concurrent document access. They do not, however, provide **version control**. They do not limit the actions that can be taken by any particular user, and they do not give control over the changes to documents to particular users.

With version-control systems, each team member is given an account with a set of permissions. Shared documents are placed into shared directories, sometimes called **libraries**. For example, on a shared site with four libraries, a particular user might be given read-only permission for library 1; read and edit permission for library 2; read, edit, and delete permission for library 3; and no permission even to see library 4.

Furthermore, document directories can be set up so that users are required to check out documents before they can modify them. When a document is checked out, no other user can obtain it for the purpose of editing it. Once the document has been checked in, other users can obtain it for editing. Figure CE2-9 shows a user (Lori McGovern—see the welcome message in the top banner of the screen) checking out a document named Problem_Definition_Rickey. Of course, for the system to allow the checkout the user must have permission to edit that document.

Numerous version-control applications exist. **Microsoft SharePoint** is the most popular for general business use. Other document-control systems include MasterControl (*www.mastercontrol.com*) and Document Locator (*www.documentlocator.com*). Software development teams use applications such as CVS (*www.nongnu.org/cvs*) or Subversion (*http://subversion.tigris.org*) to control versions of software code, test plans, and product documentation.

By the way, SharePoint includes many collaboration features and functions besides document check-in/checkout. In addition to support for document libraries and lists, it has features for creating and managing the following team work products: surveys, discussion forums, wikis, member blogs, member Web sites, and workflow (see next section).

FIGURE CE2-9
Example of Document Checkout

Source: Microsoft Office SharePoint Designer 2007. Reprinted with permission from Microsoft Corporation.

For any but the most trivial team project, SharePoint is exceedingly useful. Unfortunately, installing SharePoint requires a publicly accessible server and more skill, experience, and knowledge than most college students are likely to have. Accordingly, Prentice Hall, this text's publisher, has set up SharePoint sites for you to use. See your instructor for information about how to create and use one of these SharePoint sites.

Q4 How Can You Use Collaboration Systems to Control Workflow?

So far you have learned how information systems can be used to facilitate team communication and manage content. It is possible to gain even more control by using information systems to manage workflow.

Figure CE2-10 shows a simple workflow example. This workflow is called a **sequential workflow** because activities occur in sequence. First, Burrows reviews the document, then McGovern, and finally Reynolds, one after the other in sequence. In a **parallel workflow**, the reviews would occur simultaneously. There are numerous other types of workflow that we will not consider here.[1]

You *can* manage a workflow such as that shown in Figure CE2-10 manually. Someone, perhaps the group's manager, sends an email to Burrows requesting the review, possibly with the document as an attachment. After Burrows finishes the review, the manager sends the reviewed document to McGovern, and so forth. If Burrows forgets to do the review, the manager would send a follow-up email, and so forth. As you can imagine, manual enforcement of workflows is an administrative nightmare.

However, a number of collaboration tools are available that will manage workflows for you. Microsoft SharePoint is one. Look again at Figure CE2-9. The user is about to click the *Check Out* command. However, from this same menu, the user could also click *Workflows* (two commands below *Check Out*) to define a workflow on this document.

---

[1]For more information about workflows and the Windows Workflow Foundation, see David Mann, *Workflow in the 2007 Microsoft Office System* (Berkeley, CA: Apress, 2007).

If the user were to click *Workflow*, the screen shown in Figure CE2-11 would appear. The user would fill out the entries in this form and in the one in Figure CE2-12 to define the workflow. Note in Figure CE2-12 that the workflow is defined as sequential; the form is also used to identify the users who will review the document.

Once this workflow is defined, SharePoint will manage it. SharePoint will send an email to Burrows requesting the review and a copy of that email to the person who defined this workflow. SharePoint will also create a task in a new task list defined for this workflow. When Burrows completes his review, he will check the document back in, and SharePoint will mark the task as complete and send an email to McGovern, requesting her review. Copies of these emails will be sent to the workflow creator. If Burrows does not complete the task within 5 days (see the bottom of the form in Figure CE2-12), SharePoint will send him a reminder as well as an advisory email to the creator of the workflow.

If you create a **SharePoint site**, you can define workflows just like the one described here for your group. You can use this capability to ensure that all of your teammates perform the work they are requested to do.

FIGURE CE2-11
Defining a SharePoint
Workflow, Part 1

Source: Microsoft Office SharePoint Designer 2007. Reprinted with permission from Microsoft Corporation.

Add a Workflow: Laptop Problem Resolution Documents

Use this page to set up a workflow for this document library.

Workflow

Select a workflow to add to this document library. If the workflow template you want does not appear, contact your administrator to get it added to your site collection or workspace.

Select a workflow template:

Approval
Collect Feedback
Collect Signatures
Disposition Approval

Description:

Routes a document for review. Reviewers can provide feedback, which is compiled and sent to the document owner when the workflow has completed.

Name

Type a name for this workflow. The name will be used to identify this workflow to users of this document library.

Type a unique name for this workflow:

Problem Definition Document Workflow

Task List

Select a task list to use with this workflow. You can select an existing task list or request that a new task list be created.

Select a task list:

New task list

Description:

A new task list will be created for use by this workflow.

History List

Select a history list to use with this workflow. You can select an existing history list or request that a new history list be created.

Select a history list:

Workflow History

Description:

History list for workflow.

Start Options

Specify how this workflow can be started.

☐ Allow this workflow to be manually started by an authenticated user with Edit Items Permissions.

☐ Require Manage Lists Permissions to start the workflow.

☐ Start this workflow to approve publishing a major version of an item.

☑ Start this workflow when a new item is created.

☐ Start this workflow when an item is changed.

FIGURE CE2-12
Defining a SharePoint Workflow, Part 2

Source: Microsoft Office SharePoint Designer 2007. Reprinted with permission from Microsoft Corporation.

Customize Workflow: Problem Definition Document Workflow

OK Cancel

Workflow Tasks

Specify how tasks are routed to participants and whether to allow tasks to be delegated or if participants can request changes be made to the document prior to finishing their tasks.

Assign tasks to:
- ○ All participants simultaneously (parallel)
- ● One participant at a time (serial)

Allow workflow participants to:
- ☐ Reassign the task to another person
- ☑ Request a change before completing the task

Default Workflow Start Values

Specify the default values that this workflow will use when it is started. You can opt to allow the person who starts the workflow to change or add participants.

Type the names of people you want to participate when this workflow is started. Add names in the order in which you want the tasks assigned (for serial workflows).

Reviewers... | William Burrows; Lori McGovern; Jordan Reynolds

- ☐ Assign a single task to each group entered (Do not expand groups).
- ☑ Allow changes to the participant list when this workflow is started

Type a message to include with your request:

Please look at this version of the document and annotate it with your comments. SharePoint will pass it along, with your comments, to the next person in the group.

Due Date

If a due date is specified and e-mail is enabled on the server, participants will receive a reminder on that date if their task is not finished.

Tasks are due by (parallel):

Give each person the following amount of time to finish their task (serial):

5 Day(s) ▼

By the way, SharePoint has several other default workflows that you can use. With some time and patience, you can also learn how to define custom workflows using Windows Office SharePoint Designer. And, if you are a programmer, you can use Visual Studio to create custom workflows that are limited only by your knowledge and programming skill.

Q5 What Are the Differences Among Google Docs & Spreadsheets, Microsoft Groove, and Microsoft SharePoint?

Figure CE2-13 compares and contrasts Google Docs & Spreadsheets, Microsoft Groove, and Microsoft SharePoint. The advantages of Google Docs & Spreadsheets are that it is easy to use, free, and requires only a browser. However, it can be used only with Word and Excel files. In contrast, you can use Microsoft Groove to share

FIGURE CE2-13
Comparison of
Collaboration Products

Collaboration Product	Strengths	Weaknesses	Best for
Google Docs & Spreadsheets	• Easy to learn • Free • Thin client (only need a browser)	• Use only with Word and Excel documents	• Sharing a few Word or Excel documents
Microsoft Groove	• Share many types of documents • Share calendars, discussions, meeting spaces • Automatic reconciliation of offline changes • Multi-party text chat • VoIP • Secure communications	• Licensed product that must be installed • Cost	• Virtual meetings with multi-party text chat
Microsoft Sharepoint	• Supports all the collaboration tools in Figure CE2-14 • Thin client (only need browser) • Highly customizable • Highly marketable skill	• Must be set up by an IS professional • Initial learning curve	• Complicated projects • Large teams • Project management

Word and Excel files as well as many other types of documents, calendars, meetings spaces, and diagrams. If you work on a Groove document offline (while not connected to the Internet), Groove will reconcile your changes with changes made by others when you next sign on to the Internet. Groove provides chat and VoIP, and all Groove communications are secure, even those sent from public places, such as coffee shops. The disadvantage of Groove is that it is a licensed product that must be purchased and installed.

Microsoft SharePoint is the largest and most complex of these three products. With SharePoint, you can create all of the collaboration tools listed in Figure CE2-14 with only the browser on your computer. SharePoint is also highly customizable. Finally, because of its popularity in industry, SharePoint skills are highly marketable.

FIGURE CE2-14
Recommended Uses for
Collaboration Tools

Collaboration Tool	Recommended Uses
Survey	Introduce team members Verify understanding of goals or other critical topic Wrap up project
Document Library	Single repository for team documents
Version-controlled Documents	Record history of document changes Track document contributors
Workflow-controlled Documents	Ensure all team members review or approve documents
Discussion Forum	Asynchronous, virtual discussion of any issue Track comments Share knowledge
Wiki	Create team glossary Show relationship of team's terms Document team knowledge
Lists	Track to-do items Keep inventory List of Web links

The downside to SharePoint is that it must be set up by a professional and you must learn basic skills before you can use it. SharePoint is well suited for large, complicated collaborations and for project management.

Q6 What Are Recommended Uses for Particular Collaboration Tools?

Figure CE2-14 lists common collaboration tools and recommends potential applications for them. Surveys are good for getting to know your teammates, for verifying understanding of project goals and other topics, and for deciding when to wrap up the project. Document libraries overcome the disadvantages of sharing documents using email. If the libraries are version controlled, then the tool will track changes, and if they are workflow controlled, the team can ensure that all members review or approve documents.

Discussion forums provide a means to asynchronously discuss any issue—and to track the comments made by different authors. They can also be used to share knowledge. The team can use wikis to create a team glossary, to show the relationships among defined terms, and to document the team's knowledge. Finally, lists can be used to track items that need to be completed; to keep an inventory of documents, tasks, or other resources; and to maintain a list of Web links to documents, videos, or other items.

Active Review

Use this Active Review to verify that you understand the material in the chapter. You can read the entire chapter and then perform the tasks in this review, or you can read the text material for just one question and perform the tasks in this review for that question before moving on to the next one.

Q1 Why use information systems for collaboration? Explain the difference between a collaboration program and a collaboration information system. Summarize the reasons that your team might want to use a collaboration system for its work. Explain how you can use skills you already possess, and give an example of how knowledge of one collaboration tool can give you a competitive advantage.

Q2 How can you use collaboration systems to improve team communication? Explain why communication is important to student collaborations. Define *synchronous* and *asynchronous communication*, and explain when each is used. Name two collaboration tools that can be used to help set up synchronous meetings. Describe collaboration tools that can be used for face-to-face meetings. Describe tools that can be used for virtual, synchronous meetings. Describe tools that can be used for virtual, asynchronous meetings. Compare and contrast the advantages of email, discussion forums, and team surveys.

Q3 How can you use collaboration systems to manage content? Describe two ways that content is shared with no control, and explain the problems that can occur. Explain how control is provided by the following collaboration tools: wikis, Google Docs & Spreadsheets, and Microsoft Groove. Define *workspace*, and explain how Groove uses workspaces. Explain the difference between version management and version control. Describe how user accounts, passwords, and libraries are used to control user activity. Explain how check-in/checkout works. Identify major features in Microsoft SharePoint.

Q4 How can you use collaboration systems to control workflow? Explain the difference between content management and workflow control. Give an example of a sequential workflow. Describe why manual enforcement of workflow is an administrative nightmare. Explain how Microsoft SharePoint can be used to enforce sequential workflow.

Q5 What are the differences among Google Docs & Spreadsheets, Microsoft Groove, and Microsoft SharePoint? Using Figure CE2-13 as a guide, compare and contrast Google Docs & Spreadsheets, Microsoft Groove, and Microsoft SharePoint. Explain how you could use this

figure to describe the advantages of collaboration to your boss.

Q6 What are recommended uses for particular collaboration tools? Using your experience from prior team projects, describe an appropriate application for each of the collaboration tools in Figure CE2-14. Explain how your team might have been more effective by using that tool. Use Hackman's definition of *team effectiveness* (page 329) in your answer.

Key Terms and Concepts

Asynchronous communication 338
Conference calls 338
Discussion forums 339
Email 339
FTP 341
Google Docs & Spreadsheets 342
Libraries 344
Microsoft Office Groove 343

Microsoft SharePoint 344
Multiparty text chat 338
Parallel workflow 345
Sequential workflow 345
SharePoint site 346
Synchronous communication 338
Team surveys 339
Version control 344

Version management 341
Videoconferencing 338
Virtual meetings 338
Voice over IP (VoIP) 343
Wiki 341
Workspace 343

Using Your Knowledge

Reflect on your experience working on teams in previous classes as well as on collaborative teams in other settings, such as a campus committee. To what extent was your team collaborative? Did it involve feedback and iteration? If so, how? How did you use collaborative information systems, if at all? If you did not use collaborative information systems, describe how you think such systems might have improved your work methods and results. If you did use collaborative information systems, explain how you could improve on that use, given the knowledge you have gained from this chapter extension.

1. This exercise requires you to experiment with Google Docs & Spreadsheets. You will need two Google accounts to complete this exercise. If you have two different email addresses, then set up two Google accounts using those addresses. Otherwise, use your school email address and set up a Google Gmail account. A Gmail account will automatically give you a Google account.

    a. Using Microsoft Word, write a memo to yourself. In the memo, explain the nature of the communication collaboration driver. Go to *http://docs.google.com* and sign in with one of

your Google accounts. Upload your memo using Google Docs & Spreadsheets. Save your uploaded document and share your document with the email in your second Google account. Sign out of your first Google account.

(If you have access to two computers situated close to each other, use both of them for this exercise. You will see more of the Google Docs & Spreadsheets functionality by using two computers. If you have two computers, do not sign out of your Google account. Perform step b and all actions for the second account on that second computer. If you are using two computers, ignore the instructions in the following steps to sign out of the Google accounts.)

    b. Open a new window in your browser. Access *http://docs.google.com* from that second window and sign in using your second Google account. Open the document that you shared in step a.

    c. Change the memo by adding a brief description of the content-management driver. Save the document from your second account. If you are using just one computer, sign out from your second account.

d. Sign in on your first account. Open the most recent version of the memo and add a description of the workflow-control communication driver. Save the document. (If you are using two computers, notice how Google warns you that another user is editing the document at the same time. Click *Refresh* to see what happens.) If you are using just one computer, sign out from your first account.

e. Sign in on your second account. Re-open the shared document. From the File menu, save the document as a Word document. Describe how Google processed the changes to your document.

2. This exercise requires you to experiment with Microsoft Groove. To perform it, you need to work with a classmate. Both you and your classmate must install a copy of Microsoft Groove. Check with your instructor to learn how to download a license-free version using the MSDN Academic Alliance. In the following, one of you should take the role of user A and the other should take the role of user B.

a. User A should open the Groove launch bar and create a new workspace. Select *Standard*. In the lower right-hand second of the new workspace, invite user B to join the workspace by entering user B's email address. While you are waiting for user B to respond, use Word to write a memo briefly summarizing the need for version management. Save the memo using the file name *VersionManagement* and add it to the workspace by clicking *Add Files*.

b. User B will receive an invitation to join the workspace. All user B needs to do is to click the link provided. The workspace will open. User B should write a memo summarizing the need for

version control. Save that memo with the name *VersionControl* and add it to the workspace.

c. User A should then open the chat window in the lower right-hand corner and enter a chat message asking user B to read *VersionManagement* and make comments.

d. User B should respond to user A's chat and send a chat message to user A asking for a review of *VersionControl*. Make a few changes and save the document.

e. User A should open and review *VersionManagement*. User B should open and review *VersionControl*. Make a few changes and save the document.

f. Using chat, coordinate your efforts so that both users attempt to open the same document at the same time. Note what happens.

g. Add a sketchpad tool to the workspace by clicking the icon (in the lower right-of-center section of the workspace) that shows a document and a green plus sign and selecting *Sketchpad*.

h. Using chat, coordinate your efforts to modify the sketch at the same time. Note what happens.

i. Using chat, describe your experiences. Both users should comment on what they have seen.

j. Save your chat transcript as a file. Right-click in the chat window, and select *Chat/Print transcript*. In the print window, select *Print to file*. Submit your chat transcript as your answer to this exercise.

3. If your instructor has enabled a Microsoft SharePoint site for your class, you can perform exercises using SharePoint. Go to *www.pearsonhighered.com/kroenke* and find the file *Chapter 2 SharePoint Exercise*. Perform the exercises shown there.

GLOSSARY

10/100/1000 Ethernet A type of Ethernet that conforms to the IEEE 802.3 protocol and allows for transmission at a rate of 10, 100, or 1,000 Mbps (megabits per second). p. 123

Access A popular personal and small workgroup DBMS product from Microsoft. p. 105

Access control list (ACL) A list that encodes the rules stating which packets are to be allowed through a firewall and which are to be prohibited. p. 136

Access devices Devices, typically special-purpose computers, that connect network sites. The particular device required depends on the line used and other factors. Sometimes switches and routers are employed, but other types of equipment are needed as well. p. 129

Access point (AP) A point in a wireless network that facilitates communication among wireless devices and serves as a point of interconnection between wireless and wired networks. The AP must be able to process messages according to both the 802.3 and 802.11 standards, because it sends and receives wireless traffic using the 802.11 protocol and communicates with wired networks using the 802.3 protocol. p. 125

Accurate information Information that is based on correct and complete data and that has been processed correctly as expected. p. 26

Activity The part of a business process that transforms resources and information of one type into resources and information of another type; can be manual or automated. p. 25

AdSense A Web 2.0 product from Google. Google searches an organization's Web site and inserts ads that match content on that site; when users click those ads, Google pays the organization a fee. p. 202

Adware Programs installed on the user's computer without the user's knowledge or permission that reside in the background and, unknown to the user, observe the user's actions and keystrokes, modify computer activity, and report the user's activities to sponsoring organizations. Most adware is benign in that it does not perform malicious acts or steal data. It does, however, watch user activity and produce pop-up ads. p. 294

AdWords A Web 2.0 advertising product from Google. Vendors agree to pay a certain amount to Google for use of particular search words, which link to the vendor's site. p. 202

Agile enterprise An organization that can quickly adapt to changes in the market, industry, product,

law, or other significant external factors; the term was coined by Microsoft. p. 270

Analog signal A wavy signal. A modem converts the computer's digital data into analog signals that can be transmitted over dial-up Internet connections. p. 127

Analysis paralysis When too much time is spent documenting project requirements. p. 264

Antivirus programs Software that detects and possibly eliminates viruses. p. 93

Application software Programs that perform a business function. Some application programs are general purpose, such as Excel or Word. Other application programs are specific to a business function, such as accounts payable. p. 86

As-is model A business process model that documents the current business process; teams then change that model to make adjustments necessary to solve process problems. p. 164

Asymmetric digital subscriber lines (ADSL) DSL lines that have different upload and download speeds. p. 128

Asymmetric encryption An encryption method whereby different keys are used to encode and to decode the message; one key encodes the message, and the other key decodes the message. Symmetric encryption is simpler and much faster than asymmetric encryption. p. 134

Asynchronous communication Information exchange that occurs when all members of a work team do not meet at the same time, such as those who work different shifts or at different locations. p. 338

Asynchronous transfer mode (ATM) A protocol that divides data into uniformly sized cells, eliminates the need for protocol conversion, and can process speeds from 1 to 156 Mbps. ATM can support both voice and data communication. p. 133

Attribute (1) A variable that provides properties for an HTML tag. Each attribute has a standard name. For example, the attribute for a hyperlink is *href*, and its value indicates which Web page is to be displayed when the user clicks the link. (2) Characteristics of an entity. Example attributes of *Order* would be *OrderNumber, OrderDate, SubTotal, Tax, Total*, and so forth. Example attributes of *Salesperson* would be *SalespersonName, Email, Phone*, and so forth. p. 196

Auctions Applications that match buyers and sellers by using an e-commerce version of a standard, competitive-bidding auction process. p. 190

Authentication The process whereby an information system approves (authenticates) a user by checking the user's password. p. 292

Beta program A prerelease version of software, used for testing. The beta program becomes obsolete when the final version is released. p. 198

Beta testing The process of allowing future system users to try out the new system on their own. Used to locate program failures just prior to program shipment. p. 258

Binary digits The means by which computers represent data; also called *bits*. A binary digit is either a zero or a one. p. 77

Biometric authentication The use of personal physical characteristics, such as fingerprints, facial features, and retinal scans, to authenticate users. p. 293

Bit The means by which computers represent data; also called *binary digit*. A bit is either a zero or a one. p. 77

Blog (Web-log) An online journal, which uses technology to publish information over the Internet. p. 3

Broadband Internet communication lines that have speeds in excess of 256 kbps. DSL and cable modems provide broadband access. p. 129

Brooks's Law The famous adage that states: *Adding more people to a late project makes the project later.* Brooks's Law is true not only because a larger staff requires increased coordination, but also because new people need training. The only people who can train the new employees are the existing team members, who are thus taken off productive tasks. The costs of training new people can overwhelm the benefit of their contribution. p. 248

Browser A program that processes the HTTP protocol; receives, displays, and processes HTML documents; and transmits responses. p. 194

Bus Means by which the CPU reads instructions and data from main memory and writes data to main memory. p. 78

Business intelligence (BI) system A system that provides the right information, to the right user, at the right time. A tool produces the information, but the system ensures that the right information is delivered to the right user at the right time. p. 214

Business process A network of activities, resources, facilities, and information that interact to achieve some business function; sometimes called a business system. p. 24

Business process management (BPM) The systematic process of creating, assessing, and altering business processes. p. 163

Business Process Modeling Notation (BPMN) A standard set of terms and graphical notations for documenting business processes, created by the Object Management Group (OMG). p. 168

Business system Another term for *business process*. p. 24

Business-to-business (B2B) E-commerce sales between companies. p. 190

Business-to-consumer (B2C) E-commerce sales between a supplier and a retail customer (the consumer). p. 189

Business-to-government (B2G) E-commerce sales between companies and governmental organizations. p. 190

Byte (1) A character of data; (2) An 8-bit chunk. p. 78, p. 100

Cable modem A type of modem that provides high-speed data transmission using cable television lines. The cable company installs a fast, high-capacity optical fiber cable to a distribution center in each neighborhood that it serves. At the distribution center, the optical fiber cable connects to regular cable-television cables that run to subscribers' homes or businesses. Cable modems modulate in such a way that their signals do not interfere with TV signals. Like DSL lines, they are always on. p. 128

Cache A file on a domain name resolver that stores domain names and IP addresses that have been resolved. Then, when someone else needs to resolve that same domain name, there is no need to go through the entire resolution process. Instead, the resolver can supply the IP address from the local file. p. 78

Central processing unit (CPU) The CPU selects instructions, processes them, performs arithmetic and logical comparisons, and stores results of operations in memory. p. 75

Channel conflict In e-commerce, a conflict that may result between a manufacturer that wants to sell products directly to consumers and the retailers in the existing sales channels. p. 192

Chief information officer (CIO) The title of the principal manager of the IT department. Other common titles are *vice president of information services*, *director of information services*, and, less commonly, *director of computer services*. p. 272

Chief technology officer (CTO) The head of the technology group. The CTO sorts through new ideas and products to identify those that are most relevant to the organization. The CTO's job requires deep knowledge of information technology and the ability to envision how new IT will affect the organization over time. p. 273

Clearinghouse   Entity that provides goods and services at a stated price, prices and arranges for the delivery of the goods, but never takes title to the goods. p. 190

Clickstream data   E-commerce data that describes a customer's clicking behavior. Such data includes everything the customer does at the Web site. p. 217

Client   A computer that provides word processing, spreadsheets, database access, and usually a network connection. p. 82

Cloud   Computing services that provide processing, data storage, and specific application functions over the Internet. p. 83

Cluster analysis   An unsupervised data-mining technique whereby statistical techniques are used to identify groups of entities that have similar characteristics. A common use for cluster analysis is to find groups of similar customers in data about customer orders and customer demographics. p. 223

Cold site   A remote processing center that provides office space, but no computer equipment, for use by a company that needs to continue operations after a natural disaster. p. 305

Collaboration   The situation in which two or more people work together toward a common goal, result, or product; information systems facilitate collaboration. p. 327

Columns   Also called *fields*, or groups of bytes. A database table has multiple columns that are used to represent the attributes of an entity. Examples are *PartNumber*, *EmployeeName*, and *SalesDate*. p. 100

Commerce server   A computer that operates Web-based programs that display products, support online ordering, record and process payments, and interface with inventory-management applications. p. 194

Competitive strategy   The strategy an organization chooses as the way it will succeed in its industry. According to Porter, there are four fundamental competitive strategies: cost leadership across an industry or within a particular industry segment, and product differentiation across an industry or within a particular industry segment. p. 44

Component design phase   The third phase in the SDLC, in which developers determine hardware and software specifications, design the database (if applicable), design procedures, and create job descriptions for users and operations personnel. p. 249

Computer hardware   One of the five fundamental components of an information system. p. 5

Computer-based information system   An information system that includes a computer. p. 6

Conference call   A synchronous virtual meeting, in which participants meet at the same time via a voice-communication channel. p. 338

Cost feasibility   One of four dimensions of feasibility. p. 251

Cross-functional processes   Processes that involve activities among several, or even many, business departments. p. 165

Crowdsourcing   The process by which organizations use Web 2.0 technologies such as user-generated content to involve their users in the design and marketing of their products. p. 206

Curse of dimensionality   The more attributes there are, the easier it is to build a data model that fits the sample data but that is worthless as a predictor. p. 217

Custom-developed software   Tailor-made software. p. 87

Customer relationship management (CRM)   The set of business processes for attracting, selling, managing, and supporting customers. p. 165

Data   Recorded facts or figures. One of the five fundamental components of an information system. p. 5

Data administration   A staff function that pertains to *all* of an organization's data assets. Typical data administration tasks are setting data standards, developing data policies, and providing for data security. p. 296

Data channel   Means by which the CPU reads instructions and data from main memory and writes data to main memory. p. 78

Data marts   Facilities that prepare, store, and manage data for reporting and data mining for specific business functions. p. 221

Data mining   The application of statistical techniques to find patterns and relationships among data and to classify and predict. p. 222

Data-mining system   Information system that processes data using sophisticated statistical techniques such as regression analysis and decision-tree analysis to find patterns and relationships that cannot be found by simpler operations such as sorting, grouping, and averaging. p. 215

Data safeguards   Steps taken to protect databases and other organizational data by means of data administration and database administration. p. 296

Data warehouses   Facilities that prepare, store, and manage data specifically for reporting and data mining. p. 217

Database   A self-describing collection of integrated records. p. 100

Database administration   The management, development, operation, and maintenance of the database so as to achieve the organization's objectives. This staff function requires balancing conflicting goals: protecting the database while maximizing its availability for authorized use. In smaller organizations, this function usually is served by a single person. Larger organizations assign several people to an office of database administration. p. 296

Database application   A collection of forms, reports, queries, and application programs that process a database. p. 109

Database application system   Applications, having the standard five components, that make database data more accessible and useful. Users employ a database application that consists of forms, formatted reports, queries, and application programs. Each of these, in turn, calls on the database management system (DBMS) to process the database tables. p. 105

Database management system (DBMS)   A program used to create, process, and administer a database. p. 105

Database tier   In the three-tier architecture, the tier that runs the DBMS and receives and processes SQL requests to retrieve and store data. p. 193

DB2   A popular, enterprise-class DBMS product from IBM. p. 105

Denial of service (DOS)   Security problem in which users are not able to access an IS; can be caused by human errors, natural disaster, or malicious activity. p. 289

Dial-up modem   A modem that performs the conversion between analog and digital in such a way that the signal can be carried on a regular telephone line. p. 127

Digital subscriber line (DSL)   DSL uses voice telephone lines with a DSL modem; it operates so that the signals do not interfere with voice telephone service. DSL provides much faster data transmission speeds than dial-up connections. Additionally, DSL is an always-on connection, so there is no need to dial in. p. 128

Dirty data   Problematic data. Examples are a value of *B* for customer gender and a value of *213* for customer age. Other examples are a value of *999-999-9999* for a U.S. phone number, a part color of *gren*, and an email address of WhyMe@GuessWhoIAM-Hah-Hah.org. All these values are problematic when data mining. p. 216

Discussion forum   A form of asynchronous communication in which one group member posts an entry and other group members respond. A better form of group communication than email, because it is more difficult for the discussion to go off track. p. 339

Disintermediation   Elimination of one or more middle layers in the supply chain. p. 191

Drive-by sniffers   People who take computers with wireless connections through an area and search for unprotected wireless networks in an attempt to gain free Internet access or to gather unauthorized data. p. 288

DSL modem   A type of modem. DSL modems operate on the same lines as voice telephones and dial-up modems, but they operate so that their signals do not interfere with voice telephone service. DSL modems provide much faster data transmission speeds than dial-up modems. Additionally, DSL modems always maintain a connection, so there is no need to dial in; the Internet connection is available immediately. p. 128

Dual processor   A computer with two CPUs. p. 82

E-commerce   The buying and selling of goods and services over public and private computer networks. p. 189

Effective team   A team characterized by its ability to accomplish assigned goals and objectives, improve its capability, and enable team members to gain knowledge and skills from one another. p. 335

Electronic exchanges   Sites that facilitate the matching of buyers and sellers; the business process is similar to that of a stock exchange. Sellers offer goods at a given price through the electronic exchange, and buyers make offers to purchase over the same exchange. Price matches result in transactions from which the exchange takes a commission. p. 190

Email   A form of asynchronous communication in which participants send comments and attachments electronically. As a form of group communication, it can be disorganized, disconnected, and easy to hide from. p. 339

Email spoofing   A synonym for phishing. A technique for obtaining unauthorized data that uses pretexting via email. The *phisher* pretends to be a legitimate company and sends email requests for confidential data, such as account numbers, Social Security numbers, account passwords, and so forth. Phishers direct traffic to their sites under the guise of a legitimate business. p. 288

Encapsulation   Isolating all of the logic for a given business process within a particular service. The logic is hidden from service users and thus can be changed as long as the data to and from the service remain the same. p. 177

Encryption The process of transforming clear text into coded, unintelligible text for secure storage or communication. p. 134

Encryption algorithms Algorithms used to transform clear text into coded, unintelligible text for secure storage or communication. Commonly used methods are DES, 3DES, and AES. p. 134

Enterprise DBMS A product that processes large organizational and workgroup databases. These products support many users, perhaps thousands, and many different database applications. Such DBMS products support 24/7 operations and can manage databases that span dozens of different magnetic disks with hundreds of gigabytes or more of data. IBM's DB2, Microsoft's SQL Server, and Oracle's Oracle are examples of enterprise DBMS products. p. 114

Ethernet Another name for the IEEE 802.3 protocol, Ethernet is a network protocol that operates at Layers 1 and 2 of the TCP/IP–OSI architecture. Ethernet, the world's most popular LAN protocol, is used on WANs as well. p. 123

Exabyte 10^{18} bytes. p. 213

Expert system Knowledge-sharing system that is created by interviewing experts in a given business domain and codifying the rules used by those experts. p. 215

eXtensible Markup Language (XML) A document standard that separates document content, structure, and presentation; eliminates problems in HTML; and offers advantages over EDI. Most believe XML will eventually replace EDI. p. 182

Facilities Structures used within a business process. p. 25

Fields Also called *columns*, groups of bytes in a database table. A database table has multiple columns that are used to represent the attributes of an entity. Examples are *PartNumber*, *EmployeeName*, and *SalesDate*. p. 100

File A group of similar rows or records. In a database, sometimes called a *table*. p. 101

Fire-and-forget pattern A business process pattern in which the activity sends a message or request ("fires" it) and then forgets about it, not checking on the outcome of the message or request. p. 170

Firewall A computing device located between a firm's internal and external networks that prevents unauthorized access to or from the internal network. A firewall can be a special-purpose computer or it can

be a program on a general-purpose computer or on a router. p. 135

Firmware Computer software that is installed into devices such as printers, print services, and various types of communication devices. The software is coded just like other software, but it is installed into special, programmable memory of the printer or other device. p. 88

Five-component framework The five fundamental components of an information system—computer hardware, software, data, procedures, and people—that are present in every information system, from the simplest to the most complex. p. 5

Five-forces model Model, proposed by Michael Porter, that assesses industry characteristics and profitability by means of five competitive forces—bargaining power of suppliers, threat of substitution, bargaining power of customers, rivalry among firms, and threat of new entrants. p. 44

Foreign keys A column or group of columns used to represent relationships. Values of the foreign key match values of the primary key in a different (foreign) table. p. 103

Form Data entry forms are used to read, insert, modify, and delete database data. p. 109

Frame Relay A protocol that can process traffic in the range of 56 kbps to 40 Mbps by packaging data into frames. p. 133

FTP See *File Transfer Protocol*. p. 341

Functional processes Processes that involve activities within a single department or business function such as accounts payable or inventory management. p. 164

Gigabyte (GB) 1,024 MB. p. 78

Google Docs & Spreadsheets A version-management system for sharing documents and spreadsheet data. Documents are stored on a Google server, from which users can access and simultaneously see and edit the documents. p. 342

Granularity The level of detail in data. Customer name and account balance is large granularity data. Customer name, balance, and the order details and payment history of every customer order is smaller granularity. p. 217

Grid A network of computers that operates as an integrated whole; the grid appears to be a single computer. p. 83

Hacking Occurs when a person gains unauthorized access to a computer system. Although some people hack for the sheer joy of doing it, other hackers invade systems for the malicious purpose of stealing or modifying data. p. 289

Hardening   The process of taking extraordinary measures to reduce a system's vulnerability. Hardened sites use special versions of the operating system, and they lock down or eliminate operating systems features and functions that are not required by the application. Hardening is a technical safeguard. p. 299

Hardware   Electronic components and related gadgetry that input, process, output, store, and communicate data according to instructions encoded in computer programs or software. p. 75

Horizontal-market application   Software that provides capabilities common across all organizations and industries; examples include word processors, graphics programs, spreadsheets, and presentation programs. p. 86

Hot site   A remote processing center, run by a commercial disaster-recovery service, that provides equipment a company would need to continue operations after a natural disaster. p. 305

HTTPS   An indication that a Web browser is using the SSL/TLS protocol to ensure secure communications. p. 135

Human safeguards   Steps taken to protect against security threats by establishing appropriate procedures for users to follow for system use. p. 297

Hyperlink   A pointer on a Web page to another Web page. A hyperlink contains the URL of the Web page to access when the user clicks the hyperlink. The URL can reference a page on the Web server that generated the page containing the hyperlink, or it can reference a page on another server. p. 196

Hypertext Markup Language (HTML)   A language that defines the structure and layout of Web page content. An HTML tag is a notation used to define a data element for display or other purposes. p. 196

Hypertext Transfer Protocol (HTTP)   A Layer-5 protocol used to process Web pages. p. 194

Identification   The process whereby an information system identifies a user by requiring the user to sign on with a user name and password. p. 292

IEEE 802.3 protocol   This standard, also called *Ethernet*, is a network protocol that operates at Layers 1 and 2 of the TCP/IP–OSI architecture. Ethernet, the world's most popular LAN protocol, is used on WANs as well. p. 123

IEEE 802.11 protocol   A wireless communications standard, widely used today, that enables access within a few hundred feet. The most popular version of this standard is IEEE 802.11g, which allows wireless transmissions of up to 54 Mbps. p. 125

IEE 802.16 protocol   An emerging wireless communications standard, also known as *WiMax*, that enables broadband wireless access for fixed, nomadic, and portable applications. In fixed mode, it enables access across a several-mile or larger region. See also *WiMax*. p. 126

If/then rule   Format for rules derived from a decision tree (data mining) or by interviewing a human expert (expert systems). p. 364

Implementation phase   The fourth phase in the SDLC, in which developers build and integrate system components, test the system, and convert to the new system. p. 249

Information   (1) Knowledge derived from data, where *data* is defined as recorded facts or figures. (2) Data presented in a meaningful context. (3) Data processed by summing, ordering, averaging, grouping, comparing, or other similar operations. (4) A difference that makes a difference. p. 25

Information system (IS)   A group of components that interact to produce information. p. 5

Information technology (IT)   The products, methods, inventions, and standards that are used for the purpose of producing information. p. 7

Input hardware   Hardware devices that attach to a computer; includes keyboards, mouse, document scanners, and bar-code (Universal Product Code) scanners. p. 75

Instruction set   The collection of instructions that a computer can process. p. 84

Intangible benefit   A benefit of an IS for which it is impossible to compute a dollar value. p. 275

Intelligence gathering step   A step where decision makers determine what is to be decided, what the criteria for the decision will be, and what data are available. p. 356

Internal firewall   A firewall that sits inside the organizational network. p. 136

Internet   When spelled with a small *i*, as in *internet*, a private network of networks. When spelled with a capital *I*, as *Internet*, the public internet known as the Internet. p. 121

Internet service provider (ISP)   An ISP provides users with Internet access. An ISP provides a user with a legitimate Internet address; it serves as the user's gateway to the Internet; and it passes communications back and forth between the user and the Internet. ISPs also pay for the Internet. They collect money from their customers and pay access fees and other charges on the users' behalf. p. 127

Interorganizational processes   Business processes that cross not only departmental boundaries, but organizational boundaries as well. Such processes involve activities among organizations having different owners. p. 165

IP spoofing   A type of spoofing whereby an intruder uses another site's IP address as if it were that other site. p. 288

Islands of automation   The structure that results when functional applications work independently in isolation from one another. Usually problematic because data is duplicated, integration is difficult, and results can be inconsistent. p. 165

Just-barely-sufficient information   Information that meets the purpose for which it is generated, but just barely so. p. 27

Key   (1) A column or group of columns that identifies a unique row in a table. (2) A number used to encrypt data. The encryption algorithm applies the key to the original message to produce the coded message. Decoding (decrypting) a message is similar; a key is applied to the coded message to recover the original text. p. 102, p. 134

Key escrow   A control procedure whereby a trusted party is given a copy of a key used to encrypt database data. p. 296

Kilobyte (K)   1,024 bytes. p. 78

Knowledge management (KM)   The process of creating value from intellectual capital and sharing that knowledge with employees, managers, suppliers, customers, and others who need that capital. p. 215

Last mile problem   The difficulty involved in getting the capacity of fast optical-fiber transmission lines from the street in front of buildings into the homes and smaller businesses located in those buildings. Digging up the street and backyard of every residence and small business to install optical fiber is not affordable; it is hoped that WiMax technology will be able to solve the problem of making the network connections of "the last mile." p. 126

Library   In version-control collaboration systems, a shared directory that allows access to various documents by means of *permissions*. p. 344

License   Agreement that stipulates how a program can be used. Most specify the number of computers on which the program can be installed and sometimes the number of users that can connect to and use the program remotely. Such agreements also stipulate limitations on the liability of the software vendor for the consequences of errors in the software. p. 86

Linkages   Process interactions across value chains. Linkages are important sources of efficiencies and are readily supported by information systems. p. 49

Linux   A version of Unix that was developed by the open-source community. The open-source community owns Linux, and there is no fee to use it. Linux is a popular operating system for Web servers. p. 86

Local area network (LAN)   A network that connects computers that reside in a single geographic location on the premises of the company that operates the LAN. The number of connected computers can range from two to several hundred. p. 121

Localizing   The process of making a computer program work in a second language. p. 146

Lost-update problem   An issue in multi-user database processing in which two or more users try to make changes to the data but the database cannot make the changes because it was not designed to process changes from multiple users. p. 111

MAC address   Also called *physical address*. A permanent address given to each network interface card (NIC) at the factory. This address enables the device to access the network via a Level-2 protocol. By agreement among computer manufacturers, MAC addresses are assigned in such a way that no two NIC devices will ever have the same MAC address. p. 122

Mac OS   An operating system developed by Apple Computer, Inc., for the Macintosh. The current version is Mac OS X. Macintosh computers are used primarily by graphic artists and workers in the arts community. Mac OS was developed for the PowerPC, but as of 2006 will run on Intel processors as well. p. 85

Macro virus   Virus that attaches itself to a Word, Excel, PowerPoint, or other type of document. When the infected document is opened, the virus places itself in the startup files of the application. After that, the virus infects every file that the application creates or processes. p. 92

Main memory   A set of cells in which each cell holds a byte of data or instruction; each cell has an address, and the CPU uses the addresses to identify particular data items. p. 77

Maintenance phase   The fifth and final phase in the SDLC, in which developers record requests for changes, including both enhancements and failures, and fix failures by means of patches, service packs, and new releases. p. 249

Malware   Viruses, worms, Trojan horses, spyware, and adware. p. 294

Malware definitions   Patterns that exist in malware code. Anti-malware vendors update these definitions continuously and incorporate them into their products in order to better fight against malware. p. 294

Management information system (MIS)   An information system that helps businesses achieve their goals and objectives. p. 6

Manual system   An information system in which the activity of processing information is done by people, without the use of automated processing. p. 31

Margin   The difference between value and cost. p. 48

Market-basket analysis   A data-mining technique for determining sales patterns. A market-basket analysis shows the products that customers tend to buy together. p. 215

Mashup   The combination of output from two or more Web sites into a single user experience. p. 199

Media access control (MAC) address   See *MAC address.* p. 122

Megabyte (MB)   1,024 KB. p. 78

Memory swapping   The movement of programs and data into and out of memory. If a computer has insufficient memory for its workload, such swapping will degrade system performance. p. 79

Merchant companies   In e-commerce, companies that take title to the goods they sell. They buy goods and resell them. p. 189

Metadata   Data that describe data. p. 103

Microsoft Office Groove   A collaboration product that includes version management and other useful tools. Users can access and edit documents at a workspace; the software automatically propagates changes made by one user to other users' computers. p. 343

Microsoft SharePoint   A version-control application that includes many collaboration features and functions, including document check-in/checkout, surveys, discussion forums, and workflow. p. 344

Microsoft Surface   Hardware-software product from Microsoft that enables people to interact with data on the surface of a table. p. 84

Modem   Short for *modulator/demodulator*, a modem converts the computer's digital data into signals that can be transmitted over telephone or cable lines. p. 127

Moore's Law   A law, created by Gordon Moore, stating that the number of transistors per square inch on an integrated chip doubles every 18 months. Moore's prediction has proved generally accurate in the 40 years since it was made. Sometimes this law is stated that the performance of a computer doubles every 18 months. Although not strictly true, this version gives the gist of the idea. p. 13

Multiparty text chat   A synchronous virtual meeting, in which participants meet at the same time and communicate by typing comments over a communication network. p. 338

Multiuser processing   When multiple users process the database at the same time. p. 111

My Maps   A Web 2.0 product that provides tools with which users can make custom modifications to maps provided by Google; My Maps is an example of a mashup. p. 199

MySQL   A popular open-source DBMS product that is license-free for most applications. p. 105

Narrowband   Internet communication lines that have transmission speeds of 56 kbps or less. A dial-up modem provides narrowband access. p. 129

Network   A collection of computers that communicate with one another over transmission lines. p. 121

Network interface card (NIC)   A hardware component on each device on a network (computer, printer, etc.) that connects the device's circuitry to the communications line. The NIC works together with programs in each device to implement Layers 1 and 2 of the TCP/IP–OSI hybrid protocol. p. 122

Network of leased lines   A WAN connection alternative. Communication lines are leased from telecommunications companies and connected into a network. The lines connect geographically distant sites. p. 129

Neural network   A popular supervised data-mining technique used to predict values and make classifications, such as "good prospect" or "poor prospect." p. 223

Nonmerchant companies   E-commerce companies that arrange for the purchase and sale of goods without ever owning or taking title to those goods. p. 189

Nonvolatile   Memory that preserves data contents even when not powered (e.g., magnetic and optical disks). With such devices, you can turn the computer off and back on, and the contents will be unchanged. p. 82

Object Management Group (OMG)   A software-industry standards organization that has sponsored the creation of many technology standards including the Business Process Modeling Notation (BPMN), a standard set of terms and graphical notations for documenting business processes. p. 168

Object-relational database   A type of database that stores both OOP objects and relational data. Rarely used in commercial applications. p. 103

Off-the-shelf software   Software that can be used without having to make any changes. p. 87

Off-the-shelf with alterations software   Software bought off-the-shelf but altered to fit the organization's specific needs. p. 87

Onboard NIC   A built-in NIC. p. 122

One-of-a-kind application   Software that is developed for a specific, unique need, usually for a particular company's operations. p. 86

Open-source community   A loosely coupled group of programmers who mostly volunteer their time to contribute code to develop and maintain common software. Linux and MySQL are two prominent products developed by such a community. p. 86

Operating system (OS)   A computer program that controls the computer's resources: It manages the contents of main memory, processes keystrokes and mouse movements, sends signals to the display monitor, reads and writes disk files, and controls the processing of other programs. p. 79

Optical fiber cable   A type of cable used to connect the computers, printers, switches, and other devices on a LAN. The signals on such cables are light rays, and they are reflected inside the glass core of the optical fiber cable. The core is surrounded by a *cladding* to contain the light signals, and the cladding, in turn, is wrapped with an outer layer to protect it. p. 123

Oracle   A popular, enterprise-class DBMS product from Oracle Corporation. p. 105

Organizational feasibility   One of four dimensions of feasibility. p. 251

Output hardware   Hardware that displays the results of the computer's processing. Consists of video displays, printers, audio speakers, overhead projectors, and other special-purpose devices, such as large flatbed plotters. p. 77

Packet-filtering firewall   A firewall that examines each packet and determines whether to let the packet pass. To make this decision, it examines the source address, the destination addresses, and other data. p. 136

Parallel installation   A type of system conversion in which the new system runs in parallel with the old one for a while. Parallel installation is expensive because the organization incurs the costs of running both systems. p. 259

Parallel workflow   A workflow in which activities occur simultaneously. p. 345

Patch   A group of fixes for high-priority failures that can be applied to existing copies of a particular product. Software vendors supply patches to fix security and other critical problems. p. 92, p. 260

Payload   The program code of a virus that causes unwanted or hurtful actions, such as deleting programs or data, or even worse, modifying data in ways that are undetected by the user. p. 92

People   As part of the five-component framework, one of the five fundamental components of an information system; includes those who operate and service the computers, those who maintain the data, those who support the networks, and those who use the system. p. 5

Perimeter firewall   A firewall that sits outside the organizational network. It is the first device that Internet traffic encounters. p. 136

Personal DBMS   DBMS products designed for smaller, simpler database applications. Such products are used for personal or small workgroup applications that involve fewer than a 100 users, and normally fewer than 15. Today, Microsoft Access is the only prominent personal DBMS. p. 114

Personal identification number (PIN)   A form of authentication whereby the user supplies a number that only he or she knows. p. 293

Petabyte 10^{15} bytes. p. 213

Phased installation   A type of system conversion in which the new system is installed in pieces across the organization(s). Once a given piece works, then the organization installs and tests another piece of the system, until the entire system has been installed. p. 259

Phishing   A technique for obtaining unauthorized data that uses pretexting via email. The *phisher* pretends to be a legitimate company and sends an email requesting confidential data, such as account numbers, Social Security numbers, account passwords, and so forth. p. 288

Pilot installation   A type of system conversion in which the organization implements the entire system on a limited portion of the business. The advantage of pilot implementation is that if the system fails, the failure is contained within a limited boundary. This reduces exposure of the business and also protects the new system from developing a negative reputation throughout the organization(s). p. 259

Plunge installation   Sometimes called *direct installation*, a type of system conversion in which the organization shuts off the old system and starts the new system. If the new system fails, the organization is in trouble: Nothing can be done until either the new system is fixed or the old system is reinstalled. Because of the risk, organizations should avoid this conversion style if possible. p. 259

Point of presence (POP)   The location at which a line connects to a PSDN network. Think of the POP as the phone number that one dials to connect to the PSDN. Once a site has connected to the PSDN POP, the site obtains access to all other sites connected to the PSDN. p. 132

Point-to-Point Protocol (PPP)   A Layer-2 protocol used for networks that involve just two computers, hence the term *point-to-point*. PPP is used between a modem and an ISP as well as on some networks of leased lines. p. 128

Pretexting   A technique for gathering unauthorized information in which someone pretends to be someone else. A common scam involves a telephone caller who pretends to be from a credit card company and claims to be checking the validity of credit card numbers. Phishing is also a form of pretexting. p. 288

Price conflict   In e-commerce, a conflict that may result when manufacturers offer products at prices lower than those available through existing sales channels. p. 192

Price elasticity   A measure of the sensitivity in demand to changes in price. It is the ratio of the percentage change in quantity divided by the percentage change in price. p. 191

Primary activities   In Porter's value chain model, the fundamental activities that create value—inbound logistics, operations, outbound logistics, marketing/sales, and service. p. 48

Procedures   Instructions for humans. One of the five fundamental components of an information system. p. 5

Product quality assurance (PQA)   The testing of a system. PQA personnel usually construct a test plan with the advice and assistance of users. PQA test engineers perform testing, and they also supervise user-test activity. Many PQA professionals are programmers who write automated test programs. p. 258

Protocol   A standardized means for coordinating an activity between two or more entities. p. 121

Public key/private key   A special version of asymmetric encryption that is popular on the Internet. With this method, each site has a public key for encoding messages and a private key for decoding them. p. 134

Public switched data network (PSDN)   A WAN connection alternative. A network of computers and leased lines is developed and maintained by a vendor that leases time on the network to other organizations. p. 132

Quad processor   A computer with four CPUs. p. 82

Query   A request for data from a database. p. 109

RAM   Stands for *random access memory*, which is main memory consisting of cells that hold data or instructions. Each cell has an address that the CPU uses to read or write data. Memory locations can be read or written in any order, hence the term *random access*. RAM memory is almost always volatile. p. 77

Records   Also called *rows*, groups of columns in a database table. p. 100

Regression analysis   A type of supervised data mining that estimates the values of parameters in a linear equation. Used to determine the relative influence of variables on an outcome and also to predict future values of that outcome. p. 223

Relation   The more formal name for a database table. p. 103

Relational database   Database that carries its data in the form of tables and that represents relationships using foreign keys. p. 103

Relevant information   Information that is appropriate to both the context and the subject. p. 27

Replicated databases   Databases that contain duplicated records. Processing of such databases is complex if users want to be able to update the same items at the same time without experiencing *lost-update problems*. p. 148

Report   A presentation of data in a structured, meaningful context. p. 109

Reporting system   A system that creates information from disparate data sources and delivers that information to the proper users on a timely basis. p. 214

Requirements analysis phase   The second phase in the SDLC, in which developers conduct user interviews, evaluate existing systems, determine new forms/reports/ queries, identify new features and functions, including security, and create the data model. p. 249

Resources   Items of value, such as inventory or funds, that are part of a business process. p. 25

Router   A special-purpose computer that moves network traffic from one node on a network to another. p. 129

Rows   Also called *records*, groups of columns in a database table. p. 100

Schedule feasibility   One of four dimensions of feasibility. p. 251

Secure Socket Layer (SSL)   A protocol that uses both asymmetric and symmetric encryption. SSL is a protocol layer that works between Levels 4 (transport) and 5 (application) of the TCP–OSI protocol architecture. When SSL is in use, the browser address will begin with https://. The most recent version of SSI is called TLS. p. 135

Security threat   A problem with the security of an information system or the data therein caused by human error, malicious activity, or natural disasters. p. 287

Sequential workflow   A workflow in which activities occur in sequence. p. 345

Server   A computer that provides some type of service, such as hosting a database, running a blog, publishing a Web site, or selling goods. Server computers are faster, larger, and more powerful than client computers. p. 82

Server farm   A large collection of server computers that coordinates the activities of the servers, usually for commercial purposes. p. 83

Server tier   In the three-tier architecture, the tier that consists of computers that run Web servers to generate Web pages and other data in response to requests from browsers. Web servers also process application programs. p. 193

Service   A repeatable task that a business needs to perform. p. 175

Service pack   A large group of fixes that solve low-priority software problems. Users apply service packs in much the same way that they apply patches, except that service packs typically involve fixes to hundreds or thousands of problems. p. 260

Service-oriented architecture (SOA)   Processing philosophy that advocates that computing systems use a *standard method* to declare the services they provide and the interface by which those services can be requested and used. Web services are an implementation of SOA. p. 175

SharePoint site   A facility constructed and shared by Microsoft SharePoint, a component of Windows Server. A SharePoint site is a collection of libraries, lists, discussion boards, surveys, Wikis, and other collaboration tools. SharePoint sites support workflows, which are important for content management. A SharePoint site can have multiple sub-sites, and those sub-sites can have multiple sub-sites as well. p. 346

Smart card   A plastic card similar to a credit card that has a microchip. The microchip, which holds much more data than a magnetic strip, is loaded with identifying data. Normally requires a PIN. p. 293

Sniffing   A technique for intercepting computer communications. With wired networks, sniffing requires a physical connection to the network. With wireless networks, no such connection is required. p. 288

SOAP   A protocol for exchanging messages encoded in XML. SOAP sits on top of any available transport protocol, such as HTTP, HTTPS, or FTP. SOAP is independent of any device, network, vendor, or product. p. 181

Social networking (SN)   Connections of people with similar interests. Today, social networks typically are supported by Web 2.0 technology. p. 202

Software   Instructions for computers. One of the five fundamental components of an information system. p. 5

Software as a service (SAAS)   Business model whereby companies (such as Google, Amazon.com, and eBay) provide services based on their software, rather than providing software as a product (by means of software-usage licenses). Software as a service is an example of Web 2.0. p. 197

Special function cards   Cards that can be added to the computer to augment the computer's basic capabilities. p. 77

Spoofing   When someone pretends to be someone else with the intent of obtaining unauthorized data. If you pretend to be your professor, you are spoofing your professor. p. 288

Spyware   Programs installed on the user's computer without the user's knowledge or permission that reside in the background and, unknown to the user, observe the user's actions and keystrokes, modify computer activity, and report the user's activities to sponsoring organizations. Malicious spyware captures keystrokes to obtain user names, passwords, account numbers, and other sensitive information. Other spyware is used for marketing analyses, observing what users do, Web sites visited, products examined and purchased, and so forth. p. 294

SQL Server   A popular enterprise-class DBMS product from Microsoft. p. 105

Storage hardware   Hardware that saves data and programs. Magnetic disk is by far the most common storage device, although optical disks, such as CDs and DVDs, also are popular. p. 77

Strong password   A password with the following characteristics: seven or more characters; does not contain the user's user name, real name, or company name; does not contain a complete dictionary word, in any language; is different from the user's previous passwords; and contains both upper- and lowercase letters, numbers, and special characters. p. 14

Structured Query Language (SQL)   An international standard language for processing database data. p. 108

Supervised data mining   A form of data mining in which data miners develop a model prior to the analysis and apply statistical techniques to data to estimate values of the parameters of the model. p. 223

Support activities   In Porter's value chain model, the activities that contribute indirectly to value creation—procurement, technology, human resources, and the firm's infrastructure. p. 48

Swim-lane layout   A type of business process diagram. Like swim lanes in a swimming pool, each role is shown in its own horizontal rectangle. Swim-lane layout can be used to simplify process diagrams and to draw attention to interactions among components of the diagram. p. 169

Switch   A special-purpose computer that receives and transmits data across a network. p. 122

Switching costs   Business strategy of locking in customers by making it difficult or expensive to change to another product or supplier. p. 52

Symmetric encryption   An encryption method whereby the same key is used to encode and to decode the message. p. 134

Symmetrical digital subscriber lines (SDSL)   DSL lines that have the same upload and download speeds. p. 128

Synchronous communication   Information exchange that occurs when all members of a work team meet at the same time, such as face-to-face meetings or conference calls. p. 338

System   A group of components that interact to achieve some purpose. p. 5

System conversion   The process of *converting* business activity from the old system to the new. p. 259

System definition phase   The first phase in the SDLC, in which developers, with the help of eventual users, define the new system's goals and scope, assess its feasibility, form a project team, and plan the project. p. 249

Systems analysis and design   The process of creating and maintaining information systems. It is sometimes called systems development. p. 245

Systems analysts   IS professionals who understand both business and technology. They are active throughout the systems development process and play a key role in moving the project from conception to conversion and, ultimately, maintenance. Systems analysts integrate the work of the programmers, testers, and users. p. 254

Systems development   The process of creating and maintaining information systems. It is sometimes called *systems analysis and design*. p. 245

Systems development life cycle (SDLC)   The classical process used to develop information systems. These basic tasks of systems development are combined into the following phases: system definition, requirements analysis, component design, implementation, and system maintenance (fix or enhance). p. 249

Table   Also called a *file*, a group of similar rows or records in a database. p. 101

Tag   In markup languages such as HTML and XML, notation used to define a data element for display or other purposes. p. 180, p. 196

Tangible benefit   A benefit of an IS that can be measured as a dollar value. p. 275

Team   A small group of people with complementary skills who are committed to a common purpose, goals, and work approach. p. 329

Team survey   A form of asynchronous communication in which one team member creates a list of questions and other team members respond. Microsoft SharePoint has built-in survey capability. p. 339

Technical feasibility   One of four dimensions of feasibility. p. 251

Technical safeguards   Safeguards that involve the hardware and software components of an information system. p. 292

Terabyte (TB)   1,024 GB. p. 78

Test plan   Groups of sequences of actions that users will take when using the new system. p. 258

Thick client   A software application that requires programs other than just the browser on a user's computer—that is, that requires code on both a client and server computers. p. 88

Thin client   A software application that requires nothing more than a browser and can be run on only the user's computer. p. 88

Three-tier architecture   Architecture used by most e-commerce server applications. The tiers refer to three different classes of computers. The user tier consists of users' computers that have browsers that request and process Web pages. The server tier consists of computers that run Web servers and in the process generate Web pages and other data in response to requests from browsers. Web servers also process application programs. The third tier is the database tier, which runs the DBMS that processes the database. p. 193

Timely information   Information that is produced in time for its intended use. p. 26

Transport Layer Security (TLS)   A protocol, using both asymmetric and symmetric encryption, that works between Levels 4 (transport) and 5 (application) of the TCP–OSI protocol architecture. TLS is the new name for a later version of SSL. p. 135

Trojan horse   Virus that masquerades as a useful program or file. The name refers to the gigantic mock-up of a horse that was filled with soldiers and moved into Troy during the Peloponnesian Wars. A typical Trojan horse appears to be a computer game, an MP3 music file, or some other useful, innocuous program. p. 92

Tuned, Tuning Adjusting information systems from time to time to accommodate changes in workload. p. 271

Tunnel A virtual, private pathway over a public or shared network from the VPN client to the VPN server. p. 137

Unauthorized data disclosure When a person inadvertently releases data in violation of policy. p. 288

Unix An operating system developed at Bell Labs in the 1970s. It has been the workhorse of the scientific and engineering communities since then. p. 86

Unshielded twisted pair (UTP) cable A type of cable used to connect the computers, printers, switches, and other devices on a LAN. A UTP cable has four pairs of twisted wire. A device called an RJ-45 connector is used to connect the UTP cable into NIC devices. p. 122

Unsupervised data mining A form of data mining whereby the analysts do not create a model or hypothesis before running the analysis. Instead, they apply the data-mining technique to the data and observe the results. With this method, analysts create hypotheses after the analysis to explain the patterns found. p. 223

User-generated content (UGC) In Web 2.0, data and information that is provided by users. Examples are product ratings, product problem solutions, product designs, and marketing data. p. 203

User tier In the three-tier architecture, the tier that consists of computers that have browsers that request and process Web pages. p. 193

Usurpation Occurs when unauthorized programs invade a computer system and replace legitimate programs. Such unauthorized programs typically shut down the legitimate system and substitute their own processing. p. 289

Value chain A network of value-creating activities. p. 48

Version control Use of software to control access to and configuration of documents, designs, and other electronic versions of products. p. 344

Version management Use of software to control configuration of documents, designs, and other electronic versions of products. p. 341

Vertical-market application Software that serves the needs of a specific industry. Examples of such programs are those used by dental offices to schedule appointments and bill patients, those used by auto mechanics to keep track of customer data and

customers' automobile repairs, and those used by parts warehouses to track inventory, purchases, and sales. p. 86

Video conferencing Technology that combines a conference call with video cameras. p. 338

Viral marketing A marketing method used in the Web 2.0 world in which *users* spread news about products and services to one another. p. 198

Virtual meeting A meeting in which participants do not meet in the same place and possibly not at the same time. p. 338

Virtual private network (VPN) A WAN connection alternative that uses the Internet or a private internet to create the appearance of private point-to-point connections. In the IT world, the term *virtual* means something that appears to exist that does not exist in fact. Here, a VPN uses the public Internet to create the appearance of a private connection. p. 136

Virus a computer program that replicates itself. p. 92

Voice-over IP (VoIP) A technology that provides telephone communication over the Internet. p. 343

Volatile Data that will be lost when the computer or device is not powered. p. 82

Waterfall The fiction that one phase of the SDLC can be completed in its entirety and the project can progress, without any backtracking, to the next phase of the SDLC. Projects seldom are that simple; backtracking is normally required. p. 261

Web 2.0 Generally, a loose cloud of capabilities, technologies, business models, and philosophies that characterize the new and emerging business uses of the Internet. p. 197

Web farm A facility that runs multiple Web servers. Work is distributed among the computers in a Web farm so as to maximize throughput. p. 194

Web pages Documents encoded in HTML that are created, transmitted, and consumed using the World Wide Web. p. 194

Web server A program that processes the HTTP protocol and transmits Web pages on demand. Web servers also process application programs. p. 194

Web Services Description Language (WSDL) A language that services can use to describe what they do and how other computer programs can access their features. p. 181

Web storefront In e-commerce, a Web-based application that enables customers to enter and manage their orders. p. 190

Web-log See *Blog*. p. 3

Wide area network (WANs) A network that connects computers located at different geographic locations. p. 121

Wiki A common-knowledge base maintained by its users; processed on Web sites that allow users to add, remove, and edit content. p. 341

WiMax An emerging technology based on the IEEE 802.16 standard. WiMax is designed to deliver the "last mile" of wireless broadband access and could ultimately replace cable and DSL for fixed applications and replace cell phones for nomadic and portable applications. See also *IEEE 802.16*. p. 126

Windows An operating system designed and sold by Microsoft. It is the most widely used operating system. p. 95

Wireless NIC (WNIC) Devices that enable wireless networks by communicating with wireless access points. Such devices can be cards that slide into the PCMA slot or they can be built-in, onboard devices. WNICs operate according to the 802.11 protocol. p. 124

Workspace In Microsoft Groove, an electronic "space" consisting of tools and documents that enable users to collaborate. p. 343

Worm A virus that propagates itself using the Internet or some other computer network. Worm code is written specifically to infect another computer as quickly as possible. p. 92

Worth-its-cost information Information in which an appropriate relationship exists between the value of the information and the cost of creating it. p. 27

WSDL See *Web Services Description Language.* p. 181

XML See *eXtensible Markup Language.* p. 182

XML document A file of XML tags and data. p. 180

XML schema An XML document that specifies the structure of other XML documents. An XML schema is metadata for other XML documents. For example, a SalesOrder XML schema specifies the structure of SalesOrder documents. p. 180

INDEX

Page numbers with f indicate figures; those with n indicate footnotes.